KARL R. WALLACE
Professor of Speech
University of Massachusetts, Amherst
ADVISORY EDITOR TO DODD, MEAD & COMPANY

Man Speaking

A RHETORIC OF PUBLIC SPEECH

Man Speaking

A RHETORIC OF PUBLIC SPEECH

DONALD K. SMITH

University of Minnesota

Dodd, Mead & Company

NEW YORK   TORONTO   1969

Editor's Introduction

Three features of this textbook make it unique. First, its author possesses special qualifications. He is an unusually experienced teacher of speechmaking; he has counseled hundreds of students and a number of successful political speakers in the art of responsible communication. He has spoken many times in the public arena for himself, and occasionally he has spoken and written for others. As a result of all such experience, he has developed the ability to *observe* speakers in action and to appraise them and their methods in terms and tone that are almost objective. The student who will live awhile with this book stands a good chance of acquiring an objective attitude toward his speaking and that of others.

Another feature of this book is to be found in its point of view toward public utterance. Speaking is seen as a social act. Like any act, it can be formal or informal, prepared or spontaneous, solemn or humorous, responsible or irresponsible, good or bad. An utterance, whether it is a President's inaugural address or a bit of conversation, must always be a product and function of the communicative situation that calls it forth. An utterance reveals the speaker's purposes (whether these be apparent or not) and the expectations of listeners; it reveals the materials and forms the speaker chooses to employ for the achievement of his purposes and goals. It reveals, too, the social and linguistic constraints within which the speaker makes his choices. Through such constraints as well as through his own particular resources, a speaker discovers the scope of his choices, the extent of his freedom and creativity, and the relation of his public and private selves.

Viewing speech as a social act allows Professor Smith to give more attention than is usual in books on speechmaking to the influence of social organizations and institutions on speech practices. As a result the book joins contemporary perspectives on communication with perspectives drawn from traditional rhetorical theory.

The third unusual aspect of this book is its tone. Professor Smith speaks to the student as would a good adviser and counselor. He asks the student above all to understand the act of public speaking as one that reflects both himself and his society. Through such understanding comes the ability to appraise the utterance not merely of others but of one's self with frankness and justice.

KARL R. WALLACE

Foreword

College courses in public speaking usually serve two related objectives: first, assisting students in their search for personal excellence in speaking; second, assisting students to understand more fully the nature of the significant human activity known as public speaking. This book was written with the hope that it will be useful to students and teachers pursuing these objectives.

The importance of the first objective, the search for excellence in speaking, is so widely accepted as to need little explanation. The man or woman skilled in public speaking enjoys obvious advantages in positions of professional, social, or political leadership—advantages which seem to complete his capacity to serve as teacher or businessman, lawyer or civic leader, preacher or politician or administrator. For this reason the formal study of public speaking has been one of the more ancient and persistent studies associated with higher education.

But when one asks about the kind of theoretical materials appropriate to the study of public speaking, the most serious educational questions emerge. For example, is it educationally sound practice for a college course in public speaking simply to offer students a body of good advice on ways to go about choosing a topic; finding, organizing, and amplifying materials; and preparing for presentation? Or should such a course seek to help students understand as fully as possible the rationale underlying the choices men make when they engage in acts of public discourse? Is it enough for the mature student of public speaking to cast himself only in the role of practitioner of a practical art? Or should he also see himself as one who, through participation in the public discourse of his society, serves as judge of his own practices and the practices of others—and ultimately as guardian of the standards of public communication acceptable to his society? Is it possible for any teacher of public speaking, however wise, to set forth in book or lecture the choices a host of individual speakers *should* make when they confront multifarious personal and societal realities? Or should the teacher try in an organized way to uncover the generality of constraints and possibilities affecting the choices of speakers and listeners, while reserving treatment of the varied personal problems of student speakers to individual conferences, written comments, and occasional class discussions built around particular acts of speaking?

I have tried in this book, and particularly in the eight chapters of Part I, to provide an answer to pedagogical questions such as those in the foregoing paragraph. The answer rises not only from some two decades of experience in trying to teach public speaking, but also from observations about the responses of college students to various types of public speaking materials, from a growing confidence that a college public speaking course can and should teach more about public speaking than a set of immediate performance skills, and from a conviction that the most fundamental progress toward personal excellence in public discourse is made by students who become interested, not simply in their own personal needs and goals, but in the social and public dimensions of all acts of public discourse.

I think I have learned that most college students accept readily the proposition that the study of rhetoric, or the theory of public discourse, is as intellectually demanding and important as the study of linguistics, history, literature, anthropology, or psychology. They can accept this proposition when they are encouraged in their reading and discussion to see acts of public discourse as both a function and an expression of societal customs, organizations, and purposes, and to see that public speakers, themselves included, are inevitably enmeshed in a series of *choices* as to when to speak and when to be silent, positions to be taken and to be avoided, relationships to be cemented and to be abandoned. From such a perspective, the study of the theory of public speaking becomes more than a search for good advice as to how to improve one's own habits. It becomes an avenue for increased understanding of the way in which men form, sustain, and transform social organizations, and the way in which they respond, in acts of judgment, to that union of circumstances commonly thought of as speaker-audience-subject-occasion. I would say that college students have an appetite for studying public speaking in this larger context.

Moreover, I think it true that students who study a theory of public discourse which goes beyond the immediate exigencies of classroom performance can find such study fully supportive of their search for personal excellence. For some years I have approached students in class as one who wishes to discuss with them in a public way, not primarily their personal triumphs and shortcomings, but rather the fundamental problems that the citizen-speaker and the citizen-judge face when they wish to do two things: improve themselves as effective and responsible speakers and thus to assume more significant roles in our kind of society; and improve themselves as interpreters and judges of their own speechmaking and that of others. I have talked with students *about* speakers, and *about* speeches—both those occurring in class and in the world they know—and *about* the problems of choice confronting speakers, the possible reasons for the choices made, and the alternative choices that might have been possible. I have tried to emphasize the point of view that no man is ultimately qualified to tell another mature adult when he should speak, or why, or in what manner. The responsibility for such choices must ultimately rest with the man who speaks. I have tried to emphasize to students that they should consider my advice and that of their fellow students as well-intentioned, but that they must always carry final responsibility for deciding whose advice to heed, and whose to disregard. And I have tried to confine my exercise of the teacher's prerogative as preceptor, director, and judge to the personal conference, brief written reactions to speeches, and occasional public outbursts of enthusiasm or dismay about particular performances. I have been encouraged to believe that students who catch a vision of themselves as public figures, engaged in a public action of some importance, and responsible for choosing how to place and conduct that action, try harder to make significant speeches. They also try harder to understand the speeches of others, and to concern themselves with the standards of public communication in their society.

This book reflects the foregoing educational and pedagogical assumptions. Part I, the major portion of the book, is not concerned with how to prepare and present a public speech, but with the nature of public speech; its reason for being; the structure of speaking events; the underlying nature of positions and points of view taken by speakers; the structure, movement, and forms of enforcement found in acts of speaking; the dimensions of style, or manner, expressed by speakers; and the relationship of speakers and audiences. Since the act of public speaking inevitably takes on a social-ethical dimension, the problem of ethics is discussed explicitly. All such matters are considered from the point of view of the "third person" observing speech practices in our society, rather than from the point of view of one giving advice to a particular speechmaker, or from that of one expounding simply his own preferences in developing or presenting speeches. The discussion focuses on uncovering the choices facing speakers as they go about the business of speechmaking, and reflexively the choices facing audiences as they seek to understand the nature of the actions in which they participate. Part I is concerned rather liberally *about* speakers and speechmakers, and invites the student to contemplate his own particular problems of choice. But it does not direct him to undertake such contemplation, nor direct him to reach certain "wise" decisions. Such matters, I believe, are better managed through personal dialogue between teachers and students.

The theory in Part I is intended to be coherent with aspects of communication theory which college students may be studying in courses in linguistics, literature, sociology, anthropology, or psychology. However, the terminology and manner of treating ideas is drawn from the rhetorical tradition, with only occasional borrowings from more recent academic disciplines. I have tried to write a book which is clearly a work in rhetoric, but which will not seem irrelevant to, or inconsistent with, other courses which treat the theory of language and communication from a different point of departure. Part I may also serve as a college-level rhetoric of sufficient scope to meet the needs of students who may not have additional opportunity for the study of communication theory, or sufficient to provide a foundation for more specialized courses in argumentation and persuasion, or in the history and criticism of public address.

The three short chapters in Part II examine in a compressed fashion the problems of choice and management commonly faced by college students who prepare and present speeches. These chapters are intended as a review of the kinds of "good advice" commonly given to students seeking to develop effective public speeches. But the advice here is meant to flow naturally from the more fundamental study of speech acts undertaken in Part I. Hence, the chapters are derived from a larger theory of public discourse rather than forming the foundation of that larger theory.

The chapters in Part II provide little amplification or illustration since I am persuaded that they treat of manners which have already been studied by most college students. High school courses in speech or the English language arts commonly present a minimal rhetoric on the preparation and presentation of public discourse. College courses in speech fundamentals or English composition commonly treat at least some of the problems of finding topics, and selecting, organizing, and amplifying materials. From this point of view it might have been possible to have omitted the materials in Part II altogether, but I have included them partly to emphasize the derivative nature of the so-called first principles of speechmaking, partly to aid students in recalling matters they may have studied before, and partly to provide students using this book with a common terminology for treating matters of speech preparation organization, amplification, and delivery. Given the nature of the materials in Part II, some teachers may prefer to assign the reading of these chapters concurrently with the study of Part I; others may wish to make the study of Part II optional.

I hope this book will prove useful to the many teachers of public speaking who believe that public discourse is too important a part of the fabric of civilization to be thought of simply as the function of a personal skill possessed in varying degrees by different men. I hope it will also prove useful to the many college students who are ready to join their search for personal excellence to their concern for understanding why speeches occur, what they tell us about the public life of any society, and what problems of human choice, judgment, accommodation, and responsibility they entail.

Many of the adjustments made in the final text of this book reflect my indebtedness to colleagues in the speech field who have read and reacted to earlier versions. I am particularly grateful for the encouragement and advice of Professor Karl R. Wallace. The responsibility for shortcomings in conception and expression is, of course, mine.

DONALD K. SMITH

Contents

PART I

Perspective, Choice, and Responsibility

> *Let him see that his speech is not different from action;*
> *that when he has spoken, he has not done nothing, nor*
> *done wrong, but has cleared his own skirts, has engaged*
> *himself to wholesome exertion.*
>
> —EMERSON

INTRODUCTION

Thucydides, the historian of the Peloponnesian war, saw public speeches as an inseparable part of the movement of great political and military events. The pages of his remarkable history of the great war between the Athenian empire and her enemies are filled with speeches of statesmen and warriors. The texts represent, as Thucydides explains, his method of "keeping as closely as possible to the general sense of the words that were actually used, to make each speaker say what, in my opinion, was called for by each situation." [1]

One of the more familiar texts in Thucydides' history is the Funeral Oration he attributes to Pericles, delivered in 430 B.C.—at the end of the first year of the war—on the occasion of the traditional Athenian ceremony in honor of those who had fallen in combat. The text is still read by Americans, at least in part because its memorable statement of the ideals of a free and democratic society has resonance for our own age. The Funeral Oration takes on added interest for Americans because the response of Pericles to his nation's honoring of its war dead inevitably invites comparison and contrast with President Abraham Lincoln's response on a similar occasion at Gettysburg.

However, our purpose here in recalling the Funeral Oration is not to

---

[1] Thucydides, *The Peloponnesian War*, translated by Rex Warner (Baltimore, Maryland: Penguin Books Inc., 1965), p. 25.

1

pursue any detailed analysis of its historical significance. Rather, we turn to a résumé of the major movements in a speech delivered more than two millenniums ago as a way of seeking some insight into the reasons public speeches occur and into the nature of their being. The résumé and interpretations will, in turn, provide a preliminary glimpse of the perspective from which this book examines public speaking.

It is worth noting that Pericles spoke because it was the custom of his people each year to hold a public ceremony for the soldiers slain in battle in the previous year. The ceremony was explicit in its contemplation of the reality of violent death. The bones of the slain were brought to a tent and offerings were made. The remains of the soldiers from each tribe were placed in a cypress coffin, and an empty coffin was provided to symbolize the missing soldiers. A funeral procession and public burial followed, after which a man chosen by the city for his intellectual gifts and reputation made an appropriate speech of praise for the dead. This was the role which Pericles was asked to fill, and this the occasion to which he responded. His speech opens with explicit reference to the speaker's role, a familiar recognition of the hazards of speech on such an occasion, and a direct observation about the varied responses likely from his listeners. (The passages cited are from Rex Warner's translation.)

Many of those who have spoken here in the past have praised the institution of this speech at the close of our ceremony. It seemed to them a mark of honor to our soldiers who have fallen in war that a speech should be made over them. I do not agree. These men have shown themselves valiant in action, and it would be enough, I think, for their glories to be proclaimed in action, as you have just seen it done at this funeral organized by the state. Our belief in the courage and manliness of so many should not be hazarded on the goodness or badness of one man's speech. Then it is not easy to speak with a proper sense of balance, when a man's listeners find it difficult to believe in the truth of what one is saying. The man who knows the facts and loves the dead may well think that an oration tells less than what he knows and what he would like to hear: others who do not know so much may feel envy for the dead, and think the orator over-praises them, when he speaks of exploits that are beyond their own capacities. . . . However, the fact is that this institution was set up and approved by our forefathers, and it is my duty to follow the tradition and do my best to meet the wishes and expectation of every one of you.

After a brief transitional passage in praise of the accomplishments of Athenian ancestors, Pericles states the purpose and order of his address, and continues with his first major movement, an extended passage in praise of the Athenian spirit and democratic way of life.

What I want to do is, in the first place, to discuss the spirit in which we faced our trials and also our constitution and the way of life which has made us great. After that I shall speak in praise of the dead, believing that this kind of speech is not inappropriate to the present occasion, and that this whole assembly, of citizens and foreigners, may listen to it with advantage.

Let me say that our system of government does not copy the institutions of our neighbours. It is more the case of our being a model to others, than of our imitating anyone else. Our constitution is called a democracy because power is in the hands not of a minority but of the whole people. When it is a question of settling private disputes, everyone is equal before the law; when it is a question of putting one person before another in positions of public responsibility, what counts is not membership of a particular class, but the actual ability which the man possesses. No one, so long as he has it in him to be of service to the state, is kept in political obscurity because of poverty. And, just as our political life is free and open, so is our day-to-day life in our relations with each other. We do not get into a state with our next-door neighbour if he enjoys himself in his own way, nor do we give him the kind of black looks which, though they do no real harm, still do hurt people's feelings. We are free and tolerant in our private lives; but in public affairs we keep to the law. This is because it commands our deep respect.

Pericles continues with praise for his city in the longest part of his speech, then summarizes this movement, and continues, as he had promised, with a passage in praise of the slain. We continue with his interim summary and transition to the second major division.

This, then, is the kind of city for which these men, who could not bear the thought of losing her, nobly fought and nobly died. It is only natural that every one of us who survive them should be willing to undergo hardships in her service. And it was for this reason that I have spoken at such length about our city, because I wanted to make it clear that for us there is more at stake than there is for others who lack our advantages; also I wanted my words of praise for the dead to be set in the bright light of evidence. And now the most important of these words has been spoken. I have sung the praises of our city; but it was the courage and gallantry of these men, and of people like them, which made her splendid. Nor would you find it true in the case of many of the Greeks, as it is true of them, that no words can do more than justice to their deeds.

To me it seems that the consummation which has overtaken these men shows us the meaning of manliness in its first revelation and in its final proof. Some of them, no doubt, had their faults; but what we ought to remember first is their gallant conduct against the enemy in defence of their native land. They have blotted out evil with good, and done more service to the commonwealth than they ever did harm in their private lives. No one of these men weakened because he wanted to go on enjoying his wealth: no one put off the awful day in the hope that he might live to escape his poverty and grow rich. More to be desired than such things, they chose to check the enemy's pride. This, to them, was a risk most glorious, and they accepted it, willing to strike down the enemy and relinquish everything else. As for success or failure, they left that in the doubtful hands of Hope, and when the reality of battle was before their faces, they put their trust in their own selves. In the fighting, they thought it more honourable to stand their ground and suffer death than to give in and save their lives. So they fled from the reproaches of men, abiding with life and limb the brunt of battle; and, in a small moment of time, the climax of their lives, a culmination of glory, not of fear, were swept away from us.

So and such they were, these men—worthy of their city.

Pericles continues his praise of the dead, offers words of comfort for their parents, observes the struggle living sons and brothers must face to approach the honor achieved by the fallen, admonishes the widows of their duties, and concludes abruptly as one who has carried out the action demanded by the occasion.

I have now, as the law demanded, said what I had to say. For the time being our offerings to the dead have been made, and for the future their children will be supported at the public expense by the city, until they come of age. This is the crown and the prize which she offers, both to the dead and their children, for the ordeals they have faced. Where the rewards of valour are the greatest, there you will find also the best and bravest spirits among the people. And now, when you have mourned for your dear ones, you must depart.

For the student of public speaking, there is much in the Funeral Oration which must remain hidden. We cannot know that the words of the text were those actually uttered by Pericles, although there is no reason to doubt the accuracy of the sentiments Thucydides attributes to the Athenian statesman. We have little reason to concern ourselves with the choice or ordering of words, since we are limited to a translation, variously rendered, from the language of ancient Greece. We cannot know the speaker's manner of delivery. Nor can we know whether the variety of audience response anticipated by the speaker actually occurred, nor how his audience regarded the speech in comparison with others heard on similar occasions. Yet, with so much obscured, there is still much to note which may be productive of insight into the general nature of public speeches.

There is, for example, the fact that the speech, like most public speeches ancient and modern, grew out of the customs and demands of the institutional life of a society. The speaker was chosen to play a particular role defined by the ceremonial customs of the Athenian state, and his action is at once a response to tradition, and a response to a particular set of circumstances and a particular audience. Tradition and the general nature of the occasion determined the most obvious purpose of the speech. But Pericles was also the leading citizen of a state in the midst of war, a major architect of the decision to go to war, and a formulator of the policies for conducting the struggle. The traditional purpose of the speech is extended by the particular circumstances surrounding its presentation. Pericles could not have been insensitive to the importance of the speech for maintaining the morale of his audience, and for securing or strengthening his own reputation. His extended praise of the Athenian way of life had more than ceremonial implications.

Pericles, like all public speakers, faced both constraints limiting his action, and the opportunity to choose among many alternative possibilities. He was constrained in the sense that tradition defined the central purpose of his speech. He could choose, however, the emphasis to be given the various movements in his speech, matters to be treated and to be ignored, and the tone or manner of treatment. He might have chosen, for example, to be less candid about the possibility that he would disappoint many listeners, or about the probable personal shortcomings of the men being honored. He could have been less blunt in reminding the widows present of their duties, or have avoided, as Lincoln would many centuries later, references to the enemy and the inferiority of their way of life. We can observe his bluntness, speculate on the reasons for his choosing as he did, and on the possible nature of an audience for whom such an approach would be appropriate.

We notice also the speaker's sense of the affiliations of many of those present and their need for personal words of recognition. This assuredly is a characteristic of the action of public speakers who understand their role—their search for an action that will join the requirements of an occasion to the needs of a particular audience. The speaker must know that his language is not an object set apart from people or events, but more properly is an instrument for encompassing all aspects of an immediate situation.

If we can assume that the speaker is a man knowledgeable about, and sensitive to the values of his society, we may see the speech as a reflection of some of the character of the Athenian society. There is, for example, the indication that Pericles assumed that such topics as duty and honor would be important to his listeners, and that they would respond to the vision of their state as one devoted to justice, personal freedom, respect for public law, the cultivation of beauty, wisdom, prudence, and generosity. We may suspect that this vision of Athens is touched by the irony of a society never able to achieve its own ideals. Yet we know that public speakers, at least on ceremonial occasions, often assure people that they are what they aspire to be. We can also note in the speech the somber reflection of a society accustomed to war as a part of life, and foredoomed by its inability to achieve peaceful accommodation with its neighbors. Public speeches often reflect not only the values held important by a speaker, but also the values held in common by speaker and audience.

Because of the clarity of its structure and statement, the Funeral Oration invites closer examination of the method by which the speaker advances his ideas. Pericles announces the divisions of his speech to his audience, and moves through these divisions with the ease of one who knows precisely the action he proposes. He is plainspoken, exemplifying abstract ideals of duty and justice and freedom with commonplace illustrations of the way in which his people live. We note that his tone is somber, almost harsh, and yet touched with concern for the welfare of his city and the audience he addresses. Even through the screen of a written and translated record of a living, human action, we sense something of the strength and assurance of the man speaking.

These reflections on a speech given long ago are preliminary to the discussion of public speaking to be undertaken in Part I of this book. The discussion in that part, in broadest outline, will seek *perspective* on the nature and reason for being of public speeches. It will observe the variety of *constraints* speakers confront, and the *choices* available to them. And it will consider the *responsibility* speakers carry for an action which involves the well-being of their listeners.

Public Speaking as Social Action

We live suspended in language.
—NIELS BOHR

Section I examines the nature of public speaking, specifically, its basis in the distinctive human behavior called "speech," its necessity to the life of social organizations, its status as an art of choosing wisely, and the purposes served by its study and practice. Public speaking is viewed as a complex social action, and a set of terms and concepts useful in understanding this action is presented. These terms and concepts also introduce the student to the problems of constraint and possibility, of judgment and choice faced by all public speakers.

The materials of Section I are presented in two chapters: "Man Speaking" and "The Act and Its Parts."

CHAPTER 1

Man Speaking

A SPEAKING WORLD

Historian Lynn Case has observed that most of man's "significant wrestling with his social environment has been by voice. Down through the ages the warnings of prophets, the sermons on the mount, the commands of caesars, the dialogue of philosophers, the orations of statesmen, the battle cries of warriors, the howling of mobs, the weeping of widows, the laughter of children, the judgment of magistrates, the curses of the damned—all the tongues of men and angels have swelled the chorus of history 'to the last syllable of recorded time.' " [1] Professor Case obviously views man speaking with a somewhat larger lens than may be appropriate for the student of public speaking. But even if we trim away the battle cries, howls, tears, laughter, and curses, we are left with the fact that both the nature of man and the history of his social organizations and institutions are inextricably linked to the human capacity for speech.

It will be useful, therefore, to begin our search for understanding of public speaking with a brief inquiry into the nature of speech. This behavior, apparently unique to man, makes possible the development of an art of public speaking. Its importance to man also gives rise to some of the deepest impulses, necessities, and problems of the public speaker.

THE NATURE OF SPEECH

We have called speech a "behavior." We observe it as our most common way of acting in the presence of others or when stimulated by some physical event in our environment.

At first glance this behavior is deceptively simple. This deceptive impression is encouraged by the universality of speech among men, and by the inconsequential amount of physical energy required for its production. Since all normal men talk, indeed since they usually begin talking

---

[1] Lynn M. Case, "Voices From the Past," *Quarterly Journal of Speech*, XXXVI (1950), 77.

before they are two years of age and become remarkable producers by age four or five, we may tend to be inattentive to implications derived from an understanding of how speech is learned, the multiple functions it serves, and its linked power and fragility.

A Learned Behavior

Speech, which seems natural to man, is nevertheless a learned behavior. It is learned as an elaborate structure of conventions, or "rules," for meaningful utterance. These rules are transmitted to children initially by the adults who care for them, with later elaborations probable from the influence of peers. Psychologist Roger Brown refers to this learning process as "the original word game," requiring for play a tutor, a pupil, and a set of rules which are reflected in the behavior of the tutor. These rules are both arbitrary and obligatory for the pupil who wishes to play the game.[2]

Thus the child who learns American English must learn to recognize the approximately 46 discrete categories of sound known as "phonemes," and to produce noises which will be recognized by those with whom he talks as belonging to these 46 categories. The child is quite capable of producing noises so at variance with these 46 categories as to be useless for the production of English words, although some of them might be conventional and useful for other languages. Thus the child experiences early the constraints placed on the behavior of one who hopes to communicate with his fellowmen. He must learn to recognize and interpret a growing number of words, and the rules by which these words are used to designate categories of objects and events in his environment. He must further learn the sentence patterns of his language—the rules for placing different form classes of words in meaningful sequences. The child who says, "Red is the green by surrounded house flowers," may get some attention from a concerned mother and might possibly arouse hope that he is a budding poet. But his chance of getting a response suggesting that he has been understood will be greatly improved by the pattern, "The green house is surrounded by red flowers."

The pupil has other rules to master. He must learn to interpret and use the conventions of vocal rate, force, pitch, inflection, and quality which his tutors use to modify, emphasize, or change the interpretation to be given to words and sentences. He must also learn the conventions of facial expression, bodily set, and gesture which are used for similar purposes, or are used frequently as substitutes for words or sentences. And finally, he becomes an initiate in the elaborate sequences of utter-

[2] Roger Brown, *Words and Things* (Glencoe, Illinois: The Free Press, 1958), Chapter I.

ance and rejoinder which reflect the expectation of his tutors that certain forms of statement ask for certain forms of response: the question asks for answer; the command for obedience, acknowledgment, or rebuff; the appraisal asks agreement, doubt, or disagreement, and so forth.

One may properly marvel that most children before they enter a period of formal schooling have mastered such an elaborate structure of behavior and the rules governing its deployment in meaningful speech. The speed with which this massive learning task is accomplished elicits the interest of scientists in the peculiar readiness of the maturing human organism for language acquisition, and the interest of philosophers and artists in the distinctively human need to act toward and with one's environment through use of symbols.[3]

But it is of more immediate concern to the student of public speaking to observe the sense in which the process of speech acquisition foreshadows the tensions of constraint and possibility faced by every public speaker, the multiplicity of functions served by public speeches, and the problem of communication implicit in every speaking situation.

Constraint and Possibility

The requirement of speech is that one acts through conventional forms known to one's listeners, forms which are the possession of a social group rather than an individual. In this sense, no one is free to talk as he wishes; he begins with the necessity of using forms which are obligatory in the language he employs, and his behavior is constrained by the expectations of an audience, whether that audience be one or two other people in a primary social group or the larger assembly typically faced by the public speaker. To speak effectively is to join some social group by accepting and acknowledging in one's own behavior the constraints placed by the conventions and expectations of that group.

The possibility of speech, however, lies in the fact that the shared forms of language, with all the obligations they impose on the speaker, have potential for endless productivity in creating new ways of treating objects, events, and relationships in one's environment. The potential productivity of a limited number of conventional linguistic forms is most easily illustrated by the observation that the 46 phonemes of English have been used to create approximately 600,000 words in current use by some speakers of this language. Furthermore, speakers of English continue to use this limited repertory of phonemes in the production of new terms for naming newly perceived features of their environment. The sense of the limitless productivity possible through language grows as one moves from the smallest language gestures to larger units of dis-

[3] See references at the end of Part I for further readings on such matters.

course. The speaker may stay within the phonemic, lexical, and grammatical conventions of his language. He may acknowledge the social expectations of his listeners. But he may also create new ways of interpreting objects and events—ways which may be unfamiliar to his listeners but nevertheless comprehensible. And he can create visions of a world which neither he nor his listeners have ever experienced. All orders of reality in nature, all visions of man become possible within the conventions of speech.

The tension of constraint and possibility is faced by every speaker. He can choose to talk only in ways which mirror the existing habits and views of his listeners, or he can choose to move from these to utterance making new possibilities available to those listeners. The competing claims of convention and creation make the speaker's choice difficult, and every public speaker seeking deliberate mastery of his art must learn to reconcile them. If he chooses to talk only in ways already known to and accepted by his listeners, he risks little, but he also counts for little.

MULTIPLE FUNCTIONS

The process of speech acquisition has three major consequences for the learner. It enables him to discover his identity—the answer to the all-important question of "who am I?"; it provides an instrument for giving form and order, and therefore meaning to his environment; and it gives him some capacity to communicate with his fellow human beings. These three major functions of language learning and behavior are not mutually exclusive; each depends upon the others for its fulfillment. But an understanding of all three functions is important to grasping both the necessities and the problems of the speaker.

The Discovery of Self

We often overlook the sense in which speakers, as they talk with other people, are engaging in acts of self-discovery. This function of speech is difficult to conceptualize, yet it serves the most pressing need of every human being. In his provocative work, *Mind, Self and Society,*[4] George Herbert Mead explores the way in which man acquires a concept of self, of a personal identity, through acts of communicating with others. Simply stated, we all learn to know who we are by seeing our selves mirrored in the actions others take toward us: in the value they grant to our statements, in their expectancies from us, in the responses they

[4] George Herbert Mead, *Mind, Self and Society* (Chicago: University of Chicago Press, 1934).

make to our acts of assertion. Thus as the child learns to talk with others, to understand their responses to his efforts to communicate, and to interpret their verbal efforts to elicit his response, he comes to see himself as worthwhile or worthless, responsible or erratic, creative or conventional.

For the child, this mirrored image of self may give rise to a quite unselfconscious sense of identity, especially if he lives with parents who obviously value him, his needs, and his efforts to communicate. For the adolescent moving into new social relations and subject to new needs, expectancies, and evaluations, the question of "who am I?" is likely to be agonizingly reawakened, never to be fully or comfortably answered as he pursues his lifelong quest for knowledge of his place in the universe. For the adult who speaks in public, each speech becomes a testing of whatever identity he brings to the occasion; the speaker may assert implicitly in his discourse that "I am this kind of person," and find in the response of others either confirmation or rejection of this self-appraisal. Or he may find his own uncertainty about who he is as a public person mirrored in the ambiguity of audience response.

There is a paradox in the fact that each man can come to know himself as unique, separate from, or different from other people only by using conventional forms of symbolic behavior which he shares with others. To be an identifiable person capable of creative acts is also to be a person joined to others by the social conventions of speech. In his quest for identity, the speaker faces once more the tension of constraint and possibility. He can find himself only by acknowledging the habits and expectancies of others; he can assert uniqueness only by moving beyond that which is already known and expected by those with whom he talks.

Giving Meaning

A second function of speech is that of giving meaning to our environment. Observe the three-year-old child busy at naming the objects he sees, searching to state their interrelationship and purpose, acting out his attitudes toward them, and you will understand the sense in which speech is an action to give meaning. Observe also the pleasure children take in repetitive acts of naming, even when no other person seems to listen or respond, and you will sense the deep importance of talk to the speaker, even apart from any response by a listener. Apparently we all use language to transform the "buzzing confusion" of our environment into knowable order. And apparently this very act of naming, or talking about, objects and events gives us a sense of relationship with them, or even a feeling of control over them.

This seemingly universal experience with the pleasure and power of naming may account for the prevalence of the belief in "word magic." Primitive people almost universally believe that physical events can be affected by symbolic actions directed at them, as in the case of rain dances, or hexes and incantations directed at the health or fortune of another person. Persons living in so-called advanced civilizations in which study of the physical and biological sciences is well regarded, discount the idea that words can affect directly the shape of a mountain, or bring on an attack of beriberi. But the shadows of belief in word magic are everywhere evident in our own civilization. The belief is recalled, with varying degrees of seriousness, by every baseball fan who warns that it will affect the fortunes of the pitcher in the midst of a no-hit game if the radio announcer discusses the no-hit possibility. It is reflected in the verbal behavior of the man who abuses the boulder over which he has tripped. It is subtly reinforced by our experience that a man who is told repeatedly that he doesn't look well is likely to begin to feel somewhat ill. And it may be reflected in the behavior of the public speaker who, having talked loudly and at length to an audience, assumes without further evidence that his listeners have been greatly affected by his discourse.

The question of the formative effect of speech on events external to the speaker is a complex one, and one which we will pursue later in this book in discussing the relationship of public speakers and their audiences. Certainly it is true that abusing a rock is not likely to make the rock feel guilty. But it is also true that objects named take on a different substance to the person who accepts the propriety of the name. Events talked about in a new way are never again the same to the talker, or to others persuaded of the legitimacy of his talk; the speech has given a new meaning to objects and events in the speaker's environment.[5] Thus, to speak is to give form, order, and meaning. This is an act, important to the speaker even if no one listens. The philosopher John Dewey is alleged to have commented on one occasion, as he completed a long and somewhat obscure discourse on a difficult problem, "I now understand my topic somewhat better than I did when I began talking." The whole goal of the public speaker who claims the time and attention of others can scarcely be limited to such self-edification. But it is helpful to observe that the act of talking to give meaning to oneself underlies and supports the further ambition of the public speaker to be understood by others and to shape their views.

[5] Apparently we all "see" the world through a particular filter provided by our way of talking about it. For futher discussion of this function of language, see the readings at the end of Part I.

③ Communication

The overarching function of language is communication. The child learning to talk is learning also to manage his relationships with other people. He not only discovers his identity as he learns to understand what others are saying to him; he also gives identity to others in his gestures toward them. The form, order, and meaning that speech gives to his environment is one he seeks to share with others. He learns quickly the comfort of shared information and attitudes, the power implicit in speech which elicits a desired response from others, and the frustrations of misunderstanding or requests which are denied.

From the simple fact that human beings mediate nearly all their relationships with one another through symbols, and most commonly through speech, stems all the immense power of mankind for social organization. This power is best understood if we observe that through speech two or more men can bring the not-present symbolically into common focus. They can talk of the past, real or fictional, and use its lessons in current calculations. They can talk of the future as though it were real, and make plans for future actions to be undertaken. They can seek common understanding of what ought, or ought not to be and then plan actions to bring into being the possibility created through speech.

Each of us daily uses the speech of communication for a variety of purposes: for sociability, for sharing information, for advocacy or persuasion, for inquiry, and for sharing experience. The speech of sociability is so commonplace and coterminous with daily life that we may scarcely be aware of its forms. The anthropologist Bronislaw Malinowski has given the somewhat formidable label of "phatic communion" to our use of speech to construct an atmosphere of good will, trust, or mutual appreciation. This function is observable in the social pleasantries of conversation, in "Inquiries about health, comments on weather, affirmations of some supremely obvious state of things." Such communication, Malinowski observes, brings people "savage and civilized alike into the pleasant atmosphere of polite, social intercourse." [6] The function is equally apparent in many public speeches, as the speaker acknowledges ritualistically his high regard for his listeners, and his sharing of their attitudes and purposes.

Apart from words, we may observe the symbolic importance of the speaker's manner in phatic communion. The ready smile, the firm handclasp, the look of interested attention all become forms of building soci-

[6] Bronislaw Malinowski, "The Problem of Meaning in Primitive Languages," in C. K. Ogden and I. A. Richards, *The Meaning of Meaning* 17th ed. (New York: Harcourt, Brace and Company, 1945), pp. 313–316.

ability, possibly more important than any audible utterance. Most college students, for example, come to understand how to preserve the illusion of phatic communion during a dull lecture, even if they refuse to respond in other ways.

The *information sharing* speech is almost equally commonplace. "Your shoes are in the upstairs closet," says a parent. A scientist reports his experiment. A newspaper reporter tells of an accident. A speech textbook asserts that speech is a conventional behavior. A college professor lectures on the taboos of primitive religions. These are obvious examples of information sharing, but what may be less obvious is the sense in which such sharing relates people to one another. If information is actually shared—if the labels or ways of talking about some aspect of experience are held in common by two or more people—a community has been established. The child becomes a member of the family as he learns the names of objects of household possessions. "This is a print of a painting by Van Gogh," says a host to his guest. The guest, who already thought he knew this, feels the relationship of shared information. "You are standing near a rattlesnake," says a camper to his friend, and after certain hasty movements, the friend may pause to be grateful that speech permits a ready sharing of information.

A third mode of communication is that of *advocacy,* or persuasion. The advocate asks that others share not only his information, but also certain attitudes or beliefs; or he may ask that others act in ways he recommends. In this sense, his speech includes the community-building capacity of the speech of sociability or information, but goes beyond these modalities in its explicit search for acceptance of the beliefs or actions recommended by the speaker. This is the speech of command. "The Red Coats are coming," says a fictional warrior. (He is sharing information.) "Fire when you see the whites of their eyes." (He is advocating an action he hopes others will follow in the best spirit of military cooperation.) "There are three reasons why you should not take the family car tonight," says a parent. (He is testing the power of rational advocacy or persuasion as a means of getting cooperation, perhaps hopeful that he will not be driven to command.)

Advocacy is the commonplace mode of the public platform. It is also the speech of the political campaign, the legislative assembly, and the court of law. These latter contexts usually involve the speeches of opposing advocates, each seeking a community of purpose or belief relevant to his purposes. And in the presence of opposing advocacy, the listener has opportunity to perceive speech as entering the mode of *inquiry.*

The mode of *inquiry* uses speech to search out the information, beliefs, attitudes, or actions around which community may be formed. In its simplest expression this involves no more than a question and a rejoinder. In its more complex expressions it involves the public forms of debate, discussion, or dialogue. Debates, by providing a forum for opposing advocacy, enable listeners to engage in reflective search for their own decisions. They also provide opposing advocates with the materials for negotiation—or a search for positions which they can mutually endorse. When we sense that disputants are genuinely seeking resolution of their disagreements, we ordinarily refer to the event as a discussion or a negotiation rather than a debate. The term *dialogue* is also used to designate conversation marked by a totally open search for clarification and understanding of the differences and agreements among two or more speakers. Although the mode of inquiry seems more suited to group rather than individual speaking, a lecturer or platform speaker may conduct his utterance in ways designed to stimulate search or inquiry in his listeners.

Our final mode of communication is not so easily described as the others. The storyteller in one sense seems to be sharing information, or perhaps soliciting cooperation in some belief or action. But the better the story is told and the more complete its artistry, the more we sense that the speaker is seeking our imaginative participation in the whole of some human experience, whether the experience be real or created from the materials of reality. The storyteller, the dramatist, the novelist, or the poet may engage in an action capable of evoking for a listener or reader a sense of participation in some part of life itself. His language, if skillful enough, may make tangible all the qualities of human experience with life—tragedy, conflict, humor, paradox, doubt, rage, love—all these may for a moment in time be controlled symbolically by the speaker and those who share his utterance. Such speech is often said to serve a *consummatory* rather than an *instrumental* end. The speaker does not ask for something more from his listeners after his discourse—for evidences of friendship, or remembrance, or cooperation. He asks only that they accept at a point in time that "this is the way life is."

These five modes of communication—sociability, sharing information, advocacy, inquiry, and sharing experience—appear early in the behavior of children acquiring speech. They are equally observable as the functions of adult communication. And they are used with purpose and prior calculation by public speakers seeking particular relationships with audiences.

The Fragility of Communication [7]

Because speech serves us so well in innumerable daily acts of communication, the extraordinary fragility of the effort of one man to be understood by another is often overlooked. To be sure, we have all had experience with being misunderstood or misinterpreted, or with having our best efforts at persuasion prove to be resoundingly unsuccessful. But too often we attribute such failures to the inattentiveness, stupidity, or perverseness of those with whom we are talking. And too seldom do we observe that the very nature of speech, including characteristics which give it remarkable power, tends to make all efforts at communication at least partially unsuccessful.

The difficulty in communication begins with the fact that we learn our speech as a set of complex "rules of the game," as the game is played by some primary social group in which we achieve membership. These rules and the behavior they justify always vary subtly, and sometimes dramatically, from group to group. In the very process of achieving membership and identity with one social group, we acquire behaviors which mark us as something of a stranger to groups with different habits. The verbal gestures which worked as well as possible in our family, for example, may not work well at all with the members of other families. The habits of pronunciation which made us inconspicuous in one social group or one section of the nation may make us conspicuous in a different group or different locale. The objects, events, and actions which enjoy high value in the groups with which we identify, and the language used to designate these values, may be given quite different scales of importance in a different social group. Consider, for example, the communication problem faced by the speaker who believes meekness a higher value than aggressiveness in talking to listeners who reverse this order.

The notion that all speakers of American English talk the same language is a part truth; it is equally true to say that they speak as many varieties of this language as there are different social groups in this nation, varied according to their educational, recreational, vocational, religious, or economic experiences. One of the major problems of every public speaker is that of finding a language, a view of reality, an order of values, an identity which will somehow be understandable or interpretable to the members of a given audience. If the speaker compre-

---

[7] Because effective and efficient communication is so essential in our increasingly complex world, the study of communication failure and barriers to communication has expanded greatly in our century. We touch only briefly on this important topic in this section of the book. For further discussion, see the readings at the end of Part I.

hends the varied experiences with language his listeners are likely to have had, he will also understand the difficulty of his enterprise, as well as understanding the amount of work prior to speaking which may be needed to assure some success and the fact that some residue of failure with some listeners will attend even his best efforts.

The difficulty in communication is also inherent in the fact that words are not the equivalents of the objects or events being talked about; rather they are symbols which abstract from reality certain features or aspects. Thus, even the simplest of words, such as "cat," refers not to the total reality of some specific furry and four-legged creature, but rather to those attributes of a class of objects which enable us to categorize certain creatures as cats, and to differentiate these creatures from dogs, birds, trees, and snakes. By abstracting from reality, and establishing categories of objects and events, language achieves its immense power to create form, order, and therefore meaning. With the single word "cat" we can direct attention to the similarities of a tomcat and a mountain lion, and by metaphoric extension we can even use the term to characterize some human beings. By the similar power of abstraction from reality, we can develop a way of communicating about events as complex as forms of government—such as democracies, dictatorships, and the like—or about concepts as elusive as freedom, or justice, or beauty. Using such terms, men are able to develop shared intentions concerning matters of political organization or to seek shared valuations concerning different objects, ways of living, or ways of behaving toward one another.

Symbols abstract from reality, and this gives them their immense power for organizing human thought and action. But the fact that they do abstract also creates difficulty between speakers and listeners. Can any speaker be sure that the precise set of attributes he has in mind when he calls a government a "democracy" are the attributes that his listener has in mind? When he says "all men are born equal," does he hold attributes for the concept of equality which are necessarily those selected by his listener? And does he place the same value on equality as that placed by his listener? The public speaker who believes he has been misinterpreted may not be confronting stupidity in his listeners, but only the fact that they have given attributes and values to his language which were not at all those he had in mind.

A third problem of communication rises from the fact that speech is the behavior by which men discover and announce their identity, and by which they attribute identity to others. Speakers and their listeners are forever involved in the business of seeking to classify themselves for others, or in seeking to classify others. This process is part of the fundamental language functions of self-discovery and giving order and meaning to one's environment. But there is no certainty that the "self" a speaker claims is the one which will be granted him by any given listener. He may believe himself to be a man of good will, and therefore worth listening to, but he may encounter listeners who find in him attributes they associate with men who are deceptive, or exploitative in their treatment of others. His listeners may discount or reject his utterance not because of its substance, but because of what they believe to be true of the speaker. Listeners who attribute unwholesome character or intentions to a speaker may find it more comfortable to act contrary to his advice rather than cooperatively, or to believe the contrary of that which he asserts to be true. Thus most Americans in recent years have been notably unsympathetic listeners to speakers they identify as Communists; working men may be skeptical of the intentions of their employers; Democrats and Republicans have a notable penchant for not understanding one another; young men have been known to be inattentive to the advice of their elders, and so forth. Public speakers face the fact that part of their identity may be already known to their listeners before they begin talking, and that this identity will either support or hinder their chances of being understood. They face the problem and opportunity of affecting the judgments of others concerning their identity by the manner in which they conduct their speeches.

A fourth problem of communication also stems from the fact that we use language to give order and meaning to our environment. The speaker who talks about our environment may threaten our security, especially if he talks about events external to us in ways which are unfamiliar, or which present an order of reality which conflicts with the one we have known. For this reason, we may find it more comfortable to forget what he says or to distort what he says rather than to seek real understanding of his utterance. The fact that listeners will forget or distort information contrary to their biases, or contrary to an order of reality they have accepted, has been well established by a growing body of experimental evidence. Similarly, listeners will attend to, accept, and remember information which fits into an order of reality already accepted. This tendency is so powerful that it distorts the critical powers of listeners, making them receptive to the most dubious statements of alleged fact that comfort them. Equally, they tend to reject the most reputable and well supported statements of fact that threaten them. Apparently, none of us likes to hear or remember "bad news," but we are eager for "good news" and quite uncritical about its truth.

The tendency to distort what one hears presents the public speaker with some of his most troublesome ethical and tactical choices. He can

often win applause and immediate credence from an audience by statements which will comfort their existing beliefs, even when he thinks such
statements to be half truths at best. But of course the speaker who
chooses this course becomes a deliberate partisan of deception. His
choice may give him an immediate problem of living with himself and
may damage his credibility with other audiences. The speaker can also
choose a kind of success with an audience by not troubling their biases.
If he does, he rejects the greater and more difficult task of helping listeners to grow beyond themselves, to find some new order of reality which,
by the speaker's art, can be made both tenable and memorable.

FROM SPEECH TO PUBLIC SPEAKING

Our brief exploration of the nature of speech has been preliminary to
the central concern of this book with the art of public speaking. But at
least one general perspective on public speaking should emerge from the
exploration conducted thus far. *There is no fundamental discontinuity
between the necessities, opportunities, and problems of the public
speaker, and those confronted by every person using speech in the conduct of his daily affairs.*

Speech is a human behavior, a distinctively human mode of acting toward one's environment and one's fellowmen. So is public speaking. We
sometimes think of public speeches merely as artifacts created by men,
and somehow standing outside man, to be contemplated as one might
examine a painting or piece of sculpture. We would do better to think of
the public speech as a human action, undertaken in greater or lesser degree by all men, and involving the inseparable unity of a man and his
utterance, the unity of man speaking. In this sense, a manuscript or a
text is not a public speech, although it may be an important fossil or
consequence of a given human action. In this sense also there can be no
real separation in a public speech of the speaker and his utterance, the
man and his message. The public speaker seeks to enter into a relationship with other human beings, to know and be known by them, to share
human concerns about the form of an external world of objects and
events, and an internal world of values and plans. Man speaking is more
than a man giving a speech.

Speech is a learned behavior, and so is public speaking. The child
must come to understand the "rules" of the language game as it is
played by his tutors; the public speaker must seek to know the habits
and expectancies of his audience as the beginning point of his hope to
understand and be understood by them. Both speech and public speaking involve man in the tension of constraint and possibility, in knowl-

edge of what he must do to be understood, and simultaneous knowledge of the productivity possible through language behavior. Speech serves multiple functions, and so does public speaking. And the overriding function of communication, so central to the art of public speaking, is a fragile human enterprise beset with problems which are inherent in the very factors which give it such power.

THE NATURE OF PUBLIC SPEECH

In thus emphasizing the fundamental continuity of public speaking and speech generally, we should not overlook the factors which enable us to set some events apart from the whole of human speaking and call these events "public speeches."

A number of the criteria for differentiation are obvious enough. Public speeches are usually thought of as somewhat formal events in which one person talks for some period of time with the presumption that he won't be interrupted. The criteria of *formality and duration* are, of course, very loose ones. Mr. Blodgett's public speech to the P.T.A. on the need to serve more orange juice during the free lunch period may be quite informal, while a President's inaugural address will be surrounded by highly formal and traditional rituals. Similarly, Lincoln's Gettysburg Address probably took less than three minutes in delivery, while the summation of lawyer Clarence Darrow in the well-known Leopold and Loeb murder case took the better part of a working day.

A more important demarcation is the fact that public speeches typically differentiate sharply the role of the speaker and the role of the audience, as contrasted with the changing roles assumed by conversationalists or participants in a discussion. This polarization of speaker-audience roles serves to center attention on the speaker and to make his character and behavior the central event of a social situation. It should increase the speaker's sense of responsibility, and it is likely to increase his nervous tension.

Polarization, and the centering of attention on a given speaker, also leads to many of the social conventions which have come to be associated with public speaking events. There is, for example, the convention of having the speaker introduced so that his identity may be established in ways useful to his purpose, and there is the reciprocal problem public speakers often experience in responding gracefully to either an overly lavish or awkward introduction. There is the convention that public speakers stand while talking, to increase the ease with which they may be seen and heard by the audience, and to dramatize the importance of their role. This convention is sometimes ignored if the speaker finds standing a physical burden, as was the case with President Franklin Roosevelt. It is sometimes violated by design if the speaker wishes to reduce the formality of his relationship with the audience. And it is sometimes violated because of the speaker's timidity, which he may hope will be regarded by the audience as either informality or winning diffidence.

The characteristic polarization of speaker and audience in the public speaking situation sometimes seems to have unfortunate consequences. The speaker may forget that he is engaged in an effort to talk with his listeners, to interact with them much in the manner of conversation even though there is no overt exchange of language. The speaker not only stands apart from his listeners; he may emphasize the fact that he is standing apart by performing for them rather than talking with them, or by reading a manuscript as though the piece of typescript rather than the speaker was doing the talking. Such responses to polarization may be thought of as characteristics of bad public speeches, but not as criteria differentiating the public speech from good conversation or discussion.

Two other factors serve to distinguish public speaking from speech generally. These are the general association of public speaking with the ongoing life of public organizations or institutions, and the general presumption that the public speaker's behavior is deliberately and purposefully chosen. These characteristics of public speech are of such importance to its art that they will be given somewhat more extended consideration.

Public Speaking and the Life of Public Institutions

One cannot study the history of any of man's public institutions without noting the way in which their life is linked to speechmaking. Political institutions create the forums for the public speeches of politicians and statesmen; religious institutions have their preachers and prophets; courts of law, their jurists and attorneys; and schools, their teachers, students, and administrators. Businessmen gather to hear speeches, as do labor unions, clubs, and the variety of civic and cultural organizations characteristic of American public life. The occasion and setting for the public speech is ordinarily provided by some public institution or organization.

The coexistence of speechmaking and the life of our social institutions is more than a matter of accident or custom. Rather it is the case that public discourse is the instrument by which human institutions are formed, by which they are maintained, and by which they are either destroyed or changed. Organizations can be formed because a group of men have discovered through language that they hold certain purposes in common, and that they can reach agreement as to the way in which they will cooperate to achieve those purposes. Organizations are maintained by speeches which remind members of their common purposes and values and which rekindle their enthusiasm for participation in some common enterprise. Organizations are transformed by speeches which seek modification of the purposes, values, and forms of action agreed to by members; and they are destroyed by the thrust of criticism which induces disaffection from members. Speechmaking thus becomes part of the fabric of man's social organizations and institutions. One may know much of the history of any social organization by examining the speeches to which its members attend. One may know much of the purposes and problems of any public speaker by asking about the nature of the social organization which provided the occasion for his discourse.

The dependence of organizations on public speeches is readily illustrated in ancient societies. The first books on the art of public speaking known to the Western world were written in ancient Greece, and reflected the important status of this art as one which served the needs of political organization. Thus the political system of Athens centered in the gathering of citizens to hear, judge, and respond to deliberative speeches advocating proper policies for the state. They also gathered to hear ceremonial speeches evoking remembrance of values which bound the people of the state in common cause. Similarly, the Athenian legal system established a system for judging the merits of allegations of wrongdoing, or disputes over property, by hearings before magistrates and juries in which the litigants pleaded their own cases. To the Athenian citizen, deliberative, ceremonial, and forensic public speeches were part of the essential life of the state, and of the system of social organization identifying that state. To be a citizen and to take part in the life of the state meant also to be a speechmaker, and a judge of public speeches.[8]

The organization of Athenian public life was comparatively simple compared with the organization of public life in contemporary America. The public speaker in America no longer finds his only forum in political or legal organization. The institutional context for his speech may involve the purposes of a church or a school, of a business corporation, a garden club, or a society to preserve old buildings. It is not entirely true that to be a citizen means to be a speechmaker, although to be an influential citizen means the making of speeches and acting as judge of public speeches. We cannot describe as readily as the Athenians the occasions for public speeches, or the particular institutional constraints

[8] For further discussion of the relationship of speechmaking and social organization, see the readings at the end of Part I.

and expectancies which may be faced by a given speechmaker. But we can observe that today, as in the ancient world, public speeches find their occasion in the life of some social organization; that their general purpose has to do with the formation, maintenance, and modification of social organizations and institutions; and that their effective conduct requires that the speaker understand the constraints and expectancies of the organization which provides his forum.

Public Speaking as a Purposive Art

The final, and perhaps most important characteristic of public speaking is its status as a purposive and deliberate art. To be sure, all speech performs some function, but in the give and take of everyday conversation, speakers often act without forethought or without conscious awareness of any specific purpose. The public speaker, however, is presumed to have a specific purpose. His audience, which is granting him the central position in some social situation, may properly assume that he has thought in advance about the way he will use his time and that each part of his utterance has been chosen because the speaker believes it will best serve his purpose. Thus it should be possible to ask a public speaker why he selected a particular way of opening his address rather than some possible alternative, or why he chose one argument rather than another in support of his thesis. It is even reasonable to ask him what he hoped to accomplish with his discourse, although if the public speaker feels that his purpose should have been perfectly clear, the question may irritate him.

The presumption that the public speaker has a purpose, and that he has deliberately chosen both the substance and the manner of his utterance, makes it possible to think of public speaking as an art. It is essentially an art of choosing wisely from the alternative possibilities open to the speaker in every situation he confronts. Thus the study of public speaking becomes ultimately the study of why men might choose to act in given ways in a specific speaking situation, of the alternative choices open to them, and of the possible consequences of these options. This study has traditionally been named *rhetoric.* It is a study which can inform the practice of men who wish to perfect the art of speaking effectively and responsibly, as well as shaping the judgment of all those who listen and respond to public discourse.

VALUES IN STUDYING PUBLIC SPEAKING

In our discussion thus far we have observed how speech is prerequisite to the development of a sense of identity, and how public speech serves to establish, maintain, and modify social institutions. We conclude this opening chapter with an application of these concepts to the question of the values which may be achieved through the study of public speaking.

Students of public speaking often state that through study and practice they hope to become more self-confident in public situations. This aspiration is worthy, but alone it does not justify study of the art.

We have suggested that speech is the instrument through which we discover an answer to the question, "who am I?" We suggest here that public speaking is the instrument through which we discover the answer to important related questions: "Who am I as a public person? What is it that I know, or believe, with sufficient certainty that I sense the importance of sharing this knowledge or belief with others? What will be the nature of my influence and participation in the public affairs of my society?" The study of public speaking, and participation in public speaking makes available some part of the answer to these questions. It is extraordinarily difficult for any person to "know what he knows" until he has submitted this knowledge to the discipline of putting it into a publicly communicable form, and submitted it to insights provided by the responses of others. Just as we see the answer to the question "who am I?" reflected in the way others respond in our presence, so we test the clarity, appropriateness, and persuasiveness of our knowledge by submitting it to the public response of an audience. The preparation of a public speech, if carefully undertaken, becomes in itself a way of achieving control over some aspect of our environment. It is a way of converting vague thoughts, jumbled information, and half-held beliefs into clear, orderly, and precise positions. The public testing of information and ideas becomes a means of discovering the terms on which we can enter publicly into effective interaction with others.

But we set our discussion of the significance of speech in a social as well as personal context. From the point of view of society the study of public speaking is concerned not simply with the personal goals of individuals, for it has a bearing on the health of all social institutions that depend in part upon public communication for their maintenance and development. It is doubtless more than a cultural accident that the study of public speaking was a central concern of the educational systems of the earliest efforts at democratic society—in ancient Athens, and in the Roman republic. A political system that depends for its strength upon the public deliberations of its citizens needs articulate citizens. A society which assumes that free discussion can produce wise decisions lives with an illusion unless a reasonable proportion of its citizens are able effectively to take part in such discussion. A society that assumes that the guarantee of free speech will insure both that power is prudently distributed and that decision-making will be subjected to constant correction—such a society places its faith in an illusion unless people who are free to speak are also competent to speak.

Finally, the condition of public communication in any society becomes a product not so much of the capability of those who speak as of those who make up the audience. An audience generally ignorant of what a speech could or ought to be, passive in the presence of incompetence, patient in the presence of vagueness, eager for the comforting sounds of flattery and old slogans—an audience uncritical because it has never thought seriously about the purposes of speechmaking and has no vision of the means suitable to these purposes—such people will generate, and will deserve, a low standard of public communication. Their society will be the poorer for it.

It is commonly observed that great drama requires a great audience. It must be equally true that good speaking demands a good audience. If the standards of public address in twentieth century America are lower than they should be—a possibility which has often been voiced—then the cause might lie not so much in those who speak as in the lack of a sufficient audience of those who have studied public speaking. Citizens are the caretakers not only of their private interests, but also of the standards of public communication in their society.

SUMMARY

Public speaking finds its basis in the distinctively human behavior known as speech. This behavior is acquired by all normal men early in life under conditions which impose on the speaker a set of socially accepted conventions or "rules" for meaningful behavior, but which also give to the speaker a system of behavior capable of almost limitless possibilities for discovering new meanings, new ways of giving order to one's environment, and new forms of social cooperation.

The acquisition of speech has three important consequences: it enables the learner to discover his identity; it provides him with an instrument for giving form and order, and therefore meaning to his environment; and it serves his efforts to communicate with his fellowmen. These major functions of language are not mutually exclusive, but depend on one another. Men communicate for purposes of sociability, sharing information, soliciting cooperation, sharing experience, and inquiry. This enterprise of communication, so central to public speaking, is a fragile one. The characteristics of language which give it such great power also make probable some residue of misunderstanding.

The necessities, opportunities, and problems faced by men in any speaking situation also apply to public speaking. But although public speaking is clearly only a particular variant of speech, certain criteria enable us to designate some acts as public speeches. Public speeches are characterized by some level of formality and some duration. They are also characterized by polarization of the role of speaker and listener, with the central position in a social situation given to a particular speaker. The polar roles assumed by a public speaker and his audience lead some speakers to lose sight of the essential fact that to speak effectively they must interact with their listeners and not simply perform before them. In this sense, the public speech remains at its best a case of "man speaking," and not of "man making a speech."

Two very important characteristics also differentiate public speech from the generality of speaking. First, public speeches are part of the life of public institutions. They make social organization possible; they serve to maintain, modify, and sometimes to destroy social organizations. The public speaker usually finds the occasion for and general purpose of his action in the life of some social organization or institution. Second, public speeches are presumed to be purposive acts in which the speaker has selected with forethought his goals, his materials, and his manner of address. In this sense, the public speaker may be said to be practicing an art. This art is ultimately an art of choosing, of selecting from alternative possibilities the materials and manner most likely to achieve a given purpose. Thus the student of public speaking should seek to become proficient in the art of choosing wisely.

The study of public speaking, and the search for excellence in its practice are demonstrably matters of great importance, both to the individual and to society.

CHAPTER 2

The Act and Its Parts

OBSERVING PUBLIC SPEECHES

The English literary critic Matthew Arnold thought that the basis of his art lay in the capacity to see things as they are. This same capacity, Arnold believed, was a requirement for civilized living, since no man could know how to act toward objects and events unless he understood their whole nature.[1]

An analogue of Arnold's requirement for civilized living would seem worth considering by the student of public speaking. Underlying the speaker's capacity to choose wisely how to act in any given situation is his picture of the nature of that situation. For this reason the study of public speaking both begins and ends in the effort to see speeches for what they are, to understand as fully as possible the nature of their being and action.

The most serious difficulties, however, attend the search for a genuine understanding of public speeches. These difficulties begin with the fact emphasized in Chapter 1: that a public speech is not an object or artifact which can be contemplated at leisure; rather it is a human action taking place in a particular social situation which brings together a speaker, listeners, and purposes in a relationship which is always, in some respects, unique. As we observe a speaker trying to manage a particular situation, we necessarily confront a complex interplay of forces which affect the speaker's behavior and the response of his listeners. We must ask such questions as these: Who is the speaker, for whom does he speak, and for what purpose? How does he perceive his listeners, their expectations of him, and the requirements of the occasion? Who are the listeners, and what purposes, perceptions, and expectations do they bring to the occasion? What events have gone before, and what events will come after, which may affect our understanding of the action in process? The answer to each question is important to our effort to know a speech for "what it is," and yet these answers involve information which is likely to be only partially available to us.

[1] Matthew Arnold, "The Functions of Criticism in the Present Time," from *Essays in Criticism* (New York: The Macmillan Company, 1880), pp. 3–38.

The difficulty in understanding a particular public speech resides also in the fact that we are either a participant in its action, or else cut off from much that is important to the action. If the speech is in process, we are there as speaker or audience member, affecting the event by our presence. However, if we study the speech by reading the text and by examining historical records about the speaker, audience, and occasion, we have at best an incomplete picture of the event.

Clearly the task of understanding a public speech is difficult. Its action is complex and is grounded in particular and varying historical circumstances; its purposes may be obvious or hidden; its consequences may be apparent or obscure, fleeting or enduring. Yet the whole action, the whole event, is the complicated reality that public speakers must work with in choosing the substance and manner of their discourse. This is also the reality that listeners confront as they respond to or form judgments about the event. We can, however, acknowledge this difficulty— confronting the probability that no one is ever likely to understand the totality of any given speech—and still accept the necessity of seeking to perfect our capacity to understand. To get on with this necessary task, we shall first propose a general perspective for observing public speeches, and then turn to a set of terms and concepts useful in uncovering in detail the nature and action of a public speech.

A CONTINGENT ACTION

The most useful general perspective for viewing a public speech is one which emphasizes the contingency of each aspect of the event and each choice made by the speaker. Each aspect and each choice can be understood and appraised only if one observes its relationship to all other aspects, and to other possible choices by the speaker. Thus it is not the case that a given person is a better speaker than another person for all audiences, for all purposes, and on all occasions. For example, President Franklin Roosevelt was justly famed for his speaking skill, but one may properly wonder if he knew as well how to manage the understanding and aspirations of rural Louisiana voters as did a contemporary of his, Governor Huey Long. However, Roosevelt has taken his place in history as one of the great public speakers of our century, and Long as a skillful demagogue. These disparate classifications warn us of the difficulty of understanding public speeches. When we praise a speaker's skill, we may mean that we cannot conceive of a situation, an audience, a purpose, or a type of subject matter that he could not handle with superlative effectiveness. If so, we have given very high praise indeed. But it is more likely that our praise carries with it implicit assumptions: that we see this speaker as greatly effective with audiences we believe to be judi-cious, with subject matter we believe to be important, and for purposes we find worthy.

Similarly, each choice made by a speaker on a particular occasion is good or bad, effective or ineffective, only in relation to the social field for which the choice is made. The contingencies affecting a speaker's choices will be given much more attention in this book than the consid-erations which make one speaker better suited than another for a given audience or occasion. Obviously speakers cannot be certain that they will be asked to talk or will wish to talk only on occasions for which they are better suited than any other person. And even if this were the case, each occasion faced by a speaker is in some sense new or unique; his artistry is to be freshly tested as he chooses for a particular case the substance and manner of his utterance.

In a commonsense way most of us understand that a speaker's choices are contingent. With minimal thought we would know why Abraham Lincoln, as President, did not in his inaugural or ceremonial addresses make use of the homely anecdotes which served him so well as conversationalist, frontier lawyer, or candidate for public office in Illinois. We can understand why it would have been wrong for President Lyndon Johnson to have used the language of President Dwight Eisen-hower's inaugural address for his own inauguration, even aside from the impropriety of plagiarism. The disproportion in political philosophy of the two men, and the differences in the expectations of their supporters and of the nation's circumstances called for different language. We can observe how a speaker might appropriately praise one audience for its generosity and wisdom, and seem either fulsome or ironic if he used the same language with a different audience. We can see that a speaker might need models or pictures to serve as analogies in explaining the structure of the atom to an audience of college freshmen, but be able to talk more efficiently and accurately to an audience of professional physi-cists by using only mathematical formulations. We might find it appro-priate for a speaker to thunder defiance of his nation's enemies in a time of war, but be struck by the absurdity of the same tone in a discourse on the depredations of the coyote.

Yet despite this commonsense understanding, we are too much given to talking about a speaker's choices as though they were by definition, or in some immutable way, the right or wrong choices. "Jones is a good speaker," we aver, "because he gives a humorous twist to all his com-ments," but a few days later we may discover that Johnson is a good speaker because of the high seriousness and manifest sincerity of his manner. "Brown is a good speaker," we assert, "because he makes clear at the very outset of his talks exactly what he wants his audience to know, believe, or do." But on another occasion we find ourselves full of praise for Swanson's skill in leading an audience to a conclusion which he has avoided announcing or asserting. If we try hurriedly to convert our own pleasure in a particular speech into statements about "the principles or rules for good speaking," we may simply be deluding ourselves as to the nature of public speech. To the extent that we seek some immutable rules for successful public speaking, we blind ourselves to the fact that speakers must choose from among alternative ways of encompassing the particular contingencies of a given situation. Each choice takes account of these contingencies in a different way. No choice is inevitably "right" for all situations. If we hope to extend our power to see public speeches for what they are, to choose wisely in our own speaking, and to respond wisely to the speaking of others, then we must lay aside the easy search for rules. We must undertake the more difficult task of exploring imaginatively the alternative choices available to a speaker on a given occasion, seeking to uncover the potentialities and limitations of each alternative.

Speeches and Games

The general perspective for observing a complex social action such as a public speech is similar to the point of view we bring to the observation of games. Psychologist Viktor Frankl calls attention to the importance of contingencies in judging the meaning or value of any human behavior by using the analogy of a chess game. He points to the inherent foolishness of asking a chess champion this question: "Tell me, Master, what is the best move in the world?" Frankl goes on to comment: "There is no such thing as the best or even a good move apart from the particular situation in a game and the particular personality of one's opponent." [2]

Once we have learned the purpose and rules (constraints on choice) for a particular game, most of us find pleasure in observing the game by examining players' moves in a particular situation. At a given moment in a chess game, a player may have available several possible moves. At times one of these is so clearly the best choice that we may be appalled if the player fails to make it; another may be so clearly a disastrous choice that we would be equally appalled if the player selected it. But oftentimes the player has several possible moves available, each of which takes account of the contingencies in a different way. One may be a "gambling" move—a thrust for quick success carrying heavy risk. An-

[2] Viktor E. Frankl, *Man's Search For Meaning* (New York: Washington Square Press, Inc., 1963), p. 71.

other move may be cautious—it risks little and seeks more knowledge about the response of the opponent before further choices are made. Neither move is inherently good or bad, but each fits into a set of complex relationships in a different way. The favorite perspective of the informed observer of games—whether of chess, or tennis, or football—is that of asking why one choice was made by a player rather than another.

The analogy of the public speech and a competitive game can, of course, be carried too far. The speaker who thinks of his listeners as opponents rather than people likely to be willing to cooperate with him in a search for common understanding has already made a choice potentially destructive to his purpose, although there are, of course, many speeches set within an explicit or implicit context of debate between opposing ideas and opposing lines of argument. Similarly, the speaker who thinks of his action as simply recreational demeans the personal and social importance of the art he practices.

If, however, one abstracts from the theory of games only the idea of a human action taking place within a social field—including purpose, rules or constraints, and a sequence of contingent choices—then the analogy becomes not only plausible but also instructive. The public speaker enters a social field for certain purposes, some of which he may choose and some of which may be given by the occasion. He must observe certain constraints—obligations laid down by the linguistic system available to him and his listeners, and more or less restrictive pressures laid down by the nature of the occasion and the expectations of his audience. He has a variety of choices open to him which take into account, in different ways, the contingencies of the situation. He is relatively successful or unsuccessful in relation to his purpose. His "game" is assuredly more complex, more significant, more subject to reconstruction of purpose and possibility than even the most complicated recreational games invented by man. But the speech, like the game, can be viewed both in prospect and retrospect as a human action seeking to encompass for certain purposes, through a sequence of choices, the contingencies of a particular social situation. This is the general perspective most useful for observing public speeches and for developing wisdom in conducting or responding to such events.

A SET OF TERMS FOR ANALYZING SPEAKING EVENTS

Informed understanding of a public speech requires not only a general perspective for viewing such an event, but also a set of terms or concepts useful in uncovering its details. The exploration of terms which follows is preliminary in the sense that each of the items to be discussed will be used further or given further analysis in subsequent chapters. Thus the purpose here is only to define a structure of terms which can serve as a frame of reference for the more detailed and limited subject matter of the chapters which follow.

Four major dimensions of public speeches can be observed directly. These are the *speaker,* his *speech* (utterance or discourse), the *audience,* and the *occasion.* The second dimension, the speech, can be analyzed in terms of *purpose, position, movement, structure, forms of enforcement,* and *style.* Since speeches are purposive actions, a dimension of *effect* also becomes important, even though observations about effect often take the form of indirect inferences. And since public speeches tend to be associated with the life of public institutions and organizations, a theory of types of speeches also becomes useful. We shall advance the somewhat traditional concepts of *expository, persuasive,* and *ceremonial* speeches as a set of types sufficient to our purposes.

These fourteen terms are all in common usage in the discussion of public speeches, and most of them would seem to provide few problems of definition. But even such obvious questions as "who is the speaker?" and "who is the audience?" turn up unexpected complications.

THE SPEAKER

The *speaker* seems clearly enough the person doing the talking on the occasion of a public speech. But certain curiosities attach themselves to the person of the speaker, sufficient to make answer to the question "who is talking?" less than immediately clear. On some occasions speakers talk only for themselves. On other occasions they speak as representatives of some other person or of an institution. For example, the President of the United States in recent decades has employed a press secretary. During the administration of President Dwight Eisenhower, his press secretary, Mr. James Hagerty, often explained to the press the "official" position of the administration or the President on matters of public policy. Mr. Hagerty was there. He spoke. But the significance of his utterance rested less in the person of Mr. Hagerty than in the shadow of the President or the administration standing behind the speaker. The point is a simple but important one: the speaker may be viewed simply as a person, or he may be viewed as a person representing some other person or group. If the speaker serves as a representative, his substance has been altered somewhat. As "spokesman" he is limited in the choice of what he may say, indeed in the very attitude he may reflect, by the obligations he has assumed toward the person or institution he represents.

The speaker is a man or woman. He may also be a symbol. Most of us have had occasion to observe the King or Queen of England speaking in public and have noted the use of the pronoun "we" in such utterance. "We deem it appropriate," says the Queen, and by the use of "We" she indicates that she speaks not simply as woman or person, but as representative of a venerable institution. This is not Queen Elizabeth seeking reelection or seeking to express her personal views on some current bit of legislation. The former role would be irrelevant; the latter role, altogether inappropriate for the Queen as Queen. This is an abstract institution speaking. The British monarchy has been made animate and visible in the person of the Queen. It must speak through her, and she must speak as she thinks the monarchy would speak.

The distinction between speaker as person and speaker as representative may seem at first to be of little importance to the student seeking development of his own public speaking skills. But a larger view of the development of every public speaker reveals the sense in which each of us as a person speaks also as a representative. As "person" we all enter into the business of a public speech with certain capabilities and limitations. Some of these capabilities and limitations are scarcely modifiable. We may believe that we would be better public speakers if we were taller, or if our voice carried the resonance of a basso profundo. But we know that elevator shoes can modify one's stature only within limits (and is it worth it?), while the human voice is modifiable only within certain limits laid down by its physical structures. "Person" as a physical being is only the easiest and most obvious aspect of the self we know, and which we take with us into a public speech. But we also take into some speaking situations some concept of ourselves as "representative," even when we are not really required to act as representative. Each of us as a public person, early in life, begins to act in varying ways as a representative of different groups with which we can identify ourselves—our church, our government, certain social and recreational groups, etc. The final conception we have of ourselves as a public person represents a long period of interaction between certain aspects of person or personality which we believe are uniquely ours, and the roles we take from our membership in a variety of public groups. Similarly, the identity we are given by listeners is in part based on their knowledge of the groups or institutions we represent.

The question "who is speaking?" is not easily answered. It raises such problems as the way in which the speaker's person limits or makes possible certain choices, and also the way in which his role as representative constrains or permits certain conduct and, ultimately, influences audience response.

THE SPEECH

The language commonly used for talking about public speaking tends to separate the speaker from his utterance. We often talk about a "man making a speech" as though the speech had some separate existence and could be thought of as one would think of a chair or painting. This tendency to perceive a speaker's discourse as separate from his person is reinforced by the extraordinary importance of written documents in our culture and also, more subtly, by the technologies of film, audio recordings, and video recordings.

We insisted in Chapter 1 on the necessity of seeing man as inseparable from his talk, and the public speech as a human action rather than a document or artifact. This perspective is necessary if we are to perceive fully the interaction between the speaker's person and role, and his utterance, and if we are to understand that audience response to a public speech is always to a man talking, and not simply to his language. We should no more think of a "man making a speech" than we think of a "man making a walk," or a "man making his heart beat."

In a commonsense way, however, the term *speech* is often used to designate the speaker's utterance or discourse—the audible and visible symbols he produces in the presence of the audience. For this reason, subsequent chapters will examine in some detail the problems of substance, arrangement, and style faced by speakers in the construction of their discourse. Analysis of these problems requires an additional set of terms useful for looking inside the substance and form of the speaker's utterance.

Purpose

Presumably public utterance is purposive action. One of the most serious charges against any public speech is that it seemed aimless. But aimless speeches occur often enough to justify the venerable anecdote of the hard-of-hearing listener who attended an extended public harangue only to find himself unable to hear the speaker. At the end of the evening, he asked a neighbor, "what was the speaker talking about?" His neighbor's reply was: "I don't know. He didn't say."

Almost equally serious is the charge that the purpose of a speech was unsuited to the audience or occasion; or that the speech embraced several purposes, some of which were contradictory; or that the means selected by the speaker were unsuited to his announced purpose; or that the purpose selected, while achieved, was either unworthy or contradictory to larger purposes the speaker ought to have held. Conversely, it is high praise to say of a speaker that his end was both just and judicious, that his sense of purpose was clearly marked, and that he did all those things, and only those things, suitable to the accomplishment of his purpose.

Often one must infer a speaker's purpose from observation of the ideas he chooses to emphasize, or from the direction of attitude or thought suggested by his statements. Sometimes, to be sure, speakers announce the purpose of their utterance very clearly. Indeed there is some reason to believe that if speakers observed this custom more universally the result might be agreeable both as a means of regulating the speaker's action and as a means of relieving certain ambiguities between speaker and audience. But obviously such announcements are not always made nor when made are they always to be trusted. The politician who says that his purpose is to make clear the causes of urban riots in the United States may have in mind another purpose—an action which will endear him to a majority of the voters in his district, say, or which will affect the fate of legislation which he favors or dislikes.

We have also referred to purpose as the "intended end" of the speaker. But sadly enough speakers may have intentions of which they are scarcely themselves aware. We have all had experiences with this phenomenon. The speaker says, "The purpose of my speech is to explain the financial crisis now confronting Brazil," but as we listen we say to ourselves, "His real purpose is to demonstrate that he is a very funny fellow. The man is a confirmed comic showoff, less interested in our learning about Brazil than in our applauding him." We may have some confidence that we perceived the "real" intention of the speech, and less certainty that the speaker himself was fully aware of this intention.

The entire action of a speech may be viewed as "the means selected for the achievement of some end or purpose." In this sense, the speaker's purpose does not automatically define or limit narrowly the subject matter of his utterance, although it will make some kinds of subject matter irrelevant or destructive. Clearly, however, four speakers might have the purpose of arousing an audience to a sense of the gravity of world population expansion; each might give a somewhat different speech using somewhat different materials; and yet each speech might move clearly toward the common purpose. We may judge "the means" selected by a speaker in relation to its end, but we should not assume that the selection of a purpose limits sharply the materials a speaker may select. Purpose does define, should define, only the direction of movement in a speech.

We have thus far taken the common point of view that purpose is a choice of the speaker. But properly viewed this category links speaker to audience and occasion. Speakers select their purposes, but audiences too have their purposes and not infrequently select speakers to fulfill those purposes. A national political convention chooses its keynote speaker to achieve purposes belonging to the party. To be sure, keynote speakers may and do use the same occasion for promoting their personal aspirations. Furthermore, occasions as well as audiences have their purposes. The party convention serves to illustrate this as aptly as it illustrates purpose in the audience. Church services gather both audience and speaker in terms of the purpose of the occasion, as do ceremonial gatherings such as commencements. We look to a speech to uncover the speaker's purpose, but we must do so with full awareness that the speaker's purpose must somehow encompass a total situation in which both the audience and the occasion act to direct or limit the choices of the speaker.

Position

If a speaker announces the central idea, or thesis of his utterance, this announcement identifies his central *position*. Among all of the possible statements he could have made concerning his subject, the speaker chose to organize his utterance to support a particular statement. Thus he has taken a position vis-à-vis the subject matter under discussion.

We observe a speaker taking a position most readily when he asserts a central idea concerning a subject under dispute. The attorney who says "My client is innocent," is taking a position. The legislator who says, "Federal aid to education will improve the quality of our schools," is taking a position. The position of the speaker may be less obvious if his utterance seems designed to share information or experience. But even in such cases, the speaker's utterance proceeds from some assumption or point of view (a *position*) which can be located. We shall examine the application of the term *position* to the full range of public speeches in Chapter 3. We shall also have occasion then to observe the complexity of positions taken by speakers, to see how much positions have within them attitudinal inclinations toward the speaker's audience and the occasion as well as toward his subject matter. Often it is not possible to define a speaker's position in a single sentence, and often it is not possible to define the speaker's position without referring to his style or manner of utterance.

If a speaker's purpose defines the direction of movement his utterance will take, his position defines and limits the materials useful to his utterance. Having taken a position, the speaker should seek only the utterance which defines and supports that position, while avoiding utterance which is irrelevant to, or nonsupportive of it.

Movement

The speech is an action in time. That is, it has duration, and it occurs not as an event immediately and wholly under scrutiny but as a sequence of events unfolding before the listener. It seems to have a beginning and end, and between these points the speaker moves in an intellectual and linguistic sense. In the sense that the speech has movement it resembles more the action of an orchestra playing a symphony than it does the action of an artist painting a picture. The painter presents the result of his action as a single event, capable of being observed at a single moment in time. The orchestra starts, proceeds, and finishes; it is perceived in action. The customary formal language which describes the parts of a musical selection may be more appropriate to a speech than the language about discourse which gives to the divisions of the speech such static terms as "introduction," "body," and "conclusion." Terminology such as "opening movement," "major movement," and "concluding movement" would maintain our sense of the speech as an action, moving toward some purpose, and encompassing an audience and occasion.

Public speaking, unlike the fine art of music, is a practical art embedded in the ongoing life of social institutions. While one may think of the movement of a speech as beginning when the speaker rises to address his audience and concluding when he sits down, this view may be too limiting to grasp the full sequence of events important to a speech. The point is easily illustrated. We might not understand the opening movement of a particular discourse in a parliamentary debate without having heard the speech that preceded it, any more than we would understand the second act of a play after missing the first act. Thus, the proper boundaries to be used in examining the movement of a particular utterance may be broader than the moments that mark the beginning and ending of that discourse. The public speaker's choices often reflect his knowledge of what has gone before and what will come after his utterance. Listeners seeking to understand his action must also see it within these broader dimensions.

Structure

An event which occurs in time can also be viewed in retrospect as a single structure or form. We may observe that the whole of some discourse has structure. Its parts, or movements, may be perceived as constituents of an overall pattern or form.

We have already used some of the simple and vague terms often employed to describe the structure of a speech. One can observe that it has an "introduction, body, and conclusion"; or a "beginning, middle, and end"; or an "opening movement, major movement, and concluding movement." Such categories tell us little about the variety of structures used by public speakers to give form to their discourse, or about the necessary relationships between structure and purpose, substance and purpose, or substance and audience. We cannot therefore talk in an a priori way about the "good" structure for a public speech. But what we can do in Chapter 4 is talk about a variety of structures commonly employed by public speakers, the types of subject matter they are suited to manage, and the problems attending their use.

Forms of Enforcement

Within the structure of a speech, one may observe a relationship between statements making a major assertion or generalization, and statements designed to support, clarify, or amplify the major assertions or generalizations. Speakers use a great variety of verbal constructs for purposes of proof, clarification, or amplification; and to the extent that we can perceive commonalities of form in many of these statements, we can also identify the *forms of enforcement* characteristic of public speeches. For example, one of the common forms used by speakers to clarify or amplify a general assertion is the use of an illustration or anecdote; thus, we identify the "illustration or anecdote" as a form of enforcement. As another example, speakers often seek to "prove" the worth of some generalization by showing that important or prestigious people have supported the generalization. Thus, we may identify "testimony" as a form of enforcement.

Because the resources of language are enormous, the concept of forms of enforcement is susceptible to great elaboration. There is ample historical evidence that observers are capable of perceiving more varieties of forms of enforcement within a speech than may be useful either to the tasks of speaking or of understanding a speech. For example, rhetoricians of the medieval world observed and named more than two hundred different "figures of speech," all of which could be thought of as variant forms for amplifying ideas. We shall set a somewhat more modest goal in Chapter 5 and discuss there only the major forms of proof or amplification characteristic of public discourse.

Style

The final category useful for analysis of the speaker's utterance is that of *style.* This is in many ways the most elusive and comprehensive term used in examining discourse: elusive because it has been employed in widely varying ways for more than 2,000 years, comprehensive because it invites an observer to make inferences about a speaker based on all of the manifest characteristics of his person and utterance.

We shall use the term *style* as a concept applicable to the total manner of the man speaking—to his physical conduct or delivery, as well as to his selection and ordering of words. All speeches reveal a style. Our description of a speaker's style is an inference drawn from observation of his appearance, his gesture and movement, the language he selects, and the way he makes his ideas available to others. In this sense, as we characterize a speaker's style, we are also describing his manifest public character. Thus we may find one speaker to be direct, clear, economical, uncomplicated, and friendly in his manner of address. Close examination of his physical demeanor and his selection of language would lead us to the details of behavior which generate this response to the man. Another speaker may seem to us colorful, complex, verbose, and arrogant. Once more we can uncover the objective sources for our inference through close examination of his utterance.

In applying the term *style* to the speaker's manner, we seem to say that it is possible to separate the manner of utterance from its substance. It is more accurate to say that we can look at utterance from the perspective of the speaker's manner; that this may direct our attention to some characteristics of his discourse which seem to have little to do with substance; but that if we carry the study of manner very far, we inevitably move into consideration of the speaker's substance—his selection of purposes, positions, structures, and forms of enforcement. In other words, each of the terms useful in the analysis of discourse is but a perspective for approaching the task of analysis, and each perspective ultimately involves all of the others in the unity of an action, a man speaking.

THE AUDIENCE

The third major dimension of a public speaking situation is the audience. A group of listeners can be viewed as simply the most important part of the speaker's environment. Presumably the speaker's purpose is an end to be achieved with or through those who listen. Thus, the audience, more than any other aspect of the environment, influences the choices available to the speaker. The audience also is frequently the reason for being of the speech. Speakers may choose audiences or announce their intention to speak to anyone willing to listen, but audiences as often choose speakers and set for the speaker certain assumptions as to his purpose. We readily observe speakers acting purposefully toward audiences. We should be as ready to observe audiences acting purposefully in their selection of a speaker and in the demands they make of him. The intimate interrelationship of speaker and audience—each serving as a stimulus to the other, each serving as response to the other, is readily apparent.

The identification of the speaker's audience involves certain complexities. For example, the audience assembled to hear a speech at a particular time and place may not be the audience of primary concern to the speaker. The President of the United States may use a commencement speech at some university as the occasion for a major address on the foreign policy of his administration. The speaker may be interested in his present audience, but he is keenly aware that his important audience includes Congress, the voting public, and persons abroad concerned with American foreign policy.

While a speaker may seek his purpose in the reactions of his immediate audience he may be equally or more concerned with a remote audience listening or viewing on radio or television. He may at times speak for an audience to be reached by the immediate effect of his speech, and at other times seek an effect mediated through some other communication channel. Thus, a political speaker may want to initiate a newspaper story concerning his attitude on civil disobedience and may use the occasion of an address to any available audience as a means of getting the newspaper story written.

It is characteristic of the public speech, as contrasted with such other possible speech forms as the dialogue or conversation, that the speaker talks not with individuals but with groups. The real audience for the speaker—that is, that audience he can conceptualize and interact with—consists not of the full range of individuals addressed, but rather of a range of group tendencies or group interests presumed by the speaker to be represented in his audience. We shall accordingly treat the audience not in terms of the psychology of individual behavior, but in terms of the group structure of American society, the kinds of analysis speakers make of that group structure, and the kinds of evidence used for such analysis. Public speakers do not for the most part talk to "Tom, Dick, and Harry"; they talk to farmers, businessmen, women, students, Catholics, Protestants, Jews, Afro-Americans, the League of Women Voters, Democrats, Republicans, the educated, the ignorant, Americans, Canadians, etc. In short they talk *to* a concept of the way in which the members of certain groups will respond to certain forms of utterance. They also talk *from* a concept of group purposes, positions, movements, structures, and styles. That is, the speaker talks not simply as an unique individual, but as the representative of the group of people with whom he finds common substance.

THE OCCASION

Speakers are limited in their choices, or have those choices determined for them by the occasion for the speech, as well as by the audience. For example, a speaker invited to make a commencement address for Hoffbrau High School could theoretically make this the occasion for a discussion of "the superiority of dry fly fishing as a form of recreation." The choice would be unusual, however. It would violate so sharply the expectations of the audience as to what the occasion calls for, that the theoretical choice is effectively closed to the speaker.

The occasion both inhibits and facilitates certain kinds of choices by the speaker. It also may serve to reinforce or limit the effectiveness of the utterance chosen. In this sense it is useful to divide the concept of occasion into consideration of the "immediate occasion" and of "the historical-cultural setting for the speech."

The immediate occasion includes not only the data implied by some special title given to the occasion, as in the case of a commencement, after-dinner speech, speech of nomination, or lecture. It also includes the physical environment for the speech and the events immediately preceding the speech. The size of the room, its acoustical characteristics, its ventilation, its decorations, the presence of a band—all of these may become important events conditioning the speaker's choices and the effects of his choice.

The significance of the historical-cultural setting is less obvious but not less important. A public lecture given in 1920 on drug addiction would take place in a historical-cultural setting quite different from our own, and it would be impossible to understand the nature of the speaker's choice of position, forms of support, or style without understanding the influence of that setting. A public lecture on the same subject in 1968 would occur in a changed cultural-historical setting, and would presumably bring about a different order of choices by the speaker. Consideration of LSD and the amphetamines (unknown in 1920) might be indicated, together with the phenomenon of student interest in marijuana. Of course these presumed differences affect the speaker's utterance only to the extent that our speakers in 1920 and in 1968 perceive themselves as operating within different historical-cultural settings. Some speakers talk for a context which no longer exists. The fault is a grave one.

The category of occasion is important enough to public speaking to have been used as a point of departure for classifying types of speeches. Thus Aristotle in his *Rhetoric* defined three types of public speeches:

deliberative, forensic, and ceremonial. Each type was associated with certain kinds of subject matter, certain ultimate purposes, and with events of the future, the past, or the present. The names seem clearly to have been based on the major settings, or occasions, for Athenian public speaking. Deliberative speaking occurred when policies of state were under consideration; forensic, when some accusation of wrongdoing was being judged; ceremonial, when some national celebration, triumph, or disaster was being observed. The occasion and audience for each type of speech was well established by the customs of the Greek city state. The Greek terms are still in use; we have little difficulty identifying legislative, legal, or ceremonial occasions in our own society. We have also added a variety of names for loose classifications of types of speaking. We can readily visualize the usual occasion for a "sermon," or the variety of occasions which elicit "campaign speaking" in American political life.

EFFECT

A public speech requires a speaker, his speech, an audience, and an occasion. But interpretation of the event requires also that we inquire on the one hand into its purpose, and on the other hand into its consequences. The relationship between the effect intended or hoped for, and the effect achieved becomes an important sign of the speaker's skill. If we could know all of the effects of any speech, we would have the most powerful evidence for generalizing about the merit of the choices made by the speaker. Such knowledge is not possible, and the evidence available to us about the effect of any given speech is likely to be not only fragmentary but ambiguous. Nevertheless, this evidence is so important to our judgments of the speaker's selection of purpose, substance, and method that we need zealously to seek it out, and to give it the most careful interpretation.

The most obvious evidences of effect often seem to be such matters as the manifest attentiveness, responsiveness, and applause offered by the audience. Such matters are important to the speaker, although he is likely to know better when he is failing with an audience than when he is succeeding. Manifest inattention is seldom sought by a speaker, but manifest attention and responsiveness may not be a secure evidence of success. For example, the applause of an audience gives little indication of the extent to which the speaker's information will be remembered, or his ideas appropriated and acted upon. It may not even be an accurate indication of gross audience approval for the speaker. Partisan audiences meeting for occasions they believe important to their purposes are notably generous with applause even in the presence of speaking they regard as indifferent or poor. They may respond not so much to indicate approval as from the hope of stimulating the speaker to a better effort, or from the hope of impressing "outsiders" with the morale and solidarity of their group. The most arduous effort may be needed to get objective evidence of particular effects. Speakers seeking to inform audiences may get this through carefully constructed post-speech examinations. Teachers commonly employ this method, often to the mutual distress of speaker and audience. Speakers seeking to affect audience values and conduct may find evidence of effect in behavior changes on the part of some listeners or of changes of attitude as registered on opinion polls or attitude scales. Such methods for gathering evidence are seldom available to the speaker unless his activity is associated with the purposes of a large organization with financial and technical resources, and with a strong interest in the effects of speeches made by its members. Thus political speakers may operate in the context of carefully conducted opinion polls, designed to test the effects of positions advanced. And thus evangelist Billy Graham keeps careful records of the number of conversions attributable to his sermons, including follow-up studies on the subsequent church affiliations of the converts and on church attendance. Many teachers now seek student evaluations of their instruction, which may tell little about how much students did or didn't learn, but tell much about their affection for the substance and manner of the teacher's discourse.

If gathering evidence on the effect of a speech is difficult, this evidence as it relates to the quality of the speech is at least equally troublesome. A naive view of public speaking might hold, for example, that the overt response of a present audience provides an ultimate or absolute criterion for judging the speech's merit. "A public speech seeks an end in the audience," it might be argued. "If it does not achieve that end, the speech is a failure and is not worthy of esteem." The capriciousness of such a judgment and its failure to square with common sense becomes apparent upon reflection. Some speaking situations permit an easy victory for the speaker. His listeners like and respect him; their ideas are substantially harmonious with those of the speaker; they have come to cheer the speaker and to make the event successful. Given such favorable circumstances, the speaker can avoid the appearance of overt success only by a dramatic display of incompetence. Conversely some situations are loaded against the speaker. Unless we assume that it is wrong for speakers to attempt a difficult task of persuasion, we should have to assume that the speaker who achieves partial success against great odds may well have spoken with great skill. Even if the speaker fails with his present audience, he still may have done his work well. Abraham Lincoln's first inaugural address unquestionably sought to check the movement of American history toward Civil War. In this purpose the speech failed. But could anyone have produced a more artistic effort to achieve an unrealized goal? If the speaker has used artistically the means of persuasion available to him, then we must grant the merit of his speech even in the absence of evidence that the speech succeeded with its present audience. The speaker's lack of success may cause us to ask about the wisdom of the choices represented by his speech or may cause us to ask if he left certain available resources unused, but lack of success by no means requires that we find the speaker deficient in judgment or conduct.

A further complication in examining the effect of a speech lies in the unstable relationship between immediate and long-term effects. We have already indicated that a speaker may be more interested in the judgment of an audience which is not physically present for his discourse than in the judgment of the present audience. Similarly, the speaker may be less interested in immediate effect than in potential long-term influence. Speakers occupying public positions must live with the products of their speeches, with the written documents or recordings which the speech generates. And it profits such speakers little if the present audience applauds words which will subsequently prove an embarrassment to the man who uttered them. In achieving success with one audience, a speaker may preempt the possibility that he can influence a wider audience. For example, William Jennings Bryan's "Cross of Gold" speech at the 1896 Democratic National Convention is presumed to have stampeded the convention to nominating Bryan for the Presidency. This is one of the few occasions in history in which a single speech seems to have affected decisively the action of a large political gathering. The same speech so alarmed financial and business interests in the United States as to cause them to work for Bryan's defeat with rare unanimity, energy, and resourcefulness. Did the speech that won Bryan the nomination make it impossible for him to be elected president? Answer to such a question would be difficult at best, but the question reveals the complexity of judging speeches from evaluation of their effect.

Observations of the effect of a speech will be incomplete and open to varying interpretations. This does not mean that such observations are without value. Speeches do seek effect, and evidence of their success or lack of success may direct our attention to aspects of the speech which we might otherwise have overlooked. If we say of a speech that "it should have succeeded, but didn't," we are alerted to the possibility that we have overlooked features of the action which were of decisive importance.

TYPES OF SPEECHES

We have thus far emphasized the point of view that each public speech is in some sense unique. It brings together a collection of human beings unlikely to be precisely repeated, and an interplay of purposes and expectations different in some degree from all others that have occurred or will occur. However, while it is useful to keep in mind the uniqueness of each speech, it is equally useful to look for the similarities of purpose, method, and occasion which permit classification of a large number of speeches as members of a given type or genre of public speeches.

A number of alternative approaches have been used to categorize public speeches. We have already referred to Aristotle's classification of speeches as deliberative, forensic, and ceremonial—a system which linked the major occasions for public speaking in Athenian society to certain major purposes for speaking. It would also be possible to talk of speeches in terms of their relationship to the organizations which provide their setting and shape their purposes. Thus one can classify speeches as sermons, campaign speeches, scholarly lectures, popular lectures, legislative discourses, ceremonial discourses, and so forth. These classifications are useful in emphasizing the link between public speeches and the life of social organizations and institutions, but the system tends to become unwieldy because of the large number of classes it involves.

For purposes of this book, we shall propose three types of speeches, using labels which direct attention to the major classes of purpose held by public speakers, to the major classes of expectation held by their listeners, and to certain broad lines of difference in the method used by speakers. Thus we shall say that all speeches may be usefully examined in terms of the question of whether or not they are *expository, persuasive,* or *ceremonial.*

The adjectives *expository, persuasive,* and *ceremonial* are commonly used in discussions of speech types to designate the major purposes of speakers. Thus we observe that speakers engage in utterance in order to share information with their listeners, or in order to lay out the lines of evidence and reasoning that might be used to support some inference. The speaker may say, "My purpose is to inform you about the historical events leading up to the battle of Gettysburg," or "My purpose is to make known to you the arguments used by Anselm to prove the existence of God." We can say then that the speaker's purpose is *expository*, and that he has no desire for his audience other than that they be better informed after listening to his discourse. On other occasions, we observe speakers soliciting an audience to join the speaker in some belief, or to act in a specified way. The politician may say "vote for me" or "support my program for urban renewal," and we mark his purpose as *persuasive*. He is asking for a change in the belief or action of his audience. At other times we see speakers engaged in utterance appropriate to clarifying the values an audience should honor on a given occasion—at a Fourth of July rally, a centennial celebration, a funeral, or a recognition dinner. The speaker is saying that we should honor (or excoriate) certain historical events, the lives of certain men, or the nature of a given institution; and we mark his purpose as *ceremonial*. Lurking in the shadows of the names "exposition," "persuasion," and "ceremony" is the ancient triad of knowing, acting, and feeling, as forms of human consciousness.

Proper use of the terms *expository, persuasive,* and *ceremonial* in classifying types of speeches requires, however, that we observe that each term may be used to designate not only a speaker's purpose, but also the way in which his audience perceives his discourse and the nature of his language and manner. If a speaker's intention is to inform an audience, if he uses utterance which is appropriate to the presentation of information, and if his audience accepts his subject matter as informative, then classification is a simple matter. The speech is expository in intent, in method, and in audience perception. But such a happy correlation of events may not take place. A politician says, "I am here only to present the facts about the 'poverty bill' now before Congress." But his information may be selected and ordered in such a way as to suggest powerfully that only a hardhearted scoundrel would vote against the bill. A sophisticated listener may decide that the speaker has neither been totally candid about his purpose nor totally unaware of the persuasive potential of his method.

The disparity between the speaker's intent and the audience's recognition of it may be much more subtle. We can visualize a speaker who generally conceives his purpose to be expository, lecturing on the hypothesis of evolution, and of a listener perceiving the discourse as an unsubtle attack on the Biblical account of creation, and therefore an effort at persuasion. In this case, the same speech might be viewed as clearly expository by one audience and clearly persuasive by another. Moreover, both interpretations give us valid information about the nature of the speech act in all of its potential relationships with different listeners.

The difficulties we have observed in classifying expository speeches apply also to ceremonial speeches. In Shakespeare's version of Mark Antony's funeral oration over the body of Julius Caesar, for instance, the occasion is ceremonial; and as the speech begins the language and substance of the speech seem appropriate to the occasion. But as the speech goes on, we see that it is one of powerful persuasive intent and effect, artistically developed.

The terms *expository, persuasive,* and *ceremonial* seem to merge as one seeks application to particular speeches. Nevertheless they are useful terms for directing our attention to the differing purposes of speakers, the differing forms their statements take, and the differing interpretations audiences place on the speaker's utterance. We can apply the terms unequivocally to the classification of a speech which seems clearly univocal in intent, in method, and in audience perception. We can use the terms strategically to uncover the workings of a speech which cannot be readily classified. Thus the merit of the three terms derives less from their power to differentiate mutually exclusive classes of speeches than from the set of perspectives they provide for examining any particular speech. They become ways of talking about the nature of a speaker's purpose, the nature of his speech, and the perception an audience brings to it.

ANALYSIS AND SYNTHESIS

The fourteen terms introduced in this chapter provide a useful frame of reference for analyzing the nature and action of any public speech. But it should be clear that these terms do not label events which exist independently in nature. One cannot conceive of a speaker without a speech, or of a public speech without an audience and occasion. Neither can one conceive of inquiry into the purpose of an act without concern for its consequences, nor of a study of a speaker's style which does not move toward concern for his purpose and position, for the structure and methods of enforcement found in his utterance. In the final analysis, each of the terms proposed for examining public speeches is but a perspective on speechmaking which, pursued far enough, brings one into the study of the whole action of the speech. One does not understand a public speech by thinking of it as a structure built up from a set of discrete parts, each of which may be studied in isolation. Rather, understanding comes from accepting the essential unity of the whole act, while approaching its study from a variety of perspectives. The most important of these perspectives serve as the subject matter for the chapters which follow in Parts II and III of this book.

SUMMARY

A public speech is an action designed to take into account the contingencies of a particular social situation. In this sense a speaker's choices must be viewed as good or bad, effective or ineffective, in relation to all aspects of the situation he confronts.

Speakers need to work toward full understanding of the nature and action of public speeches in order to have a proper basis for choosing how to conduct themselves as speakers. Listeners have equal need for understanding in order to govern their reactions to discourses. This search for understanding starts with an examination of the various aspects of a public speech and the terms used to designate these aspects.

The events objectively necessary to the public speech are a *speaker,* his *speech* or utterance, an *audience,* and an *occasion.* The speech itself may be analyzed in terms of *purpose, position, movement, structure, forms of enforcement,* and *style.* Since public speeches are purposive acts, their study also involves inquiry into *effect.* And since public speeches constitute almost infinite range of events, each of which is in some sense unique, their study is aided by seeking to perceive commonalities of intent, audience expectation, and method brought to various types of speeches. The terms proposed to designate types of speeches are *expository, persuasive,* and *ceremonial.*

Each of the fourteen terms advanced for the analysis of public speeches reveals some problems of interpretation. For example, speakers need to be viewed both as individuals and as representatives; occasions, as involving both the immediate setting for a speech and the broader historical-cultural context; audiences, as individuals related to one another by the group structure of American society; and effect, as both an immediate and long-term consequence of a particular utterance. None of the fourteen terms designates an event existing independently in nature, and in this sense each is but a perspective for looking into the whole action of a speech.

FOR FURTHER STUDY

SPEAKING, WRITING, OR DISCUSSION EXERCISES

1. Report on the trial and death of Socrates. In your report try to show how the customs and assumptions of political life in ancient Athens affected

the nature of the speaking by Socrates and others during his trial, and made possible the choices available to Socrates after he had been sentenced to death.

2. Describe the problems of communication which may arise when speakers and listeners are divided for one of the following reasons:

   a. Because they occupy different status levels in a bureaucratic organization, as would be the case with managers and workers in a business, professors and students in a college, doctors and nurses in a hospital, etc.

   b. Because they belong to different reference groups separated by language habits or value assumptions, as in the case of some young people and their elders, members of different socio-economic groups, etc.

   Insofar as possible, base your report on a specific situation and try to explain how differences brought to the situation by the different groups caused speakers to behave in ways which were meaningless, irrelevant, or irritating to listeners. *Readings* listed below under number 4 will help in preparing your report.

3. From your own experience, identify one or more situations in which the level of abstraction of a speaker's language led to misunderstanding or confusion in the interpretation of his utterance.

4. Prepare a report discussing the evidence that our language habits either constrain or determine the kind of "reality" we are able to perceive in the world we experience. The *readings* listed below under numbers 2 and 3 will help in preparing the report.

5. Classical rhetoricians talked of "the speaker" as the person who originated the content of his discourse, and also encoded this content in language and gesture. Modern communication theorists often define the "message source" as a category different from the "encoder," suggesting that the person or agency giving expression to ideas may not be the source of the ideas. How do you account for this emphasis on the difference between message source and message encoder in contemporary communication theory? Would contemporary public speaking provide examples of speakers who are not the source of their messages?

6. Report on a speech which seems to have revealed a complex relationship between artistry and effect, or between various types of effect, as:

   a. A speech which seems to have been artistic but a failure with its audience.

   b. A speech which seems to have been inartistic but successful with its audience.

   c. A speech which seems to have been unsuccessful with its immediate audience, but successful with subsequent audiences.

   d. A speech which seems to have been successful with the immediate audience, but subsequently damaging to the speaker's reputation.

READINGS

1. Concerning the interrelationship of public speaking and social institutions:
   a. George Kennedy, *The Art of Persuasion in Greece* (New Jersey: Princeton University Press, 1963). See especially Chapter 1.
   b. H. D. F. Kitto, *The Greeks* (Baltimore: Penguin Books, Ltd., 1951). See especially Chapters 5, 7, 9, 12.
   c. Kathleen Freeman, *The Murder of Herodes and Other Trials From Athenian Law Courts* (New York: The Norton Library, 1953). See especially Chapters 1–3 for an account of the Athenian legal system and the speaking it generated.
   d. A. W. Plumstead, ed., *The Wall and the Garden, Selected Massachusetts Election Sermons, 1670–1775* (Minneapolis: University of Minnesota Press, 1968), pp. 3–37.
2. For discussion of the significance of man's unique capacity for symbolic behavior:
   a. Charles D. Hockett, "The Origin of Speech," *Scientific American,* September, 1960, pp. 3–10.
   b. Leslie A. White, "The Symbol: The Origin and Basis of Human Behavior," in S. I. Hayakawa, ed., *Language, Meaning and Maturity* (New York: Harper and Bros., 1954), pp. 252–263.
   c. Ralph Ross, *Symbols and Civilization* (New York: Harcourt Brace & World, Inc., 1962). Chapter 9, on "Communication, Symbols and Society," includes a perspective on the functions of symbols different from that presented in Chapter 1 of this book.
3. For further discussion of the effects of language habits on our perception of the reality of events:
   a. Roger Brown, *Words and Things* (Glencoe, Illinois: The Free Press, 1958). See Chapter 7, "Linguistic Relativity and Determinism."
   b. John C. Condon, Jr., *Semantics and Communication* (New York: The Macmillan Co., 1966), Chapter 2.
   c. John B. Carroll and Joseph B. Casagrande, "The Functions of Language Classifications in Behavior," in Alfred G. Smith, ed., *Communication and Culture* (New York: Holt, Rinehart and Winston, Inc., 1966), pp. 489–504.
4. For discussion of the difficulties in communication inherent in the nature of language:
   a. F. R. Roethlisberger, "Barriers to Communication Between Men," in S. I. Hayakawa, ed., *The Use and Misuse of Language* (Greenwich, Conn.: Fawcett Publications, Inc., 1962).
   b. Ralph Ross, *Symbols and Civilization,* Chapter 2.
   c. John C. Condon, Jr., *Semantics and Communication,* Chapters 3 and 4.

d. Irving Lee, "They Talk Past Each Other," in Haig A. Bosmajian, ed., *Readings in Speech* (New York: Harper and Row, 1965), pp. 35–46.

5. Other sets of terms for describing the parts of an act of communication, and the interrelationships of the parts:
   a. J. L. Aranguren, *Human Communication* (New York: McGraw-Hill World University Library, 1967), pp. 11–69.
   b. David Berlo, *The Process of Communication* (New York: Holt, Rinehart, and Winston, Inc., 1960), Chapter 2.
   c. Kenneth Burke, *A Grammar of Motives and a Rhetoric of Motives* (Cleveland World Publishing Co., 1962), pp. xvii–xxv, 3–20.
   d. Lee Thayer, *Communication and Communication Systems* (Homewood, Ill.: Richard D. Irwin, Inc., 1968), Chapters 1–3, 6.

6. For further interpretation of speech purposes, types, and functions:
   a. David Berlo, *The Process of Communication.* Chapter 1 provides a critique of traditional language used in describing communication purposes.
   b. Lee Thayer, *Communication and Communication Systems.* Chapters 13–16 describe four applied functions of instrumental communication.
   c. John F. Wilson and Carroll C. Arnold, *Public Speaking as a Liberal Art* (Boston: Allyn and Bacon, Inc., 1964), Chapter 7.

7. Other views on the personal and social importance of the study and practice of public speaking:
   a. Otis Walter and Robert Scott, *Thinking and Speaking* (New York: The Macmillan Co., 1962), pp. 3–12.
   b. John F. Wilson and Carroll C. Arnold, *Public Speaking as a Liberal Art* (Boston: Allyn and Bacon, Inc., 1964), Chapters 1 and 2.

Analytical Perspectives

Section II explores in some depth the structure of the speaker's utterance. The perspective is essentially analytical, with attention to the various categories of choice speakers may make on matters of position, organization, and enforcement, and with attention to the implications of various choices relative to the speaker's person, purpose, audience, and occasion. While the point of view of Section II is generally that of the person observing a public speech, the discussion has clear implications for the practitioner who wishes to achieve more than superficial control over the preparation and management of his own discourse.

The materials are presented in three chapters: "The Position of the Speaker," "Structure and Movement," and "Patterns of Enforcement."

CHAPTER 3

The Position of the Speaker

POSITION: THE CENTRAL DECISION

The central decision of the public speaker is his choice among various possible positions. This choice represents the speaker's selection of: (a) the central content, or organizing statement of his utterance, and (b) the point of view, or stance from which he will conduct his utterance. To the extent that the speaker assumes a position, he makes a choice that will shape the selection of both the substance and manner of his total discourse. He also asserts some part of his own public identity, for men are known publicly in large measure by the positions they take on public matters.

The student speaker has opportunity to "try on" positions, and to modify or abandon those which prove to be unhappily susceptible to sound criticism, or which seem inconsistent with the student's emerging image of himself as a public person. This opportunity is one of the major perquisites of the student. It frees him in some measure to explore the consequences of asserting and developing in public various assertions, and of assuming various points of view toward himself, his auditors, and different types of subject matter.

Men or women who have assumed identifiable roles in public life have more difficulty in "trying on," abandoning, or modifying positions they take. Theodore Sorenson, who served as special assistant to President John Kennedy, observed that any public position taken by an American President must be considered as the President's commitment to the public. In this sense each position taken becomes a precedent controlling or shaping all subsequent Presidential statements or actions. Through time, of course, people in public life modify their positions. We may properly honor the public man who remains a student to the extent that he studies and changes his positions in the light of new circumstances and new information. But such changes are not to be undertaken lightly by those who take their public responsibilities seriously. We "know" a public man by the positions he takes; our trust in him rests on the assumption that he speaks candidly and with forethought, and that he will honor his commitments.

The significance of taking a public position is such that a speaker with many resources, such as a President, may "try on" positions by having them tested publicly by other members of his administration. The so-called trial balloon technique, beloved by politicians, follows this procedure. A speaker other than the President presents a position on some public policy. Public reaction to this position can then be examined before the President himself makes a final decision on the position he will personally articulate. The technique raises some ethical questions, but we shall not pursue these at the moment. Our point here is that the existence of the technique is testimony to the unusual importance speakers give to the search for public positions.

Position, then, is the central choice of the speaker, controlling the content and form of his utterance, and modifying his subsequent choices. For this reason we should give close attention to the concept of position, the general nature of the choices represented by positions, and the considerations affecting choice.

THE CONCEPT OF POSITION

The speaker's *position* is the central content and stance of his action. In this sense, the idea of position includes, but is broader than, the conception that a speech is organized around a central statement or thesis. The speaker takes a position by defining not only the central idea he wishes to communicate, but also by revealing his point of view (or stance) toward his subject matter, his audience, the occasion, and himself. Thus the speaker's position has both a cognitive dimension and an emotive dimension; it reveals not only what the speaker believes, but also the point of view and attitudes through which he expresses his belief.

We can observe the importance of both content and stance in a speaker's position by examining two statements. Suppose our first speaker says, "Technology threatens to destroy all that is best and most human in mankind." He has clearly taken a position. The statement is vague, but it has content. In a cognitive sense, we would understand that this speaker deplores the impact of technology on the character or quality of human life. The statement is also attitudinally charged. The speaker has a stance, or point of view, and we are alerted to the fact that he may be taking the aggressive and alarmist posture of a strong advocate. If he goes on to call for the systematic destruction of large-scale social and economic organization, in order to "save man's soul," we will know that his position is uncompromising and highly emotive.

A second speaker talking on the same general subject matter area might tell us that "I want to examine conflicting viewpoints about the effect of technology on the quality of human life. These viewpoints will reveal both the way in which technology has enriched human possibilities, and the way in which it may threaten certain possibilities." This statement also has content, but the speaker's stance is quite different from that expressed in the former statement. Speaker number two seems to be assuming the posture of a reporter and interpreter. He promises a balanced point of view toward technology, free from strongly emotive language. To be sure, he may move toward a more aggressive and uncompromising position, but his initial position differs from that of the first speaker not only in content, but also in stance, or point of view.

The speaker who takes a position, then, selects not only the central content of his utterance but also the stance he will take in and through that content toward his audience and the occasion. He reveals himself as a human being acting through language toward the world about him from a particular point of view, and holding particular attitudes toward his subject matter, audience, and the occasion. Thus the speaker's listeners sense his position not simply in terms of the meaning of a particular statement, but also as a revelation of how the man speaking has placed himself in relation to his environment—including the members of his audience. The audience sees the speaker as taking a position *on* population control, for example, but it also sees him as taking the position *of* a reporter or an advocate; as taking an aggressive or conciliatory stance; as attentive to the simplicity of his topic or to its complexity, and so forth. The speaker places himself for his audience by choosing a position, and the audience places the speaker by discovering that position both in terms of the central content of the utterance and in terms of the stance of the man who talks.

The Concept of Position Summarized

In summary, the speaker's position can be described with two kinds of statements: (a) statements about the central content of his discourse, and (b) statements about his stance, or point of view. We can discover in the speaker's position whether he appears as persuader, expositor, or ceremonialist; whether he "takes a stand" or chooses to avoid taking a stand; whether he is aggressive and uncompromising or conciliatory. The speaker's position is his choice of the ground he will stand on and the point of view from which he examines that ground. The choice is a crucial one. It limits the appropriateness of some utterances and sanctions others. It reveals the speaker as he will be known to his audience. It shapes all aspects of his subsequent thought and utterance. Choice of position, therefore, is the speaker's central task.

What are the considerations that govern choice of position? We turn first to some of the general characteristics of positions and their implications.

SOME GENERAL CHARACTERISTICS OF POSITIONS

The speaker's choice of position is accompanied by the problems usual to choices made in the complex game of communication. That is, any given choice is likely to have some merit and is likely to produce some difficulties. When we say that the speaker made a good choice of position, we are judging that the merits of the choice outweighed its limitations. We are in effect assuming that any alternative choice made by the speaker would have been less serviceable for his purpose than the choice he made.

That merits and defects accompany all positional choices can be understood by examining some of the general characteristics of positions. For example, we can say of a position that it is "relatively narrow or broad; relatively clear or ambiguous; relatively simple or complex." Other sets of adjectives could be applied to the general description of positions, but these three will illustrate the implications of choice.

(1) *The Narrow vs. Broad Position.* The speaker who chooses to undertake a critique of American education might limit himself to the statement that "The teaching of the social sciences in American high schools is woefully inadequate." His position would be narrower if he confined himself to a critique of the teaching of economic theory in American high schools, and still narrower if he limited himself to the teaching of economic theory in George Washington High School. His position would become progressively broader if he extended his critique to the whole of the curriculum or to the whole of the educational systems. Speakers choose positions of such cosmological breadth as "Mankind is lurching toward the extinction of all values that have made life worth living." They also choose positions of such particularity as "How Begonias can be grown in northern climates."

Presumably the narrower the speaker's position, the greater the probability that he can support it adequately. The narrow position enables the speaker to say "more about less," to bring to bear more of the total fund of pertinent information and lines of amplification, and to spend more of his time in relating relevant and interesting anecdotes. Presumably also, the narrow position increases the likelihood that the speaker will be clear. A speaker is more likely to produce a clear, concrete, and fully supported analysis of instruction about economic theory in a particular high school than to achieve similar clarity in a critique of the whole of American education. Thus speakers are often well advised to curb the impulse to encompass the whole of some complex topic in a single speech, and to choose a position on a particularly relevant aspect of that topic. For example, a speaker wishing to take a position on the proper nature of American foreign policy might well confine himself to a position on American foreign policy in Central Africa.

Narrow positions carry limitations. Foremost among these is the possibility that a position may become so narrow as to make the speech trivial, or to leave the audience vastly unsatisfied. Unless one is a patron of George Washington High School, learning that economic theory is badly taught at that high school may prompt the reply "So what?" The speaker who seeks full control over his subject matter by narrowing his position is caught by the irony of the definition applied to an expert: "One who knows more and more about less and less, until eventually he knows everything about nothing."

The merit of a broad position is its potential for bringing useful order out of a vast diversity of particular information, and thus achieving great significance for an audience. The speaker who supports a position which illuminates the whole of some vast area of human concern has achieved much. For example, the psychologist Jerome Bruner is perhaps best known for a position he has taken on the whole vast topic of human learning. His position is a broad one: that knowledge has structure, and that learning the structure of any kind of knowledge facilitates further learning.[1] The position, aptly illustrated, seems to illuminate the whole of the problem of organizing and conducting instruction in the whole of the educational system, and it thus takes on a significance impossible to a narrower position on learning. The speaker who takes a broad position risks much. He risks obscurity, the accusation that he has tried to put camels and lions into one tent, the possibility that he will lay claim to greater insight than he can make credible to his listeners, and the possibility that he has indeed allowed his vision to run beyond his knowledge. The limitations of breadth mirror the merits of the narrow position, and vice versa.

(2) *The Clear vs. Ambiguous Position*. Clarity seems an obvious merit in public speaking, so much so that any discussion of the limitations of clarity, or the possible merits of ambiguity may seem vaguely scandalous. Yet it should be observed that judicious ambiguity is a common strategy for unifying an audience, and that the speaker who makes his position "too clear" on a given issue may sow discord. For example, the closing words of Lincoln's Gettysburg Address (". . . government

[1] Jerome Bruner, *The Process of Education* (Cambridge: Harvard University Press, 1960).

of the people, by the people, and for the people shall not perish from this earth") are inherently ambiguous. If one pursues philosophically what is meant by "the people," as Walter Lippmann does in his book *The Public Philosophy,* one soon appreciates the ambiguity. By "the people" do we mean all those living, or only those living who have met some qualification for voting in elections? Do we mean those living, and dead, and yet to be born who share in some national political tradition? One can be grateful that Lincoln did not seek full clarification of his abstraction on the occasion of a ceremonial address. Nor did he pause for clarification of the phrase "all men are created equal," yet the ambiguities lurking in this statement have been the subject of innumerable speeches and essays. Should we criticize Lincoln because he refrained from using a ceremonial occasion to plunge his audience into philosophic discord?

In the political context, ambiguity is often considered the device by which the politician avoids a commitment other than to virtue, and thus avoids giving offense to any potential voter. But it should be further observed that the politician who takes a clear public position on legislative issues limits his own "freedom of movement" concerning these issues, no matter how circumstances may change after the time of his speech. Thus, the candidate for state governor who announces his clear, unequivocal, and unalterable opposition to any increase in taxation may face embarrassment as he confronts subsequent realities of the balance between state obligations and state income. Shall we always cry "fault" to the speaker who, facing the uncertainties of decision making on matters of vast social complexity, chooses positions at least as ambiguous as his own lack of certainty?

The merit of clarity, like the limitation of ambiguity, is apparent. The clear position removes doubt in the relation between speaker and listener; it minimizes the possibility of misunderstanding or of subsequent disenchantment. But the service of ambiguity to certain purposes, like the limitation of clarity for these purposes, should also be apparent.

(3) *The Simple vs. Complex Position.* The speaker who says "The United States should use its full military power to destroy the capacity of North Vietnam to wage war" has taken a reasonably simple position on one aspect of U.S. involvement in Southeast Asia. Official American foreign policy in the 1950's and 1960's, on the other hand, seemed based on a more complex position which began as a commitment of goods, services, and expert advice to the formation of a stable South Vietnam, and progressed to a commitment of American military power to stop alleged North Vietnamese aggression against South Vietnam. The complex governmental position was also ambiguous, possibly with

the intention of preserving the freedom of the government to change the direction of its particular actions. The tendency of simple positions to be unambiguous and clear is not, however, a universal concomitant of simplicity. Simple positions can be both broad and ambiguous, as in the venerable toast, "My country, may she always be right, but right or wrong my country" or in Lord Acton's epigram, "All power corrupts, but absolute power corrupts absolutely."

Simple positions which are unqualified, unhedged by doubts, conditions, or discussion of possible modifications, have obvious rhetorical force. They can be compactly or even memorably worded and thus easily held in mind. Ceremonial discourse and moral discourse are filled with assertions of simple positions. Political discourse associated with aggressive political movements, or with moments of decision may also propose simple positions. One observes such positions in the rhetoric with which any American political party describes its own virtues and the faults of its opponents, as election time nears. Or similar simplicity is found in such diverse utterances as Hitler's rhetoric (assertions of Aryan supremacy, the absolute evil of the Jew, the absolute malice of the Versailles treaty after World War I, the inevitability of victory for those who have the will for victory) and the *Communist Manifesto* (history as a matter of class struggle and economic determinism, the inevitable victory of the proletariat, the inevitable movement to a classless society).

The strength of the simple position is balanced by its limitations. The most conspicuous limitation is the possibility of disproportion between the simplicity of the speaker's position and the complexity of the subject matter he discusses. Simple explanations for complex phenomena may be sheer nonsense. The speaker who asserts a simple explanation for the causes of juvenile delinquency in America may demonstrate for many listeners only the fact that he knows too little about the problem to assume the privilege of speaking in public.

In summary, positions which are narrow, clear, and simple seem generally strong. The speaker who chooses a broad position may find it difficult to provide support adequate to his statement; the speaker who is ambiguous risks misunderstanding and its fruit of disappointment; the speaker who is complex risks the difficulty of making his position clear, and the danger of seeming to be indecisive or lacking in force. Yet it is not a sound general rule that speakers should choose narrow, clear, and simple positions. Each such choice carries with it limitations; narrowness risks triviality; clarity reduces the speaker's latitude for change; simplicity may be inappropriate to complex phenomena. The particular choice of the speaker needs to be made in the full light of the speaking situation—his purpose, his subject matter, his audience, the occasion. Evaluation of the speaker's choice of position needs to be made in the light of a similar range of considerations. When we say of a speaker that his position was too narrow or too broad, too clear or too ambiguous, too simple or too complex, we are in effect proposing that he take a different position. We should propose this only if we understand the new limitations, as well as the new potentialities, that the different position will bring.

We next consider the way in which a speaker's person, his audience and occasion limit his choice of position.

THE SPEAKER'S PERSON AND HIS POSITION

We have already observed that the man in public life who takes a position must take this commitment into account in his subsequent choices. We can further observe that each speaker, by reason of his own person and biography is both limited and aided in his selection of position.

Kenneth Burke has called attention to the embarrassment possible in the relationship between the speaker's person and his utterance. For example, there is an embarrassment in these positions: the rich man praising wealth; the rich man praising poverty; the poor man praising wealth; and the poor man praising poverty. The embarrassment results from the discomfort an audience may experience at the spectacle of a speaker praising his own station in life; or conversely praising that which he has not experienced and therefore cannot know. We are familiar with the possibility that men often speak not from love of the truth so much as self-love, or not from knowledge so much as from envy or the desire to dissemble.

Examples of embarrassment in the relationship between the speaker's person and his position are legion. The college student who, from his own wisdom and insight, denounces the feeble rationality of Aristotle, Augustine, John Locke, or Arnold Toynbee may have created a public embarrassment, particularly if he seems totally unaware of a possible disproportion between his own credentials and those of the persons he denounces. The student who, with gay abandon, proposes sweeping reforms of American higher education based on his two years of college experience plus an evening of deep thought risks a similar embarrassment. In public life we are all too familiar with the unmarried speaker who lectures on the proper conduct of marriage; the worker who knows how a business should be managed, or the manager who lectures workers on the virtues of honest and uncomplaining toil; the man who has never written a play but finds all living playwrights deficient in talent; the thrice-divorced sociologist who calls for national analysis of the instability of the American home; the educator who finds that the pattern of his own education is most suitable for the production of wise and virtuous men; the politician who finds remarkable virtue in his own political party; the journalist who gives the Secretary of State sage advice on the conduct of international relations; the man who has never heard a shot fired in anger and yet questions the courage of battlefield heroes; the housewife who has spent only three weeks in Russia yet lectures on the "truth about Communism"; the elderly who denounce the young as a class, and the young who denounce the aged. The list could be extended. That so many public speakers succeed in producing embarrassment is tribute to widespread inattention to the relation between the speaker's person and his public position.

If the speaker's person limits some choice of position, it may also enhance other choices. For example, special attention seems always accorded to the positions of persons who can claim that they have been converted to the position chosen: the Democrat turned Republican; the Communist turned Anti-Communist; the atheist turned Christian; the former hoodlum supporting virtuous living; the reformed alcoholic denouncing the evils of drink. Travel abroad seems always to enhance the speaker's position on international relations, and positions which seem in some way contrary to the manifest self-interest of the speaker are also strengthened. Thus the wealthy man who calls for an increase in a progressive income tax speaks from a strong personal position.

Any position carries the possibility of embarrassment. We should not expect teachers to stop arguing the merits of education simply because they are well educated, nor students to stop claiming some special insight into educational problems if for no other reason than their experience tells them that they are part of the problem. Public speakers can and do move in ways to accomplish their purposes and hold to their desired positions while relieving potential embarrassment. The student who wishes to denounce Professor Arnold Toynbee is not required to do so on his own authority; he can present the analysis of Toynbee provided by Professor Kaufmann. The student who wishes to advance proposals for the reform of higher education will have little trouble finding a range of such proposals ably supported by men who have devoted their lives to the study of educational systems. The traveler who wants to talk on the products of his experience can report what he saw, and how he interprets it, without claiming insight into the totality of a culture he experienced briefly.

The speaker's problem, then, is not so much the search for positions which free him from embarrassment as having enough insight into the possible implications of his position to enable proper management of his relationship with subject, audience, and occasion. For example, the well-known English writer of mystery stories Dorothy Sayers addressed a vacation course in education at Oxford University in 1947, and chose to present a comprehensive critique of the entire design of British common-school education. She was fully aware of the possible tension between the audience's perception of who she was, and who might be properly qualified to undertake a broad critique of the educational system. She dealt with the problem in her introduction with a note of good natured aggressiveness:

That I, whose experience of teaching is extremely limited, and whose life of recent years has been almost wholly out of touch with educational circles, should presume to discuss education is a matter, surely, that calls for no apology. It is a kind of behaviour to which the present climate of opinion is wholly favourable. Bishops air their opinions about economics; biologists, about metaphysics; celibates, about matrimony; inorganic chemists about theology; the most irrelevant people are appointed to highly-technical ministeries; and plain, blunt men write to the papers to say that Epstein and Picasso do not know how to draw. Up to a certain point, and provided that the criticisms are made with a reasonable modesty, these activities are commendable. Too much specialization is not a good thing. There is also one excellent reason why the veriest amateur may feel entitled to have an opinion about education. For if we have not all been professional teachers, we have all, at some time or another, been taught. Even if we learnt nothing —perhaps in particular if we learnt nothing—our contribution to the discussion may have a potential value.

Without apology, then, I will begin. . . .[2]

We have explored the relationship between the speaker's person and his position, observing how a speaker's choice of position may be limited, enhanced, or modified by the particular nature of this relationship. We could explore in like manner the relationship between the speaker's position and his audience, or between his position and the occasion. For example, a strong position on the virtue of frugality would seem a peculiar choice for a speaker who had just joined fellow club members in a five-course dinner featuring imported wines and gold compacts for the ladies. But the point should not require further elaboration. The speaker works within the constraints and possibilities provided by all aspects of the situation, and he chooses a position rationally to the extent that he is aware of these constraints and possibilities.

[2] Dorothy Sayers, *The Lost Tools of Learning* (London: Methuen and Company, 1948), p. 1.

We turn next to the interrelationships of the concept of position and the conduct of expository, persuasive, and ceremonial speaking.

ISSUE, POINT OF VIEW, AND POSITION

We have previously observed that the speaker's position includes both the central content of his utterance and the point of view from which he treats that content. In this sense, the speaker's position defines the relationship he seeks with his subject matter, his audience, and the occasion. We shall now explore the interrelationship of point of view and content —the way in which various points of view assumed by speakers tend to define the central content of their utterance. To conduct this exploration we shall have need to use somewhat rigorously a rhetorical term which we have previously used only casually. The term is *issue*. We shall also have need to return to the three terms introduced in Chapter 2 to designate three broad classifications of public speeches, the terms *expository, persuasive,* and *ceremonial.*

In rhetoric, the term *issue* is used to designate a question to which different men might bring divergent or contradictory answers. A properly formulated question, to which some respondents might answer "yes" and others "no," identifies an issue, or point of tension, between these respondents. The existence of such points of tension among men is presumably the psychological cause for being of public speeches, and other forms of public discourse. That is, listeners attend public speeches because of the tension existing or potential in some issue they confront. And speakers take positions designed to be responsive to issues they and their listeners confront. In this sense, speakers find their proper subject matter only by responding to their awareness of issues present or potential for their audiences. Therefore, by looking toward the types of issues which underlie various classes of positions, we can uncover the area within which the speaker will choose his particular position.

The various classes of positions we shall be concerned with are identified by the three types of public speeches, the *expository,* the *persuasive,* and the *ceremonial.* In the remainder of this chapter we shall use these terms to designate different points of view a speaker may bring to the speaking situation. Thus, the expository speaker takes a point of view of a reporter or teacher—one who makes knowledge about man or his environment available to an audience. The persuasive speaker takes the point of view of the advocate—one who seeks to influence the attitudes or actions of his listeners. The ceremonial speaker takes the point of view of the artist or philosopher—one who seeks to uncover the values implicit in the lives of particular men, particular institutions, or particular occasions. These points of view are not mutually exclusive. Speakers can and do move from one point of view to another in a single discourse. We have all had experience with the ostensibly expository speech which drifts in and out of controversial assertions on attitudes and actions without assuming responsibility for justifying these assertions. We have also seen that a particular point of view may be a disguise assumed strategically, as in the case of the speaker who purports simply to report the facts objectively, but who selects and arranges his facts to lead toward an inescapable conclusion. However, for the present analysis, we should set aside these complexities.

Position and the Expository Speaker

At first thought, an expository speech seems to have a point of view, but seems also to lack any central ground or any necessary engagement with an issue. The central ground of a persuasive speaker who supports some assertion seems clear. The speaker who says "America should continue nuclear testing until we have perfected an anti-missile weapon" clearly has a position, and is clearly addressing himself to an issue. But what of the speaker who says "We shall examine today the major theses presented concerning the causes of the civil war, and observe the different treatments given the question of causation by different historians." He has a statement or controlling concept, and he has a mission. But does he have any position other than the point of view of the reporter or teacher?

A useful perspective for viewing the expository speech is to note that the speaker does have a position central to the selection of his content and that if his speech is to be successful, this position must be derived from certain issues implicit in the expository point of view. The position of the expository speaker can be and often is only implicit in his utterance. It must therefore be discovered by inference.

Let us examine more closely the expository speech. The speaker who purports to bring information or knowledge to an audience must necessarily make two assumptions about his utterance. The first is that he has information or knowledge which is in some sense needed by the audience. If the speaker does not make this assumption his reason for talking becomes questionable, and the product of his utterance will be limited to whatever pleasure the speaker may derive from listening to the sound of his own voice. The expository point of view does not require the assumption that the audience perceive its need prior to the speech. The speaker may move to make the audience aware of its need for his information, and in that case he may make explicit his assumption and position.

The second assumption is that the information provided for the audience is reputable or truthful. The question of what constitutes reputable or truthful description of some part of the universe is a baffling one that has haunted scholars since the beginnings of a self-conscious search for knowledge. Since our topic at the moment is the *position* of the expository speaker, rather than the nature of truth, we can avoid the knotty question "What is truth?" and center our attention on the requirements of the expository speaking situation. The speaker who purports to bring information or knowledge to an audience must necessarily take the position that his utterance has been chosen and arranged in a manner as consistent as possible with the best knowledge or "truth" available to his culture. If he takes any other position, his claim as reporter or teacher is fraudulent. If he makes statements at variance with those his audience believes to be reputable or truthful, he will be considered not as an expositor, but as an imposter. Since speakers and audiences do manage to join to one another on the assumption that they are sharing reputable knowledge, it is clear that commonsense decisions on the nature of reputable information or truthful statements are constantly being made; it should be clear too that they must be made as a precondition of exposition.

We have now proposed that the expository point of view requires a speaker to take the position that his utterance is (a) needed, and (b) reputable or truthful. For example, the speaker who says "I shall teach you how to repair a carburetor" must necessarily also be saying, implicitly or explicitly, "You need information on the repair of the carburetor," and "the information I shall give you is reputable." If the speaker cannot take a position on need, his utterance has no justification for the particular audience. If he cannot take the position on reputability, he might better be silent. In this sense, the speaker whose point of view is expository faces two inescapable issues; and he must respond to these issues, implicitly or explicitly, if he is to justify his point of view. Our analysis suggests that the speaker who assumes an expository point of view accepts a rigorous limitation on the nature of the utterance consistent with this point of view.

The importance of this required position for the expository speech can be demonstrated by showing some of its effects on the design, conduct, and results of expository speeches. These effects can be explored by a more extended treatment of the two major issues or questions to which the expository speaker gives implicit or explicit affirmation.

(1) *Is the information needed?* As we have suggested, an expository speech signals the speaker's assumption that his information is, in some sense, needed. If the speaker senses that the need for his information is

doubtful, he may choose to discuss his position with some explanation of the significance or usefulness of his material.

In the case of the expository speech which selects its audience from those who acknowledge by their presence their interest in the speaker's subject matter, the speaker can comfortably assume that the issue of "need" has been substantially resolved. Thus the speaker purporting to explain the procedures by which a manufacturer may secure a government contract for his production, and whose audience consists of businessmen interested in the possibility of securing such contracts, approaches a willing audience. This is not to say that the speaker in such circumstances will refrain from "puffing" the importance of his information. It is possible to heighten an existing appetite.

With audiences which are not selected by the speaker's subject matter, the speaker purporting to bring needed information may face some substantial problems in establishing his position. If he chooses to "inform" an audience with materials already known to many or most, his position is all but hopeless. Student speakers, choosing their information from materials drawn exclusively from the most recent issue of the local Sunday newspaper, face the certainty of substantial failure with their audience. They are merchandising boredom.

Expository speakers whose position on "need" is sustained primarily by some element of enforced attendance on the part of the audience may face a serious tension with an audience. To some extent, the college lecturer faces this situation, particularly if his audience has been recruited by some requirement in the curriculum. If the lecturer is inattentive to the need for his information, he may seem to be arguing that he should be heard only because his course is required, that learning its materials is essential to passing the examinations he will give, and that passing the examinations is essential to those who wish a college degree. In such circumstances the listener's sense of "need" may be both real and practical enough, but it is scarcely the sort of speaker-audience relationship designed to produce high rapport.

While the speaker's position on "need," whether explicit or implicit, inevitably involves the audience's question, "why should I listen?" the speaker is favored by the fact that most listeners have an all but insatiable appetite for "new" information so long as its acquisition is not attended by excessive labor. The need for information does not require that the information carry with it the promise that it will improve the listener's earning power, or increase his attractiveness to members of the opposite sex, or prolong his life—although such needs have a way of assuring unusual attention on the part of listeners. The generality of mankind seeks to search out the nature of its environment; people were curious about the structure of the atom long before the nuclear bomb demonstrated the relationship of such structure to human survival. And anyone who has ever noticed that his world is shared by spiders may have his curiosity aroused by tales of the ways in which they go about securing food and assuring the survival of their species. Without speculating at this time as to the nature of the human motivation which causes listeners to be interested in the mating habits of the stickleback fish, or the edibility of the Mediterranean octopus, or the inside story of how the Cuban crisis was handled by the White House, it may nevertheless be asserted with some confidence that the speaker whose information is genuinely capable of extending the audience's knowledge has the human quality commonly known as curiosity working on his side.

(2) *Is the information reputable or truthful?* As with the issue of need, the answer of the expository speaker to this question must be "yes." If the audience accepts the speaker's required position, the speech may proceed on a high level of acceptability. To the extent that members of the audience question the reputability of the information they are receiving, the speaker faces difficulty in maintaining his position.

The existence of the question of truthfulness accounts for the importance of the speaker's qualification as an expert, or his demonstration that he has sought expert sources for his information.

It is not necessarily the case that information which is unclear or disorderly in its manner of presentation is thereby lacking in reputability. Nevertheless the listener cannot judge the reputability of that which he does not understand. Accordingly, to sustain the position that his information is reputable, the speaker must achieve—through his language, organization, and delivery—a reasonable level of clarity with his audience.

If the expository speaker needs clarity of statement as a requisite for any claim he may make for truth, he also needs to conduct the kind of utterance that will sustain examination as to the sources of his information and as to the reasonableness of the relationship between his information and any interpretations he may make of that information. We expect the speaker who tells us the source of his information to be discriminating about his choice of sources. Hence, the expository speaker may take some pains to justify his sources. We expect that his interpretations and conclusions will be logically supported by the information he has gathered—that he will not claim to know things which could not be known from the evidence he has available. The expository speaker often therefore states his claims with the characteristic moderation of the man careful not to let his conclusions outrun his evidence. "We can draw a tentative conclusion," he says, or "one possible interpretation of this evidence would be . . ." Or he says, "while no final conclusions are possible, it seems to me likely . . ." Clearly this kind of behavior by an expository speaker is also found in persuasive speakers—particularly in those who seek to be persuasive by assuming the manner and position of the expository speaker. But by perceiving the implicit existence of the issue of reputability in every genuinely expository speech, we also perceive the significance of the kind of language practices which characterize exposition.

The general position of the expository speaker may be supplemented by other positions, implicit or explicit, present in the selection and ordering of the materials of the speech. For example, the speaker who gives us an account of the battle of Gettysburg primarily through analysis of the character, motivations, and decisions of the major commanders present at that battle has taken, at least for the moment, a position about reputable historical exposition. He is saying in effect: "The character and actions of a particular man have an important influence on the course of history." The speaker's general point of view, that of expositor, has been extended by a particular point of view about a good way, or reputable way, of knowing part of the past. The specific extensions of the expository speaker's general position need to be uncovered if we are to see his position fully. For instance, the speaker who describes human learning and behavior with information drawn from laboratory investigation of the behavior of rats or monkeys makes this assumption: that human behavior may be reputably interpreted on the basis of information about animal behavior.

Our discussion of the position of the expository speaker brings us back to the ambiguity of lines drawn between expository and persuasive speaking. When we discover that the expository speaker has a position, we understand that the success of his exposition rests on his ability to "persuade" the audience to accept this position. We are likely to perceive the persuasion in exposition, however, only at the moment some listener challenges some part of the speaker's position by asserting that his information is not needed, or that it is not reputable, or that some particular extension of his position is unwarranted. The difference in exposition and persuasion does not lie in the nature of the general process of communication being undertaken, but rather in the extent to which the expository situation tends to prescribe major aspects of the speaker's position. The speaker who purports to act genuinely as reporter or teacher accepts many rigorous constraints on his choices. Few speakers or writers meet all of these constraints successfully.

Position and the Persuasive Speaker

The prescriptive nature of the expositor's position contrasts with the relative latitude of choice available to the persuader. To be sure, the persuasive speaker must assume like the expositor that his point of view is needed, and that it is reputable; to concede otherwise would be fatal to his enterprise. But as advocate he starts with the assumption that he is discussing some matter which is a subject of controversy, that he will take a position and seek to influence others to share his position. Ten expositors purporting to give an account of the nature of atomic fission should not vary too greatly in the substance of their utterance. If they do, either some of them should not be speaking, or the status of contemporary knowledge about atomic fission is one of scandalous disarray. Ten persuaders taking a position on the banning of nuclear weapons testing may appropriately take widely varied positions, and the substance of their utterance would be expected to vary widely.

Unless the persuasive speaker moves by indirection, perhaps using the mask of exposition or ceremony, his central position should be readily apparent. This position may be expressed as the proposition or assertion for which the speaker seeks assent, and can readily be perceived as a particular choice among a number of available choices. These choices are available along the familiar pro-con continuum associated with controverted issues. Thus, if we pose the issue, "Should the state of Minnesota legalize parimutuel gambling?" the speaker can take one of a variety of positions representing varying levels of affirmative or negative response to the question. He can respond:

Unquestionably yes . . . or . . . Probably yes . . . or . . . I am uncertain . . . or . . . Probably no . . . or . . . Unquestionably no.

One could hypothesize various shadings of all these possible positions, such as the position, "Under some circumstances, which I shall describe, the state should legalize parimutuel gambling."

We have earlier made the point that the location of a speaker's position as a single assertion or statement seldom does justice to the description of the "ground" central to his utterance. Description of this central ground is more likely to require a précis or summary of the central content and stance of the speech than to be expressible in a single assertion.

At a general level, the central ground the expository speaker needs to occupy can be rather clearly designated or predicted. Interestingly enough we can also predict to some extent the area within which certain kinds of persuasive speeches will find their central ground. This prediction is based on the fact that the persuader who takes a public position on a particular controverted issue almost automatically confronts a discrete set of subordinate issues. These subordinate issues define in a priori fashion the space or area within which he will locate his particular position. It is obviously useful to explore the general ground within which the persuasive speaker finds his position. The speaker who knows generally the kinds of questions his speech must or may usefully answer is able to choose a position relevant to his purpose. The listener who knows these same questions can more readily perceive and evaluate the nature of the particular position chosen by the speaker.

Two kinds of persuasive speeches seem clearly to predict the space within which the speaker will choose his position. The first of these is the speech which is responsive to some question of social or political policy—to a proposal for change in the political or social customs of a given society. The second is the speech which is responsive to some accusation of wrongdoing—to a proposal, ordinarily in a courtroom setting, that some person has been guilty of wrongful or illegal action. We shall examine each kind of speech briefly, observing the possibility predicting the nature of the area within which the speaker may take his position.

The Speech of Policy and its Positional Area. Many persuasive speeches find their origin in some proposal for a change in social or political beliefs or actions. Proposals for changes in laws, changes in the conduct of voluntary associations, changes in customary ways of doing business or of conducting oneself all result in such speeches of policy. Thus speakers favor or oppose federal aid to education; they favor or oppose the use of an honor system for the conduct of university examinations; they favor or oppose increased public control over network programming of television; they favor or oppose changes in the laws regulating automobile driving, and so forth.

For such speeches, a general framework of issues has been developed as part of the theory of argumentation and debate. This framework has been based on a set of so-called stock issues. These stock issues presumably represent the range of questions potentially at issue whenever a proposition of policy is put forward. In other words they define the immediate area within which the speaker will take his position.

Although the stock issues pertaining to speaking about matters of policy have been variously phrased by different authors, a considerable consensus exists as to the nature of these issues. They have been embedded in political and legal controversy throughout the history of western civilization. The following statement of these issues is based on an analysis made by Professor Lee Hultzen, although his terminology has been modified.[3] The general questions to which a speech about policy responds seem to be four in number:

(1) *Is there a need for a change in policy?*

Presumably the occasion for any public discussion of policy is the belief by some speaker that there are deficiencies in existing social policies or customs. Someone must propose that "things as they are" are not all that they could be, or should be. Otherwise there is no reason for a public discussion of any proposal for a change in social policy. Since all human societies seem to have escaped perfection by a sizeable margin, the charge that there is a need for change is rather commonly raised by the speaker.

(2) *Is the proposed "need" remediable?*

To say that a social ill exists, or that some need for a change in the human condition exists, inevitably raises the question as to whether or not that ill is remediable. The speaker who argues that a need exists must inevitably propose that it is remediable. One could charge, though not without dispute, that the fact that people die of old age is a human ill which needs changing. But one does not expect a public speech to emerge from such a charge, since the need seems somewhat beyond the possibility of remedy.

The question of the remediability of an alleged need usually involves an analysis of the alleged causes of that need. Presumably only the accurate diagnosis of an alleged need can result in a proposal for change suitable to remedying the need.

(3) *Is the proposed change the best way of remedying the need?*

If it be assumed that a need for change exists and that the need describes a situation which can be remedied, the further question rises as to the nature of the change of policy best calculated to remedy the need. Public speeches on matters of policy often center on this issue, particularly when the speech proposes a policy related to some need which is rather commonly accepted. For example, American society in 1960 revealed a considerable consensus that better provision for the medical care of the aged needed to be made, and that it could be made. Any particular proposal as to how this need might be met, however, was likely to arouse strong dispute.

(4) *Would the proposed change introduce problems greater than those it solves?*

Presumably any change in policy involves the possibility of both desirable and undesirable consequences. A family without a car, for example, might perceive a need for improved transportation. The situation might seem remediable in terms of modern technology, and it might be clear that an automobile would satisfy the need better than

[3] Lee S. Hultzen, "Status in Deliberative Analysis," in Donald C. Bryant, ed., *The Rhetorical Idiom* (Ithaca, New York: Cornell University Press, 1958), pp. 97–123.

any alternative plan of action. If it were further apparent that the purchase of an automobile would jeopardize the family's ability to purchase food, the desirability of the purchase would come into question.

Professor Hultzen calls the four stock issues just described the four "frames" within which the point or points at issue in any discussion of a matter of policy will be located. The four issues are capsulized in the easily remembered quartet term of "ill, blame, cure, and cost." What illness is charged? What (or who) is responsible for this illness? What policy or action will remedy the illness? And what will be the total cost, monetary or otherwise, of the proposed policy? These issues (or frames) may be said to define the space surrounding any speech proposing or opposing a change in policy. Within this space, the speaker takes his position.

A speaker may choose to take a position responsive to all of the four issues, or he may limit his position to affirmation or negation of one, two, or three of the issues. In any extended debate over the issue of policy, we are likely to find positions emerging on all of the four issues. That is, one or several speakers will have occupied the entire positional ground for speeches on matters of policy change.

The Speech of Accusation or Defense and its Positional Area. If Citizen "A" is accused of murder, we have a situation likely to produce persuasive speaking. The most obvious location for such speaking is the courtroom, but we are all sufficiently burdened by television drama purporting to picture life on the old frontier to understand that speeches of accusation and defense also take place in settings such as saloons and street corners. Moreover, few intensely argued election campaigns are free from such speaking.

Speeches of accusation and defense seem a staple ingredient of history. The issues they involve are associated with the development of systems of law and systems for judging the merit of such accusations. Because such systems are very ancient, the positional area implied by an accusation has been more rigorously defined than that implied by any other kind of persuasive speaking. We can illustrate both the antiquity and rigor of this definition by turning to the analysis made by Cicero of the issues raised by a legal action in the Roman state.

In discussing forensic or courtroom speaking, Cicero developed a system by which a speaker could survey, in advance of the legal action, all of the issues likely to arise in the case. Through such a survey, the speaker could anticipate all of the arguments that might be raised by his opponent, and could examine the facts of a particular case with a view toward finding those statements and arguments which would best support his point of view. In the interests of historical accuracy we should observe that Cicero did not develop this system with reference to a concept of positional space, nor did he use the Latin equivalent of our term *issue* as the base of his discussion. Rather he wrote of this survey as one which would enable the speaker to discover the status of his case. By *status,* he meant simply discovery of those issues which were likely to be in contention in a particular case, or those issues which would be most advantageous to the speaker's case. In the discussion which follows, however, we shall not use the classical term *status,* but rather confine ourselves to a free interpretation of Cicero's comments on the speech of accusation or defense as these comments apply to the concept of position.

According to Cicero's analysis,[4] any accusation of wrongdoing would raise five major issues, any or all of which might figure in the defense of the accused. Thus if "A" is accused of the murder of "B," and brought to trial, the relevant questions become:

(1) *Did "A" kill "B"?*
   The question is one of *fact*. It involves two lesser questions of fact, "Is 'B' dead?" and "Was 'B' killed?" as well as the decisive question.
(2) *If "B" was killed, was his killing murder?*
   The question is one of *definition*. Not all killing is murder as defined by law. Killing in self-defense, or accidental killing, might not fall under the definition of murder, for example.
(3) *Is the court within which the trial is held legally entitled to try Citizen "A"?*
   The question is one of *jurisdiction*. Even if there is good evidence that "A" murdered "B," he could be found guilty and punished only by a properly constituted court.
(4) *Do the procedures of the trial follow those prescribed by law as necessary to a finding by the court?*
   The question is one of *procedure*. Court procedures are prescribed presumably to assure the maximum possibility that justice will be done, and if improper procedures are followed, then no finding of guilt ought to be made.
(5) *If "A" did murder "B," were there circumstances surrounding his crime, or which would surround his punishment, which ought to be taken into account?*
   The issue is one of *circumstance*. If "B" had provoked "A" unconscionably, or if "B" was a notable scoundrel, then the court might wish either to find "A" not guilty of murder, or to provide little or no

[4] As suggested, the terminology here used is a free adaption of Cicero's doctrine of status. For one Ciceronian version of the doctrine see Cicero, *De Inventione,* 1.8.10.

punishment. It is interesting to note that in a very strict legal sense, the question of extenuating circumstances should be irrelevant to the guilt or innocence of an accused person. However, Cicero made frequent use of this issue in the defense of his own clients, and to the extent that any legal system presumes to temper justice with mercy the issue becomes important.

These five issues—which can be named as the issues of fact, definition, jurisdiction, procedure, and circumstance—were the major issues which Cicero found relevant to any public problem raised by a legal action. There were other minor issues discussed by Cicero.

Certain observations are possible about the nature of the positional area defined for speeches of accusation and defense. Presumably the speaker supporting an accusation within a legal system must be prepared to affirm each of the five issues should that issue be controverted; the speaker defending against the accusation may controvert any or all of the issues. The issues thus define an area within which the accuser and defender will take their positions, but it does not indicate in advance the particular part of that area which the speaker will choose as the ground or position for his utterance. Many interesting examples are available of the way in which speakers have chosen position within this defined area. In 1961, Adolph Eichmann, a Nazi official during World War II, was tried in Israel and ultimately sentenced to death on the charge that he had joined in the conspiracy to murder millions of European Jews during the war—a so-called crime against humanity. Robert Servatius, Eichmann's German lawyer, made no effort to deny that a crime had been committed, nor to deny Eichmann's complicity in the crime. He did, however, address himself to two questions: (a) Since Eichmann carried out the wishes of his superiors in the Nazi government, should he be held responsible for his actions and punished for them? Servatius raised here the issue of circumstance. (b) Did an Israeli court have the right to try and punish Eichmann for crimes committed in a place not under the jurisdiction of that court? Here the issue was one of jurisdiction.

One of the famous defense speeches in literature finds the speaker taking his position on somewhat different ground. In the novel *The Brothers Karamazov,* Dostoevsky presents as a full speech the summation of the defense attorney in the famous murder trial of the novel. The attorney is defending Dmitri, the brother accused of the murder of his father Fyodor. The attorney argues: (a) if there was a murder, Dmitri did not commit it (the issue of fact); and (b) if Fyodor was murdered by his son, it was because he richly deserved killing (the issue of circumstance).

Positional Area and the Generality of Persuasive Speaking. If we are given speeches calling for or opposing policy changes, or are given speeches of accusation or defense, we can predict with reasonable accuracy the area within which speakers will take their positions. Such speeches are a major part of the totality of persuasive speaking. The ability to predict the positional area of advocates is useful in that it tells speakers where to look for their positions, and tells listeners the kinds of positions they might expect.

We should not assume that all persuasive speeches will reveal positions readily describable in terms of the systems of issues we have described. We have already observed the tenuous nature of the line between persuasive speeches, expository speeches, and ceremonial speeches. We can further observe that persuaders take positions which do not involve recommendations about policy or about acts of accusation and defense, and that they intermix matters of policy and accusation with matters of exposition, praise, and blame. As with the expository speech, the description of the position of a particular persuasive speech requires specific analysis of its action.

The Ceremonial Speech and its Positional Area

We have given preliminary definition of the mission of the ceremonial speaker as that of praising or blaming, or seeking to unite an audience in terms of commonly experienced values. We have further suggested that the point of view of the ceremonial speaker is akin to that of the plastic or pictorial artist. The speaker's art is discursive rather than presentational. But as he seeks to uncover the enduring values in the life of some man, or in the nature of some institution, and to give these values symbolic visibility, his work may share the aesthetic purposes of painter or sculptor.

The difficulty in defining the point of view of the ceremonial speaker as that of an artist rests in the fact that few speakers are able to sustain this point of view, or to support it with appropriate utterance. For example, many speeches in praise or blame of a person are clearly persuasive in nature. A man is praised as a model for our emulation, to prove that his enemies were wrong, or to prove that his ideas should be supported. Ceremonial speeches turn toward persuasive ends as readily as expository speeches, although the fact that a speaker uses a ceremonial occasion to seek explicitly to influence the actions and attitudes of his listeners is certainly not an automatic reason to condemn him. Moreover, many ceremonial speeches are clearly devoted to the evocation of transient or trivial values rather than the engraving of enduring values. The after-dinner speech, which seems clearly designed to entertain and has no larger pretentions, is a well-established American ritual. Such speeches, if successful, may be said to evoke a common experience with good fellowship—an experience which might be titled, "We members of the Royal Order of Old Buffalos are the world's most convivial people." The speaker who brings off this ceremony successfully is practicing a kind of art and making visible a type of human value. His art is a popular one; the values it uncovers may not be exceptionally worthy of deep contemplation. Again, we should not cry "fault" at the skillful practitioner of popular art, for by so doing we seem to argue that all ceremonial occasions are moments of high gravity served only by the action of a true artist who seeks to uncover enduring values.

Most speeches which seem primarily ceremonial in nature, then, do not adhere closely to our narrow definition of this type of speech. We can nevertheless propose a narrow definition of the ceremonial speech in order to illustrate the unique problems and possibilities in such speeches.

As a case in point consider the eulogy delivered in praise of some person, group, event, or institution. Robert Ingersoll's speech in praise of "Our Pioneer Forefathers" was such a speech. Thucydides' Funeral Oration, discussed in the foreword to Part I, was such a speech. So also was Lincoln's Gettysburg Address, or Wendell Phillips' well-known eulogy of Toussaint l'Ouverture, the Haitian liberator. The eulogy is a common type of ceremonial speaking, and the impulse to eulogize is also represented in the production of biographical writing of the type known as hagiography, as well as in many historical dramas.

The eulogist's point of view entails only one major issue which defines its positional area. That issue is represented by the question: Are there values in this man's life (this event, this institution) which are worthy of contemplation? When the eulogist has found the value or set of values he wishes to make visible, he has found the center of his discourse, the ground on which he will stand. Wendell Phillips found the life of Toussaint l'Ouverture an exemplification of courage, endurance, honor, sense, purpose, and skill crowned with success. The portrait is a stirring one. On the other hand the eulogist may choose to center on some single value epitomizing the totality of a man's life. One of the biographers of Senator George Norris of Nebraska subtitled his work, "A Study in Integrity." In it, the single human value of integrity served to give focus to the character and works of Norris, as this eulogist saw him. The eulogist may also choose to work with ironic contrast in his subject's life. For example, a eulogy of the American comedian W. C. Fields might bring out Fields' all-too-human penury, addiction to alcohol, and alienation from the generality of virtuous attitudes, and go on to relate these aspects of his life to the nature of Fields' comic vision and art. The values in Fields' life do not generate a rendering of unambiguous human virtues.

But however the eulogist selects his ground, by whatever method of utterance he makes that ground visible and secure, however explicit or implicit his evocation of value, the fact remains that the eulogist finds the content center of his discourse in the area defined by the values potentially visible in the life, event, or institution he makes his topic.

SUMMARY

Choice of position is the speaker's most crucial decision. This choice includes selection of the central "ground" or content that the speech will support, and, also selection of the stance or point of view the speaker will assume in and through that content. Thus, in taking a position the speaker chooses both what he wants his audience to remember or believe about some topic, and how he wants his audience to know him. In this sense public speakers become known by the positions they take.

Positions may be observed as varying according to certain general characteristics. That is, they are narrow or broad, clear or ambiguous, and simple or complex. A particular choice between any of these options presents the speaker with certain advantages and certain limitations.

Positions may also be observed as interacting with the speaker's person, the nature of his audience, and the occasion. That is, the merit or limitation of a particular position may be determined by its relationship to the person of a particular speaker, or to the nature of a particular audience or occasion. A position which is reinforced by the person of a given speaker may seem an embarrassment when chosen by a different speaker. Similar ratios of reinforcement or embarrassment are inherent in the relationship of a position to a particular audience or occasion.

The stance of the speaker varies in expository, persuasive, and ceremonial speaking. Moreover, each of these three types of speaking generates an abstract frame of reference within which the speaker will discover the central content of his utterance. The speaker who knows that he wishes to take the position of an expositor, or advocate, or ceremonialist can also know the kind of subject matter he needs to look for in developing the content of his position.

Each of the general types of speaking—expository, persuasive and ceremonial—can be recognized in part by differences in the speaker's point of view. Thus expository speaking entails the point of view of the disinterested reporter or teacher; persuasive speaking, the point of view of the advocate; and ceremonial speaking, the point of view of the artist. Each point of view generates certain types of issues or questions which define the area within which the speaker will find the central content of his speech. Exploration of the issues relevant to a given type of speech is useful in that it tells speakers where to look for the content of their utterance, and tells listeners the general nature of the position they might anticipate. We can chart with some accuracy the positional area available to the expository speaker, the persuasive speaker who advocates or opposes a change in policy, the persuasive speaker who accuses or defends, and the ceremonial speaker who engages in praise or blame.

Such a priori charting of the positional area available to the speaker provides a frame of reference for uncovering the position chosen by a particular speaker. It does not provide a full and specific description of the concrete position assumed by a particular speaker on a particular occasion.

CHAPTER 4

Speech Forms: Structure and Movement

FORM AND SUBSTANCE

We are accustomed to viewing objects as combining form and substance. We may observe, for example, that a sword and a plowshare are made of similar substance, but that they take on vastly different significance because of their form.

If we assume an analogy between the significance of objects, and the meaning of acts of language, we can readily accept the idea that a change in the form of an event may have decisive influence on its meaning. But it is also true that changes in form may influence meaning in certain contexts and be quite unimportant in other contexts. For example, a man who is thirsty enough is not likely to attend to the difference between a plain glass tumbler and an artistically etched goblet if each holds the desired water. The difference in form could be important, however, at a formal dinner or an exhibition of craftsmanship. Similarly, a tired traveller seeking information is more likely to attend to the substance of the information he receives than to the dialect or grammatical purity of his informant's utterance. Thus, while it is true that any change in the form of an object or event potentially alters its significance or meaning, it is also true that some changes in form are unimportant in certain contexts.

How should we view the relationship of form and substance in a public speech? One possibility is to treat the two as somewhat separable, and to conceive of the same speech substance as being arranged in different ways or cast into different structures. This view of speechmaking is commonplace, and conforms to ordinary commentary about speeches. Thus we may say, "The two speakers had the same message (substance), but one stated his ideas more clearly, with a better sense of order and movement." Or we say to a speaker, "Try to say the same thing, but say it with half as many words." This point of view does not make form unimportant, but it does suggest that questions of form and substance can be separated in the construction or criticism of a speech. Yet if a public speech is an action giving meaning, the form of that speech becomes part of that meaning, and any effort to view form and substance as ultimately separable may be misleading.

The more artistry in a public speech, the more inseparable its form and substance become. We cannot readily paraphrase Lincoln's Gettysburg Address without changing its substance in an important way. Given significant or artistic utterance, the proper analogy for viewing the relationship of form and substance becomes that of iron made into a sword. The meaning of the act becomes no less than the totality of its form and substance. The public speaker whose utterance seems to be an inevitable consequence of his position and situation will have achieved an action in which substance and form have become one entity.

If good speaking aims toward a union of form and substance, then the speaker's choice of form becomes a matter of major importance. The form he chooses for utterance is intrinsic to the meaning he chooses to place on his world. It is intrinsic to the meaning others may share. The idea that as we choose form we choose in part the meaning we would give to our experience seems strange at first. We are accustomed to viewing speech or language as a way of reflecting, or registering some reality external to language. We are unaccustomed to the notion that as we talk about our world we are choosing the meaning we shall give to it, much as the iron worker chooses the meaning a piece of metal shall have as he gives it form. Yet only the latter point of view gives us any sense of the way language really works to give meaning.

Speakers choose an "order of reality" as they speak. As they give linguistic form and structure to experience, they also give meaning. For example, the speaker who talks about a behavior called "alcoholism" may describe this behavior as an "ailment" or "disease." He may then give a structure to his utterance through discussion of the problem of diagnosis, the analysis of possible causation, the possibility of treatment, and the need for further research by medical scientists. We can observe that the speaker's utterance proceeds from a particular perspective, and that it takes on a certain structure and form which shapes the meaning he wishes to give to the phenomenon of alcoholism, and the meaning he hopes to share with others. Different perspectives and linguistic forms could be applied to the same phenomenon. The behavior could be talked of as a "sin," and examined as an expression of moral dereliction leading to immoral personal and social consequences. The two forms applied to the phenomenon of alcoholism are not necessarily mutually exclusive or contradictory, but they give somewhat different meanings to the same phenomenon.

William James made this point about language in an essay published in 1879. "A Beethoven string-quartette," he wrote, "is truly as some one has said, a scraping of horses' tails on cats' bowels, and may be exhaustively described in such terms; but the application of this description in no way precludes the simultaneous applicability of an entirely different description." [1]

OBSERVING FORM IN SPEECHES

Terminology

In Chapter 2 we observed that a public speech may be examined as an action conducted through a series of *movements*. The patterning of these movements can be described as the *structure* of the speech. Thus any movement in the speech is also a structural element. In this chapter we have introduced the term *form* as the most general label under which we can examine the various types of patterning or structure used by public speakers. We shall assert that public speeches reveal a limited number of basic forms for organizing their subject matter. Certain of these forms suggest a typical structure, or sequence of movements which the speaker might use in realizing the form, but within each basic form various structural modifications are both possible and likely to be used in particular speeches.

Form as a Microscopic and Macroscopic Concept

A difficulty in discussing the form of public speeches rises from the fact that one may properly observe that words have form, sentences have form, larger units of discourse have form, and the social construct created by a man speaking in a particular context also has a form. To elaborate, individual words are forms—a structure of sounds; physical actions used in communication are forms; the language of whole speeches reveals a form in the structure of constituent movements within the act; and the speech in relation to audience, occasion, and speaker produces a structure of social interrelationships which becomes a form. In other words, we can pursue the examination of the workings of form at levels which are variously microscopic or macroscopic.

A good case can be made for assuming that the most significant form ultimately created by a speech is the social form perceived by examining the whole utterance in relation to audience, occasion, and speaker. That

[1] William James, "The Sentiment of Rationality", from an article reprinted in *Essays in Pragmatism* by William James (New York: Haffner Publishing Company, 1951), p. 12.

is, speeches presented to an immediate and present audience characteristically employ forms or structural elements related to aspects of the immediate situation. At the most obvious level, speeches as delivered frequently include references to the audience, the occasion, and the speaker himself. We can judge the speaker's artistry only if we reconstruct the occasion of his utterance. For example, when Henry Grady, a Southerner, went north after the Civil War to address the New England Society on "The New South," he spoke from and to a particular set of circumstances. In one comment he refers to a fellow speaker on the occasion, General William T. Sherman, as one ". . . who is considered an able man in our parts, though some people think he is a kind of a careless man about fire." The skill of the allusion cannot be understood unless one knows of Sherman's "scorched earth" cavalry campaign through the South during the Civil War, and of Sherman's simultaneous status as Northern war hero and Southern scourge.

We have observed repeatedly that the interplay of purpose, speaker, utterance, occasion, and audience constitutes the final reality of any speech. They must all be observed before one knows the final form of an act of speaking. In this sense utterance by the speaker which seems merely digressive—a movement away from or unrelated to the speaker's central position—should not be hastily judged as inept or inconsequential. The so-called digression may perform an essential and skillful task in encompassing the whole of the speaking situation.

Although we shall return to the question of digressions, *form* needs some limitation if it is to be discussed systematically. Therefore, in this chapter we shall restrict ourselves primarily to consideration of the form of the whole utterance and to the structure created by the pattern or arrangement of the major movements within that utterance. We shall further limit consideration to the language of the speech, or to that part of the speaker's action which could be recorded in a text.

Speech Forms as Social Property

A basic assumption in our exploration of speech form is that most public speeches in our culture reveal one or more of a limited number of typical forms. The social nature of public speaking guarantees this assumption. That is, public speaking is a practical art, charged with the worldly task of organizing the knowledge, attitudes, and actions of social groups. Thus the speaker necessarily meets his audience through a language held in common and through ways of treating experience also held in common. We cannot hypothesize an organized society in which men would organize their experience through an unlimited number of forms; if each man sought to give some unique view of reality through his utterance, the possibility of communication and social organization would disappear. Accordingly, we would expect public speakers in any given society to use a limited number of typical forms, commonly understood and used by members of their society.

That there are a limited number of typical forms does not deny the fact that particular public speeches will reveal unusual, or atypical aspects. Speakers can and do seek to modify somewhat the habitual way in which members of an audience may structure some aspect of experience. But the assumption does permit search for a typology of speech forms, brief enough to be comprehensible, and yet sufficient to account for the forms most common to public speaking in our society. Knowledge of these will give the speaker a priori insight concerning the available ways of organizing any given body of subject matter and, furthermore, will give the listener a proper basis for understanding the implications of the speaker's method of handling his subject matter.

A TYPOLOGY OF SPEECH FORMS

If we seek the limited number of forms most commonly used by public speakers as ways of giving meaning to experience, we must necessarily look beyond the unique characteristics of any particular speech. Our search is for the "root" structures commonly used by American speakers for organizing the substance of speech, structures which may be shaped, transformed, or intermixed in a variety of ways in any particular utterance.

Moreover, if we are to understand the nature of the forms and structures we identify, we must look beyond the simple task of naming the various patterns of movement one could use in organizing a public speech. Our purpose is not simply to describe how speeches might be organized, but to examine the implications of choosing some particular pattern of organization. Thus, we will seek to observe the sense in which a speaker who chooses a particular form for his utterance also chooses to invite his listeners to participate in a particular way of giving meaning to reality, and chooses to accept certain possibilities and limitations for his utterance.

The difference between being able to name and describe various patterns of speech organization, and being able to understand the assumptions, limitations, and possibilities of these patterns, is a crucial one for the thoughtful student of public speaking. Accordingly, we should examine this difference more closely.

One can name and describe a variety of organizational patterns used by public speakers by simply observing the order and nature of the major movements in their speeches. For example, we can observe that many speakers in our society discuss so-called social problems by developing a set of major movements such as: (a) a statement and a description of the problem to be discussed; (b) an analysis of the causes of this problem; and (c) a proposal of certain action designed to alleviate the problem by getting at its causes. This pattern of movements may be elaborated by smaller movements designed to show the audience that the social problem under discussion is their problem, or that responsibility for its solution is their responsibility, or that the consequences of the action proposed by the speaker will be pleasing to members of the audience. We have now "named" a pattern of movements which could produce a clearly organized speech. We can even give a general name to the form created, calling the whole utterance a "problem-solution" speech. But even as we give these names, we raise a series of questions about the implications of choosing such a form. For example, what do we assume about the nature of social reality when we perceive certain events as a "problem," having causes and a solution amenable to human social action? What kind of subject matter seems best suited to this form? What transformations or modifications of the form are possible? What are the major problems of communication faced by speakers who choose this form for their utterance? What are the possibilities and limitations of the form? Until the public speaker confronts such questions, his employment of this form for his utterance is technological. He says, in effect, "this is a clear and recommended way of organizing a speech; I will use it." After such questions are confronted, the speaker can perceive selection of form as a genuine choice, involving the choice of certain assumptions, certain possibilities, and certain limitations.

To get at the assumptions, possibilities, and limitations inherent in certain forms, we shall propose in this chapter a set of five general forms for speeches. Each of these forms involves a somewhat different way of looking at reality; each may be observed to present certain possibilities and limitations. These five general forms may be viewed as a typology of speech forms. They should not be viewed as a necessary description of any particular speech, nor as instructions for discrete but alternative methods of organizing a speech. As we shall see, particular speeches may incorporate more than one of these "root" forms. The five forms proposed for examination, together with the point of view implicit within each form, are as follows:

(1) The pragmatic view: reality as problem and solution.

(2) The normative view: reality as value and application.

(3) The taxonomical view: naming the divisions of the whole.

(4) The dialectical view: reality as conflict or opposition.

(5) The organic view: evoking the whole of experience.

1. The Pragmatic View: Reality as Problem and Solution

In his book *Paths of Life*,[2] the American philosopher Charles Morris designates the "Promethean path of unceasing making" as a way of life receiving extraordinary emphasis in western civilization—the civilization of Europe and America. The Prometheus myth, used by Morris to name this "path of life," is suggestive. It symbolizes the inventiveness, resourcefulness, and creativity of man. Promethean man sees his world as material for reconstruction. He is in one perspective the eternal scientist: "I will ask questions, find answers, extend my knowledge, and gain new power to control my environment." He is in a related perspective the eternal problem solver: "We need food?—here is a way to get it!" "Men are unemployed?—here is the way to employ them!" "The crime rate is rising?—this will reduce it!" "You have tired blood?—vitamins will pep you up!"

One could speculate that the extraordinary prevalence of problem-solving discourse in American society reflects a kind of Promethean bias in our culture. It would be equally possible to observe that the kinds of settings in which many public speeches rise are organized for problem-solving activity. In the hurly-burly of politics and commerce, problems and their answers become the intellectual diet. We must "do this, stop doing this, refrain from doing this, or continue this"—all because the action in question has or hasn't worked, will or won't work. We must "buy this rather than that, invest here, withdraw money there"—all because these choices will or won't gratify certain desires we have. We are active and intelligent people confronted with an endless series of unsatisfied personal desires and social goals; we study these and make practical choices. The structure we give to our world is problem and solution, question and answer, or desire and its gratification. The structure is readily adapted to public speaking; it provides a familiar way of perceiving reality; it can be trimmed or expanded, transformed in many ways.

A consideration of some of the transformations of problem-solution structure increases our ability to find this form lurking behind the particularities of many speeches encompassing a diversity of movements. The speaker may attenuate the structure by spending most of his time on the analysis of a social or personal problem, suggesting a solution only in barest outline or only with such popular formulas as "educa-

[2] (New York: Harper & Bros., 1942) p. 257.

tion is the answer" or "if we but apply the historic ingenuity of the American people to this problem, assuredly a sound answer will be forthcoming." Or, in a kind of concealed desperation (which may be honest enough), the speaker may analyze his problem and leave the solution to "you the audience," or "those who are wiser than I."

The form may also be attenuated by omitting explicit analysis of a problem and moving immediately into a proposal for action, followed by a visualization of the benefits of such action. Presumably if the speaker can demonstrate that his proposal will make his listeners happier or will improve their comfort, he has implicitly revealed the kind of problem which he identifies.

The form may be expanded. The assertion of a problem invites analysis of the causes; the assertion of a solution invites visualization of the consequences of that solution. Thus the speaker describes the farm problem and presents his analysis of the causes of that problem; he proposes the kind of farm legislation (or nonlegislation) that he favors and applies this solution to the nature of the problem as he has described it. The form may also be expanded by comparative analysis of the problem or of proposed solutions. Thus the speaker may seek to define his problem by looking at it from more than one point of view. "What is the problem of the American college student?" asks the speaker. "Is he self-indulgent because food, clothing, cars, and education have been made easily available, or is he deeply disturbed and confused in a world grown too complex for understanding?" Or the speaker may point out that in response to some problem his listeners or their society have a limited number of possible actions available. This structure was popular for speeches on the Korean war during the argument over the concept of limited war. "We can do three things in Korea," said many speakers. "We can withdraw, or we can throw in our full military might to secure a full military victory, or we can fight a limited war, seeking an honorable cessation of hostilities." This movement was followed by analysis of the three possible courses of action, rejection of two of them, and affirmation of the third as the best possible answer to the situation.

The form may be concealed within some expositional device which relieves the speaker from any direct engagement with statements about a problem or its solution. A speech of prophecy, talking about the shape of "things to come," may serve to present the speaker's ideas about the problems of the present, and about the form that a solution would need to take. Thus McGeorge Bundy, in a speech delivered in 1961, took the position of a reporter commenting in 1975 on the changes that had taken place in American higher education between 1961 and 1975.[3] His "report" is a prophecy, and also a device for talking about the major problems the speaker believed were facing the universities—the rigidity of departmental structure, the peripatetic scholar spending little time on his own campus, and so forth.

If the problem-solution form can be concealed with a discourse which avoids any mention of problems or their solution, it can also be used as the form for expository as well as persuasive speeches. Thus, from the stance of a reporter or teacher, the speaker can describe the problem of water pollution in America, the actions being undertaken in response to the problem, and the further lines of action under public discussion.

Speakers find the problem-solution structure versatile enough to encompass many of their purposes. But the limitations of this form also need comment. The Promethean view of reality may not lend itself to the discussion of certain significant aspects of reality. It is not usually the form within which the speaker can celebrate the life of a person, or the significance of some ceremonial occasion. To be sure, Robert Ingersoll celebrated the virtues of the American pioneer, showing that chief among those virtues was the dauntless capacity of the pioneer to surmount all obstacles in best Promethean spirit. But the structure of his speech is not that of reporting the nature of a problem and how it was solved; rather it is the evocation of the qualities of mind and spirit allegedly displayed by a group of our ancestors.

A less obvious limitation of the problem-solution form lies in the propensity of the form to force an activist response to natural and social phenomenon. As the speaker treats some aspects of his environment as a "problem," he is suggesting to himself and any responsive auditors that human ingenuity should be able to define and undertake an action which will "solve" the problem. Thus a tornado defined as a problem is not simply a natural phenomenon to be contemplated with awe, or propitiated through prayer. It is a force to be tamed or neutralized by aggressive human countermeasures. The stance of the problem-solution form is activist and optimistic, and an implicit denial of the merit of alternative stances toward man's environment or the human condition.

For example, in the 1960's several thousand young Americans became identified with groups seeking to withdraw from participation in or support of "the establishment"—the political, social, economic, and religious institutions developed by their elders. By mid-decade, a num-

[3] McGeorge Bundy, "Report From an Academic Utopia," *Harper's*, CCXXIV (1962), 10, 12, 14–15.

ber of subgroups had developed in this dropout culture. One group seemed to emphasize a type of communal living in which survival needs would be met at a low level through primitive agricultural enterprise, while members sought personal fulfillment through various forms of artistic enterprise. Another group, known as "hippies," seemed attracted to the possibilities of drug-induced experiences as a route to self-discovery. Still other groups turned to revolutionary methods of harassing the establishment, thinking to reveal its corruption. The complex phenomenon of sizable groups of social revolutionaries and dropouts inevitably stimulated public discussion. Some of this discussion treated the phenomenon as a specific problem calling for solutions ranging from stronger enforcement of public health and drug control laws, to a return to stern discipline in the nation's colleges, to reform of established churches, to withdrawal of the United States from war in South Vietnam, to a national conscription of all young Americans for a period of public service. Alternative forms of public discourse were also applied to the same phenomenon. Some speakers, in a transformation of the problem-solution form, saw the dropout groups less as a specific problem than as a symptom for some ill-defined crisis in western civilization; they called for inquiry into the general health of America's system of values. Other speakers abandoned the problem-solution form in its entirety. They treated the dropout groups as dramatic assertions of important human values such as love, nonviolence, nonacquisitiveness, and freedom. To these latter speakers the phenomenon was not a problem calling for social action but an evocative realization of values deserving of human contemplation.

Our point here is not evaluation of alternative forms for treating a particular social phenomenon. It is rather to call attention to the way in which application of the problem-solution form to a situation promotes the proposing of social actions and inhibits other possible responses.

2. The Normative View: The World as Value and Its Application to Choice

On May 12, 1962, General of the Army Douglas MacArthur delivered a speech entitled "Duty, Honor, and Country" at the United States Military Academy at West Point. The occasion was one honoring the General and presenting him with an award. He made use of the occasion to speak on the meaning of the three words which form the motto of West Point. His speech, ceremonial in nature, moves from an assertion of the formative character of the words; to a discussion of what the words teach; to a colorful account of the fortitude and daring of men who have had their character formed by these words; to a definition of the profession of arms, its dedication to the nation, and its prayers for peace. The speech closes on a personal note of affection for the corps, and of farewell.

If we ask what form the General has used to encompass his "reality" in this speech, we must start with the nature and use made of the motto: "duty, honor, and country." The words are obviously very abstract and capable of calling up a wide range or referents. We should call them "value" words, in the sense that they label some quality or value to which human conduct can or should aspire. They could be converted into statements by which one would justify an action: "I did this because it was my duty," or "I did this because it was the honorable thing to do," or "This was an act of devotion to my country." In this perspective, then, the terms of the motto become values or standards by which actions can be judged. The form of General MacArthur's speech becomes the assertion of certain values and the application of these values both to the praise of how soldiers have acted, and to the description of how soldiers ought to act.

We have called this view of reality *normative*. Presumably each person, and each culture, is characterized by its adherence to certain standards or norms which are used to judge the worth of actions or events. When we assert these standards or norms verbally we are asserting a conception of that which is good or desirable. This conception of the good or the desirable can be described as one of our "values." Thus, if we encounter a person who talks frequently of the importance of being honest, we would be inclined to guess that he places value on honesty (however he defines it), and that he uses honesty as a standard or norm for judging the worth of certain kinds of conduct, or perhaps even for judging the worth of certain events such as a play, a novel, or a painting.

For purposes of this discussion we will not press any distinction among the terms *norm, standard,* or *value,* but rather use these terms interchangeably.

Presumably the fabric of any society (culture or subculture) is bound together by some set of values held somewhat in common by the members of that society. These values may be implied in the actions of people or they may be asserted in acts of praise, blame, or judgment by speakers or writers. They may be implied in the language of speakers or writers even though not explicitly asserted. The values held by an individual or society are numerous, and they seem to be organized in some loose hierarchy of importance. Thus a particular person may assert that he believes worldly success to be important (it is one of his values), but less important than some quality of character he calls "integrity," or living in accordance with one's best beliefs. The same person or society may simultaneously hold contradictory values. Thus the English gentleman of the sixteenth and seventeenth century asserted admiration for Christian virtue, which he in part defined as the avoidance of falsehood in one's speech. He also valued social skill and the ability to use flattery, tact, and even dissimulation to achieve social position.

Our values come to us from many sources. We learn them through participation in society, mostly as the product of symbolic interaction with others, but we may learn them as values passed on through our religion, or values rising in our form of government or social organization, or values rising from interpretations of the nature of man. The question of whether or not values exist *before and independent of society* or are simply derived *from society* has been a perennial philosophic and theological issue in western civilization. But this issue need not concern us here since our primary focus is not the ultimate nature of values, but rather the way in which values serve in a kind of structure speakers may give to their reality.

The central movements of a simple speech based on a normative view of reality are: (a) the assertion of one or more values, and (b) the application of this value or these values in some act of judgment. The form thus created may be put explicitly to work in the appraisal of a book, motion picture, play, poem, painting, or piece of music. It serves equally well in the appraisal of the quality of a man's life, or in the evaluation of a particular human action. It may also appear in the evaluation of some proposed action by government.

The particular working of the "value-application" form is also apparent in the way some speakers will treat the appraisal of a proposed legislative action. For example, the extensive rhetoric surrounding the discussion of federal aid to education in recent years tends to exhibit a preference on the part of proponents of federal aid for the problem-solution form, and on the part of opponents for a value-application form. The proponent of federal aid may often, of course, assert certain values—such as the value of equal educational opportunity and the value of quality education—and apply these to the approval of federal aid. But the form most prominent in such speeches incorporates analysis of serious deficiencies in the American educational system and the proposal that federal aid to education will ameliorate these deficiencies. Similarly, the opponent of federal aid may deny either the existence of a problem or the adequacy of federal aid to meet the problem. But his most prominent form is likely to be based on certain values—as shown in such assertions as "The power of government, and especially the federal government should be limited," or "The federal government is growing too rapidly," or "Federal control over education would move this nation closer to socialism, which is a bad thing." In the context of such values the speaker finds that federal aid to education is a bad thing, on principle, and should be rejected.

The value-application form, like the problem-solution one, is subject to attenuation, extension, and a variety of transformations. The most common type of attenuation occurs when the speaker does not state explicitly the values which are at work in his judgment. Thus in the criticism of a play, the critic might describe the plot of the play in a way designed to highlight the presence of unmotivated or improbable plot developments in the play. Implicit in his discussion is a position on some of the characteristics of a plot which he values as critic, but these are not stated. Rather, the plot is described and judged. Similarly, in a speech eulogizing a person the speaker might describe incidents from the person's life which reveal qualities of courage, or kindness, or shrewdness, and yet refrain from explicitly naming these qualities as deserving of praise.

A common form of extension of the value-application form involves the effort on the part of the speaker not merely to use certain values in his judgment, but to justify or make important these values. This kind of extension is evident in the speech by General MacArthur previously described. The General in one sense *uses* the values of "duty, honor and country" as the norm for praising the history of the West Point Officer Corps. But the opening part of his address is a movement seeking some level of definition of these values, and developing the significance of these values in the life of our nation.

One of the interesting transformations of the value-application form is presented by the speaker whose object is the revivification of some value or even the verbal creation of some value. Here the speaker, rather than asserting value as the basis for passing judgment in a particular case, uses cases or events as the basis for deriving a statement concerning some value held to be significant. For example, in a eulogy, rather than finding the values which serve to judge the man, the speaker finds in the life of the man certain values which may not have wide currency in a society but which the speaker holds to be worthy of greater attention. Thus the speaker may use the life of Gandhi to give new importance to the values of nonviolence, or pacifism, or humility to listeners who may be inclined to give higher status to contradictory values. One sees this form at work in the speech by the late Justice Jackson of the United States Supreme Court in praise of the

Nuremberg War Crimes Trials held at the end of World War II. The trials had been condemned by Senator Robert Taft in a characteristic application of norms to a particular instance. Taft used the standards or values of the American legal system as a basis for judging the trial, and found the trial defective and a shameful violation of American legal values. Jackson described the trials as part of a process of creating international law. From the underlying concept of the trial and from its conduct, he found at work a process of creating certain values in international conduct which had previously lacked definition.

The peculiar appropriateness of value-application form to ceremonial speaking needs no elaboration. Speeches of praise or blame will ordinarily be formulated within this structure. It is also apparent from the examples already given that the form appears in persuasive discourse. The speaker asks listeners to share his values and to share his judgments; and if he is successful in relating values held by the audience to some particular judgment, he has asserted a strong claim on his listeners. The form also serves for expository speeches in the sense that a speaker may "report" value applications. Indeed the speaker who tends to see reality in terms of the value-application form may tend to employ this form in giving an account of historical events. In a very broad sense, Professor Arnold J. Toynbee's *A Study of History* is an interpretation of history based on a value-application form. He sees civilizations rising as incorporations of certain value systems (religions), and dying as these value systems become insufficient to meet changing circumstance, or as they are otherwise weakened. Since historical "exposition" may incorporate the value-application form, we observe once more the ambiguity of the boundary between exposition and persuasion. To accept Professor Toynbee's interpretation of history we must also accept the idea that history can be properly viewed as value and its application, that this is the form that reality takes.

As with the problem-solution form, the value-application form provides its own set of limitations. One of these is the difficulty of stating clearly and unambiguously the values held to be relevant to a particular application. The speaker working with some value system is often moved to produce lyric prose. Whether or not he could give an adequate accounting of the meaning of his values may be another question. For example, we have used the label "courage" to designate a kind of value in human conduct generally esteemed in our society. Asked to define "courage" a speaker might turn to authority and say that "it is grace under pressure." Asked to define "grace under pressure," he may turn to example—an application—to provide his definition. If his example pleases us we may be satisfied with the definition; if it turns out to be an example of behavior we would not credit with the label of "courage" we are left in a state of confusion. Values are not easily set forth unambiguously, and the propriety of the application of a value to a given instance is a complicated matter.

The use of the form is also complicated by the existence of a large number of values, ordered in some loose hierarchy and sometimes contradictory, which are held as part of the common property of speakers and listeners. "It is wrong to take life," says a speaker. And with the flourishes of authority and example he makes his value credible. He goes on to say, "The execution of a murderer is in itself an act equivalent to murder. It is wrong and a civilized people should have no part of capital punishment." But then another speaker asks, "Shall we not feel outrage toward an act of crime?" (He too has his values.) "And is our outrage real unless we act to show it?" he continues. We shall, mercifully, drop this ancient dialogue since our purpose is only to indicate the extraordinary complexity of the process of finding the values or norms which should be applied in any concrete act of judgment.

A second, though related, limitation of the value-application form is its propensity for supporting dogmatic assertions of the adequacy of a few received social values as the basis for judging the merit of a host of concrete proposals for social change. Thus the speaker who believes it axiomatic that "that government is best which governs least" has a simple response to any proposal that the government take action to relieve some alleged social ill. All such actions become "bad" by definition because they violate some supposedly fundamental principal. In the preceding section we observed the propensity of the problem-solution form for promoting social activism. Here we observe the opposing tendency of the value-application form to support the conservation of tradition.

3. The Taxonomical View: Naming the Parts of the Whole and Observing Their Relationship

If we apply a set of terms to the description of some phenomenon we create a structure within which the phenomenon can be comprehended. Thus when a speaker says "the divisions of an act of communication are the sender, the message, the channel, the receiver, and the context," he has created a verbal structure for encompassing a certain class of phenomena. The structure provides an intellectual framework within which the speaker can elaborate his description of the phenomenon in question. That kind of structuring was undertaken in Chapter 2 of this book. The same kind of structuring can be found in almost any act of expository or persuasive discourse. Sometimes the speaker who names the parts of some whole does so within a problem-solution form or within a value-application form; but the act of naming the parts can also be carried through without reference to these forms. Accordingly, we identify "naming the parts" as a third form within which reality may be encompassed.

We call this view of reality "taxonomical," since its primary impulse is to uncover the reality of some event or system by naming its parts and by calling attention to the interrelationship of these parts.

At the simplest level, the taxonomical form attempts no more than a classification of natural events according to some system of definition. Thus biologists through the years have established elaborate classifications for the flora and fauna of our environment, starting, for example, with the notion that organisms or events in nature may be divided into the living and the inanimate, and that biologists are concerned with the former. Living organisms in turn may be classified as plants, animals, or insects, and each of these families may be subdivided into a variety of species. Taxonomical verbal structures help us to perceive or know the differences and similarities of mammals and reptiles, or spiders and beetles. Or if we turn to nonliving events, we can name the different kinds of rocks or different cloud formations. One can apply the same taxonomical structuring to actions. For example, the teachers of elocution in the eighteenth and nineteenth centuries worked on elaborate taxonomies of communicative physical action. In writing of gesture in speech, Gilbert Austin, in his early nineteenth century work on speech delivery entitled *Chironomia,* uncovered some 135 fundamental positions of the arms alone which Austin thought important to understanding this one aspect of delivery. At this simple level of naming, the taxonomist asks of each phenomenon, what is it a part of, and what are its parts?

Increasing power is given to a taxonomical form when it is used not merely to name the parts of some whole, but to explain the interactions of these parts—to explain how some process, or system works. It has been characteristic of the growing power of science in the last century, and particularly in the last few decades, to treat phenomena in terms of dynamic systems in which the names of the parts of the system are associated with discovery of how these parts affect or interact with one another. In this sense, the science of chemistry progressed from naming elements, or substances in nature, to naming the parts of matter in a system which accounted for their interaction. Thus our ancient Greek ancestors considered water one of the elements of the universe. But we are now told that pure water is a combination of hydrogen and oxygen, and we may be shown on the periodic table of chemical elements certain characteristics of hydrogen and oxygen atoms which will cause them to interact in the proportion of one oxygen atom to two hydrogen atoms. The system in nature by which water is formed, and by which it may be transformed back into its constituent gases may now be known by any grade school student. We are also familiar with the fact that contemporary science has not been content to let the atom rest unexplored, but has been at work examining the interactions of the constituents of this structure, revealing it to be only a relatively stable system.

Taxonomical activity in areas other than the natural sciences has also moved from "naming the parts" to naming the parts in order to explain the workings of a system. Thus in economics, one no longer speaks of supply and demand as the two laws governing the price of any given commodity. One examines rather the pricing system of a given society, observing the interaction of the variety of forces and decisions which may bear upon the price structure of a given field of commodities in a given market. Similarly in Chapter 2 of this book we sought to move from naming the parts of an act of communication to observing the act as a system in which the parts impinge upon and affect one another. And we earlier observed that an act of public speaking is itself only part of some larger social structure, affecting and affected by that structure.

Sources of Taxonomical Forms Used by Speakers

Whether the speaker seeks only to name the parts of some whole, or to give a more informative analysis of the operation of some system, he will find a variety of sources available for the taxonomical form he may wish to give to his utterance. We can identify some of the sources as "received systems" and some as strategic inventions of the speaker.

Received Systems. "Received systems" of naming serve as a structure for expository speaking in all academic disciplines. Thus physicists develop a set of names for explaining the structure of the atom, biologists name aspects of the process by which genetic characteristics of an organism are transmitted, literary scholars give names to various genres of literature, and linguists talk about the structure of language behavior through such concepts as phoneme, morpheme, and sentence. Much of the human activity by which the subject matter of formal education is organized consists of the development of a system of names which will be used as the "map" for some segment of knowledge and the development of definitions which will give these names a common currency in the communications of those who are knowledgeable. These systems are developed by scholars, modified and extended through time as new information or new insights become available, and "received" by the members of society who seek understanding of some aspect of knowledge. The public speaker may draw upon a current received system of naming as a structure for his exposition of some body of information and ideas. Or, since no such system is immutable, the speaker may seek to extend the power or clarity of a received system through appropriate modification or extension.

Strategic Inventions. Speakers often need to create a structure of terms which will be useful for examining some area of subject matter. When we say that the speaker creates or invents a structure of terms, we do not mean that he is engaged in the production of new words. We mean rather that the speaker brings into relationship with one another a set of words which will serve to give form to his utterance, and which may provide new insight into the subject matter treated. The terms used by the speaker may be commonplace, but the speaker's "invention" rests in his perception of a new system of relationship among the familiar terms. The form thus created by the speaker can be called "heuristic"; it is not based on any fundamental scientific discovery, as might be the case with a physicist's discussion of the structure of the atom, but it is a useful form for organizing the information and relationships which the speaker wishes to communicate.

Jacques Barzun's book, *The House of Intellect,* provides an excellent example of this kind of taxonomical activity. Barzun's subject is the American educational system. He develops his view of this system within a set of four concepts: the concepts of intellect, science, philanthropy, and art. All of the words are familiar, but using them in relationship with one another to provide a way of "seeing" our educational system is an invention of the writer. As an extensive and complex work of exposition and persuasion, the book encompasses all of the ways of structuring reality we have discussed thus far. Intellect serves as the concept for defining what education ought to be. Science, philanthropy, and art embrace the kind of estimable activity which threatens intellect. Thus, Barzun has his system of classification; he also has his set of preferred values to apply to the examination of American education; and implicitly he has uncovered the "problem of education" in America and the path that a solution must take. But Barzun's "naming of the parts of the whole" provides the fundamental structure for his book. The set of names or concepts, brought into a given relationship with one another, becomes a strategic invention by which we are asked to understand American education as the writer understands it.

Speakers may make unique and original contributions to their listeners through the invention of unusually apt or illuminating taxonomical

structures for their discourse. However, they also may invent structures which are simply systems of convenience, and which add little to
the power of the discourse. Thus, the speaker who wants to talk on
"ways of becoming rich," may organize his utterance by the simple
device of naming as many different "ways" as he can think of, or as
many as he will have time to develop in his allotted time, or as many as
he thinks he can discuss entertainingly, usefully, or provocatively for a
particular audience. The speaker who says that his subject is "three
ways to become a millionaire" usually does not purport to have discovered any truths laid down in the nature of human systems of acquisi-
tiveness. Moreover, the divisions of his discourse may have little relationship with one another other than their common property of being
"ways of becoming a millionaire." The speaker's speech structure may
seem to be an act of convenience, or even of desperation. But it does
provide a frame within which the speaker can proceed in an orderly
manner to say whatever it is that he wishes to say. Speakers often en-
liven such arbitrary systems of division with a metaphor, and the metaphor of the "key" may have become excessively popular with American speakers, as in speeches on "The Three Keys to Safe Driving" or
"The Six Keys to Better Human Relations."

4. The Dialectical View: Reality as Conflict or Opposition

Plato thought *dialectic* to be the highest of intellectual pursuits. By
dialectic he meant activity of the kind modeled in his familiar dialogues
—conversations among learned men in which examination was made of
the differing claims that men might make about the nature of the good,
or of virtue, or of truth, or of any other important matter about which
the assertions of men might differ. The Greek philosopher thought
that truth about important matters was not likely to be apprehended
through the intellectual activity of one man, but was more likely to
rise between or among men who gave rational consideration to the
conflicting answers that might be given to any important question.
The significance Plato assigned to the theory and practice of dialectic
was mirrored in educational practices developed in ancient Greece, and
continued as part of higher education throughout the ancient, medieval, and early modern periods of history.

Dialectic, or the art of rational disputation, long enjoyed high status
as a study appropriate to men who sought wisdom. Behind this status
lay some enduring observations about the nature of the matters about
which men speak.

These observations may be quite practical. Men do differ about matters of governmental policy, personal conduct, the nature of justice,

virtue, truth, and so forth. Because they differ, they need to acquire skill in ways of living together peacefully in the presence of disagreement, thus learning to avoid resort to violence in forcing unanimity of opinion where unanimity does not really exist. The theory of democratic government as a just and prudent form of social organization derives from this kind of practical observation. So does the theory underlying the organization of courts of law in western Europe and America. For that matter, the earliest textbooks on the art of public speaking developed in ancient Greece thought that the art of persuasion should be studied precisely because there were questions raised in every society for which only probable or possible answers could be provided. And every man needed to be skilled in speaking so that his "probability" might receive a fair hearing.

Behind the practical observation that men do differ rests a philosophic possibility that some of their differences are rooted inevitably in the nature of man and society. That is, the observation is made that many of the concepts, or terms, or claims that men make in giving form or order to their experience are essentially contested.[4] The mere forwarding of the concept, or term, or claim automatically postulates the existence of an opposing concept, or term, or claim. Thus the concept of *individuality* postulates a concept of *society,* and a claim or assertion made on the basis of the importance of the individual automatically invites an opposing claim about the importance of society.

We shall not pause here to explore the philosophic question of the nature of concepts or assertions which are essentially contested since our interest is in the way in which speakers use the dialectical form to give structure to their utterance.

If one examines the speeches of persons in our society that are concerned with any of the important public issues, one quickly discovers that the opposing views of different speakers include some oppositions which seem likely to persist. A speech which proposes that man must be free to do as his conscience dictates invites a counterspeech asserting that one man's freedom ends at the point where it impinges on another man's freedom. A speech proposing that there is too much conformity in our society invites a speech proposing that there is too much disorder in our society—too little voluntary accommodation to law and order. A speech proposing that a lawbreaker be dealt with justly and punished according to the dictates of the law invites the famous response of Portia in Shakespeare's *Merchant of Venice:* "The

[4] I take the term "essentially contested" from W. B. Gallie's article, "Essentially Contested Concepts," in Max Black, ed., *The Importance of Language* (Englewood Cliffs, N. J.: Prentice Hall, Inc., 1962), pp. 121–146.

quality of mercy is not strained. . . ." A speech proposing that man's highest value should be human life is opposed by "give me liberty or give me death," a sharp and not unfamiliar reordering of the value to be placed on life.

The conflict or controversy developed through such opposing speeches does not reflect the simple fact that some men believe in individual freedom, while others believe in law and order; or that some believe in justice, while others believe in mercy; or that some believe in life, while others believe in liberty. Doubtless all of the speakers involved would say that they believe in all of these values. But the values, as applied to particular questions of public policy or personal conduct may be given differing weight by different speakers, or may be viewed as applying with different force to some particular set of events. Among the body of speeches presented on any controversial issue in our society, the dialectical form of opposition—claim and counterclaim—inevitably emerges.

The same form may be used by a single speaker in a particular speech if he highlights the shape of the controversy involved in the issue with which he is dealing. Thus one may observe a dialectical form in its most simple manifestation in a speech which presents the "pros and cons" on a particular public issue. Expository speeches seeking to uncover the nature of opposing arguments on some controverted issue often take this form, and if the issue is a complex one, the speech may uncover several conflicting positions which have been taken on the issue in question.

The dialectical form may also be present in a persuasive speech in which the speaker makes clear his own position, but does so only after a careful effort to deal justly with the claims made against his position.

Obviously the form may be used to conceal an intention of the speaker. Thus the expository speech purporting to provide an accurate accounting of the oppositions present in a controverted public issue may, by slanting, seek to convince an audience that one of the opposing positions explained has unusual merit. Such a speech seeks persuasion masquerading as exposition. Moreover, if the speaker does take a position among the opposing positions he presents, he may deliberately or inadvertently do less than justice to those positions which he rejects.

It is high and rare praise for a speaker analyzing controversial subject matter to have listeners whose positions differ concede that their ideas were given full and accurate representation. However, the most fully realized dialectical form seeks this response by achieving absolute impartiality in presenting the oppositions inherent in given positions or claims. A discourse in such form is an invitation from speaker to audience that they join together in mutual understanding of the conflicts of opinion and judgment that divide men from one another. The form gives a picture of reality which implicitly criticizes the excess of partisanship characteristic of many speeches. It invites a continuing dialogue on the substance with which the speaker deals.

Only the most philosophic speaker is likely to seek a fully realized dialectical form for a particular speech. But the shadow of this form is often found in speeches which are more explicitly cast in a pragmatic, normative, or taxonomical structure. Thus a speaker who identifies poverty as a social problem requiring solution may show understanding of the fact that some listeners may not consider poverty as a problem meriting action. If the speaker treats justly the claim of some that the human spirit is less threatened by poverty than by a society which makes the pursuit of affluence a high value, then the speaker has revealed dialectical awareness in the form of his discourse. Such awareness adds texture or complexity to the form of a speech. In expository speeches, dialectical awareness reduces emphasis on the simplicity with which phenomena of systems may be described, and increases emphasis on the uncertainties in such description. In ceremonial speeches, such awareness restrains the impulse to find unqualified virtue or evil in particular men or events, and emphasizes the ambiguities of character and action. In persuasive speeches, the dialectical form moderates intense partisanship and uses language which leaves open the possibility of integration with opposing ideas. One thinks, for example, of the effect dialectical form might have had on a speech such as Patrick Henry's call to arms in his "Give me liberty, or give me death" speech to the Virginia Assembly on the eve of the American Revolution. With a different impulse and different view of reality, Henry might have paused to consider the complex inner conflicts of the English government, and to have appraised the possibility that this government might continue to modify policy toward the colonies. Or he might have considered ambiguities in the character of King George III, as well as the mortality of all particular rulers. The form would have been ill-suited to arousing fervor in an audience, but well-suited to inviting reflection, or even political accommodation short of revolution.

5. The Organic View: Analysis Rejected

We have thus far considered four fundamental ways of giving form to the realities that prompt rhetorical utterance. Each is based on a kind of structure which constitutes a form, and in this sense each may be said to be a way of analyzing or dividing rhetorical reality. It is commonplace to observe that some speakers seem to call attention to the divisions of their utterance. "It is alleged," says the speaker, "that Senator Jarvis McGillicuddy told falsehoods. How are we to judge whether or not this is true? This evening I propose first to discuss the standards by which we may judge the truth or falsity of a statement, and then I shall apply these standards to an examination of a series of the Senator's statements." The speaker has now "overviewed" the structure of his utterance. We may anticipate that he will indicate clearly when he has finished the first movement of his speech and turned to the second. The framework shows that the speech is "highly structured."

But not all speeches reveal such obvious or analytical structure. Moreover, the fact that a speech seems to lack clear divisions is not in itself an indication that the speech lacks form. The speech may seem to flow without clear divisions, yet with a satisfying sense of movement and of completeness. In retrospect one could "analyze" the form, uncovering the structure which must lie buried within it; yet the effort seems somehow to miss the essential fact that the form itself did not try to analyze reality, but rather to present itself as a single, uninterrupted, undivided movement. Such effects are common in brief but artistic ceremonial speeches, as for example Lincoln's Gettysburg Address, or Ingersoll's speech "At a Child's Grave." In contrast to the speech exhibiting an analytical structure is the speech said to reveal an organic form.

The sharpest contrast between analytical form and organic form is provided by comparison of utterance characteristic of scientific activity and that characteristic of literary activity. In broad perspective the scientist may be said to analyze his universe, to take it apart. By contrast, the poet or novelist ordinarily works within some organic form —an effort to capture some part of reality as a whole. He may be said to argue that human experience is so rich and complex that analysis destroys it. We may use language to evoke the sense of wonder or delight that one might experience. But suppose we say that "reaching the top of the mountain, John felt a sense of wonder. By 'wonder' I mean a generalized neuro-physical reaction to the unexpected which is describable in terms of heightened glandular activity, followed by certain predictable changes in muscle tone, perception, etc. Let me describe these changes in detail." The reality of the experience as experience is now abandoned in favor of analysis.

The concept that a speaker's utterance may reveal an organic rather than analytical form poses some difficulties. For example, a problem-solution speech might be presented without clear verbal "signposts" designating its divisions. Yet while an observer could note the lack of obvious "structuring" in the speaker's utterance, he could nevertheless see the speech as encompassing an analytical form. Similarly, a problem-solution speech might be structurally incoherent, with materials relating the problem and its diagnosis, the solution and its consequences, mixed together in splendid disorder. Such a disorganized or incoherent effort might baffle a listener, but this effect is not a sufficient basis for saying that the speech has an organic form. On the other hand, if the speaker turns to utterance which rejects analysis in favor of an effort to evoke some unified response appropriate to the speaker's purpose, we would miss the point of the form of his speech if we tried to force it into an analytical structure. For example, the speech based almost exclusively on an extended narration—a story—might seek to evoke through the story some sense of value or some understanding of the human condition. The narrative is a form. It has movement and upon close analysis we might uncover its underlying structure as involved in the selection of events and characters in the story and the development of their interrelationship. But our first observation about the form would be its organic nature, its effort to evoke some total experience. To force an analytical structure upon the story could be absurd. One could say, for example, that Salinger's novel *Catcher in the Rye* has an attenuated problem-solution form. It is attenuated in the sense that the writer uncovers problems of the adolescent in the modern world but offers no clear solution to these problems. One *could* say this, but to do so would be to miss the point that the novelist's object is not that of identifying problems and discovering their solutions; nor is it to state values and apply them to an appraisal of modern teenage culture; nor is it to establish some set of names for the analysis of adolescent life. The novelist's form is organic rather than analytical. He may involve us in the experience of his central character. If he gets us to contemplate the problems of adolescent search for identity, or the values important in an adolescent's world, so much the better. But these are not the primary forms used to encompass the adolescent's world.

STRUCTURAL MOVEMENTS DERIVED FROM CONTEXT

Early in this chapter we observed that each speech presents a form which may be uniquely related to the circumstance of the utterance. This form can be understood only by explicit tracing of the major movements of a particular speech and through the further effort to discover the interrelationship of the movements. Such an analysis often uncovers structural movements which seem in some sense digressions from the major line of development undertaken by the speech. But it would be unwise to conclude that such digressions are without purpose or that they do not in some sense encompass part of the reality with which the speaker is concerned.

For example, public speakers commonly acknowledge in their introductory comments some aspect of the immediate occasion. Thus, President John Kennedy, speaking on the occasion of receiving an honorary degree at Yale University, found occasion to recall the timeworn quip that he now enjoyed the best of all possible worlds, a Harvard education and a Yale degree. Similarly, innumerable commencement speakers each spring find it in their hearts to comment favorably on some specific aspect of the immediate ceremony, whether it be the unusual size of the graduating class, the cogency of the comments by the class valedictorian, or the harmony of a rendition by the girls' choir. Such conciliatory gestures have little to do with direct enforcement of the speaker's thesis, but they are important to the larger social structure of the public speech.

The speaker's recognition of his public role, and consequent relationship with a particular audience, may be the source of larger digressions from the fundamental structure of his discourse. Thus, in 1966 Vice-President Hubert Humphrey travelled to the campus of Stanford University for a convocation address on civil rights. He was greeted by pickets outside the auditorium protesting American involvement in the Vietnam war, and the Vice-President's support for such involvement. In his introductory comments, the Vice-President acknowledged the demonstration outside the auditorium by contrasting its spirit with the courtesy of the immediate audience. He also made clear that he would respond to questions at the conclusion of his formal address, thus providing the occasion for discussion of Vietnam.

A more ritualistic form of digression is commonplace in the public speeches of major political figures during campaigns. A candidate for President on a cross-country speaking tour will ordinarily have local candidates for office who are members of his party join him on the platform. He will also take occasion to add to the general substance of his address some direct recognition of these candidates, either by acknowledging his respect for and friendship with them, or by linking their efforts to some of the important legislative purposes or achievement of the party.

CHOICES AND PROBLEMS

Our discussion thus far has centered on the nature of the reality pre-supposed by various "root" forms used by speakers to give meaning to their utterance. We have also observed the transformations possible in these forms, the particular tasks they are well-suited to accomplish, their limitations, the way in which they may be intermixed in a given utterance, and the way in which the speaker's utterance may include movements or digressions consonant with the occasion of his utterance rather than with any internal organizing principle. The speaker who understands the potentialities and limitations of various forms before he plans a particular utterance knows the kind of choice he has made in using a given form. He knows, for example, that the problem-solution and value-application forms are well-suited to mobilizing strong belief or action in an audience, and may be well adapted to purposes of per-suasion or ceremony; that taxonomical forms are well-suited to in-struction or exposition, and that they are most powerful when they uncover the interacting aspects of some system; that the dialectical form when fully carried out is ill-suited to mobilizing fervor or quick action in an audience, but well-suited to negotiation or to exposition designed to increase understanding of the oppositions inherent in vari-ous positions or assertions.

To such general considerations affecting a speaker's choices can be added some particular problems in the organization of whole speeches. We turn next, therefore, to consideration of certain particular alterna-tives open to speakers in the design of the general form of their utter-ance. We shall emphasize the problems of choice which are frequently troublesome.

The speaker can choose between a manifestly structured form, as opposed to more subtle structuring, or the use of some organic form. As a genre of discourse, public speeches tend to exhibit heavier, more explicit structuring than essays prepared for print. The tendency may be instructive. Spoken utterance must ordinarily be "caught in action," except in the infrequent cases where the listener is handed a text of the speech for further study or provided with a recording for repeated lis-tening. In seeking maximum clarity speakers may therefore emphasize the divisions of their utterance. Hence such practice as announcing the divisions of the speech (the overview); signalling explicitly the begin-ning of the first major movement as announced ("my first point is . . ."); and signalling explicitly the end of one movement and the beginning of the next ("I have now defined the nature of conformity, and move next to consideration of the causes of conformist behavior"). The value of such explicit structuring for joining the speaker's intention to the audience's expectation is obvious, and indeed the merit of such activity is so great as to suggest that a speaker should abandon heavy structuring of his utterance only for good cause. The good cause may lie in the speaker's search for a more artistic sense of internal unity in his utterance. The "signposts" clarify; they may also seem lumpy and obtrusive, an interruption of the flow of the utterance.

The speaker can choose the point in his speech at which to unveil his statement. That is, he may assert his position early in his speech or delay such assertion until later. As with heavy structuring, early assertion of position has the merit of producing maximum understanding of the speaker's intention. But strategic considerations may prompt delay. The generality of advice in rhetorical theory proposes that the speaker taking a controversial or unpopular position should delay asserting that position until he has led the audience through some line of argument that is not controversial, or is inevitably popular with the audience. The advice seems sensible enough and conforms to established evidence that once an audience believes a speaker to be fundamentally wrong, it will find it easy to reject his subsequent utterance. However, the variables in the speaking situation are so many that it becomes impossible to say that the assertion of controversial positions should always be delayed. For example, if the audience can guess accurately from the speaker's reputation the position he is going to take on student dissent, the speaker gains little in delaying the assertion of his position. Indeed he may lose the opportunity to seem a bold and forthright person.

The speaker can choose between a simple or a complex form. In general audiences seem to like to learn that complex matters can be reduced to simple terms; therefore the speaker who finds a simple, obvious form for his subject matter may achieve a reputation for clarity. "The problem of disarmament," says the speaker, "reduces itself to a single, fundamental question." If we find the single fundamental question persuasive, we are likely to praise the speaker as a man who "gets at the heart of the matter." But the presumption that favors simplicity of form stands in tension with the demands of the speaker's subject. If the structure of world politics is complex the speaker may achieve simplicity only by shameful distortion. The speaker who turns complex issues into simple ones may be a genius, or he may be as ignorant as the man who turns a simple issue into some incomprehensible complexity. We can observe the speaker's choice but we must judge in the particular case whether or not the speaker's simplicity is oversimplification, or his complexity, obfuscation.

The speaker must balance the demands of time and of purpose in deciding how long he should take in getting into the heart of his speech. It is commonplace to observe that good public speakers often spend time in warming up the audience. The speaker may open his address by praising the audience or the occasion and by revealing himself as a man of goodwill, leading then by easy stages into the subject of his discourse. He may open his speech with a colorful anecdote, seeking to find in the story a bridge to his subject. Artistic introductions seem to organize audience attention, create goodwill for the speaker, and to lead, like the narrowing shape of a funnel, into the speaker's subject. Less artistic introductions may seem like springboards; the speaker finds in his introduction a way to jump to his subject. Inartistic introductions may seem dissociated from the utterance. They force the speaker to say, "and now to turn to my subject." The occasion and the total amount of time available to the speaker may suggest how much time should be assigned to the introduction. And because brevity in speechmakers is widely valued, the speaker who cannot use introductory comments to excellent purpose may well find it best to enter immediately into his statement.

Finally, the speaker must find the conclusion to his speech which meets the demands of time and purpose, and which yet gives a sense of the completion of an action—the sense of artistic closure. Assuming that the speaker has carried through the major movements appropriate to the form selected for his speech, the sense of completeness is often sought through some elevation of style, in some statement which encompasses most broadly the central impulse of the speech. For Winston Churchill in his address to the French people during the Nazi occupation, this elevation was found in the familiar rallying cry of the French nation, "Vive La France." For General MacArthur in his address on Far Eastern problems to the Congress of the United States, it was found in an intensely personal statement of farewell:

I am closing my fifty-two years of military service. When I joined the army, even before the turn of the century, it was the fulfillment of all my boyish hopes and dreams. The world has turned over many times since I took the oath at West Point, and the hopes and dreams have all since vanished, but I still remember the refrain of one of the most popular barracks ballads of that day which proclaimed most proudly that old soldiers never die; they just fade away. And like the old soldier of that ballad, I now close my military career and just fade away, an old soldier who tried to do his duty as God gave him the light to see that duty. Good-by.[5]

The conclusion has been much discussed. In using it, the speaker assumed the risks characteristic of intensely sentimental, intensely personal public comment. That is, for some listeners the passage seems to have been deeply moving. Presumably persons who identified themselves with the General's age, his position of national honor, or his fundamental values as they emerged in the speech found the personal note of the conclusion a matter of genuine sentiment. Published reports on response to the speech included references to listeners who wept at its conclusion. For other listeners the ending seemed gross sentimentality —the reduction of an occasion for discussion of national policy to a personal plea for sympathy by a public figure who neither could nor would "fade" from the national scene. The conclusion, in short, sought ultimate personal identification from listeners. With those for whom it succeeded, it succeeded greatly; for those with whom it did not succeed, it failed greatly.

FORM REVEALS THE SPEAKER

We have pictured the speaker's decisions on form as reflecting the nature of the reality which he creates. We have suggested that his choice on these matters reveals his habits of thought, his way of perceiving reality. It is interesting, although speculative, to suggest that one of the links that binds certain speakers to certain listeners is the identification which occurs among persons who share the same ways of looking at reality. That is, listeners may identify with or be persuaded by the form of a speaker's utterance, apart from any relationship they may feel toward the speaker's position. This point of view would suggest that certain groups of people in our society tend to cast the same form over their public utterances, and that one of the "signs" by which members of the group recognize one another is the sign produced by the form of public utterance used by members of the group.

The proposition that certain subgroups in our culture share certain preferences on matters of form is speculative, but it does open some interesting possibilities. For example, Professor Richard Weaver in an essay in his book *The Ethics of Rhetoric* [6] asserts a preference on the part of political conservatives for "arguing from principle." That is, Weaver believes it characteristic of a conservative that he discusses po-

[5] *Congressional Record*, p. 4125, 1st session, 82nd Congress, April 19, 1951.
[6] Richard Weaver, *The Ethics of Rhetoric* (Chicago: Henry Regnery Co., 1953).

litical problems by seeking "first principles" (values or norms), and applying these to a particular question of political action. Weaver further contends that political liberals tend to argue from circumstance. That is, they seek an expedient solution to a particular set of circumstances which might be described as a problem. Weaver applies his analysis in a curious fashion, for it leads him to observe that the British statesman Edmund Burke developed his speeches through an analysis of circumstances. Thus, for Weaver, Burke becomes a typical "liberal," even though he is more commonly treated by historians as a significant figure in the development of political conservatism. Weaver further finds that Abraham Lincoln developed his speeches from an application of "principles" to public issues. His analysis does scant justice to the whole of Lincoln's political career, but it leads Weaver to claim Lincoln as a typical conservative thinker.

Aside from the merit of Professor Weaver's particular analysis, however, one may observe that his method illustrates the possibility, previously mentioned, of group preferences for particular ways of giving form to reality. One might suggest, for example, that clergymen typically view reality in terms of values (or religious norms) and their application to the world; that politicians are inevitably caught up in the examination of problems and their political solutions; that academicians are notable producers of taxonomical structures for examining systems and dialectical structures for examining values or policies; that the whole business of analysis bores artists, who want to catch experience whole. Having proposed the possibility of such tendencies, we should be ill-advised to assume that particular preachers, politicians, academicians, or artists will necessarily be attentive to our speculation and exhibit the formal preferences we suggest.

SUMMARY

Form gives meaning. That is, we know our environment only as we organize it within some structure and form. We can abstract the substance of a speech from its form or arrangement, but in so doing we change somewhat the meaning of the speech. The more artistic the speech, the more inseparable becomes its form and content.

The form of speeches may be viewed at many levels. It is useful to keep in mind that the final reality of a speech involves the interaction of speech, speaker, purpose, audience and occasion, and that the several movements of a speech cannot be fully understood except by considering the total social form created by the speech act. However, in this chapter, consideration of form has been largely limited to consideration of the speech itself, and more particularly to the speech as it might be represented in a text based on the speaker's utterance.

The form chosen for his remarks by a speaker may be thought of as his way of encompassing or viewing reality. Five major forms within which speakers view reality are (a) the problem-solution form; (b) the value-application form; (c) the taxonomical form, or naming the parts of the whole; (d) the dialectical form, or reality as conflict or opposition; and (e) the organic form. Each of these forms is subject to a variety of transformations. In a particular speech several or all of the forms may appear as part of the total action. So-called digressive movements are also common in speeches, but the meaning of such digressions should not be judged apart from a view of the speech as related to audience, occasion, and purpose.

Common problems of choice confronting speakers with reference to form are (a) the level of obviousness to be sought in structuring the speech; (b) the location of the speaker's statement, or central idea, and whether the speech should move toward such a statement or be developed in support of such a statement; (c) balancing the tension between a search for structural simplicity and an avoidance of oversimplification of complex matters; (d) balancing the tension between time and purpose, particularly in relationship to the length of introductory remarks; and (e) finding a conclusion which establishes a sense of artistic completeness.

It is interesting to observe that listeners may identify with speakers on the basis of the form chosen by the speaker, and to suggest that one of the signs of identification which may mark certain subgroups in our culture may be a preference for certain forms for treating subject matter.

CHAPTER 5

Patterns of Enforcement

Statements may go without amplification and sometimes do. The announcement "I'm going to bed" may elicit neither rejoinder nor elaboration. But a speech cannot consist of an unelaborated statement. The speaker who is introduced, announces that "we are all in deadly peril," and then sits down is unlikely to receive much credit for wit or wisdom. Audiences expect development and if the speaker's statement is of any concern or interest to them they want development.

To an interested or concerned audience any statement by a speaker invites one or more of three major questions. The first question is "What do you mean?" Speakers amplify their statements in order to be clear, in order to be certain that the audience understands as nearly as possible the speaker's meaning. The second question is "How do you know?" Speakers support their assertions with the proof which has caused them to believe in the statement, or the proof which might be calculated to help the audience believe in it. The third question is "What difference does your statement make?" Speakers elaborate statements in order to arouse audience interest and concern, and thus assure attentive listeners.

AMPLIFICATION, PROOF, AND ENFORCEMENT

The concept of amplification is often distinguished from the concept of proof. That is, we can amplify a statement without in any sense demonstrating its truth or lack of truth. For example, in his 1932 campaign speech delivered at Detroit, Michigan, Franklin D. Roosevelt asserted:

. . . there are two theories of prosperity and well-being: The first theory is that if we make the rich richer, somehow they will let part of their prosperity trickle through to the rest of us. The second theory—and I suppose this goes back to the days of Noah—I won't say Adam and Eve because they had a less complicated situation—but, at least back to the days of the flood—there was the second theory that if we make the average of mankind comfortable and secure, their prosperity will rise up, just as yeast rises up, through the ranks.[1]

Roosevelt amplified his statement of two theories by a biblical allusion, and by a double metaphor in which one theory is associated with the feeble image of water "trickling through," and the other theory with the expansive quality of yeast. His statement takes on color, interest, and memorability from the amplification. But he cannot be said to have proved in any sense the real presence of the two theories in economic analysis, or to have begun any demonstration of their respective merit.

By contrast, in a speech entitled "Science, Technology, and World Development," delivered in 1958, Professor Harrison Brown asserted:

During the last 300 years, man has attained a remarkable degree of control over his environment. Through the achievement of a partial understanding of how nature operates, he has learned how to grow more crops on a given piece of land; he has learned a great deal about disease and how to control it; he has learned how to harness the energy of fossil fuels; he has learned how to transport himself, his ideas, and his goods rapidly.[2]

Brown amplifies his assertion with a series of examples which could be said to prove the truth of his statement. The examples are general ones, each susceptible of further amplification; but since neither Brown's assertion nor the examples would be likely to arouse dissent, the proof is sufficient.

The distinction between "amplifying" and "proving" would thus seem to be clear. But in certain contexts, and from certain perspectives, the difference becomes ambiguous. For example, from the perspective of an audience, the clarity and memorability of the speaker's discourse may induce agreement. In this sense, apt analogies, such as those developed by President Roosevelt in the foregoing illustration, can have the effect of demonstrating to certain listeners that Roosevelt's position is true. Moreover, many sciences define rigorously the kind of evidence and reasoning needed to prove assertions indigenous to a given science. But there are other areas of public discussion which admit or favor methods of proof which would be rejected by the sciences. Thus, a metaphor or analogy cannot be said to "prove" a statement about the

---

[1] Franklin D. Roosevelt, address delivered at Detroit, Michigan, October 2, 1932.

[2] Harrison Brown, "Science, Technology, and World Development," *Bulletin of the Atomic Scientists,* December 14, 1958, pp. 409–412.

properties of electrons, but this form of amplification may serve to demonstrate effectively the quality of a human emotion.

We shall not pursue here the interesting philosophic problem of differentiating modes of discourse which prove statements from those modes which simply amplify statements. Rather, we observe that the public speaker engages in amplification or proof for the single purpose of eliciting favorable audience response. He uses both amplification and proof as a method of enforcing his purposes with a particular audience. The single concept of *enforcement* comprehends, therefore, all actions of the speaker designed to enhance the interest, memorability, or plausibility of his discourse.

THE CONCEPT OF ENFORCEMENT

A major difficulty in discussing the concept of enforcement is the multiplicity of speech events which could be said to enforce the speaker's utterance. Thus the function of enforcement can be observed if the speaker phrases an idea in a particularly memorable way. President Woodrow Wilson's statement that the United States had entered World War I "to make the world safe for democracy" compressed his definition of national goals so aptly that this single phrase enforced popular belief in the idealism of the nation's purpose. The function of enforcement is also observable in nonverbal events which are part of the speaking situation. The speaker's appearance may enforce or embarrass his utterance. His delivery may enforce or detract from his language. His reputation may enforce or diminish the credibility of his discourse. Aspects of the speaking situation such as band music, banners, group singing, or a good dinner may be arranged to enforce the speaker's effect. Audience response during a speech could also be viewed as enforcement when cheers, laughter, or applause serve to assure any doubtful listeners that they are really hearing profound or witty ideas. Speakers commonly turn to pictures, charts, and various visual projections to clarify or support their utterance. In short, the concept of enforcement is potentially a comprehensive perspective for viewing the public speech. From this perspective one can observe all events which are part of the speech from the point of view of their effect on the interest, memorability, or plausibility of the speaker's utterance.

In order to give needed focus to this chapter, however, we shall limit our concern with enforcement to an examination of a limited number of patterns of forms of argument commonly employed in the development of public speeches.[3] We shall examine in some detail four major patterns of argument, designated as argument from *cause,* from *consequence,* from *comparison,* and from *definition.* Each of these patterns will be considered by defining its form, observing a variety of uses made by public speakers, and exploring the possibilities and limitations of these uses. We shall also give brief attention to two additional patterns of enforcement, argument from *authority,* and from *sign.* These latter two patterns are sufficiently evident in public speeches to deserve attention, but they can be given compressed treatment since their workings are similar to those of the patterns receiving more complete consideration.

Four reasons can be given to justify the selection of patterns of argument to be discussed in this chapter. First, each of these patterns is discoverable in the utterance of nearly all public speakers—a phenomenon which suggests that they serve as "root" patterns for the development of public discourse in our culture. Second, each pattern is substantial. While the pattern can appear in the structure of a single phrase or sentence, it can also be used to organize either a major segment of a discourse, or even an entire discourse. Third, each pattern generates a variety of transformations carrying different possibilities and limitations. The speaker who understands the possibilities and limitations of these patterns is presumably better equipped to choose a method of speech development relevant to a given set of circumstances. The listener with equal understanding brings increased critical insight to the speaking situation. Fourth, study of these and additional patterns of argument formed an important part of the instruction which was thought by classical rhetoricians to be effective in increasing a public speaker's power of invention. The instruction of ancient Greek and Roman rhetoricians was considerably more elaborate than the exposition to be provided in this chapter. However, their reasons for believing that study of patterns of argument should be undertaken by the public speaker and their method of examining various patterns were similar to the rationale and method of development followed in this chapter. A brief glance at the concept of *topoi,* as developed in classical rhetorical theory, provides a useful frame of reference for the treatment of patterns of enforcement developed in this chapter.

---

[3] Discussion of figurative language and speech delivery, which could be treated as aspects of enforcement, will be undertaken in Chapter 6 under the heading of "style." Brief discussion of other forms of enforcement, including visual aids, is provided in Chapter 10.

PATTERNS OF ARGUMENT IN ANCIENT RHETORICAL THEORY

The notion that knowledge of patterns of argument aids speakers in the discovery of the materials for speaking has its roots in ancient Greek and Roman rhetorical theory. Greek rhetoricians gave the name *topoi,* to the description of such forms, and seem to have meant that such *topoi* were the places where arguments might be found. It seemed clear to such writers as Aristotle and Cicero that a man who knew where to look for an argument was more likely to be a resourceful and imaginative speaker than one who had not observed the recurrent forms taken by arguments, whatever their substance. Both Greek and Roman theorists uncovered and described a large number of *topoi* they thought characteristic of the methods of amplification used by speakers of their day. For example, Aristotle in his *Rhetoric* listed in addition to certain general lines of argument, and certain spurious lines of argument, some twenty-seven *topoi* which he thought generally serviceable for demonstrating ideas or refuting the ideas of another person. The Aristotelian *topoi* were described with an eye to their practical possibilities for speakers, as the following examples, taken from the *Rhetoric,* demonstrate:

Another *topos* is that *a fortiori* [from degrees of more or less]. Thus you may argue that if not even the Gods are omniscient, much less are men; on the principle that, if a thing cannot be found where it is more likely to exist, of course you will not find it where it is less likely. Again, you may argue that a man who strikes his father will also strike his neighbors; on the principle that, if the less frequent thing occurs, then the more frequent thing occurs—for people strike their fathers less frequently than they strike their neighbors. . . . And you may also use this line of argument in a case of parity . . . if Theseus did no wrong [in abducting Helen] neither did Paris . . . ; or that if Hector did well to slay Patroclus, so did Paris to slay Achilles. . . .

Another *topos* is from the proportion between this and that result. For example, when they would compel the son of Iphicrates, a youth under the legal age, to discharge a public duty because he was tall, Iphicrates said: "If you make big boys count as men, you will have to enact little men into boys." So Theodectes says in his *Law:* "You enfranchise mercenaries like Strabax and Charidemus for meritorious service; will you not exile those among the mercenaries who have wrought irreparable harm?" [4]

---

[4] The passages are taken from *The Rhetoric of Aristotle,* translated by Lane Cooper (New York: Appleton-Century-Crofts, Inc., 1932), 2.23.

A complete reading of the Aristotelian treatment of *topoi* (see readings at the end of Part III) suggests the usefulness of examining the great variety of particular patterns of argument used by public speakers. However, we shall limit our discussion in this chapter to certain root forms appearing again and again in contemporary public discourse —forms which encompass a variety of particular patterns of enforcement.

THE PATTERN OF CAUSE

In 1786, Dr. Benjamin Rush, a noted American physician and scientist, addressed the American Philosophical Society on "The Influence of Physical Causes on the Moral Faculty." Dr. Rush was an enthusiastic disciple of the mechanistic view of the workings of the universe, believing that all events in nature and in man's behavior were capable of explanation and that the causes of events could be located and described, the laws governing both the natural and the moral world discovered. In the passage following an extended introduction to his speech, he begins his analysis:

The effects of CLIMATE upon the moral faculty claim our first attention. Not only individuals, but nations, derive a considerable part of their moral as well as intellectual character, from the different portions they enjoy of the rays of the sun. Irascibility, levity, timidity, and indolence, tempered with occasional emotions of benevolence, are the moral qualities of the inhabitants of warm climates, while selfishness, tempered with sincerity and integrity, form the moral character of the inhabitants of cold countries. The state of the weather, and the season of the year also, have a visible effect upon moral sensibility. The month of November, in Great Britain, rendered gloomy by constant fogs and rains, has been thought to favor the perpetration of the worst species of murder, while the vernal sun, in middle latitudes, has been as generally remarked for producing gentleness and benevolence.[5]

Dr. Rush's entire speech, with its confident linking of moral attributes to a variety of physical and physiological causes, is an interesting example of eighteenth century rationalism with its boundless confidence in the power of "scientific" explanation. We may be entertained by the confidence of Dr. Rush's assertions, his use of sweeping empirical generalization unsupported by evidence other than his own authority, and the probable acquiescence of most of his listeners. But our major concern at this time is with the form of the pattern of argu-

[5] Joseph L. Blau, ed., *American Philosophic Addresses, 1700–1900* (New York: Columbia University Press, 1946), p. 326.

ment he has started. Dr. Rush believed that events have causes and he set about locating the causes of moral conduct in man. We may find his subject matter unusual, his terminology sometimes strange, and his confidence more extensive than his information. But we are likely to find the *form* of his argument familiar.

The Form of Argument from Cause

The line of argument which develops the thesis that "event B is caused by event A" is familiar because it is omnipresent. It is doubtful that any speech concerned with social or personal problems escapes use of some variant of this line of argument. A man is ill; we seek to know why. A war occurs; we ask to know what caused it. Men are unemployed; there must be a reason. A movie star takes her own life; we ask why. The query is constant, and the supply of speeches or other discourses providing answers is at least equal to the demand. We should be careful to observe that the form of argument from cause does not require that the speaker use the word "cause." He may speak of event "B" as the result or consequence of event "A," or of "A" as being responsible for "B," as in the case of saying that "Jones was responsible for the automobile accident." The criterial attributes of the form are two in number: First, an argument from cause purports to identify an intrinsic relationship between two or more events occurring in sequence, with one event or groups of events in some sense determining, bringing into being, or making possible a succeeding event or group of events. Second, the argument applies to events which have already occurred. That is, it purports to explain a relationship between events which have happened, or have been observed. The explanation may be rigorous enough and based on enough evidence to permit the speaker to claim that he is talking about a law in nature, as "for every action there is an equal and opposite reaction." It may be as speculative as the suggestion that rats were instrumental in bringing about the decline of Athens since the rats brought the plague-carrying fleas to the city. The plague killed off not only Pericles, but also some 40 percent of the citizens of Athens, and so forth. But whether scientifically rigorous or historically speculative, the claimed relationship is made about events in existence.

The extensive use of argument from cause may reflect the fact that most people accept causality as a fact of nature, confirmed by common sense, and a necessary antecedent to rationality. We grow up in a linguistic environment in which the form is in constant use: "The hot stove burned you," or "See, you stepped on the cat's tail and that hurt him," or "The grass is turning brown because we need rain." Remove the assumption of causality and history has no meaning, the past cannot be used as guide to the future, responsibility cannot be assigned for individual actions. In short, the universe becomes chaotic. It is not surprising to find omnipresent in discourse a form so essential to the human need for understanding. Nor is it surprising to find speakers, as readily as sportswriters, taking on the role of "great explainers." The speaker who can give us a plausible accounting of the causes of crime would seem obviously able to guide us toward reducing crime. The speaker who can lead us to believe that we understand why Rome fell should be able to enlighten us concerning the perils of our own civilization. The speaker who can explain how our lack of honesty causes us to be miserable would seem to have established a case for honesty without further argument.

Scientific Versus Conventional Ideas of Causality

Argument from cause ranges from explanations of relationships which purport to be scientific or relatively conclusive to explanations which join events only within the context of some legal, moral, or conventional assumption. A speaker may observe that "Sodium pentathol in the bloodstream will cause sleep." His statement is not scientifically rigorous, and it might drive a philosopher into search for solitude, but it will not seem unusual within the context of everyday discourse. To be sure, the whole idea of causality in nature is complex if not impossible. But a speech is a response to a particular context. The patient who wants to know what put him to sleep on the operating table, and who learns that it was sodium pentathol, believes he has learned something —and so he has. He has not learned much about the complex biochemical interactions within a given environment which induce sleep, but he may have an explanation sufficient to the purpose of the situation. There is more to be said—but then there is always more to be said, including more than is known.

The speaker's explanations of relationships may not make even a strong claim to scientific verifiability. The speeding driver breaking the law who loses control of his car and gets into an accident is commonly held "responsible" for the accident. We say, "Jones caused the accident." The idea of causality here is used very loosely, and possibly quite inaccurately. But the explanation is sought and justified by legal convention which asks for an assignment of human responsibility in such events.

Hence in looking at the ways in which speakers deploy argument from cause we are not so immediately concerned with the scientific and philosophic difficulties in establishing causal relationships in nature, as with the kinds of choices speakers make in deploying their explanations.

Plausibility as a Factor of Choice

The first problem of choice apparent in argument from cause involves the question of the "surface" or prima facie plausibility of the argument. The most important source of such plausibility in an argument from cause is the "conventional wisdom" of the community to which the speaker and his audience belong. For example, in our medically-sophisticated American culture most people are familiar with the idea that germs and viruses of various sizes and dispositions are causally linked to various kinds of diseases. We are comfortable with the idea that a man suffering from a common cold has been attacked by some virus; we would be startled to hear (as our ancestors might have) that the malady had a phlogistic cause. Most of us have seen neither "phlogiston" (which we believe nonexistent) nor viruses (which we believe to exist), but the kind of wisdom which has filtered to us from medical scientists has made viruses a part of our conventional wisdom. The idea of microscopic and submicroscopic organisms producing ill health doesn't startle us. A "virus theory" for any kind of malady from cancer to gout would not startle us.

There are other kinds of surface plausibility present in a virus theory of disease. Events closely linked by time sequence, space relationships, or verbal constructs seem more plausibly related to one another than those widely separated in any of these ways. Bacteria enter a cut; later, but not much later, infection sets in. The time sequence is plausible. Bacteria, viruses, and the human organism are all coexistent physical structures; the space relationship seems plausible. All are studied by biological and medical scientists and seem joined by the verbal constructs we apply to health, disease, etc. Our tendency to leap to the perception of causal relationship in events linked closely in time, space, or verbal construct is well-known. Thus, children repeat the error of primitive tribes in perceiving thunder as causing rain. And citizens are quick to assume that the man holding the office of President at the time a national disaster occurs must somehow have caused the disaster.

Events which change together may seem to have a plausible causal connection if the linkage fits our habitual way of thinking about these events. For example, as scientists observed that the incidence of lung cancer was highest in populations in which cigarette smoking was highest they precipitated a considerable public argument over the extent to which these two co-varying events should be causally linked. The causal linkage had much plausibility. Conventional wisdom had long suspected that cigarettes were unhealthy; the smoke impinged upon human lungs so that the space relationship was obvious; the time sequence between the development of smoking and the growing incidence of lung cancer was plausible. Cautious voices observing that the link between cigarette smoking and lung cancer might be no more significant than the link between thunder and rainfall had difficulty being heard in the presence of such plausibility and, indeed, accumulating evidence constantly reinforced the assumption of causality. By contrast, during the early intensive research into poliomyelitis, it was found that the incidence of crippling was greatest in areas in which children drank the most milk. Co-variance of milk drinking and polio was treated cautiously and did not produce a spate of speeches alleging a causal relationship. Milk, unlike tobacco, had little reputation for producing bad health. It was more difficult to perceive milk impinging on nervous tissue than to see smoke irritating lung tissue. Subsequent to the discovery of certain viruses implicated in polio the most plausible account for the co-variance of polio and milk drinking held that children living in areas in which not much milk was drunk also lived in a generally unhygienic environment. They were likely to encounter early contact with polio virus and either to succumb to the virus without medical diagnosis or to develop early immunity to it.

Our illustrations of the factors which give rise to surface plausibility in a causal argument should make it clear that the plausible argument may or may not be intellectually respectable. However, a plausible argument, by definition, has rhetorical force. This is particularly the case if the plausible explanation of causality is not opposed by an alternative and equally plausible interpretation.

An argument lacking plausibility would seem, by definition, to lack rhetorical force. But surprising or incredible causal linkages may have intellectual merit, and in such cases the public speaker faces the task of turning an implausible argument into one which will seem persuasive. Public speakers have often been equal to this task.

The assertion of an implausible or unexpected linkage between events is almost automatically interesting to a listener. If the speaker can bring evidence to bear to support his "discovery," and if accepting his argument does not disturb other beliefs cherished by his listeners, then the implausible argument may become both attractive and memorable. For example, Hans Zinsser, in his book *Rats, Lice and History*,[6] seeks to show that conventional wisdom has given too much attention to the effects of political leadership, the force of ideas, the outcomes of

[6] Hans Zinsser, *Rats, Lice and History* (New York: Little, Brown and Company, 1935), p. 301.

battles, etc., on historical change. Zinsser believes that this excessive attention to the acts of men as causes of historical change has obscured the importance of the brute fact of epidemic disease as a cause of political change. As the title of his book suggests, he sees such lowly creatures as rats and lice as affecting history. Zinsser's argument is interesting. Since it bears on the interpretation of history rather than on any immediately controversial issue of public policy, a reader can follow the argument without feeling threatened. To the extent that the writer's evidence seems to make the incredible credible, the argument gains rhetorical force over and above a merely conventional interpretation of history.

Complexity as a Factor of Choice

A second dimension of choice available in argument from cause concerns its level of complexity. The speaker may seek a simple but allegedly decisive accounting of the causes of great or mysterious events. He may on the other hand explore the immense complexity of factors involved as causes in these events. The simplicity-complexity dimension has reasonably obvious application to any of the lines of argument which may be used in speaking. But its application to the argument from cause reveals some interesting aspects of this kind of argument. When one asks about the cause of any event, he has invited an answer which can potentially run on indefinitely, limited only by the speaker's resources of knowledge and imagination, and ending with "more questions needing further study." But public speakers cannot go on forever. The causal analysis they seek can be generally described as one "sufficient to the nature and purpose of the occasion." For example, we ask "how did the window in my house get broken?" The answer "Johnny threw a rock through it" may well be sufficient to our need for causal analysis. We have a physical explanation of the event—a rock broke the glass—and we have someone to blame for the misfortune. The simple answer is, however, not complete. Johnny may want to share the guilt. "I was throwing at a tree," he says, "and Bill hit my arm." Or, "Four of us planned to break the window, and I was elected to throw the rock." A social worker may observe that Johnny has aggressive tendencies brought on by tension between his parents. An amateur physicist may observe that the breakage was dependent on the brittle quality of the glass; plexiglass wouldn't have broken under a similar blow. The influence of family assemblies on the behavior of children is a matter needing explanation as well as research, and the physical properties of glass carry us into the structure of matter. In short, if one wishes to pursue the matter of causality in seemingly simple events, the circle of interacting factors constantly widens. The "full" explanation of a grain of sand becomes ultimately the story of the physical universe; the full explanation of a family quarrel becomes ultimately an accounting of the nature of biological and social men. But the speaker must stop someplace, and he usually stops at the point at which his explanation of cause is sufficient to his purpose.

Aristotle sought to classify the types of causes which might be observed in relation to some natural object or event, and identified four categories: efficient, material, formal, and final. For example, in Aristotelian terms one could say of a saw that it was produced by a toolmaker (the efficient cause); that it was made from steel with a wood handle (material cause); that it exhibited a steel blade with a serrated edge of sharpened teeth (formal cause); and that it was used for cutting pieces of wood (final cause). The categories illustrate the possibility of expanding systematically the concept of cause in relation to any natural event, but they also illustrate once again that a public speaker's interest in cause rises from the purpose of his discourse rather than from the purpose of saying all that can possibly be said.

In general the speaker's desideratum is simplicity, with its attendant virtues of clarity and memorability. But of course the occasion may dictate complexity. Johnny might prefer the most complex possible account of the breaking of a window; this would at least delay his punishment. Clarence Darrow, defending Leopold and Loeb on the charge of murder, preferred a complex account of the sociological and psychological roots of this crime. Moreover the effort to fix a single or simple decisive cause to a complex event risks the effect of disproportion. The great simplifiers of history like to furnish simple but decisive explanations of the most complex social phenomena. "Napoleon was destroyed by the bone-chilling cold of Russia's winter—and so was Hitler," says a meteorologically-inclined explainer. "The Normandy beachhead in World War II, which led to the defeat of Hitler, succeeded because Der Fuehrer couldn't have his nap interrupted to give approval to moving his Fifteenth Army," says yet another explainer. The disproportion between cause and effect in such statements gives a surface incredibility. We ask for evidence that the speaker understands that he has selected for emphasis one cause among a multitude of interacting forces, and for the evidence, or the motive in the speaking situation which justifies his selection.

Human Intention Versus Impersonal Forces in Causal Argument

Speakers may choose to emphasize human actions or intentions as causes, or they may emphasize impersonal forces of history or nature as causes. We have already illustrated in our reference to Zinsser's medically oriented interpretation of history the difference between viewing human action or intention as a cause, and viewing complex natural processes as causes. The difference in these two types of causal interpretations is interesting because it embodies an ancient but still active controversy about the proper way to interpret historical change. The speaker who emphasizes human intention and action as determining the nature of history assumes that man is in some sense free to choose and act according to his choice, and that his choices have consequences. The speaker who interprets an event as the product of the complex interaction of many events operating within some natural system tends to see man as less free than he perhaps thinks he is. The philosophic division between these two points is often seen as a controversy between "free will" versus "determinism." The dispute is a familiar one to those who have read Tolstoi's famous novel *War and Peace*. In his account of Napoleon's defeat in Russia, the novelist sought to show that wars are not won or lost by the choices of generals, or the acts of heroes, but that their outcome is determined by the complex interaction of innumerable events, as part of a vast and impersonal historical process. But the novelist also revealed that the men and women who peopled the vast panorama of his novel experienced freedom, and acted as moral or choosing agents.

There is ample evidence in contemporary American public speaking that American audiences accept both the view that some kinds of events are properly explained by reference to human intentions and actions, while other kinds are best explained by an account of the complex interactions of impersonal events within some system. The latter kind of account is associated with the activity of science, and is thought appropriate to phenomena which have been brought under rigorous scientific study. The accounts featuring human intention and actions as causes are thought appropriate to political, moral, and aesthetic matters.

For example, we seldom hear a speaker concerned with the nature of some disease talking about human intention as a cause: few Americans believe that a person catches smallpox because his neighbor cast an evil spell over him, although presumably there are cultures in which such an account would be thought credible. We are accustomed to the idea of "impersonal determinants" of some phenomenon when the phenomenon in question is one studied by natural scientists. On the other hand we are accustomed to the idea that political speeches, especially those occurring during an election campaign, will emphasize the role of human actions and intentions as affecting the most complicated kinds of social phenomena. A decisive part of the environment of campaign speaking is that it culminates in a vote—and votes are cast for or against people, and not for or against some set of impersonal forces of nature.

Political campaign speaking thus concerns itself ostensibly with subject matter of the most complex sort—international relations, economic well-being, welfare, education, taxation, etc.—but it considers such subject matter in a context oriented toward the role of human actions and intentions as an influence in history. The politician seldom speculates about the great philosophic problem of the extent to which the actions of particular men do or don't influence history; he assumes that they do. Moreover, the politician is disposed to find that historic disasters are the result of actions of the opposition party. The political situation is prestructured for causal analysis often transcending good sense in assigning human responsibility for events not totally amenable either to human understanding or control. At its best, political speaking is properly responsive to the situational motive which asks that people assume responsibility for directing social policy. At its worst, such speaking seeks a scapegoat for all human misfortune.

Politics is not the only context within which there is a situational bias toward assigning human responsibility for events. The law wants more to know "who killed cock robin?" than to know which physiological consequences from an arrow wound might result in death, although, as any close follower of Perry Mason on television knows, courtroom procedure also insists that the fact of death and the nature of the death-producing weapon be placed in evidence. And the law is much interested in the role of human intention as a cause for some misfortunes, even though the problem of establishing human intention is a notably slippery one.

The interest of politics and the law in human intention and choice as "causes" lends itself to the dramatistic interpretations of events. In literature the search for the villain of the affair is a common and dramatic transformation of argument from cause. If the villain needs identification so that he can be properly punished, or so that the tensions created by misfortune can be linked to a human agent who can be made to suffer, then we have the familiar drama of the search for a scapegoat. Political movements founded in the context of some kind of discontent find unity through the identification of a villain, and given sufficient power, they find unity also in converting the villain into a scapegoat. For example, the Nazi rise to power in Germany was marked by Hitler's identification of a whole group, the Jews, as the "villains of the story," marked for victimage and extermination after the Nazi rise to power. The form may be asserted in language less violent than that used by Hitler and may result in action less brutal, but the form is commonplace. The search for the "hero" to be linked to good fortune, and to be deserving of honor rather than victimage is also a dramatistic argument from cause.

Our brief exploration of argument from cause indicates the diversity of the materials which may be organized within such a form. The form is apparent in the exposition of scientifically verifiable "laws"; it is equally apparent in the plausible explanation of relationships which seem to need understanding even though they are not subject to the explorations of science. The form may treat the problem of causation impersonally or within the dramatistic context of the search for human purpose and action.

THE PATTERN OF CONSEQUENCE

Argument from consequence is the counterpart of argument from cause. It is to be distinguished from argument from cause only by its concern for events not yet in existence. The form we call consequence is set in the future tense. Its mode is prediction, or prophecy. As prediction, argument from consequence may seek considerable scientific rigor. The speaker may reveal a historic trend, well established by past data, and argue the probable occurrence of events. As prophecy, argument from consequence may "see" the future in the most visionary way with little effort to justify prediction by masses of evidence.

Variant Forms of Argument From Consequence

The mode of prediction or prophecy may claim that certain events or circumstances *will* come to pass. Or the mode may be that of warning, taking the form that "certain things will come to pass, unless. . . ." In using this latter form the speaker employs prophecy as the basis for advancing some statement he supports: "Grass will grow in the streets *unless* I am elected Mayor," or "60,000 people will die on our highways next year *unless* we strengthen traffic regulation." Presumably the speaker who warns of disastrous possibilities doesn't really want his hypothetical disaster to occur. However, if by chance the speaker's listeners do not heed his advice, and disaster does occur, the speaker at least gains a reputation as a man of vision. Thus Winston Churchill, in the 1930's, gave repeated Cassandra-like warnings that continued British weakness in the face of growing Nazi power would lead to a disastrous war. Churchill's call for stronger British armaments and a stronger foreign policy went unheeded. But the disaster of

World War II brought him back to political power with a formidable reputation for political vision.

Presumably also the human appetite for a look into the future is so insatiable that even a prophet with few successes to his credit may survive with honor provided he is verbally agile enough to explain his record. Tim Cohane, a sports editor for *Look* magazine explains this phenomenon as it applies to the tricky business of forecasting the results of sporting events:

To a football forecaster, infallibility is far less important than poise. Not that he should be like the alleged history expert on the TV quiz, who sought to mask his ignorance of Lincoln's assassination with the protest, "I'm no squealer." No, evasion is not needful in the forecaster, merely nimbleness. He should be able to prove convincingly that he could just as easily have been right. . . .[7]

Whether predicting some inevitable future development or warning against some unwanted possibility, the speaker usually joins argument from consequence to argument from cause, and uses both these lines of argument to establish a base for certain proposals the speaker wishes to support. For an example of an argument which predicts a probable future development, we turn to a pamphlet by Donald N. Michael entitled *Cybernation: The Silent Conquest.*[8] Mr. Michael analyzes the probable effects of automated industrial, commercial, and educational processes on the nature of American society. He gives special attention to the use of computers for managing the activities of machines and gives the name "cybernation" to the application of computers to processes now managed by human decisions. Assuming avoidance of some social cataclysm such as World War III, Michael foresees revolutionary change in the decades just ahead:

In twenty years, other things being equal, most of the routine blue-collar and white-collar tasks that can be done by cybernation will be. Our schools will probably be turning out a larger proportion of the population better educated than they are today, but most of our citizens will be unable to understand the cybernated world in which they live. . . .

There will be a small, almost separate, society of people in rapport with the advanced computers. These cyberneticians will have established a relationship with their machines that cannot be shared with the average man any more than the average man of today can understand the problems of molecular biology, nuclear physics, or neuropsychiatry. . . .

[7] "The 1962 Football Forecast," *Look,* Sept. 11, 1962, p. 31.

[8] (Santa Barbara, California: Center for Study of Democratic Social Institutions, 1962), pp. 44–45.

We can foresee a nation with a large portion of its people doing, directly or indirectly, the endless public tasks that the welfare state needs and that the government will not allow to be cybernated because of the serious unemployment that would result. These people will work shorter hours, with much time for the pursuit of leisure activities.

Mr. Michael describes his brave new world of the near tomorrow as a basis for alerting readers to the social and political decisions that must be made in the years just ahead, and to the critical inadequacy of traditional ideas to deal with problems that confronts us almost immediately. "These things will happen," he says in effect. "Therefore we must prepare for them."

By contrast we turn to an argument from consequence warning of disasters that will occur, *unless*. . . . In a newspaper column carrying his by-line, Senator Barry Goldwater addressed himself several years ago to the consequences of Communist domination of the nation of Laos. In the column, he expressed the fear that the policies of the existing Democratic national administration threatened the loss of Laos to Communism. His development of the consequences of such an event picked up a familiar form of argument from consequence:

Few Americans seem to realize the terrible consequences that could follow the loss of Laos. . . .

Now that the Communists are on the threshold of seizing power in Laos, we are in danger of seeing Communist personnel, money, materials, and orders flow unchecked deep into Thailand, Cambodia, South Viet Nam, and Malaya. . . .

Cambodia, which already has close ties with Red China, could not remain neutral if Laos falls into Communist hands. Thus Cambodia may well provide the next test of will for the United States. . . .

If Laos and Cambodia fall to Communism, the whole Eastern border of Thailand would be vulnerable. . . . All in all it is extremely doubtful that Thailand could be persuaded to maintain a strong military posture for the long pull. Our vacillating policies in Laos have already caused the Thai to doubt our determination to resist actual Communist aggression.

If Cambodia, South Viet Nam and Thailand should fall to Communism, Malaya would be exposed to infiltration and conquest. This would pave the way for a link-up with the already-strong Communist elements in Indonesia. Burma would fall like a ripe plum.

It is important for all Americans to realize that once Southeast Asia is lost, the pressure upon Japan and the Philippines, upon India, upon the Middle East and Africa, and upon Australia and New Zealand would become almost intolerable.

What I have described here is the "falling domino" thesis. I am convinced that Laos is the key domino in the pile. If it is removed the result will be the eventual crumbling of the pile.[9]

Senator Goldwater's identification of his argument as based on the "falling domino thesis" indicates that the form was not a new one. Indeed a version of this argument has appeared in public discourse at each territorial confrontation between the United States and "Communism" since World War II—over Greece, Korea, Berlin, Viet Nam, Cuba, etc. Although Senator Goldwater's argument is charged also with domestic political purposes, the ostensible purpose of the "falling domino" argument is to magnify the consequences of a particular event—in this case the loss of Laos—so as to build public demand that the event not be allowed to occur.

The "falling domino" argument joins the form of argument from consequence to the form of figurative comparison or analogy. One is asked to "see" Laos as the key domino in a line of dominos standing on end, each of which will fall if the first falls. The joining of argument from consequence to literal causal comparisons is also common. In using the past to predict the future, the speaker often engages in causal analysis of the past as a basis for his prediction. Thus, "Rome fell because her citizens lost the will to work; unless we Americans learn to enjoy hard work, the consequences are clear." Since we shall give separate consideration to argument from comparison shortly, we shall not here pursue the blending of the forms of cause, comparison, and consequence.

Another common variant of argument from consequence is that which emphasizes historical trend. The speaker seeks to use the past to predict the future by developing an account of the past based on some definable line of progression or evolution. The speaker then predicts that this trend will continue and may visualize the consequences that will follow. An historically interesting use of such a line of argument is found in Marx and Engel's *Manifesto.* The *Manifesto* purports to give an analysis of history in terms of a so-called inevitable line of development. Thus, as Marx asserted, feudal society had come into conflict with capitalist society with the resultant collapse of feudalism and triumph of capitalism and the middle class. He then found capitalism and the middle class to be in conflict with the working class or proletariat, a conflict which would end with the inevitable triumph of the proletariat and the founding of a classless society. Thus Marx predicted the form of the future as an inevitable consequence of the trend of the past. While the *Manifesto,* written in 1848, has not served subsequently

9 "How Do You Stand, Sir?" *Minneapolis Herald,* August 15, 1962.

to enhance Marx's reputation either as historian or prophet, the rhetorical form of its argument is interesting. Rather than saying "we want to build this kind of society, and therefore we must do thus and so," Marx asserts that "this kind of society will inevitably develop, therefore we should now . . . , etc." The form is reminiscent of the politician who asks that people vote for him because he is inevitably going to win.

A contemporary example of argument from historical trend is found in much of the speaking and writing concerning future population problems. In complete form the argument may trace world population figures from some given point in the past and may explain the rate of growth in terms of changing medical and public health practices, changing levels of economic productivity and political stability. With trend and cause established, the speaker then forecasts population at some future point in history. The so-called population explosion thus predicted is then used for a variety of political, social, or medical proposals.

Problems of Choice in Argument from Consequence

As with argument from cause, arguments from consequence vary in terms of surface plausibility, complexity, and attention to human as opposed to impersonal forces in history. Public speakers commonly use the same strategy for their predictions that they use in their explanations of the past. The speaker who finds the past susceptible to simple explanation is likely to see the future rather easily. And the speaker who sees human actions and intentions as significant in shaping the past is likely to stress the role of these same agents as affecting the future.

Like causal argument, prediction varies from the most rigorous kind of scientific analysis to the most cosmological kind of prophecy. We have become accustomed to the power of modern science to engage in precise predictions: an eclipse of the sun will begin at such and such a minute and end at a prestated time; the number of people to die from heart attacks in the United States in the coming year can be predicted within a certain numerical limit and so forth. This power, now commonplace, would once have been thought a sign of clairvoyance or special vision in the predictor—an idea that Mark Twain developed in *A Connecticut Yankee in King Arthur's Court.* Twain's Yankee used the commonplace knowledge and technology of the nineteenth century to gain reputation for magical power in eighth-century England. But public speakers of the twentieth century work with predictions as imprecise and unscientific as those made by speakers throughout history. Just as the past men seek to understand is more complex than those physical phenomena capable of scientific explanation, so also the future men seek to foresee encompasses all of the content of man's speculations. A speaker's prophecies have interest beyond the question of the extent to which evidence supports their probability. For they tell us much about the form of the world that the speaker wants and which he offers as a goal for his listeners. Speculative predictions, whether confirmed or denied by history, serve as goals shaping present actions and judgments.

It is in the use of the pattern of consequence to provide a vision of the future that the form often takes on its most dramatic quality. If societies move with human purpose only when animated by some commonly held vision of the future that could be, then it is obviously a high office for public discourse to provide that vision, and to provide it in a form vivid enough and memorable enough to unify society.

THE PATTERN OF COMPARISON

Perhaps the most commonplace gesture in language is the observation that event "A" is like event "B," or unlike event "C," or partly like and partly unlike event "D." The pervasive presence of comparison and contrast in linguistic activity has given rise to much speculation over the possibility that the observation of similitude and difference is the essential characteristic of human thought. Thus philosophers of the seventeenth and eighteenth centuries, wrestling with the problem of the nature of knowledge, conceived of the mind as forming concepts by perceiving similarities and differences in the content of experience. Theologians seek understanding of that which is infinite by finding analogies of the infinite in the finite forms of nature. Scientists have hypothesized that it is through analogy that they discover new hypotheses. And psychologists have viewed language learning as a process of acquiring an increasing power to perceive similarities and differences in environment and experience.

Here we observe the range of speculative interest in the relationship of thinking, linguistic activity, and the act of comparison only for the purpose of underlining the extraordinary prevalence of this form of enforcement in linguistic acts, including public speeches. Without forcing the question about the nature of thought itself, or about the processes that make knowledge possible, we can safely observe that comparison and contrast are intrinsic to the verbal activity by which men extend their understanding of their universe. We come to understand that which is new through comparison and contrast with that which is already known to the audience. We extend our insight only by finding relationships between events which previously seemed unrelated. Skillful speakers understand this and draw unusual or striking comparisons and contrasts to our attention. We remember abstract ideas only as we can root them in some kind of concrete imagery, and here again the skillful speaker comes to our assistance as he finds a simple but striking objective correlate for the shadowy or elusive concept.

Variant Forms of Comparison

A speaker makes use of comparison in a variety of ways. Comparison may be the major organizing principle of his entire speech. Thus, in a speech entitled "Education in Russia and America" we would expect the discourse to be organized around a series of comparisons, contrasts, or both. The speaker's use of comparison may also be fleeting—a mere allusion—as in the utterance, "Modern Russia, like ancient Sparta, believes that man is made to serve the state." The use of comparison may be explicit. For example, a speaker might compare the organization of medical care in the United States and Canada to show similarities and differences in the two systems. Or, if the speaker did no more than describe medical care in Canada to a United States audience, the comparison might be implicit. The United States audience presumably could be counted on to see the Canadian program in comparison with the familiar program.

The comparison might be a literal one. If the speaker compares state government in Nebraska with its unicameral legislature and government in another state with a bicameral legislature, he would presumably be making a literal comparison of two events, both in existence and both members of the common category of state governments. Or the comparison might be figurative, as in the utterance, "From every great war the hope of peace rises, like the renewal that spring brings after a bitter winter."

Because the form of comparison is used both as an explicit and literal form for "proving a case," and as a figurative or literary form, a variety of special terms have been developed for describing particular kinds of comparisons. The most general of these terms is *analogy,* which has been used as broadly as the term *comparison.* The speaker says: "The one problem the city states of ancient Greece could not solve was the problem of political unity. Unable to work together to advance their common interest, these states warred with one another, weakened one another, and fell prey to barbarian conquerors. Their problem of political unity is now the primary problem faced by the entire world. If we fail, as did the Greeks, to solve this problem, our fate will not be conquest by barbarians, but the devastation of the whole civilized world by nuclear warfare." This unit of discourse can be described as a literal comparison or literal analogy.

The speaker says: "We seem blind to the threat that automation poses to our accustomed way of life. Like ostriches in the presence of danger, we have our heads in the sand, and we hope that the threat won't notice us." The speaker's knowledge of the habits of ostriches may be defective, but his allusion is a familiar one. We can describe it as a figurative comparison or figurative analogy.

The comparison of human attitudes and the ostrich could also be called a *metaphor,* a term generally applied to any linguistic act which informs the meaning of one event or concept by introducing the perspective of an unlike event or concept. Although metaphor overlaps with figurative analogy, it also comprehends the extent to which language grows and extends its range of meaning through the interaction of events which are literally dissimilar. Thus, when we say "his thoughts were *cloaked* with gloom," the word "cloaked" is used metaphorically, since it applies a word initially associated with a physical action to a state of mind. It should also be noted that while the term *metaphor* is applied to extended acts of figurative comparison (also called "figurative analogies"), we seldom speak of the metaphors encapsuled in single words as implicit figurative analogies.

Extended figurative comparisons, especially those in which the comparison is left implicit, are called "allegories" or "fables." Thus Orwell's novel *The Animal Farm* takes the form of a story about the power structure of a barnyard assemblage, headed by a pig who shows considerable capacity for organizing and controlling power. The story is obviously intended as a commentary on the totalitarian states founded by human beings, and indeed some of the language of the allegory has found its way back into common discourse in metaphoric allusion to the affairs of men, as in the phrase, "All men are equal, but some are more equal than others." A novel by Golding, *The Lord of the Flies,* is ostensibly a story about children cast away on an island away from all adult restraint. But again the events on the island provide an obvious commentary on the structure of adult human society generally, and hence the novel becomes an allegory. While entire speeches seldom take the form of allegories, speakers do use extended narrative passages intended to develop an implicit analogy or allegory as part of the enforcement of the speaker's position.

An Extended Comparison

As an example of an extended use of comparison, we turn to a 1952 lecture by Dr. James Conant. Dr. Conant wishes to illustrate the sense in which he believes that the past half century has brought about a great change in scientific thought. He says:

To illustrate what seems to me the essence of the new departure in scientific thought, I am going to use an analogy. Let me ask you to consider not light, but heat, and to recall that somewhat more than a hundred years ago popular lectures on science fascinated their audience by demonstrating that heat was a "mode of motion."

The notion of a subtle caloric fluid that flowed from hot bodies to cooler ones could be shown to be totally unnecessary; indeed not only unnecessary but also quite incapable of accounting for a number of experimental results, such as the generation of heat by friction. Therefore, the caloric theory of heat which had been useful in its day was disproved and in its place was firmly established the concept that heat was associated with the motion of particles. Nevertheless, the caloric theory of heat has remained a useful pedagogical device. We still talk of the flow of heat, and set up mathematical expressions to formulate this flow as though there were a caloric fluid. Within a limited range of experimental facts in physics and chemistry, the caloric theory of heat is still the most convenient way of ordering these facts. Note that I said "limited range of facts," for it was the introduction of other experimental situations that destroyed the over-all usefulness of the notion of a caloric fluid. . . . In short, experiments settled conclusively, so we say, which one of the two theories of heat was "true."

At the end of the last century the nature of light seemed to be as definitely settled as did the nature of heat. Light was an electromagnetic disturbance in all-pervading ether; it was a wave phenomenon. The older idea that light was corpuscular—a stream of bullets—had been destroyed, so it was said, by a certain set of famous experiments that proved that light was in fact undulatory. Then along came certain new experimental phenomena which were as difficult to fit into a wave theory of light as had been the older set to fit into the framework of a corpuscular theory. About 1910 a highly unsatisfactory situation had developed which could be summarized by saying that light is emitted and received as though it consisted of a stream of particles and it is transmitted as though it were a set of waves. To the scientists of forty years ago this was the equivalent of saying a box was both full and empty; it was impossible, so they maintained, for light to be both undulatory and corpuscular. The fact that this appeared to be the case could only be a temporary situation. It would surely be only a matter of time before a set of experiments would be devised that would resolve the difficulty, for such a sequence of events had occurred throughout the history of science.

One is tempted to say that what has happened in the last forty years is that physicists have learned to love a situation they once thought to be intolerable.[10]

Professor Conant's use of comparison is interesting in several respects. The major statement of his lecture is that there has been a "new departure" in scientific thought in the last half century. Conant seeks to clarify this change by a comparison between the experience of scientists with theories about the nature of heat, and their contrasting experience with theories about the nature of light. The "new departure" in scientific thought is the change of attitude which makes it possible for scientists to be comfortable with their need to retain two somewhat different theories of the nature of light in order to explain existing experimental data. Conant has thus "clarified" an abstract point about scientific thinking by reference to a concrete comparison.

Within the major act of comparison, however, rest a number of additional comparisons. Conant's lecture illustrates the use of metaphor in the formulation of scientific theory: thus, the description of light as having an undulatory motion is called the "wave" theory, with the word "wave" obviously drawn from the familiar undulatory motion of water. The corpuscular theory of light is explained in passing by reference to a "stream of bullets"; the caloric theory of heat entails visualizing heat as a "fluid"; the logical principle that contradictory ideas cannot be simultaneously true is translated into the concrete statement that a box cannot be both full and empty. If the passage cited from Professor Conant's lecture seems packed with the form of comparison, this fact should not be considered remarkable. Rather it illustrates the extent to which comparison serves as a major form of enforcement in speaking.

With comparison, as with the other forms of enforcement discussed in this chapter, we shall skirt the question of the circumstances under which a comparison may be said adequately to "prove" a statement. Obviously speakers use comparisons as a form of proof. For example, speakers seek to prove that government health insurance will or will not work in the United States by showing how it has worked in England. Presumably to the extent that the speaker's description and evaluation of the English system is accepted as accurate, and to the extent that England can be considered comparable to the United States, the comparison serves as a form of proof. But we are here concerned primarily with some of the considerations which cause speakers to choose

[10] James A. Conant, Bampton lecture, delivered at Columbia University, 1952; reprinted in Walker Gibson, ed., *The Limits of Language* (New York: Hill and Wang, 1962), pp. 18–19.

certain uses of comparison, and with the potential and limitations which attend these choices.

Problems of Choice in Using Comparison

The comparison can be a simple or complex one. But this familiar dimension applies in a variety of ways to the structure of particular comparisons. The most common use of comparison by speakers is to make abstract or complicated events understandable or memorable by comparing them with concrete and familiar events. Thus the grade school textbook on electric wiring in the home may seek to make electricity and the wiring system understandable to children by comparing it with the water system. The flow of electrons is likened to the flow of water; the wires become the pipes; the electric switches become the faucets. The whole comparison doesn't add up to a particularly enlightened view of the nature of electricity, but like the caloric theory of heat it serves to explain certain phenomena at some level. The reverse use of comparison is also available for purposes of revealing the complexity of some event capable of relatively simple visualization. Thus one can simplify the visualization of the human brain by likening it to an electrical wiring circuit; or one can seek to uncover the complexity of the brain by observing that a computer containing as many interconnections as the nervous system of the brain would occupy a building seven stories high, and seven hundred yards square. The atom is simplified by calling it "the building block" of matter; it is revealed as complex by relating it to the solar system.

The simplicity-complexity dimension applies to comparisons in another sense. The comparison may be an obvious and direct one as is the case with most literal comparisons. Indeed the strength of a literal comparison lies in the claim that the events being compared are alike in essential structure. Traffic law enforcement problems in Connecticut are like similar problems in Missouri; labor problems in Germany are like labor problems in France, etc. Such literal and easily grasped comparisons seem to be simple enough to permit quick audience interpretation. But the resources of comparison permit the development of a comparison of unexpected complexity. Robert Oppenheimer's metaphor in which he likens the position of the United States and Russia in the age of nuclear weapons to that of "two scorpions in a bottle" has some unexpected depths: the scorpions, each capable of inflicting death, each unable to strike without himself accepting a fatal wound; the bottle serving well enough to dramatize the shrinking confines of the world in an age of jet aircraft and ballistic missiles; and the whole picture charged with the menace and ugliness of the world's power struggle. Allegories or extended metaphors often carry complex relationships to their object of comparison.

Closely related to the simplicity or complexity of a comparison is the dimension of the similitude or incongruity of the events compared. Literal comparisons are usually drawn from events which seem so obviously worthy of comparison that meaning can be quickly grasped. Thus in praising the productivity of American agriculture, Secretary of Agriculture Freeman uses the familiar comparison of agricultural productivity in Russia and the United States: "One agricultural worker in our country feeds 27 people. In the Soviet Union he feeds six people." [11] The fact that the comparison flatters the United States and discredits the Soviet Union adds credibility to the reference for an American audience. Given the drama of great power confrontation between the United States and Russia since World War II, the use of Russia as a point of comparison—in education, wealth, productivity, military power, medical care, housing, transportation, civil liberties, press freedom—has almost automatic interest for an American audience. As the educator Robert Hutchins observed in reviewing a new book on the USSR, "If we weren't getting ahead of Russia, or falling behind her, how would we know where we were?"

By contrast with the similitudes presented in literal comparisons, the comparison in metaphor gains its power from the superficial incongruity or dissimilarity of the events compared—as in the comparison of nations with scorpions. Indeed, it was the ability to find likeness in dissimilar events that Aristotle called the "most important point" for the poet, and "a mark of genius."

The incongruous comparison has the obvious merit of surprise, but its use—as in the metaphors of poetry—is seldom found in public speeches. One may puzzle over the poet's line, read it aloud, and read it again, and find in it a source of expanding meaning. But speakers seldom toy with obscurity. They do seek the rhetorical merit of the unexpected, however, in their use of comparison. To picture the "advance of civilization" by comparing the modern American in his fallout shelter with his ancestor, the cave man, may carry ironic surprise for the listener, at least until he hears the comparison the second time, or the twenty-second time. The speaker who pictured both Russian communism and the capitalism of western Europe as "Christian heresies" looked for unexpected similarities in movements generally viewed as antithetical to one another. But the unexpected or incongruous nature of these comparisons are matters to be explained by the speaker.

The unexpected or seemingly incongruous comparison is an available

[11] Quoted in the *Democrat*, August 24, 1962.

choice for speakers but not a common choice. The comparisons which serve as major resources for the speaker are those so sanctified by common use that both the legitimacy of the comparison and its meaning are accepted and understood. Comparisons which are much used by speakers are often called "trite" or "hackneyed." They have lost their power to surprise; the only wisdom they include is received and conventional rather than new. But they are much used, and their frequency may represent a practical judgment made by speakers rather than a deficiency of imagination. The element of practical judgment in the use of well-worn comparisons is that such comparisons tend to be accepted and understood by audiences without the necessity for long explanation. They are durable artifacts of public discourse, and once a culture has accepted a metaphor, speakers will inevitably use it and use it heavily until such time as a better choice becomes available.

Popular Comparisons Reveal Conventional Wisdom

The comparisons used freely by many speakers tell us something about the conventional wisdom of their society. For example, the most successful metaphor in American public discourse since the end of World War II has been the reference to the border between Russia and western Europe as "the iron curtain." This figure began its tour of popularity after its use by Winston Churchill in a speech delivered in Fulton, Missouri, in 1948, although its use was not an invention of Churchill's. Since that time it has become a conventional shorthand reference for the Russian border. The popularity of the comparison can be readily explained: it is brief; it reflects the western view of the secretiveness, oppressiveness, and power of the Russian state; it is uncomplicated. And it is likely to remain in current use until such time as international tensions between Russia and the West change form, or until sheer boredom calls for a replacement metaphor. Other well-worn comparisons have held long tenure in American speech.

The use of references to history as a source of "lessons" for contemporary society is also common, and comparisons of contemporary society with Roman civilization, if less popular than a century ago, continue to be used. Richard Weaver has suggested that the comparison of America with Rome was a standard topic of nineteenth-century public speaking, especially in ceremonial speaking. Audiences "knew" without proof or detailed explanation that Rome fell because her citizens became lazy and sinful. Thus sloth and vice threaten any civilization. We are no longer so certain of why Rome fell, so the comparison of Rome and the United States lacks the easy resonance it once held for audiences. But Roman history is still commonly taught in American secondary schools, and speakers still find that Rome fell for a number of reasons convenient to the speaker: from sloth or vice, welfare statism or militarism, materialism or Christianity, paganism or hedonism, ambition, or whatever else it is that the speaker wishes to excoriate. The comparison has become decorative, for the most part, rather than illuminative. That the comparison is still used indicates the extent to which language is a convention of a culture and the extent to which American culture remains self-conscious about the "causes" which nurture national power or lead to its decline.

Comparisons Reveal the Speaker's Assumptions

Comparisons in common use by many speakers inform us about the society receptive to such comparisons. Those used by a particular speaker may inform us concerning his characteristic "perspective," or manner of thought. Edmund Burke, the famous eighteenth-century English parliamentarian and essayist, had an often-noted affinity for "organic" comparisons. Society was an organism, to be likened to a tree or a living body; one should be slow to tamper with any part of it lest he affect other parts. To be sure, a diseased limb should be treated and in extreme cases removed. But one does not operate quickly or casually on any aspect of the social system any more than one operates quickly or casually on a living person. Burke's organic view of society is usually considered indicative of his conservatism, his affection for tradition. It is to be contrasted with the radicalism inherent in viewing society as a machine, constantly in need of human repair and improvement, and susceptible to useful experimentation or replacement.

The dramatistic potential of comparison and contrast is apparent. The conflict between good and evil, inherent in any morality drama, remains one of the great organizing principles for perceiving the drama of human events. Wars become dramatic, which may account for their literally fatal fascination, by providing all contestants with a dramatic conflict between absolute good (our side), and absolute evil (the other side). The drama of a courtroom trial or a political contest is heightened when the comparison presented seems to present a conflict between good and evil.

THE PATTERN OF DEFINITION

The speaker's acts of definition are designed to secure an interpretation of the meaning of a word or statement which will be useful to the speaker's intention. In broad perspective, any purposive action by a speaker is implicitly an act of definition. That is, the speaker can achieve his purpose only if his auditors interpret the meaning of his utterance as he intends. However, we are not concerned here with the sense in which all discourse involves the problem of meaning, and thus of definition. Rather our concern is with the use of explicit acts of definition by the speaker as a pattern of support for achieving the speaker's purpose.

The Form of Definition

An act of definition makes use of one set of words to clarify the meaning of another term or utterance. The act thus presupposes a term to be defined, traditionally known as the *definiendum,* and a set of words known as the *definiens,* which is directed toward clarifying the meaning of the *definiendum.* The action of the *definiens* can, of course, be supplied by a picture or chart, or by a speaker's pointing to some event. Thus the adult who says to a child, "that is a *dog,*" while pointing to a member of the species in question, is engaged in an incomplete act of definition.

The general form of a definition, then, is expressable in the formula "A" means "B," with "A" standing for the *definiendum* and "B" for the *definiens.* Any pattern of definition in a public speech will take this form, although the ambiguity of the word "means" guarantees that speakers will carry out their acts to clarify meaning in a variety of ways.

Variant Methods of Definition

In Aristotelian practice, the act of relating *definiendum* and *definiens* was an act of classification. That is, one clarified the meaning of the name for an event by first placing the event in a larger class of events to which it belonged, and then by describing the characteristics of the event in question which differentiated it from other events in the same class. Thus one came to "know" the meaning of a term by knowing the *differentiae* associated with it, or the criterial attributes of the class designated by the term. For example, if a speaker says, "A platypus is a duck-billed, egg-laying mammal," he has placed the class called "platypus" in the genus "mammal," and has identified some of the criterial attributes setting platypuses apart from other mammals. If a listener already knows that mammals are by definition warm-blooded animals that nurse their offspring, he knows an additional group of criterial attributes for the platypus. The definition hasn't moved far toward classification of the species "platypus," but the process of giving meaning to the term has been started.

Acts of definition through classification have both epistemological and rhetorical limitations. Of the epistemological limitation, we shall say little other than to observe that conceptualizing a process such as "metabolism" as a "species of events belonging to a larger genus of events" may not be a particularly accurate or informative way of getting at the meaning of "metabolism." The rhetorical limitation of formal definition, however, is a matter central to our understanding of the variety of ways speakers develop patterns of definition in the enforcement of their purpose or statement.

We speak of the "rhetorical limitation" of formal definition to point out that this pattern may not be universally adapted either to the speaker's purpose, or to the particular meaning he wishes an audience to discover in a given *definiendum*. For example, while a speaker lecturing on the nature of some member of the animal kingdom may well find a traditional exercise in genus-species differentiation well adapted to his purpose, a speaker seeking to explain the meaning of the term "alienation" in modern literary theory may have little need to try to describe a genus of events of which "alienation" is one species, and much more need to describe a theory of social structure which permits us to speak of some members of a society as "alienated." In the process of defining his central term, the speaker may find it useful to give examples of alienated groups (definition by example); he may introduce a synonym such as "estrangement," hoping that the overtones of the synonym will illuminate his *definiendum;* he may try to show how various writers or speakers have used the term "alienation," using their authority to suggest that there is a reputable and discriminating meaning in the term; or he may define the term by showing the use to which it may be put in the analysis of literature or in the analysis of social movements, thus defining his term much in the manner of one who defines a "hammer" as an instrument used to drive nails. None of these verbal processes achieves a formal classification and differentiation of the term "alienation," but each or all may establish differentiae which assist an audience in interpreting the meaning of the term in a way relevant to the speaker's intention.

Reported and Stipulated Definitions

A useful distinction may be drawn between acts of definition based on a *report* of the meaning commonly given to a particular *definiendum,* and acts which *stipulate* a particular definition for purposes of a given discourse. In a reported definition the speaker seeks to assure his listeners that he is employing a term in the sense common to the usage of their community. In a stipulated definition, the speaker acts to limit the meaning of a given term in a way congruent with the purpose of his discourse. Thus a speaker might report: "The term 'culture' is used commonly in at least two senses: First, as the sum-total of all of the behavior patterns manifest in a given society, and second, as the behaviors and values of persons with cultivated intellectual and aesthetic capacities." The speaker might then stipulate: "For purposes of this discussion, I shall use the term 'culture' only in the second sense." Stipulation gives the speaker a powerful instrument for narrowing the expansive referents which get attached to words through everyday usage. But it can also be used to extend the application of a term to events not normally part of its meaning. For example, a speaker might report: "The term 'imprinting' is ordinarily used to refer to behavior patterns laid down in the nervous system of animals as inherited, genetic systems. Thus birds of a given species will migrate to a given destination not because they have been taught to migrate, but because nature imprinted this response to their environment in their nervous system." The speaker then stipulates: "Today, I shall extend the usual meaning of the term, and speak of education itself as a process of imprinting certain response patterns in the nervous systems of children."

Definitions Concerned With Cognitive and Affective Meanings

The meaning of a term may be spoken of as having both a cognitive and an affective dimension. These dimensions are sometimes described as the denotative and connotative meanings of words. Thus, as part of its meaning, a term or utterance refers us denotatively to certain objects or events; it also disposes us, connotatively, toward certain attitudes we associate with those events. For example, the term "democracy" presumably denotes a given type of political-social system; for most Americans it also connotes an attitude of affirmation or positive value. The concern of the public speaker with the affective meaning of his utterance exists whether or not the speaker uses explicit acts of definition as a pattern of enforcement. But this concern extends to his acts of definition, which include efforts to control not only the denotations listeners will ascribe to his terms, but also their affective response. The curious reciprocal relationship of *definiendum* and *definiens* in definition by example illustrates the interplay of cognitive and affective meanings. For example, in President John F. Kennedy's book, *Profiles in Courage,* we are given a series of narratives about American politicians who chose a course of action they believed to be right even at the risk of political defeat. From one point of view the examples serve as the *definiens,* giving meaning to the abstract term "courage," by defining some of the differentia of that term and evoking certain attitudes toward it. On the other hand, the term "courage," with its honorific overtones, serves as the genus for the acts described, and thus gives the meaning the writer wishes ascribed to those acts.

An Extended Pattern of Definition

To the extent that the speaker enables listeners to join him in an act of defining, he may have established powerful enforcement for his central intention. For this reason, the pattern of definition often becomes a major movement in a speech, developed strategically in relation to the speaker's purpose and the nature of the audience. Definition may also become the encompassing pattern of an entire speech. The following example is from "What is a Classic?", presented in 1944 by the noted poet T. S. Eliot as his presidential address to the Virgil Society, a British literary organization. It illustrates both the opening of an extended argument from definition and the strategic deployment of this argument.[12]

The subject which I have taken is simply the question: "What is a classic?" It is not a new question. There is, for instance, a famous essay by Ste. Beuve with this title. The pertinence of asking this question, with Virgil particularly in mind, is obvious: whatever the definition we arrive at, it cannot be one which excludes Virgil—we may say confidently that it must be one which will expressly reckon with him.

But before I go farther, I should like to dispose of certain prejudices and anticipate certain misunderstandings. I do not aim to supersede, or to outlaw, any use of the word "classic" which precedent has made permissible. The word has, and will continue to have, several meanings in several contexts: . . . when we speak of *The Fifth Form at St. Dominic's* as a classic of schoolboy fiction, no one should expect one to apologize. And there is a very interesting book called *A Guide to the Classics*, which tells you how to pick the Derby winner. On other occasions, I permit myself to mean by "the classics," either Latin and Greek literature *in toto,* or the greatest authors of those languages, as the context indicates. And, finally, I think that the account of the classic which I propose to give here should remove it from the area of the antithesis between "classic" and "romantic"—a pair of terms belonging to literary politics, and therefore arousing winds of passion which I ask Aeolus, on this occasion, to contain in the bag.

This leads me to my next point. By the terms of the classic-romantic controversy, to call any work of art "classical," implies either the highest praise or the most contemptuous abuse, according to the party to which one belongs. It implies certain particular merits or faults: either the perfection of form or the absolute zero of frigidity. But I want to define one kind of art, and am not concerned that it is absolutely and in every respect

[12] T. S. Eliot, *On Poetry and Poets* (New York: Farrar, Straus, and Cudahy, Inc., 1957), pp. 52–74.

better or *worse* than another kind. I shall enumerate certain qualities which I should expect the classic to display. But I do not say that, if a literature is to be great literature, it must have any one author, or any one period, in which all these qualities are manifested. If, as I think, they are all to be found in Virgil, that is not to assert that he is the greatest poet who ever wrote—such an assertion about any poet seems to me meaningless—and it is certainly not to assert that Latin literature is greater than any other literature. . . .

If there is one word on which we can fix, which will suggest the maximum of what I mean by the term "a classic," it is the word *maturity*. I shall distinguish between the universal classic, like Virgil, and the classic which is only such in relation to the other literature in its own language, or according to the view of life of a particular period. A classic can only occur when a civilization is mature; when a language and a literature are mature; and it must be the work of a mature mind. It is the importance of that civilization and of that language, as well as the comprehensiveness of the mind of the individual poet, which gives the universality. To define *maturity* without assuming that the hearer already knows what it means, is almost impossible: let us say then that if we are properly mature, as well as educated persons, we can recognize maturity in a civilization and in a literature, as we do in the other human beings whom we encounter. To make the meaning of maturity really apprehensible—indeed even to make it acceptable—to the immature, is perhaps impossible. But if we are mature we either recognize maturity immediately, or come to know it on more intimate acquaintance. No reader of Shakespeare, for instance, can fail to recognize, increasingly as he himself grows up, the gradual ripening of Shakespeare's mind: even a less developed reader can perceive the rapid development of Elizabethan literature and drama as a whole, from early Tudor crudity to the plays of Shakespeare, and perceive a decline in the work of Shakespeare's successors. We can also observe, upon a little conversance, that the plays of Christopher Marlowe exhibit a greater maturity of mind and of style than the plays which Shakespeare wrote at the same age. . . .

This extended passage, from the opening movements of Eliot's address, illustrates the gradual unfolding of a pattern of definition. The speaker begins abruptly, but in a manner designed to assure the members of the Virgil Society of the relevance of his subject to their common object of interest. He continues by clearing away usages of his key term which would interfere with a proper grasp of his intention and with the suggestion that the ultimate meaning of "classic," as he will define it, is illustrated by the works of Virgil. Eliot then moves to place the meaning of "classic" within the concept of maturity, and to begin unfolding the aspects of maturity which enter into the definition of classic. As the speech proceeds, the definition of maturity becomes increasingly an instrument for the speaker's comment on a variety of writers; on the state of the English language, its literature, and the civilization it represents; on the work of poets within such a language; and on the significance of Virgil's achievements to their work. The pattern of definition is thus a major enforcement to the speaker's complete intention.

Verbal Warfare Over Definitions

The appropriateness of giving a particular name to a particular event is essentially a matter of definition. But since the name given to an event may influence the meaning of the event, public speakers give much attention to justifying their acts of naming, and inevitably become engaged in verbal warfare over the propriety of such acts.

For example, congressional debate often involves the question of the "constitutionality" of a proposed legislative act. Presumably if it can be demonstrated that a piece of legislation is unconstitutional, then that law should not be passed regardless of its other merits or defects. And presumably if the proposed act were unequivocally unconstitutional (which is seldom the case) its passage would simply invite negation by the Supreme Court. The argument involves definition; the speaker must seek to show what some portion of the Constitution means and to show that the proposed piece of legislation either conflicts with or is permitted by the Constitution. Thus used, the argument from definition permits the conclusion either that a proposed piece of legislation is constitutional and should be considered on its merits, or that it is unconstitutional and therefore unacceptable regardless of other merits or defects.

Such a pattern of enforcement has been a common feature of American congressional debate and political speaking. In his famous Cooper Union address of 1860, Abraham Lincoln raised for discussion the issue of the constitutionality of federal legislation designed to control the spread of slavery into new territories.[13] The issue had been hotly debated between Lincoln and Senator Douglas in the earlier Lincoln-Douglas debates in Illinois. Lincoln believed that federal legislation controlling the spread of slavery was constitutional, but he also believed the issue important enough to deserve careful treatment in his speech. In the Cooper Union address he argued that the vast majority of the signers of the Constitution had demonstrated both in voting practice and in statements that they believed federal legislation controlling the spread of slavery to be constitutional. None of these au-

[13] Abraham Lincoln, "Address at Cooper Union." The full text is to be found in Wayland Maxfield Parrish and Marie Hochmuth, *American Speeches* (New York: Longmans, Green and Company, 1954), pp. 284–304.

thors of the Constitution, moreover, had ever suggested a contrary meaning. Lincoln's argument was carefully developed with thorough evidence. By disposing of the argument over constitutionality, he could then go on in his speech to examine other arguments brought against the federal legislation he favored.

An argument from definition may be worked out with as much attention to evidence as Lincoln's discussion of the meaning of the Constitution. It may also be compressed into a single assertion. The "naming" of an event attended by the assumption that the name praises or blames, and that it implies certain conclusions, is an implicit argument from definition. Thus in a televised speech opposing the so-called King-Anderson bill, a proposal for financing medical care for the aged through social security, Dr. Edward Annis observed: "First I read the title—the 'Health Insurance Benefits Act.' Is it genuine insurance? No, it is not. The Supreme Court has held more than once that the Social Security system is not an insurance system. It is the way we have chosen to cushion the general economic needs of old people in this country. The Social Security tax collected from those under 65 pays benefits to those over 65. Why not be honest about it? I say any health program that calls itself insurance, and isn't, has to be bad to begin with. . . ." [14] Dr. Annis was obviously going to some trouble to point out that an act that calls itself "insurance" is not really "insurance." The problem is one of definition, and since the word "insurance" can be defined in various ways one might wonder over the quibble. Presumably Dr. Annis asserted his point because he believed that labeling the act as "insurance" constitutes some kind of argument in its favor. The argument from definition in this case would be implicitly as follows. "It is desirable that we 'insure' ourselves against unexpected costs.The King-Anderson bill is a form of insurance against unexpected medical costs. Therefore the King-Anderson bill is a desirable action." More simply we could observe that insurance is a "good" word and that things properly classified as insurance enjoy favorable response. Having sought to argue that the bill cannot be properly defined as insurance Dr. Annis can be expected to tell us what he thinks the bill "really is," and to give it a name which argues for rejection of the bill.

Because "naming" a person or event when the name arouses favorable or unfavorable response in an audience is an implicit argument by definition, it is not surprising to find political speaking filled with examples of highly intentional definition, as well as with discussion of the "proper meaning" to be assigned to given terms. The most common

[14] Dr. Edward Roland Annis, "Medical Care Through Social Security," *Vital Speeches,* June 15, 1962, p. 518.

terms used in recent decades for labeling the general orientations of politicians are *radical, liberal, conservative* and *reactionary*. Distinguishing the meaning of these terms is a tricky business at best, and the terms are more often used for their effect than discussed in terms of their meaning. Presumably the terms "radical" and "reactionary" label extremists in political life and are therefore damaging to the reputation of the person carrying the label. Thus political conservatives often apply the label of "radical" to their more formidable political opponents, and political liberals similarly apply the label "reactionary" to their opponents. Equally interesting is the effort of conservative and liberal spokesmen to define the labels they accept in a way calculated to enhance the reputation of these terms. In American political life in the 1930's, the term "liberal" seemed widely accepted by the voting public as the proper term for a politician who had energy, imagination, and humanitarian instincts. The term "conservative" carried less favorable connotations. During the long tenure of President Franklin Roosevelt, Republican spokesmen often sought to escape the label of "conservative" by alleging that they were the true liberals, in the tradition of Jefferson and Lincoln, whereas their so-called liberal opponents were really radicals or possibly reactionaries. In the 1950's however, many of the so-called conservatives changed strategy; they began to wear the label "conservative" proudly, to speak at great length on the meaning of conservatism and to attack the idea of liberalism. "If I am to be called 'conservative'," they seemed to say, "I will define the term in a way that casts favor upon me. And if my opponents are to be called 'liberal,' I will show that the definition of that term reflects unfavorably upon them." Such political warfare may seem calculated to create public confusion about the meaning of the words in question. But when we perceive the sense in which "names" become implicit arguments from definition, we are able to understand the significance of the warfare and its inevitability.

ADDITIONAL PATTERNS OF ENFORCEMENT

As suggested earlier, one can produce a considerable list of the forms of enforcement found in public speeches. We have limited our treatment, however, to a few major forms. We shall conclude this exploration with a brief examination of two additional forms.

Authority as Enforcement

Speakers use references to authorities for purposes as diverse as the embellishment of their own reputations, or as a major basis for claiming truth or significance for some part of their utterance. Thus, it is common to find speakers engaging in the practice of name dropping: "After my discussion with Mayor Brandt in Berlin, I had an opportunity to discuss some of the same problems with General Lucius Clay, at a reception at the American Embassy." Through name dropping the speaker may hope to establish some claim to being thought of as an important person with unusual sources of information. He may also wish to give his audience access to the ostensible source of some of his ideas.

Presumably the speaker enhances the force of any citation of evidence or any line of argument by crediting its source to a person who is well regarded by the audience, particularly if the person seems qualified to speak with authority on the subject at hand. Lincoln, Jefferson, and Washington—the most generally prestigious figures of American political history—serve as all-purpose authorities for their ideas on government. The common speaking practice of "discovering" what Lincoln or Washington would have thought about some current piece of legislation, circa 1968, is a somewhat disreputable method of enforcing an idea. But the frequency with which speakers make this kind of reference is tribute to the assumed power of these names. The names of Theodore Roosevelt and Woodrow Wilson show signs of attaining a similarly generalized level of prestige; Jackson and F. D. Roosevelt would be names resonant enough for Democrats, while Hoover and Eisenhower have similar potential for Republicans. On the other hand, the authority of President Polk would have little value to a speaker unless Polk's ideas were in themselves unusually memorable. The opinion of President Harding, because of his historical reputation as a notably inept President, would only diminish an idea. An authority clearly attractive to a given audience sets up an implicit pattern of reasoning. That is, "those things believed true by Lincoln are clearly true; Lincoln believed thus and so; hence by definition thus and so becomes true."

Speakers often face the problem of using qualified authorities who are unknown to an audience. Physicist A. P. Gumnowits, to take a hypothetical example, may be as qualified as any man in the world to comment on the possible effect of high-altitude nuclear explosions on radio communications, but an audience might not be much impressed unless the speaker made Gumnowits' reputation clear. Hence, one finds speakers taking the time to "puff" the reputation of their authorities. "Gumnowits is the present head of the Nuclear Propulsion Laboratory in Jamaica, and is credited by fellow physicists with knowing more about this problem than any man living."

An interesting feature of American public speaking is the extensive use of "public opinion" as authority. In a culture devoted to the hypothesis that the "people" are more often right than wrong, it makes some sense to ask what a majority of the people, as identified by public opinion pollsters, think about Vietnam, the invasion of Cuba, "right to work" laws, or reforestation. In one sense, the extensive activity of the pollsters in contemporary America has given speakers a new resource; in another sense, poll data stands as an embarrassment to speakers who are rather free and easy with references. Prior to the polls, the phrases "America believes—the people believe—everyone believes—all right-thinking people believe—" had little to commend them other than their pious acknowledgment of popular opinion. Now such phrases may run head-on into the evidence that 42 percent of a sample of the people believed one thing; 38 percent believed the opposite; 20 percent didn't know what they believed; and 96 percent didn't have enough information on the subject to warrant holding any opinion.

Argument From Sign

Certain events in nature stand as *signs* of the presence or possible presence of other events. Thus high fever is taken as a sign of illness; changes in the foliage of trees are taken as signs of changes in the season of the year; and newspapers in northern climates dutifully report each fall such signs of a hard winter ahead as thick fur on the squirrels and the early departure of robins for the southland. Fully expressed, an argument from sign states simply that the presence of event "A" implies that event "B" either has or will occur at some level of probability. If the relationship between the occurrence of event "A" and event "B" has been systematically investigated, the argument from sign can take the form of a statement of a correlation between the two events; indeed the logical form of a statement about a sign and a statement about correlation is the same. But speakers work with many kinds of signs which are accepted as meaningful by their listeners, but which have not been subjected to the systematic investigation which would permit a precise or mathematical formulation of the relationship between two or more events.

In more complex patterns, a series of signs, none of which would have particular importance in and of itself, may when taken together imply some degree of truth. Thus a series of signs or circumstantial details may be collected as proof that "A" committed a crime, or that the coming winter will be a hard one, or that it's time to buy stocks.

Argument from sign is used when the interpretation of complex data proves difficult. For example, investigation shows that people who score high on scholastic aptitude tests are more likely to succeed in college than those who score low. But the correlation between these two events is a rather weak one and is not sufficient to predict with any great certainty that a particular student will succeed in college. Thus the careful interpreter of aptitude test scores may turn to such language as "John's test scores indicate that he may have some difficulty succeeding in college." In like manner the massive investigations of economic data turn up relationships among economic events which permit economists to speak of certain "economic indicators which suggest that our economy is headed for a recession, unless. . . ."

Certain kinds of argument from sign appear in public discourse at given times with such persistence as to receive a particular name. For example, since World War II considerable public discussion in the United States has been directed to whether a particular person was or was not a Communist, or a Communist sympathizer. The discussion involved argument from definition, marked by unusual fluidity in the definitions provided; it also involved much argument from sign. One of these arguments grew out of the popular adage that "birds of a feather flock together" and alleged that a person associating with known Communists, or holding membership in organizations with Communist sympathies, should be regarded as a Communist. The argument was from sign: association with Communists was held to be a sign of Communist affiliation or sympathy. Since the charge was an extraordinarily serious one, the argument drew frequent attack. It was alleged, for example, that the argument from sign in this instance was as weak as the argument that because policemen associate with known criminals they must therefore be criminals. The argument also received its own title, "guilt by association." Although often misused, or extravagantly used in character appraisal, argument from sign remains the major form for such appraisals. That is to say, we do not measure directly a man's honesty or courage or perseverance, but we do observe signs in his behavior or appearance which seem to us indicative of his character. Napoleon was said to believe that a long nose was indicative of ability in a military officer. All of us use aspects of another person's speech as significant signs of his nature, character, or personality.

In this latter sense, the utterance of a speaker, considered as a whole or in its separate aspects, provides listeners with signs about the speaker's character. We are judged by our speech. Therefore it is not surprising that public speakers choose to incorporate into their utterance a variety of signs which may be helpful in winning audience approval. Name dropping, a practice alluded to under the use of authority, becomes a form of sign of the speaker's prominence. A speaker's allusions to literature may be taken as a sign of his erudition, even in cases in which the allusion is obscure to the listeners. References to the Bible or properly affirmative references to God may be taken as signs of the speaker's religious inclinations, and these in turn are widely held to be signs of virtue. The speaker produces signs of identification for his audience: references to his childhood on the farm for farmers, of his years of teaching to teachers, or of his affection for the old family doctor to an audience of medical practitioners.

It is also sobering, and perhaps encouraging, to realize that the speaker who engages in unusually malicious utterance, who gets his information garbled, or who produces shoddy arguments as though they were of purest merit is also producing signs to those of his listeners who are knowledgeable—signs of his malice, ignorance, and lack of judgment.

We shall have further occasion to discuss the substantial significance of the speech as a sign later in this book. We here observe the extraordinary extent to which the form of enforcement by sign is embedded in the speaker's utterance.

SUMMARY

Forms of enforcement are found within the action of the whole speech. They are the forms by which the speaker amplifies, elaborates, or proves his statement or position; and they include forms that have as their purpose the tasks of clarification, interest, and persuasion.

We have examined four major patterns of enforcement in public speeches: the forms of cause, consequence, comparison, and definition. In addition we have looked briefly at the uses of authority and signs in the enforcement of ideas. In this examination we have observed some of the transformations possible for each form as it is used in conjunction with the varying materials and purposes of the speaker and used in relationship to the expectations of audiences. The practices of many speakers in using certain patterns of enforcement inform us about the language habits of audiences.

Patterns of enforcement may be examined in a number of dimensions. The same patterns appear in discourse about the impersonal forces of nature, and about the qualities, purposes, actions, and responsibilities of human beings. They may be used for coldly scientific exposition in which evidence is interpreted according to close standards of verifiability, or in a variety of dramatistic ways which interpret history in terms of human conflict and responsibility. The forms may be used to simplify the complexities of experience, or to mirror complexity. They may find their link with an audience through the surface plausibility or clarity that they offer, or by exploiting audience interest in the implausible. In all cases the patterns indicate the ways in which speakers and listeners in a particular society seek common meanings for their world.

FOR FURTHER STUDY

SPEAKING, WRITING, OR DISCUSSION EXERCISES

1. Report on the position or positions taken by a public speaker in one or several of his important public utterances. Describe both the content of his position and the tone and attitude incorporated into development of the position. Describe the position in terms of the choices on position discussed in Chapter 3.
2. Analyze a public issue which has been treated by some speakers in terms of problem-solution analysis, and by other speakers in terms of value-application analysis. Show how these different perspectives for examining an issue may lead to quite different positions on proper public policy. Such issues as federal aid to education, governmental health insurance, governmental action on birth control, welfare legislation, civil rights legislation, tax policy, etc., have been subjected to these differing perspectives.
3. Prepare a short speech or essay based on one of the following patterns of enforcement:
   a. An analysis of the causes of a problem, leading to identification of the appropriate steps toward solution.
   b. An extrapolation from a current social trend which leads to a prediction that certain undesirable consequences will occur unless countersteps are taken now.
   c. Comparison and contrast of two events or institutions of the same general class, as two paintings, two novels or plays, two musical selections, two political systems, two educational systems, etc. The analysis should lead to evaluation of the merits of the events or institutions compared.
4. Describe an example of causal analysis which seems to you plausible but unsound, and an example of causal analysis which seems less plausible but more justified. Make clear the grounds on which you assign judgments of plausibility and soundness.
5. Study an important ceremonial speech and identify the values the speaker seeks to clarify or praise. Describe the method used by the speaker to evoke admiration for a given value.
6. Topics for discussion, or for use in speaking or writing exercises:
   a. Present an analysis of a contemporary political action organization, or

political party, in terms of the complex of positions taken by this organization on public issues.

b. Analyze a speech or essay on a controversial issue to determine the author's position, giving particular attention to the way in which the speaker modifies, limits, or extends his position.

READINGS

1. Chapter 3 considers the framework of issues within which expository, persuasive, and ceremonial speakers choose particular positions. For different approaches to this idea see:
   a. Lee S. Hultzen, "Status in Deliberative Analysis," in Donald C. Bryant, ed., *The Rhetorical Idiom* (Ithaca: Cornell University Press, 1958), pp. 97–123.
   b. Douglas Ehninger and Wayne Brockreide, *Decision by Debate* (New York: Dodd, Mead and Company, 1963), Chapter 7, "The Anatomy of a Dispute," pp. 81–97.
   c. Cicero, *De Inventione,* 1.8–14.
2. For various treatments of the structure or arrangement of the whole speech see:
   a. James H. McBurney and Ernest J. Wrage, *The Art of Good Speaking* (New Jersey: Prentice-Hall, Inc., 1953), pp. 225–244, 248–253, 275–278, 290–299. Includes discussion of the structure of discourse serving the functions of inquiry, information, and advocacy.
   b. Alan H. Monroe, *Principles and Types of Speech* (Chicago: Scott, Foresman and Co., 1962), pp. 280–303. Presents a generalized schema for the organization of speeches according to audience needs.
   c. John F. Wilson and Carroll C. Arnold, *Public Speaking as a Liberal Art* (Boston: Allyn and Bacon, Inc., 1964), pp. 191–221. Presents a variety of organizing principles for developing speech structure.
3. The discussion of the "dialectical" view of experience in Chapter 7 suggests the possible inevitability of continuing public controversy over certain kinds of assertions. For development of this thesis see:
   a. W. B. Gallie, "Essentially Contested Concepts," in Max Black, ed., *The Importance of Language* (New Jersey: Prentice-Hall, Inc., 1962), pp. 121–146.
4. For various treatments of the concept of the enforcement of ideas see:
   a. Aristotle, *Rhetoric,* translated and edited by Lane Cooper (New York: Appleton-Century, Crofts, Inc., 1960), 1.2 (on the modes of persuasion); 2.23–24 (on 28 demonstrative and refutative topics, and nine "sham" lines of argument).
   b. Edward P. Corbett, *Classical Rhetoric for the Modern Student* (New York: Oxford University Press, 1965), pp. 94–141.
5. For discussion of the form and uses of definitions:
   a. Harold C. Martin and Richard M. Ohmann, *The Logic and Rhetoric*

of Exposition (New York: Holt, Rinehart, and Winston, Inc., 1963), pp. 9–44.

b. Charles L. Stevenson, "Persuasive Definitions," in Martin Steinmann, Jr., ed., *New Rhetorics* (New York: Charles Scribner's Sons, 1967), pp. 214–225.

6. Chapter 5 presented a number of patterns for the enforcement of ideas and commented on the variety of ways in which speakers use such patterns. When speakers enforce assertions which may be controversial for listeners, the adequacy of the speaker's enforcement as a demonstration or "proof" of his assertions may be raised by his listeners. Forms of enforcement used by speakers are therefore frequently criticized in terms of their formal or material sufficiency. For discussion of the grounds on which the sufficiency of arguments or forms of enforcement may be criticized, see:

a. Ehninger and Brockreide, *Decision by Debate,* Chapter 12, "Detecting Deficiencies of Proof," pp. 168–188.

b. Albury Castell, "Analyzing a Fallacy," in Haig A. Bosmajian, ed., *Readings in Speech* (New York: Harper and Row, 1965), pp. 174–192.

SECTION III

Synoptic Perspectives

Section III examines three perspectives on public speaking which lead to the most comprehensive questions about the effect and worth of the speaker's action. These perspectives are called "synoptic," using the word in the sense that each perspective invites consideration of the greatest possible range of information about the speaker's public role, his relationships with his audience, and the ethical merit of his action. Thus while the materials of Section II moved analytically toward examination of progressively smaller units within discourse, the materials of Section III move toward the largest and most difficult questions of choice confronting the public speaker.

Section III is presented in three chapters: "Style: The Speaker's Manner"; "The Speaker's Audience"; and "The Problem of Ethics." It should be pointed out that the designation of the chapter on style as a synoptic perspective is ambiguous if one considers the history of this topic. The study of style has led many writers to consider the smallest details of a speaker's choice and ordering of language, and thus to engage in the most analytical treatment of discourse. We shall give some attention to this kind of analysis in Chapter 6, but the major thrust of the chapter will be toward a conception of the speaker's style as the summation of his entire manner.

Style: The Speaker's Manner

*Style . . . is the last acquirement of the educated mind;
it is also the most useful.*

—ALFRED NORTH WHITEHEAD

STYLE AS A MANNER OF ADDRESS

Physicist J. Robert Oppenheimer spoke in 1948 on the matter of style:

The problem of doing justice to the implicit, the imponderable, and the
unknown is . . . not unique to politics. It is always with us in science,
it is with us in the most trivial of human affairs, and it is one of the great
problems of writing and of all forms of art. The means by which it is solved
is sometimes called style. It is style which complements affirmation with
limitation and humility; it is style which makes it possible to act effectively,
but not absolutely; it is style, which, in the domain of foreign policy
enables us to find a harmony between the pursuit of ends essential to us and
the regard for the views, the sensibilities, the aspirations of those to whom
the problem may appear in another light; it is style which is the deference
that action pays to uncertainty; it is above all style through which power
defers to reason.[1]

Oppenheimer spoke of style as the total manner of man's action toward his environment, and toward those with whom he sought relationship. He spoke also of *a style*—the manner that he thought essential to
man's purposes in the twentieth century. His conception of style is
broad, and yet no narrower conception does justice to the sense in which
a man's manner of address comprehends at once all the particularities of
his actions, and goes beyond these particularities to an image of the man
himself.

The tragic assassination of President John F. Kennedy in November,
1963, produced a public response to the man that gave sharp emphasis

[1] J. Robert Oppenheimer, *The Open Mind* (New York: Simon and Schuster,
1955), p. 146.

to the sense in which "manner" can become at once the most abstract and concrete, the most elusive and most enduring impress of a speaker's public utterance and public actions.

John Cogley, who called himself ". . . an almost scandalously faithful supporter of John F. Kennedy . . ." had this to say of the sources of his admiration:

. . . my sympathy for the President had something to do with style, the most enduring of his qualities. It may be true, as one national columnist recently pointed out, that a preference for style over substance is a deadly political weakness. However in Kennedy's case I never thought of style in such terms. The style of Kennedy was the man Kennedy, and, I believe, it had a great deal to do with the substance of his leadership.

The Cuban confrontation, for example, depended mightily on his style. Any suggestion of either unsureness or bellicosity on his part could have been fatal. Making Khrushchev's capitulation possible, saving the loser's face, so to speak, was another exercise of the Kennedy style which proved to have great substantial significance; though the President tested the limits of deterrence, he did not try to test the limits of human perversity. . . .

The sudden realization of this style had affected us as a people, and how we would miss it, accounted, I believe for the phenomenal sense of loss at the time of his death.

It is no use trying to say what I mean by the Kennedy style. Style is not something one can define exactly, or prescribe for another. . . . It has something to do with taste, something to do with restraint and control, and something to do, finally, with grace and gallantry.[2]

One examines this reaction to the Kennedy style with a growing sense of the importance and difficulty of the concept. Pursued in relation to any particular speaker, the concept of *style* encompasses half a hundred or more particularities. The image of a man speaking is an image of total manner: of details of voice and its use; of appearance and manner of standing and moving; of language and the manner of choosing and ordering words; of topics talked about and the tone and attitude of that talk. If we say of Sir Winston Churchill that he was a bold, colorful, and imaginative leader, our comment may be partly grounded in details of his appearance and the management of his voice and action; partly in his choice of vivid and dramatic language; partly in his capacity to formulate bold positions on public policy. Whatever the range of detail going into our judgment, we perceive his style ultimately as a unified image of the man. The speaker's style is thus his manifest personality and it controls the way others will know him as a public person.

[2] John Cogley, "J. F. K.—A Final Word," *The Commonweal*, LXXX (May 8, 1964), 191.

Style as the Management of Both Language and Delivery

In defining style as the total manner of the speaker's address, we are expanding the concept to include both consideration of the speaker's language and of his delivery. Traditionally the idea of style has been limited to matters of choosing and ordering words, as in Jonathan Swift's definition of style as a matter of "proper words in proper places." The distinction between "language" and "delivery" is reasonably clear if one thinks of "language" as having to do with that part of the speaker's action which can be readily represented in print, and "delivery" as those aspects of vocal and physical symbolism which enforce or modify meaning, and which are only implicit in a printed text. But while one can distinguish the concepts of "language" and "delivery" as aspects of a speaker's action, the concept of style properly calls attention to speech as a single, unified human action. One may observe, for example, that a speaker's language reveals simultaneously the information and ideas he wishes to share with listeners, and aspects of his own personality—his attitudes toward his subject matter and listeners, his energy, his simplicity or ornateness, and so forth. A speaker's delivery is an equally complex symbolic action: it enforces and shapes the information and ideas presented, and it reveals information about the speaker himself. A speaker's style ultimately provides listeners with an image of the speaker himself, and this image is an interpretation of the expressive symbolism of both language and delivery.

VARIANT APPROACHES TO STYLE

While the ultimate purpose of this chapter is a unified view of style as "total manner of address," we can best reach this goal by examining three approaches to the study of style. The first of these is a traditional approach to style as a matter of choosing and ordering words to achieve certain qualities thought to be "good" or useful in speaking or writing. This approach is only inferentially concerned with the concept of "total manner," as perceived by listeners or readers. The second approach to be developed is one which examines style in terms of certain "dimensions of manner" which listeners perceive in the address of speakers. This perspective is useful in revealing the general range of stylistic choices speakers have available. The third approach will examine the concept of style as a form of role behavior developed by the speaker. This perspective gives a fully unified view of style as the source of an audience's image of the man speaking.

We shall conclude the chapter with observations about the process by which speakers may seek a useful, personal style.

TRADITIONAL ANALYSIS OF THE PROBLEM OF SELECTING AND ORDERING LANGUAGE

In limiting discussion of style to word choice and arrangement, classical rhetoricians typically set forth certain qualities that should characterize a good or effective style. Thus Aristotle in his *Rhetoric* observed that an effective style should be correct, clear, lively, and appropriate.[3] This list of precepts has been frequently modified by writers since Aristotle's time, either by the selection of different names for the qualities recommended, or by addition of other qualities such as force, economy, or vividness. But regardless of the terms selected, the effort is always one which identifies certain general qualities of style held to be good, and therefore worthy of emulation. Naming the qualities of a good style also generates names for stylistic faults. Thus, if it is commendable for a speaker's language to be correct, clear, lively, and appropriate, then it follows that one should censure the speaker whose language is incorrect, vague, dull, or inappropriate.

Such stylistic prescriptions have their uses. One may note the unusual clarity and animation of Jonathan Swift's style in *Gulliver's Travels,* and seek to account for the way he achieves such qualities. Similarly, one marks the vivid and rolling eloquence of Winston Churchill's oratory and historical writing, the economy and clarity of Abraham Lincoln's Presidential addresses, or the passion and exuberance of Wendell Phillips' public utterance. The labels designate the qualities achieved through the management of language by skilled writers and speakers. They direct our attention to the details of management which might account for the qualities. And they set goals toward which one might wish to move in the management of one's own language.

The difficulty with prescriptions is that the lists usually contain the quality of "appropriateness." The idea that a good style must be appropriate—suitable to the speaker, the subject, the audience, and the occasion—marks the essential contingency and limitation of all other prescriptions. Thus, we may concede that economy in the use of words is generally a desideratum of a good style and point to the terse eloquence of Lincoln's *Gettysburg Address,* or of Jonathan Edwards' sermons to demonstrate the potential power of economy. But we also mark the expansion of language, the redundancy, in speeches of Robert Inger-

---

[3] Aristotle, *Rhetoric,* 3.1404–41.

soll, Daniel Webster, Alfred Beveridge, or Martin Luther King. Are these latter speakers lacking in stylistic virtue, or is it rather the case that they used the greatly enlarged flow of illustrative material to immerse the listeners deeply in the drama of the great issues they treated? Prolixity, or a piling on of language, is clearly a fault if we see no purpose for the piling on. But what are we to say of abundance when it fits the purpose of the speaker, or the expectations of an audience, or when the abundance itself evokes some mood? At this point, we must take refuge in the quality of appropriateness as the universal modifier of all qualities.

To illustrate the way in which lists of precepts may be applied to the study of style, we shall select four traditional precepts and present a brief account of the particular problem in selecting and ordering words to which these precepts direct our attention. Our discussion will be brief because the literature of stylistic analysis is both extensive and readily available. Moreover, the major emphasis of this chapter will be on a somewhat more synoptic treatment of style as the total manner of the speaker's address.

Good Style Observes the Standards of Public Usage

George Campbell, who was one of the most influential of the eighteenth- and nineteenth-century British rhetoricians, set forth three criteria for determining good usage. Campbell thought that speakers and writers should prefer usage which was *national, current,* and *reputable.* These abstract criteria imply two major types of considerations affecting choice of words.

The first consideration is one of communication. In order to share meaning with an audience, a speaker must use words in the sense familiar to the audience. Campbell thought that the English nation included a community of educated people who shared common habits in the use of language, and that the student of speaking or writing should study the current practice of members of this community in order to be able to communicate easily and clearly. Thus if a speaker says, "from these data I *imply* that the moon is covered with dust," he has used the word "imply" in a sense usually reserved for the word "infer." His audience may be momentarily confused. Similarly the speaker wishing to praise the invigorating effects of steam baths who says, "a steam bath is remarkably *enervating,*" may have misled his audience completely as to his intention.

One may distinguish a national standard of usage from habits of usage peculiar to particular sections of a nation or of a given social group. The dialect held in common by members of some social group may serve admirably for communication among members of that group, but becomes inefficient and obtrusive when addressed to persons holding membership in other groups. Public speakers are commonly warned against using the familiar or specialized lexicon of their social or vocational groups when addressing a public audience including members from a variety of age groups, social groups, educational levels, and occupations. The utterance, "my feedin' hand's been bit so often than I'm near tooth-proof," may be a familiar usage for members of a particular subculture, but seems exotic or ambiguous to members of other groups. One may view Campbell's concept of a current, national standard of usage as an effort to identify the "public language" of a national community—the language familiar to the largest number of persons who carry responsibility for conducting the business of public institutions. Such usage is in one sense the dialect available for those who seek to assume public responsibility, and who therefore seek a style familiar to the largest number of persons also carrying public responsibility.

The second consideration implicit in Campbell's three criteria of good usage is that of usage as a sign of social class or status. When Campbell wrote of good usage as "reputable," he suggested that the modes of speech represented in the writing of the majority of celebrated authors could serve as the touchstone for judging reputable usage. This concept —that good usage is the usage of the best writers and speakers—is the most venerable bit of circular wisdom about style employed in instruction in composition. It is also a remarkably vague concept, and one which has produced endless argument about the proprieties of English usage. The concept is vague because the usage of celebrated speakers and writers changes through time. It is also vague because celebrated writers and speakers of any one age seldom imitate one another slavishly. This was true in Campbell's day; it is increasingly true in contemporary America. The concept is argumentative because it superimposes upon the difficult question of how people may understand one another the even more difficult question of when one man is justified in asserting that another's usage is uncultivated, wanting in taste, or disreputable. When *Webster's Third New International Dictionary* faithfully reported the different uses made of various words by Americans from many occupational and social groups, the dictionary was roundly attacked by many critics for not judging whose usage was to be preferred.

The student of public speaking needs to note the fact that social judgments are made on a basis of the sign provided by a speaker's usage; that some listeners will judge a speaker to be uneducated or uncouth if the speaker violates a precept of usage learned by the listener. For this reason a public speaker may well seek control over the public dialect, to the extent that this dialect can be known, even as he understands that some of the most commonplace forms of contemporary public usage may irritate listeners addicted to a different form. Donald Lloyd calls attention to this habit in listeners and readers:

There is at large among us today an unholy number of people who make it their business to correct the speech and writing of others. When Winston Churchill says, "It's me" in a radio address, their lips purse and murmur firmly, "It is I," and they sit down to write bitter letters to the *New York Times* about What is Happening to the English Language. Reading "I only had five dollars," they circle *only* and move it to the right of *had,* producing "I had only five dollars" with a sense of virtue that is beyond the measure of man. They are implacable enemies of "different than," of "loan" and "contact" used as verbs, and of dozens of other common expressions. They put triumphant exclamation marks in the margins of library books. They are ready to tangle the thread of any discussion by pouncing on a point of grammar.[4]

Lloyd laments that there is widespread ignorance of the way in which usage changes as speakers and writers seek to adapt language to new ways of treating reality, and he is critical of the prevalence of social judgments based on narrow application of "rules of good usage." But he also calls attention to the fact that such judgments are commonplace, a fact of some importance to public speakers.

Good Style Is Clear

The speaker's search for clarity begins with his choice of usage familiar to his listeners. To this extent the precept of clarity is included within the foregoing discussion of the standard of public usage. But the precept of clarity also directs attention to the importance of sentence structures which are free from unintentional ambiguity, of avoiding locutions which are inherently vague, and of locutions which help listeners perceive connected utterance as coherent.

An utterance is ambiguous if it makes two or more interpretations of meaning available to a listener. Speakers may choose to be ambiguous to achieve certain purposes. But the speaker who is unintentionally ambiguous may be properly accused of lacking a clear style. Thus the speaker who says, "the gallery was crowded with fat men and women drinking soda pop" creates a double ambiguity. Did he mean that both the men and women were fat, or only the men? And were both sexes drinking soda pop, or only the women? The speaker who says "my proposal will aid public schools and private schools providing effective

---

[4] Donald J. Lloyd, "Snobs, Slobs, and the English Language," *The American Scholar,* XX (Summer, 1951), 279–288.

education" leaves listeners in doubt as to whether the phrase "providing effective education" is meant to apply to both private and public schools, or only to the private schools.[5] Similarly the speaker who says "hopefully we will achieve our objective" is thoroughly ambiguous. Does he mean that he hopes we will achieve the objective in question, or that we will achieve it, while exuding hope?

An utterance is vague if its meaning is indefinite to the point that the utterance seems unrelated to any clear referent. Whereas an ambiguous statement permits two or more clear interpretations, a vague statement does not suggest any clear interpretation. Extemporaneous speakers, particularly those who are ill prepared, may produce a number of vague locutions, seemingly for the purpose of agitating the air with reassuring sound. For example, the speaker who says, "If we really believed in freedom, and things like that, and followed out our beliefs, we would accomplish all kinds of good in this world," has achieved a remarkable level of vagueness. The term "freedom" by itself has enough capacity for vagueness without being burdened by the indefinite category of "things like that." The phrase "all kinds of good" all but defies interpretation.

Obscure statement reduced to writing may be neither ambiguous nor vague when subjected to patient reading, rereading, and interpretation. But an obscure style in a public speech is almost inevitably vague. Listeners must catch utterance on the wing, without the assistance of a dictionary for interpretation of unusual terms, or recourse to a reexamination of a statement to untangle complicated verbal structures. For this reason the speaker seeking clarity has particular need to prefer a short word to a longer one when either is sufficient to his meaning; to prefer sentences unfreighted by an unusual number of long qualifying phrases; and to ground his use of abstract concepts such as freedom, dignity, truth, justice, courage, or style in concrete illustrations. The speaker who asserts, "existentially speaking, I am of the opinion that interpersonal transactions, at least for the most part, constitute the essential reality of experience" may have said something profound. But unless his elaborate, polysyllabic construction is supported by concrete illustrative material, he has achieved only an inflated form of vagueness.

As a final comment on the precept of clarity, we shall consider briefly the way in which speakers develop coherence by carrying the thought of one statement forward into the statement which follows. We say a speaker has been clear when it is easy to follow the forward movement

[5] See Norman Stageberg, "Some Structural Ambiguities," *English Journal,* XLVII (November, 1958), 479–486. The article defines and illustrates some twenty kinds of ambiguities produced by careless sentence structures.

of his thought; to see how each item of his utterance flows from that which has preceded it, and leads into that which follows. This effect must begin with the capacity of a speaker to develop a single line of thought, without permitting extraneous notions to interrupt its flow. But the effect is supported by a style which makes liberal use of verbal devices for relating successive sentences to one another. Such verbal devices include the common conjunctions of English, such as "and" and "but," and the conjunctive adverbs, such as "however," "nevertheless," "furthermore," "also," "therefore," and "notwithstanding." These devices can be extended by the speaker's repetition of a key term or concept of one sentence in the sentence that follows. The process may be illustrated by the opening passage of a speech by Professor Edmund Morgan, delivered at Yale University to the entering freshman class in 1959. Certain words are italicized in the passage which follows to call attention to the closely articulated flow of Morgan's thought:

The world does not much like curiosity. *The world* says that *curiosity* killed the cat. *The world* dismisses *curiosity* by calling it idle, or mere, idle, *curiosity*. Parents do their best to extinguish *curiosity* in their children, because it makes life difficult to be faced every day with a string of unanswerable questions about what makes fire hot or why grass grows, or to have to halt junior's investigations before they end in explosion and sudden death. *Children* whose *curiosity* survives parental discipline and who manage to grow up before they *blow up* are invited to join the Yale faculty. *Within the University they* go on asking questions and trying to find the answers. In the eyes of a scholar, that is mainly what a *university* is for. *It is a place* where the *world's* hostility to *curiosity* can be defied.[6]

Morgan introduces the key term "curiosity" in the opening sentence of his address, and uses this term along with other linking concepts in carrying forward the movement of his thought.

Good Style Is Lively and Vivid

The foregoing passage from Morgan is *lively* in the sense that the speaker's thought moves quickly forward. The effect is similar, if less impassioned than the effect of one of Winston Churchill's most familiar passages from an address to his nation in the early days of World War II:

Even though large tracts of Europe and many old and famous States have fallen or may fall into the grip of the Gestapo and all the odious apparatus of Nazi rule, we shall not flag or fail. We shall go on to the end. We shall

---

[6] The full text of Professor Morgan's speech is printed in *Saturday Review*, January 23, 1960, pp. 13–14.

fight in France, we shall fight in the seas and oceans, we shall fight with growing confidence and growing strength in the air; we shall defend our island whatever the cost may be. We shall fight on the beaches, we shall fight on the landing-grounds, we shall fight in the fields and in the streets, we shall fight in the hills; we shall never surrender; and even if, which I do not for a moment believe, this Island or a large part of it were subjugated and starving, then our Empire beyond the seas, armed and guarded by the British Fleet, would carry on the struggle, until, in God's good time, the New World, with all its power and might, steps forth to the rescue and liberation of the old.[7]

Churchill's eloquence is animated by the series of short, parallel statements, each carrying forward the speaker's cry of defiance. The utterance is also *vivid* for listeners caught in the tragic drama of a great struggle.

Aristotle observed that the power of utterance to move listeners was related to the speaker's capacity to set events "before the eyes" of listeners and show these events in a "state of activity." This observation led the Greek philosopher to suggest that in their address speakers should prefer "actuality" or reference to concrete events and actions known to their listeners. He also suggested that speakers study the power of such figures of language as *metaphor* and *antithesis* to give vividness to their thought.

We have previously described the metaphor as a kind of comparison or figurative analogy in which one is asked to view one event from the perspective provided by a quite different event. In current usage, the term *metaphor* is often restricted to linguistic forms in which the comparison is implicit, and an actual identity between the two unlike events is expressed, while the term *simile* is applied to explicit statements of comparison. Thus the statement "the tax cut lit the fuse of an economic explosion" is metaphoric: the comparison of an economic process to an explosion is implicit in the language, and we are asked to visualize an abstract set of economic events from the perspective of explosion. On the other hand, to say "the tax cut set off economic growth in the same way as a fuse sets off a bomb" would be a simile since the comparison is now made explicit. Whatever the distinctions one makes in naming such comparisons, their potential for making utterance lively and vivid rests in the color, suspense, or surprise that a fresh perspective can bring to an event or concept.

The second figure of language emphasized by Aristotle, that of *antithesis,* brings into juxtaposition two dissimilar or contrasting events.

[7] The text is from Winston Churchill, *The Second World War,* Vol. II, *Their Finest Hour* (Boston: Houghton Mifflin Company, 1949), p. 118.

Such immediate contrasts may be said to "set things before the eye" of a listener in the same manner that juxtaposing contrasting colors such as red and yellow in a painting may heighten our awareness of each. This verbal process is represented in President Kennedy's familiar phrase, "Ask not what your country can do for you—ask what you can do for your country." The process is carried to great length in the wry comment of President Clark Kerr of the University of California on the contrasting qualities that a university president must bring to his work:

He should be firm, yet gentle; sensitive to others, insensitive to himself; look to the past and the future, yet be firmly planted in the present; both visionary and sound; affable, yet reflective; know the value of a dollar and realize that ideas cannot be bought; inspiring in his visions yet cautious in what he does; a man of principle yet able to make a deal; a man with broad perspective who will follow the details conscientiously; a good American but ready to criticize the status quo fearlessly; a seeker of truth where the truth may not hurt too much; a source of public pronouncements when they do not reflect on his own institution.[8]

The Aristotelian figures of metaphor and antithesis are part of a corpus of language analysis which was pursued with increasing fervor throughout the history of ancient, medieval, and renaissance writing about style. Rhetoricians have traditionally been attracted by the ways in which speakers and writers manipulate their utterance to achieve unusual or striking effects. In ancient times they set about naming as many different figures of language as they could identify and define. This process led to the identification of more than two hundred different figurative devices, a result that no doubt dismayed students who were supposed to name, recognize, and use these figures in their speaking and writing. One may properly question the productivity of an analytical passion which gave the name *asyndeton* to the deliberate omission of conjunctions between a series of related phrases, as in Lincoln's ". . . government of the people, by the people, for the people, shall not perish from the earth," or the name *polysyndeton* to the addition of conjunctions not grammatically required. Yet the ancient study of figures did call attention to the unusual potential of language for imaginative manipulation and to the particular sources of some of the effects of surprise, or delight, or insight that good speakers achieve. Presumably a taste for such resources in language improves one's chances of achieving a vivid or lively style, and we shall provide a brief account of some of the more common figures.

    [8] Clark Kerr, *The Uses of the University* (Cambridge: Harvard University Press, 1964), p. 30.

Schemes. In the rhetorical tradition the name *scheme* was applied to a figure achieved by deviation from the ordinary pattern or arrangement of words. Thus one may select words deliberately to achieve the schematic effects of *rhythm* or *rhyme,* common to poetic form, or to achieve *alliteration*—repetition of initial or medial consonants in a series of words, as in the utterance, "The government *c*lings to us, *c*laws at us, *c*lamors for our attention, and *c*laims our service." Repetition is also evident in the use of parallel structure for phrases or sentences—a scheme illustrated in the passages from Churchill and Kerr cited earlier in this section, or in the structure of the sentence of President Kennedy's inaugural address previously used as an example of antithesis. *Asyndeton* and *polysyndeton* also provide examples of schemes.

Tropes. Rhetoricians use the name *trope* for figures which achieve their effect by using words in a way different from their ordinary signification. Thus *metaphors* and *similes* are the most commonly identified tropes. One may also identify a special kind of metaphor in *synecdoche,* a figure in which some part of an event is used to stand for the whole, as in the utterance, "The Captain hired ten *hands.*" Synecdoche turns into *metonomy,* a figure in which the meaning of an event is signified by naming an event closely related to it, as in the familiar parliamentary phrase, "I have a question to address to the *chair.*" The general figure of metaphor is also present in *personification,* or attributing animate life to inanimate objects or concepts, as in "The voice of duty calls to us," or "The tornado stretched its long and deadly finger toward the city." Similarly, *periphrasis* is a particular kind of metaphor, involving the use of some descriptive phrase as the substitute for a proper name, as in, "The Wizard of Ooze is making another speech today"; or of a proper name to denote qualities that have become associated with that name, as in, "Churchill was the *Cassandra* of Parliament in the 1930's."

While not all tropes are properly viewed as species of metaphors, we have emphasized metaphor as a generic name for the most used and useful of the figures. The liveliness and color given to concepts or events perceived from an unexpected perspective, and the power of new perspective to "set things before the eye" makes metaphor a common resource of vivid speech.

Good Style Is Appropriate

We have already called attention to the precept of appropriateness as limiting or modifying all other stylistic precepts. Good public usage may be of little value in addressing an audience unfamiliar with the dialect of public responsibility; freedom from ambiguity may be a doubtful virtue for a politician seeking to please all members of an audience whose members have sharply divergent views on national policy; vividness may become questionable if the speaker's subject matter offends the taste or sensibility of many of his auditors. In short, the problem of appropriateness in style involves all the relationships among speaker, purpose, utterance, audience, and occasion. One should not interpret this observation to mean, however, that such precepts as good public usage, clarity, and liveliness are useless; the speaker's power to choose is implicit in the precept of appropriateness, but this power is academic if the speaker cannot choose to be clear or vivid. And while the problem of appropriateness in style is inseparable from the problem of choice faced by the speaker, there are two special considerations affecting appropriateness in the management of style which may be usefully discussed at this point.

Appropriateness of tone. One observes that speakers in their manner reveal a particular attitude toward their subject matter. We refer to this quality of utterance as the speaker's *tone.* Thus we may say that the speaker's tone was sarcastic, deferential, pious, strident, ironic, casual, and so on. Such tonal qualities are made manifest both in the speaker's choice and ordering of words and in his delivery. The obvious desideratum of tone is that it be appropriate to the speaking situation. Thus the speaker who reports a baseball game with the solemnity, gravity, and richness of figurative language which might be usual for reporting a decisive battle may have found a tone quite inappropriate to his subject matter. Or it may be appropriate if he is seeking a comic effect through deliberate parody.

Certain tonal devices in language are so commonplace that they have been named and classified as figures of speech. Thus a speaker is said to be using *irony* if his language implies a meaning quite different from the obvious meaning expressed. For example, Shakespeare's version of Mark Antony's address over the body of Caesar is heavily ironic in tone. "But Brutus was an honorable man" says Antony repeatedly, while suggesting with growing force that Brutus was anything but honorable. The idea of irony is extended to include utterance in which one person's evaluation of a situation is in contrast with an evaluation held by an onlooker. A speaker, for instance, may show us a man who aspired to riches and fame, while we see a man who found deep unhappiness. The heavy-handed use of praise in an effort to blame is a form of irony, often named as *sarcasm.* The speaker may use overstatement, or *hyperbole,* for comic effect, and may use understatement, or *meiosis,* for the same purpose. Thus Mark Twain's famous comment after an erroneous newspaper account of his death, "the reports of my death are greatly exaggerated," is a form of comic understatement. Speakers engage in *apophasis* when they use the device of mentioning some event by disclaiming any intention to mention it, as: "I will not in this debate discuss the fact that my opponent was once convicted of a felony, for to bring up such information would lead us from our purpose. . . ."

Appropriateness of attitude. In public speaking we can distinguish the speaker's *tone* as his disposition toward his subject matter and his *attitude* as his disposition toward his audience. Thus the speaker may be angry or aggressive toward some flaw in the shape of the world, but deferential or friendly toward his listeners. The preacher who berates sinners while making it clear that none of his present audience deserve to be called sinners, may be said to have chosen an angry tone and a conciliatory attitude. Such complexes of tone and attitude are common in public speeches. The public speaker seeks to enlist the audience in adopting the tone of his utterance; his manner is often one which says that "we are being angry, or ironic, or comic," and not one which says "I am angry with you, or ironic at your expense." Listeners respond favorably to the speaker when he brings to his discourse the tone which they would choose for the subject under discussion. This is true even in those somewhat exceptional speaking situations in which an audience, perhaps suffering from an unusual burden of guilt, grants to the speaker both the right and responsibility to denounce, or warn, or ridicule the audience.

PRESCRIPTION TO DESCRIPTION

To this point we have explored the concept of style in ways traditional to rhetorical theory. The approach is prescriptive in that it asserts certain qualities thought characteristic of a good style, and analyzes particular attributes in the selection and ordering of words useful in achieving these qualities. The approach is useful for the student wishing to improve his own style by emulating the style of successful speakers and writers. The analytic terminology provides an instrument for uncovering the particular characteristics of the prose he may wish to use as a model. The traditional approach to style also has obvious uses for the close critic of speaking or writing.

We turn now to two relatively contemporary approaches to the study of style, each of which proceeds not from an effort to prescribe the qualities of a good style, but from the effort to uncover the ways in which audiences perceive variations in the manner of address revealed by speakers. These approaches should not be thought of as supplanting or conflicting with the traditional approach. Indeed, they often call to our attention the same details in the management of language thus far discussed. But they do provide two perspectives capable of summarizing, in synoptic fashion, the broad range of choices available in the speaker's manner of address. Thus these approaches define the speaker's problem of choice rather than prescribing behavior he should emulate. They also provide a more unified picture of the speaker's language and his delivery as inseparable aspects of his manner of address.

STYLE PERCEIVED AS DIMENSIONS OF MANNER

There are some empirical grounds for believing that listeners actually perceive a speaker's manner in terms of a limited set of contrasting qualities. Armed with this information, a speaker could set about controlling his choice of language and delivery in ways designed to evoke the response he seeks.

In a study of the stylistic evaluations of readers, Professor John Carroll sought to uncover the limited number of dimensions of manner actually identified by the readers.[9]

Although his study dealt with printed materials, Carroll's findings are nevertheless of interest to the student of public speaking. He asked eight so-called expert judges to evaluate some 150 passages of English prose in terms of 29 adjectival scales. Thus the raters judged each prose passage on scales bounded by such contrasting terms as "subtle . . . obvious"; "succinct . . . wordy"; "original . . . trite," and so forth. By subjecting all ratings to statistical analysis, Carroll was then able to discover within the large body of ratings those which worked so closely together that they seemed to represent a single cluster of evaluation. Carroll's analysis seems to show that while readers (or listeners) use a large number of adjectives to describe language behavior, they really react to only a limited number of stylistic dimensions. The 29 scales used by his raters operated in terms of only five factors, or dimensions of evaluation. Carroll names and describes his five factors as follows:

(1) A "general stylistic evaluation" factor. This factor may be named by the dimension of variation good . . . bad. Such dimensions as pleasant–unpleasant; strong–weak; interesting–boring; precise–vague; elegant–uncouth; ordered–chaotic; graceful–awkward; varied–monotonous; vivid–pale; original–trite; succinct–wordy; natural–affected; profound–superficial; and vigorous–placid seemed to relate to one another in the judgments of raters. We recognize in all of these di-

[9] For a complete account of his study, see John B. Carroll, "Vectors of Prose Style," in Thomas Sebeok, ed., *Style in Language* (Boston: Institute of Technology Press, 1960), pp. 283–292.

mensions the language of praise and blame commonly used in describing some speaker's language.

(2) *An "abstractness" dimension.* This factor may be named by the dimension *abstract . . . concrete.* Other dimensions closely related to this kind of judgment were subtle–obvious; profound–superficial; complex–simple; hazy–clear; original–trite; elegant–uncouth; and remote–intimate.

(3) *An "ornamentation" factor.* This factor may be named by the dimension *ornamented . . . plain.* Other dimensions closely related to this kind of judgment were florid–plain; wordy–succinct; lush–austere; affected–natural; complex–simple; and elegant–uncouth.

(4) *A "personal affect" factor.* This factor may be named by the dimension *personal . . . impersonal.* Other dimensions which seemed closely related to this kind of judgment were intimate–remote; emotional–rational; vigorous–placid; and to a lesser extent, vivid–pale and opinionated–impartial.

(5) *A "seriousness" factor.* This factor may be named by the dimension *serious . . . humorous.* Other dimensions closely related to this kind of judgment were earnest–flippant; meaningful–meaningless; profound–superficial; and, surprisingly, masculine–feminine.

Carroll's factors are of interest in several respects. First, as we have already indicated, they suggest the probability that readers (or listeners) apply only a limited number of dimensions to their perception of style. Second, they indicate the variety of stylistic details which may enter into each dimension. Thus as two readers or listeners apply the same set of stylistic terms to a given piece of discourse, they may be reacting to somewhat different stimuli. For example, if we call a speaker florid or say that his style is ornate, what are we actually trying to say? Do we mean that he gestures dramatically, or that his voice exhibits dramatic variety—that he thunders and whispers? Do we mean that his language is complex, or subtle? Do we mean that he seems to inflate his ideas with long or unusual words, or that he uses many striking metaphors which attract our attention? We might mean any or all of these things. In other words, the fact that we perceive only a limited number of dimensions of variation in the style of speakers does not eliminate the wealth of stylistic detail encompassed by these dimensions. Rather we are left with the conclusion that in observing the style of a speaker we find first a series of general impressions and upon close examination we may be able to locate the particular complex of details which gives rise to these impressions.

STYLISTIC DIMENSIONS

Carroll's factors also lend themselves to a description of the general dimensions of choice available in relation to style. That is, each factor summarizes a dimension along which a particular speaker's style may be located or along which a speaker may choose to place his manner. Since we have emphasized the public speaker's art as one of choosing positions, arrangements, and methods of enforcing ideas, we can usefully add an interpretation of the range of stylistic choices available and of the relationship of these choices to the speaker's purpose, subject matter, and audience.

We turn, therefore, to discussion of the four specific stylistic factors identified in Carroll's research, omitting discussion of his "general evaluation" factor, which serves only as a summary of a listener's or reader's approval or disapproval of a given style. We shall define each factor in terms of the dimension of choice it entails, describe some of the specific details in the management of language and delivery encompassed by each dimension, and suggest implications of the dimension for the practice of public speaking.

Abstract . . . Concrete

Speeches vary as to the level of abstractness or concreteness revealed in the speaker's manner, as well as in his words. The idea of abstractness is, of course, commonly applied to the description of words and statements, but after some discussion of this concept as it relates to a speaker's language, we shall also observe its relevance to delivery.

Two related kinds of observations about words give rise to the dimension of "abstract . . . concrete." First, some words are observed to have tangible referents or referents which are directly available to the sense organs. Thus the names of objects such as "car" or "horse," of actions such as "running" or "jumping," or of attributes such as "red" or "sour" or "acrid" all have tangible or sensory referents. Such words, or statements built up with such words, are called *concrete,* and are contrasted with words having referents which cannot be observed as readily or touched, tasted, or smelled. Thus concepts such as "honesty" or "democracy," or "freedom" or "materialism" do not denote events directly available to the senses. Such words, or statements built up with such words, are called *abstract.* Kenneth Burke gives the name "positive words" to the group we have called *concrete.* And he gives the interesting name of "dialectical words" to the group we have called *abstract.* His use of the term "dialectical" calls attention to the linguistic fact that

we can name an object such as a chair or water without necessarily con-
ceiving of the opposite of this object. However, we can scarcely name a
concept such as "honesty" without simultaneously proposing another
value to be named "dishonesty." Concrete language is built from names
for events within our sense experience; abstract language is built from
the linguistic activity we call "thought," as we construct interpretations
of our experience, our history, our values and purposes.

A second type of observation applies to the "abstract . . . concrete"
dimension. Even within a grouping of words with objective referents
(which we have called "concrete" words), we observe varying levels of
generality. Thus the terms "writing instrument," "pen," and "ball-point
pen" all have the same general class of objects as referents. But clearly
the word "pen" is more general than "ball-point pen," since it includes
the latter group of objects, but includes other objects as well. Similarly,
the even more general term "writing instrument" includes the referent
categories of "pen" and "ball-point pen," but includes additional groups
of objects, such as pencils, as well. Such a series of related terms can be
ordered as to level of abstraction, with "writing instrument" in this case
the most abstract of the three terms and "ball-point pen" the most concrete. The larger the referent category of events for a particular word or
phrase, the more abstract that word or phrase. This second interpretation of the dimension "abstract . . . concrete" is related to the first in
the sense that abstract concepts such as "democracy" seem obviously to
denote an enormously complex referent category, built up historically
from descriptions of political systems and interpersonal attitudes and
behaviors. Thus just as the referent category for "writing instrument" is
larger than that for "ball-point pen," so the referent category for "democracy" *seems* larger than that for "writing instrument." But we
should observe that we must make this kind of ordering through use of
the indecisive term "seems," since there is no way of counting the variety of objects encompassed by a concept such as democracy. The abstractness of this concept is not simply a matter of the number of objects
or events it entails, but more significantly a matter of the specificity of
response the term elicits in a group of listeners or interpreters.

Speakers are commonly advised to seek concreteness in style, and to
avoid excessive abstractness. The advice is based on two rather obvious
merits found in concrete words or statements. First, concrete words tend
to achieve a more common response from a group of listeners than abstract words. If the speaker says, "we must destroy communism," he
sets up an enormously varied set of possible referents for his listeners,
not all of which can be close to whatever it was the speaker had in mind.
However, if he says, "I propose to swear out a complaint against my

neighbor, Henry Smorgasboard, have him arrested, and put him behind bars in the Jefferson County Jail," his statement permits less variation of interpretation.

Not only does concrete language tend to organize audience response in a more unified manner, it also tends to be more interesting. Language which involves directly the capacity of a listener to see, hear, feel, taste, or smell some concrete event is more likely to involve the attention of that listener—and this is as durable a generalization about probable listener behavior as rhetorical theory has produced. A speech telling the story of an honest man tends to be more interesting than a speech praising the quality of honesty; a speech detailing the nature of skid row in the listener's home town should grip his imagination more than a generalized statement about "conditions in the metropolitan areas of the continental United States." The idea that concrete language involves the listener, and makes listening an experience rather than a sedative, is well-established in the theory of imaginative literature. Thus dramatists are criticized if their characters find it necessary to produce long speeches explaining to the audience the nature of their attitude toward life; drama comes nearer to its possibilities if the action of the play itself permits the audience to see the character living his attitude. The novelist who labels abstractly the experience of his characters is perhaps less an artist than the novelist who finds the objective details in experience which enable the reader to experience the feeling. By the artistic selection and ordering of concrete details, the writer or speaker "evokes" an experience in the listener or reader rather than merely telling the reader or listener what it is, in an abstract sense, that he should know. The speaker uses language effectively when he selects concrete details within some larger unit of experience and by setting forth these details evokes a listener's sense of the total experience. T. S. Eliot, in analyzing the art of poetry spoke of the writer's search for the "objective correlative" of the experience he seeks to evoke through language. The speaker who says "the thought of atomic warfare fills me with horror" has given an abstract label to his own experience, but he has not found the objective correlative of that experience which might help a listener to share the speaker's feeling. The speaker who can describe in concrete terms some selected events following an atomic explosion, as the novelist John Hersey did in his book on *Hiroshima,* has sought the objective correlate of the experience he wishes to communicate.

In praising concreteness, we should also be aware of the limitations of discourse which is merely concrete. A demonstration speech on the art of tying Christmas packages may be admirably concrete, but we are not likely to spend much time praising the speaker's style when that style encompasses mundane or trivial purposes. An interesting aspect of the growth of language skill in children is that the earliest language of the child tends to be relentlessly concrete. The increasing use of abstract language involving abstract concepts marks the growth of maturity and intellectual sophistication. Thus children, or childlike adults, live in a world of things and talk concretely. Adults, particularly educated adults, live more in a world of ideas, and talk more abstractly. The problem of style for an adult speaker is not simply the problem of talking concretely. Any child can do that. The problem rather is to achieve a sufficient or appropriate level of concreteness while dealing with positions, themes, or concepts which are in themselves abstract. In one of his earlier works on language, Stuart Chase was much troubled by the abstractness of such concepts as democracy, fascism, communism, and the like. He called these "blah" words, indicating the extent to which they were used to mean whatever a speaker chose them to mean, and to mean different things for all who heard them, thus contributing to confused public discussion. But it is not enough to caution against abstract language if the purpose of such cautioning is to suggest that such words are not needed or should be avoided. We can scarcely talk about political systems without recourse to the broad and abstract concepts man uses to label these systems; nor about human values without the abstract language of evaluation. We properly admire the concreteness of a speaker's style when we observe his skill in taking abstract and difficult ideas and making them clear and available to us by driving them back on more concrete levels of experience. Thus, if it is no trick to talk concretely about tying Christmas packages, it is a work of great style to talk concretely about a concept such as the "fourth dimension." Note how C. S. Lewis visualizes a speaker accomplishing this latter feat:

"You," [the speaker] may say, "can intuit only three dimensions; you therefore cannot conceive how space should be limited. But I think I can show you how that which may appear infinite in three dimensions, might nevertheless be finite in four. Look at it this way. Imagine a race of people who knew only two dimensions—like the Flatlanders. And suppose they were living on a globe. They would have no conception, of course, that the globe was curved—for it is curved round in that third dimension of which they have no inkling. They will therefore imagine that they are living on a plane; but they will soon find out that it is a plane which nowhere comes to an end: there are no edges to it. Nor would they be able even to imagine an edge. For an edge would mean that, after a certain point, there would be nothing to walk on; nothing below their feet. But that *below* and *above* dimension is just what their minds have not got; they have only backwards and forwards and left and right. They would thus be forced to assert that their globe, which they could not see as a globe, was infinite. You can see perfectly well that it is finite. And now, can you not see that as these flat-landers are to you, so you might be to a creature that intuited four dimensions? Can you not conceive how that which seems necessarily infinite to your three dimensional consciousness might none the less be really finite?" [10]

Lewis moves an all but incomprehensible abstraction at least to the point at which a glimmering of understanding might come to the listener, and he does so by driving the abstraction back on a metaphor or comparison.

We can move then from the easy generalization that concrete utterance is more vivid, clearer, more interesting, and more memorable than abstract utterance to the more difficult generalization that neither concreteness nor abstractness per se are necessarily good. The work of the speaker is to find the meaning he seeks, and the language suitable both to the statement of that meaning and to the work of making it available to others. If the speaker's subject matter is important, this usually means that he moves through varying levels of abstraction in his utterance. We sense the general nature of his style as concrete to the extent that he seeks urgently and consistently to drive his abstract concepts back on concrete materials—personal experiences, anecdotes, metaphors, or the language of sense experience. We sense the general nature of his style as abstract if this "driving back" process is not so evident, or so consistently evident. And we evaluate the merit of the style we observe by finding the nature of the speaker's choice, examining it in the context of the particular speaking situation, and asking if a different choice might have been more suitable.

Before turning from the dimension "abstract . . . concrete," we should observe once more the impact of the particular speaking situation on the nature of the speaker's language. Certain speeches, removed from the context of their original utterance, may seem impossibly abstract; placed within that context we may discover that the abstract language of the speaker was rooted not within concrete materials provided by his utterance, but within concrete experiences shared by members of his audience, and subject to ready evocation by abstract reference. Thus, the abstractness of Lincoln's Gettysburg Address is seldom noted. One does not hear it said of this speech that it lacks clarity, color, or vivid imagery, that it is devoid of narrative material, that it asserts broad generalizations about the nature of American government and the nation's purpose without driving these assertions back on concrete details. If it seems a paradox that a speech so much praised should be lacking in

[10] C. S. Lewis, "Bluspels and Flalansferes" from *Rehabilitations and Other Essays* (London: Oxford University Press, 1939).

concrete language, the answer rests in the relationship between the abstractions of the speech and the experience of both its first and subsequent audiences. As a speech of dedication, Lincoln's address found its concrete referent not simply within language, but within the very setting for the speech—the battlefield still fresh, the war which touched all lives, the challenge to national purpose posed by so great a crisis. The speech still evokes much of this concrete reference from the best known of Civil War battles, and history has if anything enriched the reference in the sense that its language now recalls the image of Lincoln, most respected of American heroes.

As we have indicated, the dimension "abstract . . . concrete," is seldom applied to matters of the speaker's delivery. The application is useful, however, inasmuch as it reveals a major source of concreteness in public speaking as contrasted with writing, and a major dimension of variation in the delivery habits of speakers.

The speaker has resources not available to the writer for making the tone and attitude of his utterance clear to an audience. By modeling physically and vocally his own reaction to the substance of his utterance, the speaker may make vivid the emotional tone of that utterance even while using relatively abstract language. Similarly he may clarify the attitude he holds toward his listeners. Both kinds of clarification can be achieved through the resources of vocal quality, vocal intonation, and physical expressiveness. Thus an abstract or vague description of an object can be made more concrete by gesture defining the shape and size of the object, and by vocal intonation or quality clarifying the nature of the object by reflecting its emotive effect on an observer. It is in this sense that the skillful actor makes concrete that which is merely implicit or vague in language, and that he does so through gesture or voice. Just as ostensibly abstract language may find its sources of concreteness in the situation of the utterance, so also may it take on concreteness through the speaker's delivery.

Clearly, however, speakers vary in the level of concreteness manifest in their style of delivery. Impassivity in the speaker's voice or demeanor is in itself a characteristic of abstractness in delivery. The speaker who neither smiles nor frowns, neither looks puzzled nor irritated—who avoids any of the thousand variations of attitude possible in physical manner or facial expression—such a speaker presents an abstraction rather than a concrete personality to his audience. Similarly, the speaker's voice can be drained of expressiveness. Abstract manner in delivery renders the speaker vague or ambiguous; his listeners must supply the concrete personality which has been hidden from them or remain in doubt as to the nature of the man speaking. Or they simply concentrate on hearing the words as they would wish to hear them spoken without influence from the speaker's person.

Speakers sometimes employ an abstract manner in delivery through lack of skill in managing the physical and vocal resources of speech or as an act of concealing themselves from the audience because of timidity. In such cases, the manner of speaking has not really been chosen by the speaker; his manner is abstract because he has no other resources available. But it is all too easy to assume that abstractness in delivery is not, on occasion, a plausible and artistic choice. We have had occasion earlier to observe both the limitations of clarity, and the uses of ambiguity in the relationships of speakers and listeners. Abstractness can be chosen because, for a variety of purposes, the speaker wishes to remain something of a mystery to others. We should further observe the artistic potential of a variety of relationships between the speaker's language and delivery. From a stylistic viewpoint, the clearest speech would be one combining concreteness of language and concreteness of delivery with total congruity between the speaker's language and delivery. In this sense the speaker's delivery would support the speaker's language in tone, attitude, descriptive efficiency, and so on, producing a single, coherent, clear statement. Clarity is no mean virtue in public speaking; rhetorical theorists have commonly placed it first among the virtues of style.

However, it is an injustice to the complexity of speeches to fail to perceive the resources present in varying relationships between language and delivery. For example, brilliantly concrete language delivered in a neutral or abstract manner can accomplish certain artistic ends. It can achieve the effect of "removing" the speaker from the scene to the greater emphasis of the language, or suggest that the speaker wishes the audience to have full freedom in hearing and visualizing an utterance without the pressure of the speaker's forcing a type of concrete interpretation through his own delivery. Moreover, incongruous delivery is in itself a source of artistic effect. The public roles of some speakers emphasize this contrast, as for example in the seemingly humorless comic, or the bland angry man. Classical rhetoricians made much of a figure of thought known as an *oxymoron*—a combination of words joining opposites—as in the phrase "cruel kindness," or "passionate neutrality," or, to take a more recent political example, "dynamic conservatism." The figure takes its effect from the tension of juxtaposed opposites. Similarly, the whole of a speaker's style may find effect in the tension of contrasting levels of abstraction in language and delivery. Passionately concrete delivery, joined to language characterized by a high level of abstractness, is a common stylistic characteristic of ceremonial or occasional speeches designed to move audiences powerfully. Presumably men can be powerfully aroused in the presence of mystery, and aroused not so much by the clarity of that which is held before them as by the very lack of clarity in combination with strong emotion. Prophets have known this, so have poets, and so have demagogues. Edmund Burke, the famous British statesman and author, commented at length on this matter in his chapter on "Obscurity," from *The Sublime and the Beautiful.* Burke had observed the power of language with the most obscure qualities of reference or imagery to move audiences greatly, ". . . So far is clearness of imagery from being necessary to an influence on the passions," he wrote, "that they [the passions] may be considerably operated on without presenting an image at all." [11]

Ornate . . . Plain

Speeches vary stylistically as to the relative ornateness or simplicity of the speaker's language and delivery. The dimension seems easily defined by casual observation. Some speakers seem plainspoken, both in choice of language and in delivery. They prefer the short word to the polysyllable when either might do; they give a sense of saying no more than needed, of restraint in the use of imagery, and of restraint in the use of vocal variety or physical activity. Other speakers seem to be seeking a heightened use of the resources of language, to load their utterance with figurative forms and vivid images, to support such richness of language with an extension of the resources of vocal intonation and physical activity. At his best the speaker using an ornamented style seems to be talking with increased imagination. His style does not call attention to itself, but rather gives a richness of texture and vividness of imagery in the development of thought. At worst, the ornamented style seems a seeking for effect, a reaching for the unusual expression when a simpler form would be clearer, or an effort on the part of the speaker to call attention to his own verbal resources or his own person without regard to the necessities of purpose of subject. Simplicity has an equal range of merit and limitation. Advice to speechmakers in our own century has tended to emphasize the merit of a simple style, asserting that short, common words will be more clearly and easily understood, that audiences value brevity, that the important idea caught in a few carefully chosen words has greater power than the same idea buried in verbiage. But the generalization has to be a contingent one. Simple speech may be insufficient to capture the texture of an experience; a feeble imagination

[11] Edmund Burke, "On the Sublime and the Beautiful," in *The Works of Edmund Burke, I* (Boston: Little and Brown, 1839), pp. 74–206.

may achieve brevity at the expense of vividness. Nor is an addiction to short simple words, or to freedom from imagery a guarantee of brevity.

One may sense a general preference for ornateness in one speaker and a contrasting preference for simplicity in another speaker. But skillful speech is likely to display movement within this range. The force of an imaginative extension of language is heightened if the extension is preceded and followed by plain or simple passages. Similarly, plain talk finds its greatest force in the midst of ornate speech. The point is well illustrated by Shakespearean speech. Shakespearean language seems generally ornate to the contemporary ear, yet it is possible to observe simple, direct address in the most eloquent passages of his plays. One marks the same variety of manner in Lincoln. He is generally thought of as a plainspoken man, but the best remembered of his speeches turn also to the resources of richly ornamented language, with strong biblical overtones, as in the passage preceding the conclusion of his second inaugural address:

Fondly do we hope—fervently do we pray—that this mighty scourge of war may speedily pass away. Yet, if God wills that it continue, until all the wealth piled by the bondsman's two hundred and fifty years of unrequited toil shall be sunk, and until every drop of blood drawn with the lash, shall be paid by another drawn with the sword as was said three thousand years ago, so still it must be said "the judgments of the Lord are true and righteous altogether."

Passages from contemporary speeches by Senator Everett Dirksen of Illinois reveal the same variety, even if his speeches are unlikely to be as long remembered as those of Lincoln. Senator Dirksen's style has evoked much comment, not all of it complimentary. In general he has been marked as a speaker who prefers ornamentation, or as a twentieth-century politician who looks and speaks in the manner of the nineteenth century, with a preference for euphemism, bombast, and using more language than needed. But in examining his rhetoric, *Time* magazine found unexpected variety, and cited the following contrasting passages as illustrative. The first passage was taken from an address to the Senate:

The moving finger writes, and the fortunes of politics will probably result in a change of some faces when we return in January. . . . Old faces go and new faces come, but somehow, like Tennyson's brook, the free republic continues to go on with vitality, vigor, and an energized faith, as it moves to newer heights and newer achievements for its people in the great moral climate of freedom. . . . So au revoir. We shall see you on the home diamond somewhere; and when it is all over, all the healing waters will somehow close over our dissidence, and we shall go forward as a solid phalanx once more.

This passage moves slowly, heavily, burdened by words, by literary allusions, by multiple adjectives intermixed with a fantastic variety of comparisons. But the Senator could be colloquial and plainspoken when he wanted to be, though never terse, and never free from a deliberate search for imagery. Following is a passage from a speech on Ireland:

Good old Ireland! I have tried to hold up the flag for Ireland. I introduced a resolution to try to memorialize the whole wide world, if that could be done, to compel Great Britain to give Ireland her undivided freedom. That is the way I feel. I like my freedom straight. I am like little Johnny. His teacher asked him, "How do you spell straight?" He said, "S-T-R-A-I-G-H-T." The teacher then asked, "What does it mean?" He said, "Without ginger ale." That is the way I take my freedom, I take it without ginger ale. I take it straight. So I am for the Irish people, who want the united freedom.[12]

Variation in terms of ornateness and simplicity are as observable in delivery as in language. One speaker displays remarkable range in vocal quality, pitch, and intonation. His use of gesture and action is profuse. In theater, such ornateness in delivery has been associated with the high style in Shakespearean interpretation, or with the comedy of manners. It was the style associated with melodrama in the nineteenth century, a style which may seem comic today. Another speaker may provide an audience with only the minimal range of intonation and gesture—a manner sometimes associated with comfortable conversation, and a manner much praised in contemporary advice on the delivery of speeches.

The virtue of simplicity is much praised in abstract commentary on use of language or on manner of delivery. This virtue is commonly associated with the quality of concreteness. Thus, H. W. and F. G. Fowler in their widely read *The King's English* (London: The Clarendon Press, 1938, third ed.) give the following advice on word choice: "1. Prefer the familiar word to the far-fetched. 2. Prefer the concrete word to the abstract. 3. Prefer the single word to the circumlocution. 4. Prefer the short word to the long. 5. Prefer the Saxon word to the Romance." Presumably such advice must always be qualified by an assumption that all other things being equal, one should adopt these preferences. But in matters of style, all other things are never equal. We have observed that abstractness and concreteness are both genuine options strategically available to speakers in relation to their purposes and the speaking situation. A similar observation should be made about ornateness and simplicity. One may observe a generalized preference for stylistic ornamentation in British and American speakers of the

12 *Time*, September 14, 1962, p. 29.

eighteenth and nineteenth centuries, as compared with most public speakers in our own century. But such observations must be qualified by observation of stylistic variation among notably effective speakers in each of these centuries, or by observation of variation within the practice of a single speaker. In our own century the speeches of British Prime Minister Sir Winston Churchill seem ornate if contrasted with the speeches of President Dwight Eisenhower; Churchill is much the more given to colorful metaphor, to polysyllabic words, and to use of the actor's resources of variety in voice and physical manner. The greater emotive power of Churchill's speeches cannot be dissociated from his willingness to go beyond the limits that a simple preference for simplicity might have dictated. If ornateness of style is a genuine choice for the speaker, it remains a fault when it becomes obtrusive. The speaker whose vocal and physical gyrations call attention simply to the versatility of his management of these resources risks much. At the very least he risks the chance that his manner will be remembered far longer than the substance of his utterance. At most he risks being thought pretentious and self-centered.

Personal . . . Impersonal

The personal style is characterized by the speaker's frequent use of references to self and to the audience, by the use of colloquial language characteristic of informal conversation, and by the unstudied spontaneity of delivery which is also characteristic of friendly conversation. The public speaker who opens his address by talking about the circumstances which brought him to the platform, who illustrates his ideas with personal experiences, or who reports conversations with members of the audience is using a "personal" style. The speaker who uses colloquial language or slang which he believes common to the informal conversation of his listeners is also personal; such diction is an announcement that he thinks he knows and belongs to the social group represented in his audience. The speaker is not acting as an outsider or guest or stranger, but rather as a member of the group—a conversationalist who has been given the floor.

An impersonal style is characteristically stripped of references to self or audience. The speaker does not talk about himself, or "you" or "we," but about events and persons external to the immediate situation. His usage is formal, conforming to the standards of good public usage as he understands that usage, and avoiding the informal or colloquial diction. His delivery is formal—the courteous propriety of the guest or stranger meeting others for the first time, and not presuming the informality of long acquaintance.

In a very general sense one may observe that written discourse tends to be more impersonal than spoken discourse; that authors when speaking tend to use more personal pronouns ("I," "you," and "we") than when writing for publication, and tend also when speaking to make greater use of personal experience and colloquial diction. The tendency is a natural one, but it is scarcely a universal distinction between spoken and written discourse. An author's purpose, the formality of the occasion for his discourse, and the way in which he visualizes his relationship to his audience may have more influence on the personal-impersonal dimension of style than any question of speaking versus writing. For example, newspaper columnists giving advice to the troubled commonly produce public writing with an intensely personal style. They write to the strangers who write to them and to anyone else who cares to read such exchanges as though all had gathered at a coffee party to receive sage advice. Similarly, one may observe the impersonal manner of the editorials in most newspapers, and contrast these with the personal tone of columnists. One may equally contrast the personal manner of speeches developed for informal occasions with the more impersonal manner generated by formal public occasions. In short, while spoken discourse may tend to be more personal than written discourse, the differences within each type of address are as sharply delineated as the differences between the two types.

One should avoid assuming that a personal style is necessarily concrete and vivid, and an impersonal style inevitably abstract and obscure. One may be impersonal in the sense that his usage is formal and his references external, rather than to references to self and audience. At the same time his style may be vivid and clear.

The two opening paragraphs of Herbert Muller's book *The Uses of the Past* are similar in their clarity, but illustrate a movement from an impersonal manner in the first paragraph, to a much more personal manner in the second:

When Henry Adams studied the glorious medieval cathedrals he was inspired to work out his "dynamic theory of history," and in particular his contrast between the Virgin and the Dynamo, as the symbol of medieval unity and modern anarchy. He came to feel that the love of the Virgin Mary, which had raised the cathedral of Chartres, was the "greatest force the Western world ever felt," or even "the highest energy ever known to man." As a philosopher of history, he resolved to concentrate on the Virgin's "mental and physical energy of creation," and not to yield to the charm of the "adorable mistress"; but he was obviously smitten. He ended by drawing his wistful, charming picture of the Middle Ages, which has become still more charming as men have grown appalled by the folly and evil of our own age. Quite a few writers are now saying that the thirteenth century was the greatest of all centuries, the apex of Western civilization; and a chorus swells with the obvious religious moral.

I thought of Henry Adams when I was working a few years ago, in the cathedral of Hagia Sophia, in Istanbul. Here was the great monument of Eastern Christendom, in which the Virgin had also been the favorite object of worship. From its famous dome one might get a still longer and larger view of history, for it was completed by the Roman Emperor Justinian in the year 537—six centuries before Chartres—and it looks down on both Europe and Asia. And so I too began to ponder the meanings of the past. Only, my reflections failed to produce a neat theory of history, or any simple, wholesome moral. Hagia Sophia, or the "Holy Wisdom," gave me instead a fuller sense of the complexities, ambiguities, and paradoxes of human history. Nevertheless, I propose to dwell on these messy meanings. They may be, after all, the most wholesome meanings for us today; or so I finally concluded.[13]

The movement from an impersonal to a personal style is obvious in terms of the writer's references to self in the second paragraph. Yet apart from the colloquial use of "messy" in the second paragraph, the whole passage is generally formal even as it seeks a vivid and concrete way of introducing an abstract subject. The style as a whole contrasts with the intensely personal style of Clarence Darrow, the celebrated American trial lawyer, in the opening movement of his address to the inmates of Cook County Jail:

If I looked at jails and crimes and prisoners in the way the ordinary person does, I should not speak on this subject to you. The reason I talk to you on the question of crime, its cause and cure, is because I do not in the least really believe in crime. There is no such thing as a crime as the word is generally understood. I do not believe there is any sort of distinction between the real moral condition of the people in and out of jail. One is just as good as the other. The people here can no more help being here than the people outside can avoid being outside. I do not believe that people are in jail because they deserve to be. They are in jail simply bcause they can not avoid it on account of circumstances which are entirely beyond their control and for which they are in no way responsible.

I suppose a great many people on the outside would say I was doing you harm if they should hear what I say to you this afternoon, but you can not be hurt a great deal anyway, so it will not matter. Good people outside would say that I was really teaching you things that were calculated to injure society, but it's worth while now and then to hear something different from what you ordinarily get from preachers and the like. They will tell

[13] Herbert Muller, *Uses of the Past* (N. Y.: Oxford University Press, 1952), pp. 3–4.

you you should be good, and then you get rich and be happy. Of course we know that people do not get rich by being good, and that is the reason why so many of you people try to get rich in some other way, only you do not understand how to do it quite so well as the fellow outside. . . .[14]

The personal tone of Darrow's introduction is asserted both in his direct references to self and audience, and by his colloquial diction. The manner suggests that he assumes a friendly and responsive audience, one able to identify with his well-known thesis that human behavior is determined by man's environment. He approaches his audience as a member of their community.

Public speakers are frequently advised to seek development of a personal and informal style. Such a manner may bring the speaker close to his audience; it acknowledges the general desire of audiences to know speakers personally. Successfully pursued, the style may elicit strong identification between speaker and audience so that the speech becomes a "conversation among friends." But the situational limitations of such advice are apparent. The speaker who chooses a strongly personal style may achieve much, but he risks much. Not all audiences believe that the speakers should seek to become one of them. Colloquial diction will seem obtrusive if the colloquialisms are not those of the audience. The speaker who spends too much time talking of his own experiences may seem egocentric, and the speaker who talks too much about what his audience believes may offend listeners who think that the speaker assumes too much. Furthermore, one should be aware that an impersonal manner has its uses. The speaker who wishes to suggest his own objectivity, and to invite equal impartiality from his audience, may be well advised to choose a somewhat formal and reserved manner of delivery, and to choose language free from a strong emotive tone or attitude.

Serious . . . Humorous

Man may or may not be the only animal capable of laughter. But in any event, the capability is a conspicuous temptation for public speakers. Presumably the speaker who provides humor, by intention rather than misadventure, has revealed control over a resource for unifying audience response and achieving immediate rapport. There is little evidence that comic inventiveness is essential to effective public speaking. Nevertheless, the speaker capable of entertaining an audience is a familiar figure on the American public platform. Such nineteenth-century lecturers as Mark Twain and Artemus Ward practiced a type of public

[14] The full text of the address is reprinted in Carroll C. Arnold, Douglas Ehninger, and John Gerber, eds., *The Speaker's Resource Book* (Chicago: Scott Foresman and Co., 1961), pp. 136–142.

speaking which had more to do with entertainment than with exposition or persuasion. In our own century, popular lecturers often observe the cliché of introducing their speeches with a series of humorous anecdotes which may or may not be stylistically or thematically related to the major substance of the speech. Moreover, the humorous anecdote may serve, much as its serious counterpart, to clarify or support a position of the speaker. But we are less concerned here with the isolated anecdotes used by speakers than with the differential characteristics of serious and humorous styles.

Listeners seldom doubt their ability to distinguish a serious style from a humorous one. But if one asks about the differentia of a serious and humorous manner, the answer becomes extraordinarily complex. An indication of the complexity is given by the fact that listeners are often amused by a speaker when he thinks they should not be, and unamused when the speaker hopes they will be. This phenomenon seems associated with the fact that audiences are entertained by sequences of statements which take a surprising turn, as with the "punch line" for a joke; they are also entertained by statements which provide incongruous or unexpected ways of looking at familiar events. Thus the humorous manner in some sense always plays with the serious or ordinary expectations of listeners, and the manner succeeds only if the speaker has gauged accurately the twist of manner which will genuinely surprise or delight his listeners.

Direct vs. Indirect Utterance. If we are right in observing that a humorous manner rises in a departure from the expected or the familiar, it follows that the most general characteristic of such a style is its use of indirection. That is, speakers may look at events in a straightforward way, stating facts in customary relation to one another, and placing the speaker's attitudes and positions directly before an audience. Such a manner is essentially serious; it assumes that the world makes sense, that the speaker's opinions are important, and that speakers and listeners should try to understand one another with as little diversion as possible. But speakers may also play with the expectation of directness. They may seek an unusual perspective for perceiving ordinary events, thus exaggerating some features of the event and diminishing others, as in the caricature of a familiar public figure, or in the parody of the language or actions of others. Consider, for example, the way in which Mark Twain plays with the ordinary expectations of his audience in the following passage from a speech entitled "Advice to Youth:"

Now as to the matter of lying. You want to be very careful about lying; otherwise you are nearly sure to get caught. . . . Some authorities hold that the young should not lie at all. That, of course, is putting it rather stronger than necessary; still, while I cannot go as far as that, I do maintain, and I believe I am right, that the young ought to be temperate in the use of this great art until practice and experience has given them that confidence, elegance, and precision which alone can make this accomplishment graceful and profitable.[15]

There is incongruity in the seeming directness of Twain's advice and the actual intention of his utterance, and surprise in the easy movement from moral admonition to the picture of lying as one of the graces of maturity. Twain is engaging in a form of indirection known as irony; he appears in the role of one giving good advice to the young, but actually points our attention to the customs of adult society, and to the disproportion between the conduct of adults and their readiness to give moral guidance.

One observes a similar use of complex indirection in a brief passage from an address by Adlai Stevenson at a senior class banquet at Princeton University in 1954:

I was delighted to witness a moment ago your emphatic approval of my program for Princeton some thirty-two years ago—unlimited cuts, non-compulsory Chapel, and student firing of the Dean. I always considered that it was wise in politics to have—shall we say—a popular program. The trouble is that when I went into politics it appears that I changed my views.[16]

There is incongruity in Stevenson's picture of himself as a thoroughly pragmatic undergraduate politician, and his well-known position as a Presidential candidate that it was necessary to "talk sense" to the electorate. And there is irony in his indirect reference to his own lack of success as a candidate for the Presidency.

While the two passages cited illustrate the use of incongruity or an unusual perspective in language, one may observe an analogous source of comic inventiveness in the speaker's delivery, or in the relationship between delivery and language. The speaker who accompanies passionate and aggressive language with a gentle and ingratiating physical manner or vice versa, creates comic disproportion. And the speaker who relates garish or comic anecdotes with the utmost seriousness creates for the audience an ironic picture of one unaware of the comic aspects of his language.

Humor and High Seriousness. In calling attention to the elements of surprise, incongruity, or disproportion in a humorous manner, we

[15] Mark Twain, *Mark Twain's Speeches* (New York: Harper and Brothers, 1923), p. 105.
[16] Adlai Stevenson (March 22, 1954).

should observe these same elements in utterance seeking highly emotive seriousness. The speaker who departs imaginatively from the ordinary seriousness expected in utterance may do so with comic intentions, or with an effort to charge his seriousness with the shock of surprise or disproportion. The speaker achieves a comic manner if his utterance seems relatively free from such tonalities as anger or outrage. But the affinity of the comic manner and high seriousness is such that speakers may seek a genuine ambiguity of manner, and utterance which entertains even as it shocks, saddens, or angers.

The Problem of Choice. The speaker with a controlled comic manner has a resource of obvious merit. But the decision to use this manner is a difficult one, and one involving considerations beyond the obvious fact that on some occasions and for some purposes the use of humor is obviously inappropriate.

The speaker needs to confront two considerations more subtle than obvious impropriety. The first of these is that the humorous manner, or for that matter the search for high seriousness, involves use of a style inherently more complex and difficult to interpret than a manner which is wholly direct or serious in an ordinary sense. The speaker who is ironic or who dissembles may delight listeners who catch on to his game. In like proportion he may delude listeners who lack the imagination to participate in his irony, or outrage listeners who "catch on" only after they have been misled and who thus suffer the humiliation of one whose simplicity has been exposed.

The second consideration has to do with the nature of audience response to the speaker with a reputation for humor. That listeners like to be entertained, and have regard for those who entertain them cannot be doubted. But it is less clear that audiences reserve their highest trust for the person who delights in the complexities of humor, or who avoids commonplace seriousness. Professor J. Jeffery Auer has dealt with this question in an article concerning Tom Corwin, a pre-Civil War Ohio Congressman with remarkable powers of comic inventiveness, including a formidable capacity for invective. Corwin was widely regarded as one of the most versatile and brilliant speakers of his day, and if his reputation has not survived, this is in part because of his leadership in the ill-fated Whig party. He was apparently haunted, however, by the belief that his reputation as an entertainer had limited his political career, and perhaps blocked his path to the Presidency. Auer quotes Corwin's comment to Roscoe Conkling, just before his death in 1865, that "I am old and infirm, and in the common way of life I must soon die. Men will remember me as a joker!" And Auer also cites Corwin's comment to Carl Schurz on the matter of humor:

I want to say something personal to you. At Allegheny City I heard you speak, and I noticed that you can crack a joke, and make people laugh if you try. I want to say to you, young man, if you have any such faculty, don't cultivate it. I know how great the temptation is; I have yielded to it. One of the most dangerous things to a public man is to become known as a jester.

People will go to hear such a man, and then they will be disappointed if he talks to them seriously. They will hardly listen to the best things he offers them. They will want to hear the buffoon and are dissatisfied if the buffoon talks sober sense.[17]

Corwin's gift for exaggeration was part of his comic inventiveness, and he exhibits this gift in his rejection of his own style. Nevertheless, he does pose the issue of the extent to which a speaker who wishes to be known as more than an entertainer should use a humorous manner.

The four dimensions of style thus far discussed do not necessarily form a set of dimensions sufficient for the description of all variations in the speaker's manner. Other dimensions could be readily supplied. Such dimensions as profuse–economical, partisan–impartial, and aggressive–conciliatory come readily to mind. Each gives a somewhat different perspective to the observation of style, and each opens a possible line of inquiry for judging the merit of a particular speaker's choice in a particular speaking situation.

STYLE AS PUBLIC ROLE

The discussion thus far has examined *style* from the traditional perspective of precepts for effective style, and from the perspective of dimensions of stylistic choice available to the speaker. Both perspectives are analytical; neither supports readily a summation or characterization of the image of the man speaking. We turn therefore to a synoptic perspective on style, viewed as the public role of the speaker.[18]

[17] The discussion of Corwin's career, including the original citations of the passages quoted appears in J. Jeffery Auer, "Tom Corwin: Men Will Remember Me as a Joker," *Quarterly Journal of Speech*, XXXIII (February, 1947), 9–14.

[18] An approach to viewing style as public role is that of seeking to identify broad classes of manner which are fulfilled by the characteristic language behavior of a writer or speaker. Thus Walker Gibson gives the labels, *tough, sweet,* and *stuffy* to three styles which he finds evident in contemporary prose writing. In these terms, Gibson writes, "The Tough Talker . . . is a man dramatized as centrally concerned with himself—his style is *I*-talk. The Sweet Talker goes out of his way to be nice to us—his talk is *you*-talk. The Stuffy Talker expresses no concern either for himself or his reader—his style is *it*-talk."

Walker's terms could be used as labels for the public roles assumed by speakers. We will explore labels which suggest more of the different vocational or social contexts within which speakers fulfill their roles. See Walker Gibson, *Tough, Sweet and Stuffy* (Bloomington: Indiana University Press, 1966), p. 179.

This point of view assumes that speakers tend to organize their behavior in terms of a public role, or set of roles, which they hope to fulfill. The speaker discovers his role or roles through experience with audience reactions, joined to his perceptions of the expectancies held by his audiences and the expectancies created by the occasions or social situations in which he appears. Thus the speaker may come to see himself standing in relation to his audiences as "the wise teacher" (reflective, erudite, tentative), or the "bold or charismatic leader" (colorful, direct, tough, aggressive), or "the good agent" (cordial, attentive, searching to serve), and so forth. His self-image will be influenced by his perception of the expectancies of the situations in which he speaks. Thus, role expectancies may vary for the person who fills the position of teacher, politician, lawyer, preacher, or businessman; and speakers who hold these positions will have their behaviors shaped by their concept of the expectancies provided by such contexts. The speaker's self-image will be further shaped by his experience with favorable and unfavorable audience response to his efforts and by the limitations and possibilities of his personal resources of appearance, voice, and language. The speaker's manner becomes a manifestation of his self-image. His audience's image of the man speaking becomes an interpretation of his total manner.

Presumably, speakers can learn to manage several public roles suited to different contexts and audiences. Skilled actors can assuredly do this, although they work with language provided by others and work strenuously at the management of new roles. Skilled public speakers seem generally to carry many of the marks of a personal or individual manner into all of the public contexts in which they appear. Thus one could perceive differences in the speaking style of Harry Truman the Senator, and Harry Truman the President of the United States, but one could also perceive the continuity of style in the direct and plainspoken manner characteristic of the man. Similarly, the style of Hubert Humphrey as Vice President of the United States differed from the style of Hubert Humphrey as Senator or Mayor of Minneapolis. But the qualities of exuberance, aggressiveness, fervor, warmth, and prolixity were marked in all these contexts.

One could develop an extensive list of public roles taken by American public speakers, and could observe in each the sense in which the style of speakers filling it reflects the expectancies of the role as well as the individuality of the speaker. A reasonably adequate taxonomical description of such roles would become a book in itself, since it would reflect the institutional structure of our entire society. Our purpose here is not to present such a description of the style of the major social roles taken by American public speakers, but to describe briefly the interaction of role and style in two familiar and contrasting contexts. The illustrative materials for the discussion will be drawn from a few speech manuscripts. Illustration is thus limited to style as revealed in the choice and ordering of words.

The Academic Manner

Presumably the academic manner reflects a concern for ideas, a capacity to perceive and reflect the complexity of experience, an affection for language and its uses, and resourcefulness in commanding the materials provided by received knowledge. Educational institutions are supposed to respect *erudition* as the product of long hours of study of the best that has been thought and said, *rationality* as the product of skill in the handling of evidence and reasoning, and *moderation* as the product of experience with the complexity of human experience, the variety of human beliefs, and the impermanence of many "truths" once held to be self-evident or imperishable. The manner produced by the expectancies of the academy tends toward *abstractness* in its concern for fundamental ideas, *complexity* in its respect for largeness of vision, *irony* in its perception of the disproportion between reality and appearances, and *formality* or *reserve* in its respect for the privacy or independence of other persons.

At its best the academic manner seeks to join the abstractness of concern for large or important ideas to the concreteness of vivid examples, of metaphors which embody the ideas in question, or of carefully drawn line of argument. It seeks to join complexity of thought to clarity of thought so that difficult subject matter becomes ultimately intelligible. It seeks to moderate the passion of strongly-held beliefs by respect for contrary opinion. If the academic world asks for reserve and formality, it also asks for cordiality and candor.

At its worst the academic manner turns toward pedantry or the excesses of language sometimes termed "pedagese." Pedantry is marked by lack of engagement with the audience; "it is enough," the pedant seems to say, "that I announce my subject matter without particular concern for its availability, use, or interest to any particular set of listeners." To the pedant, formality of manner is an excuse for lack of any engagement with listeners; the complexity of truth is an excuse for obscurity; the abstractness of large ideas is an excuse for the absence of commitment, or of a strong tone or attitude in the speaker's utterance; and the pious respect that erudition demands is an excuse for lack of wit. The pedant honors abstract ideas by his disinterest in those who listen, and seeks to praise the cool strength of human reason by affecting lack of passion or commitment.

"Pedagese" or academic jargon marks the inflation of small thoughts with excess verbiage, seeking a false sense of profundity. "It is the case," says the speaker, "supported by the estimable research of Professor Whorstsniffle, that members of familial assemblies revealing a high degree of interpersonal rapport engage in a markedly greater number, at a highly statistically significant level, of mutually supportive verbal interactions than do members of familial assemblies in which interpersonal rapport is lacking." In other words, members of families who like one another say nice things to one another.

For an example of the academic manner in an elaborately formal, yet genial speaker of the nineteenth century, we turn to the introduction to a ceremonial speech given by Henry James, Sr., on the Fourth of July, 1861, to a public audience at Newport. In his introduction James plays with a concept of "spread-eagle" oratory, a style often associated with Fourth of July ceremonies. In the nineteenth century spread-eagleism implied passionate and elevated tributes to the greatness of the American, unqualified by any sense of limitation for this nation, and holding that Divine Providence had marked America for greatness in all its worlds. James is not unaware of the expectations created by an Independence Day ceremony, nor does he really fail to respond to these expectancies. But he does set the stage for a somewhat more philosophic venture into patriotic affirmation of America's greatness.

A friend observed to me a few days since, as I accepted the invitation with which your Committee of Arrangements had honored me, to officiate as your orator on this occasion, that I could hardly expect, under the circumstances, to regale my auditors with the usual amount of spread-eagleism. I replied, that that depended upon what he meant by spread-eagleism. If he meant what was commonly meant by it, namely, so clearly defined a Providential destiny for our Union, that, do what we please, we shall never fall short of it, I could never, under any circumstances, the most opposed even to existing ones, consent to flatter my hearers with that unscrupulous rubbish. No doubt many men, whose consciences have been drugged by our past political prosperity, do fancy some such inevitable destiny as this before us,—do fancy that we may become so besotted with the lust of gain as to permit the greatest rapacity on the part of our public servants, the most undisguised and persistent corruption on the part of our municipal and private agents, without forfeiting the Providential favor. From that sort of spread-eagleism I told my friend that I hoped we were now undergoing a timely and permanent deliverance. But if he meant by that uncouth word an undiminished, yea, a heightened confidence in our political sanity and vigor, and in the fresh and glowing manhood which is to be in yet larger measure than ever the legitimate fruit of our institutions, I could assure him that my soul was full of it, and it would be wholly my fault if my auditors did not feelingly respond to it.

I never felt proud of my country for what many seem to consider her prime distinction, namely, her ability to foster the rapid accumulation of private wealth. It does not seem to me a particularly creditable thing, that a greater number of people annually grow richer under our institutions than they do anywhere else. It is a fact, no doubt, and like all facts has its proper amiable signification when exposed to the rectifying light of Truth. But it is not the fact which in a foreign land, for example, has made my heart to throb and my cheeks to glow when I remembered the great and happy people beyond the sea, when I thought of the vast and fertile land that lay blossoming and beckoning to all mankind beyond the setting sun. For there in Europe one sees this same private wealth, in less diffused form, it is true, concentrated in greatly fewer hands, but associated in many cases with things that go every way to dignify it or give it a lustre not its own,—associated with traditional family refinement, with inoffensive un-ostentatious manners, with the practice of art and science and literature, and sometimes with the pursuit of toilsome and honorable personal adventure . . .

No; what makes one's pulse to bound when he remembers his own home under foreign skies, is never the rich man, nor the learned man, nor the distinguished man of any sort who illustrates its history, for in all these petty products almost every country may favorably, at all events tediously, compete with our own; but it is all simply the abstract manhood itself of the country, man himself unqualified by convention, the man to whom all these conventional men have been simply introductory, the man who—let me say it—for the first time in human history finding himself in his own right erect under God's sky, and feeling himself in his own right the peer of every other man, spontaneously aspires and attains to a far freer and profounder culture of his nature than has ever yet illustrated humanity.[19]

From the perspective of the twentieth century, James' style seems elaborate, particularly in its use of long periods with an extensive piling on of both extensions and modification of his ideas. English professor Walker Gibson, writing in *The Limits of Language,* observes a movement of style in our century toward greater informality and spontaneity, toward a greater mixture of standard and colloquial diction in the address of academicians.

A passage from a speech by David Horne, executive editor of the Yale University Press, will illustrate this shift. Horne spoke in a 1962 meeting of the American Association of University Professors in Palo Alto, California. His title was "I'd Rather Be Right Than Webster," and

[19] The full text appears in Joseph Blau, ed., *American Philosophic Addresses, 1700–1900* (New York: Columbia University Press, 1946), pp. 234–36.

the title, a verbal play with a hackneyed bit of political piety ("I'd rather be right than President"), illustrates the prevalence of casual irony in contemporary academic speaking. Horne is discussing the controversy stirred up by the publication of *Webster's Third New International Dictionary*. *Webster's Third* had featured a greater presentation of linguistic data on the actual writing and speaking practices of Americans than had any of its predecessors; and as such it had been the subject of sharp attack by critics who wanted a dictionary to set standards of usage and pronunciation, rather than report usage. In his introduction Horne plays with a variety of topical allusions, all of which assume a literate and well-read audience: reference to C. P. Snow's speech "The Two Cultures," which was a discussion of communication problems between scientists and humanists in the modern world; reference to a speech by President Kennedy at Yale University; and reference to Noah Webster as an historical person.

The other day I sat down behind a table weighted with the epitomes of two cultures—not C. P. Snow's but G. and C. Merriam's—and pondered gloomily the assignment which had been given me: to start a discussion of Webster's Third as opposed to the Second, and to raise a question of an editor's proper use of dictionaries and style books.

As I tried to think of what to say that would be interesting even if not new, I remembered President Kennedy's quip of the week before in New Haven—that he now had the best of two worlds; a Harvard education and a Yale degree. We have something like that situation in Webster's Second and Webster's Third: The Second, with its emphasis on tradition, on authority, on philology, and the Third, with *its* emphasis on fashion, on current usage, on linguistics. Since Noah Webster was a Yale man with Harvard leanings, it's fitting—if not fashionable—that a representative of Yale should be asked to attempt an eclectic approach to the problems raised by the Third Edition as those problems affect all university press editors.

The issue I intend to raise is so important that its cuts to the heart of the editing process. Ultimately, how one decides it depends on one's temperament. The question can be raised in many different ways. For example, in your own attitude toward grammar, diction, good usage, do you tend to be prescriptive or descriptive? Would you rather be right than modern? Are you at all interested that D. D. Eisenhower and S. J. Perelman helped to legitimatize the word *finalize?* Do you disapprove of *legitimatize* and itch to change it to *legitimize?* Do you deplore that both words are in Webster's Third, and so, for that matter, are *legitimist, legitimism,* and *legitimation?*

The recent bad press of the Third has caused many conscientious prescriptive editors to wonder whether they should buy *in* six at $47.50

or buy *up* one of the remaining copies of the Second at the going rate of $39.50.

At Yale we were lucky: our science editor was given a copy of the Third, and she makes it available to the staff. A poll taken just before I left showed that she was the only one who had consulted it; possibly the rest of us are too lazy to walk over to her office. I still rely on the easily heftable 5th-edition Collegiate.

Yet this 1936 Collegiate is outdated by the 1961 Collegiate and by such recent abridged dictionaries as the New World and the American College, as well as by the unabridged Third. Is it then foolish to consult the Collegiate, and dangerous to rely on it?

(1) What should a dictionary do?

(2) How much and in what way should an editor use a dictionary, and tools like the "Chicago Style Manual"?

(3) How does his use of such tools affect his editing?

(4) From an editor's point of view, what *is* right and what wrong?

I'd like to generalize (not finalize) some tentative answers to these big questions. . . .[20]

In speaking of the academic manner, or in examining texts said to illustrate some of the characteristics of that manner, one must be careful to distinguish manner as a group role from the manner of particular academicians. We have been discussing tendencies in the style of academic speakers which might be derived from the expectations held for the role of the scholar or the man of learning. But scholars or men of learning are clearly a diverse set of individuals given to a great variety of personal styles. It is observable that academicians of the nineteenth century, at least as we know them from the texts of their speaking, seemed to share many characteristics of manner in the management of language. They also shared a somewhat common education, based on the study of a common literary heritage; a common study of the classical languages; and a common study of grammar, rhetoric, logic, and philosophy. It is equally observable that academicians in our own century pursue such highly specialized bodies of knowledge and methodologies of research that they may have little education in common except a similar experience with the rigorous intellectual exercise of study. Growth and specialization of knowledge has had a profound effect on the extent to which scholars today start with similar assumptions, use similar language, refer to a similar body of historical precedent. Today individuality of style among academicians may seem a more apparent phenomenon than the commonalities of style suggested by an academic role and manner.

[20] An edited text of David Horne's speech appears in *Publishers' Weekly*, CLXXXII (July 16, 1962), 24–27.

Nevertheless academicians in our century continue to "recognize" one another from signs provided by manner or style. For example, it was not simply a matter of political philosophy or program that caused the general academic community in the United States to reveal so much enthusiasm for the Presidential candidacy of Adlai Stevenson in the 1952 and 1956 Presidential elections, and to reveal a corresponding lack of enthusiasm for the man who won both these elections, President Dwight Eisenhower. Stevenson's manner of speaking—often tentative in dealing with complex political problems, frequently ironic in its reference to political platitudes or pieties, rich in its use of historical knowledge—was the manner of academicians. The manner was never completely obscured by Stevenson's role as a practicing and often successful politician.

The Journalistic Manner

If academicians are supposed to live with the unhurried contemplation of large ideas, journalists are supposed to live with the hurly-burly of daily events and the task of making these events so interesting and exciting as to enchant an audience, and so clear as to make a mass audience believe itself better informed. The expectancies surrounding the role of the journalist in American life tend to be set by the press rather than the public platform, but these expectancies permeate the role of any public speaker who sees immediacy of audience response as a primary criterion of effective style. If the academician seeks profundity, the journalist seeks color, human interest, or excitement. If the academician seeks to transcend conflict by placing it in historical or philosophic perspective, the journalist seeks to sharpen conflict. If the academician is fond of the ironic tone of contemplation, the journalist enjoys the eristic tone of men strongly engaged in any topic of the day. If the academician abhors the oversimplification of complex questions, the journalist abhors the absence of immediate clarity in the treatment of any question. The academician may use an example to clarify an abstract generalization derived from a more tedious analysis of evidence; the journalist may use an example or two to demonstrate or suggest some general truth. The academic manner may, to its detriment, tend to ignore the requirements of a present audience in its concentration on the demands of subject matter. The journalistic manner may, to its detriment, tend to ignore the demands of any subject in its concentration on pleasing the present audience. The signs of the journalistic manner are concreteness, the use of colorful or affecting anecdotal materials, a taste for the excitement of conflict and the extremes of human misery or triumph, strong assertiveness, informality, and spontaneity.

At its best the journalistic manner achieves clarity, excitement, and an immediate engagement with the listener, joined to a sense of proportion and the difference between the important and the merely exciting. At its worst the style descends to "journalese," a counterpart of pedagese. In journalese, excitement and color become their own ends, and the trivial is cloaked not by an excess of academic jargon, but by the pretense that the human appetite for stories of violence, success, and the sentimental makes all such stories profound.

For an example of journalistic style in speaking we turn to the introduction to a speech entitled "Censors and Their Tactics" presented by Jack Nelson, a reporter for the Atlanta *Constitution,* to a conference on "Freedom of Information" sponsored by the University of Missouri School of Journalism, November 6–7, 1963. Mr. Nelson is a practicing journalist facing an audience including many academicians. He is himself an author, well-informed in his subject.

You and I have a common cause—the pursuit of truth—and we face a common enemy in that pursuit. For those that would censor the books that students read would just as surely censor the press. They oppose any free exchange of ideas or publication of facts they consider obnoxious.

My subject is the activities of these censorship forces and the damage they do to our educational system by pressuring for the banning and alteration of books.

Today the United States is in the midst of a great social revolution. It affects every American. It has been building up for years. Yet it seems to have come suddenly and many people are at a loss to understand it—not only in the South, but in the North, in all sections of the country.

In this age of exploding knowledge, when man is reaching for the moon and we talk about brinksmanship and a nuclear war that could devastate civilization, we still publish high school history books that refer only to the War Between the States, a euphemism to please Southern ears. For that matter many Southern newspapers eschew the name "Civil War."

Shortly after the Civil War a New York publisher advertised: "Books prepared for Southern schools by Southern authors, and therefore free from matter offensive to Southern people."

But times have changed and regional texts have given way to books competing for a national market. So now the trick is to offend as few people as possible. The result is that many books lack vitality and are too dull to interest the students. Controversial subjects are treated superficially or not at all.

An American history text, complete through the 1960 election, deals with Southern resistance to the Supreme Court in a single sentence. It is little wonder that the Negroes' rebellion against second-class citizenship catches many Americans by surprise.

To read many textbooks you would think Americans are all white, Anglo-Saxon, Protestant, white-collared and middle class. Two university professors, after perusing a number of social studies books, concluded that students would get the impression that "all Americans live on wide, shady streets in clean suburban areas, occupy Cape Cod style houses, drive a new automobile, have two children (a boy and a girl, of course), and own a dog."

Problems of non-English-speaking migrant workers, smog, water shortages, crowded housing, slums, poverty, crime and disease are glossed over in many texts.

Now textbook publishers do not avoid publishing information about controversial subjects because they believe this is the best way to promote education. They do it because in some cases it is not only the best, but the only way they can sell their product.

The publishers face a dilemma. Every time they show the courage to explore controversial subjects in depth they risk economic setbacks caused by censorship forces. Even relatively minor matters can cost them sales. For example, in Bastrop, Louisiana, recently, the school board, learning that Macmillan planned a new line of readers in 1965 which would ignore an old taboo and show white and Negro children playing together, banned the books and urged the rest of the state to do likewise.

In our research for *The Censors and the Schools,* Gene Roberts and I found that the pressures for the elimination of censorship of "unpleasant" ideas or facts often come from diametrically opposed forces. . . .[21]

As with our discussion of the academic manner, one must distinguish discussion of tendencies in the journalistic manner from discussion of the manner of particular journalists. Academicians, politicians, ministers, and businessmen may all seek the journalistic manner in their public address; practicing journalists include men who reveal a wide variety of individual styles.

Varied Roles

The discussion of the academic and journalistic styles has been illustrative of the possibility of ascribing group stylistic tendencies produced by the expectancies present in the public roles assumed by a variety of public speakers. The same kind of analysis could be applied to other public roles: the politician, the business leader, the minister, the professional public lecturer, the creative artist turned lecturer. For reasons earlier described we shall not pursue this line of inquiry further. Rather, we turn briefly to question: Is there a general and preferred American style of public speaking?

[21] The full text of Mr. Nelson's speech appears in a pamphlet entitled *Six Speeches, Sixth Annual Freedom of Information Conference* (Columbia, Missouri: Freedom of Information Center, School of Journalism, University of Missouri, April, 1964), pp. 1–7.

The General Role of the Public Speaker

The easiest observation about successful American public speakers is that their styles vary greatly. This is the case, and the case is supported by our general analysis of the variety of purposes, situations, institutional relationships, and audience expectancies which set limits to the prudent choices possible to speakers. American culture is conspicuously pluralistic rather than homogeneous. It features and values variety and individuality. Public speaking is both the child of culture and the agent of social organization as part of culture. Given a pluralistic culture as the setting for public speaking, the safest generalization to make about a good style is the one frequently given in this book: the good style is one prudently adapted to the speaker's person, his purpose, his subject, his audience, and the occasion. Only by an analysis of the interaction of these five variables in a given case can one derive specific statements about a good style for that case.

Granting the impossibility of generating a concrete description of a "good style," applicable to all speakers and all occasions, it is nevertheless possible to make some statements about the general role of the public speaker in American society, statements which in turn imply some of the stylistic tendencies likely to be valued regardless of the particularities of the situation.

The public speaker is expected to take command of a situation. For the duration of his address he is the focal point of an event and he alone is capable of giving definition to that event. The nature of the speaker's general role suggests a certain ascendancy of manner; a force and firmness revealed physically, vocally, and through language which is greater than that required by casual conversation. Physical, vocal, and verbal animation are essential to the act of taking command.

The public speaker is expected to give attention to his audience. The event lacks definition if the audience is not intrinsic to its action. Attention to the audience suggests a considerable measure of physical and verbal directness. The speaker should look to his audience with the intention of seeing its members as people. He should acknowledge physically and verbally any response in the audience which represents courtesy, warmth, or regard for the speaker. He should feature person-to-person language, references to the audience, to self, to shared perspectives. The pronouns "you," "we," and "I" are common to the style of direct public address. So are the verbal gestures recognizing the status, experiences, and dispositions of listeners.

The public speaker is an object of audience attention. We have repeatedly emphasized that audiences gather to hear a man speaking, not simply to hear exposition on some given body of subject matter. Audience interest in the speaker as a person is intrinsic to the event and is justly a part of the event. The role of the public speaker is to make known not simply information or opinion, but to make known his own manner of thought and feeling. Good style requires a definiteness of tone and attitude, a certain physical, vocal, and verbal spontaneity which renders the speaker as a person knowable to his listeners. We have also suggested earlier in this chapter some of the considerations of judgment governing speakers' choices as to the level of spontaneity or openness suitable to a particular occasion. We suggest here that the total avoidance of spontaneity, of personal commitment to tone and attitude by the speaker, is a denial of the nature of the speaking situation and the general expectancies concerning the role of the speaker.

Other comments can be made on the general and preferred role for American public speakers derivable from the nature of values widely honored by American culture. We shall, however, defer such discussion to the next chapter, in which consideration will be given to the American audience, and turn briefly here to consideration of the problem of acquiring a style.

STYLE AS A PERSONAL SEARCH

Abraham Lincoln's address at Cooper Union, given in 1860, has been marked as both transitional and formative in Lincoln's life. Prior to this address his audience had been largely regional—his speaking characterized by the casual, colloquial, and ancedotal style of the country lawyer and by the appeals to regional self-interest evident in his campaigns to represent the State of Illinois in Congress. At Cooper Union Lincoln spoke as a national figure, to an audience concerned with the constitutional and political crisis of an entire nation. The "voice" Lincoln found in 1860 preceded his nomination for the Presidency; it was never forgotten in the set of singularly eloquent speeches Lincoln gave as the nation's President.

Lincoln's search for and discovery of a new "voice" served to fulfill his career. His successor as President, Andrew Johnson, also carried a voice he had discovered into the Presidency, but with disastrous consequences. James D. Barber, in an analysis of Johnson's Presidential style, calls attention to the circumstances in Johnson's career which addicted him to aggressive, emotive, dogmatic public speaking.[22] A subdued, generous, patient, and tentative man in office, Johnson was "wild on the

---

[22] See James D. Barber, "Adult Identity and Presidential Style: The Rhetorical Emphasis," *Daedalus*, LXXXXVII, No. 3 (Summer, 1968), 938–968.

stump," his flights of oratory filled with the pride and passion of office; and venomous attacks on his political enemies contributed no little to his impeachment.

There is no evidence which would justify a view of either Lincoln or Johnson as men who self-consciously sought after the style which marked their later years. But it would be quite accurate to picture their lives as embodying a process of search and discovery culminating in possession of those styles. So it becomes for all persons who move vigorously to the public platform. Their style is not so much a property they carry with them into their first experiences with speaking; it is rather the culmination of a process of personal growth and discovery—a public self not to be known at once, but to be sought after and ultimately known.

The importance, even the fatefulness, of the search for a style needs acknowledgment. Until the search has been undertaken and becomes in some measure productive, the speaker himself cannot be reckoned as a genuine force in the total speaking event. We have repeatedly observed the speaking event as embracing a set of situational variables, each of which makes its demands on the speaker. It is not too far from such a view of a public speech to a position so limiting to the speaker's role as to make him seem only a dependent variable responding to some social process which has chosen him to talk, and which will choose another if he does not serve the blind forces energizing social process and change. Such a view sees the speaker, as Emerson put it, as one armed with skills ". . . only a degree higher than the coaxing of an auctioneer." [23]

A different view of the speaker sees him as entering the speaking situation as a free man, in full possession of his own positions, his own view of reality, his own voice or total manner. This speaker has a style in some sense different from that of all other men. It is his own—won by study, by experience, by engagement in public affairs. He has become an independent force in human history capable of confronting or challenging an audience, an occasion, a situation, rather than merely serving all those circumstances which bear upon him.

SUMMARY

Style is the total manner of the man speaking. The concept embraces manner as found in the vocal and physical aspects of speech delivery, and in the selection and arrangement of words. Such a view makes style at once the broadest perspective from which to view the public speech,

[23] Ralph Waldo Emerson, *Society and Solitude* (Boston: Houghton Mifflin and Company, 1893), p. 75.

and the perspective directing our attention to the greatest number of concrete details about the speaker. No smaller concept does justice to the sense in which listeners come to know the speaker as a person whose total manner of address embraces and transcends the substance and structure of his content, and makes him knowable as a person.

Style has often been studied only as a matter of word choice and arrangement. Such studies have been characteristically prescriptive. They have set forth and illustrated certain qualities of style thought to be good, such as good public usage, liveliness, and appropriateness; or bad, such as obscurity, colorlessness, lack of energy, prolixity, or inappropriateness of usage or tone. Such treatments of style also analyze the variety of resources available through the creation of figures of speech or figures of thought. The traditional accounts of style have their uses, although they tend to be reductive in that they attend strongly to some part of the speaker's total manner without seeking a view of the whole nature of his action.

Style may also be studied from the point of view that the manner of a speaker is a choice lying at some point along certain dimensions of manner. Thus speakers are relatively abstract or concrete, ornate or simple, personal or impersonal, and serious or humorous.

A further perspective on style may be gained by examining the speaker's manner as related to the expectancies attached to the speaker's public role. This viewpoint assumes the possibility of identifying a cluster of characteristics of manner observable as tendencies in groups of speakers who take public positions as academicians, journalists, ministers, politicians, entertainers, and so forth. It is possible to posit a general and preferred public manner for speakers in American society, derived from an examination of the general expectancies attached to the act of speaking.

The acquisition of a style may be viewed as a process of search and discovery. The search and its product is fateful for the speaker. His existence as a genuine force in public life demands that he take possession of a voice which is his own, and not a mere reflection of the demands of other aspects of the speaking situation.

CHAPTER 7

The Speaker's Audience

The fundamental fact of human existence is neither the individual as such nor the aggregate as such. Each, considered by itself, is a mighty abstraction. The individual is a fact of existence insofar as he steps into a living relation with other individuals. The aggregate is a fact of existence insofar as it is built up of living units of relation.

—Martin Buber

PUBLIC SPEAKING AND THE AUDIENCE

Many of the most crucial problems of choice facing the speaker rise from his estimate of the nature of his audience and the accommodation he will make to it. The accommodation may be quite unselfconscious—a bringing together of speaker and audience who identify with one another so closely in matters of style and position that the speech seems simply an expression of all that is already latent in the audience. But speakers do not often enjoy such an easy common substance with all members of their audience. The art of speaking then becomes a conscious search for proper accommodation.

Some devices of accommodation are obvious enough. We have already observed the custom of speakers to be pleased to find themselves addressing a particular audience; their search for ways of acknowledging any special merit that may be found in members of the audience; their habit of announcing points of "common ground" with the audience ("I was born on a farm," or "I recall my own days of service in the armed forces"); their custom of presenting attractive and undisputed truths as an entry into positions that may be controversial. These devices recognize the general truth that the speaker must find a link between purposes, attitudes, and values already present in the audience, and the purposes, attitudes, and values the speaker wishes to be accepted. The audience will act for its own reasons, which are not necessarily those of the speaker; and the use of rhetoric is to acknowledge the proper claim of this fact.

Behind the devices of accommodation, and behind the general truth these devices acknowledge, lie the problems of method: How may speakers usefully come to know their audience and how may they view the variety of possible relationships they might form with a particular audience? We turn in this chapter to these major questions.

HOW AUDIENCES MAY BE KNOWN

Some books on public speaking approach study of the audience through study of the general nature of human behavior. A theoretical account may be given of how any person acquires purposes, needs, and values, and how these shape his response to the speaking of others. Thus we commonly observe that all men have needs or motives, partly determined by their biological nature, and partly by the impress of experience. Certain needs seem common to persons in our culture: the need for physiological security; the need for emotional security—for recognition, group membership, and status; the need for self-approval, or living in accordance with one's own values; and the need to carry out habitual ways of responding to one's environment. Although these general needs may be common to all men, each person may perceive a particular need in ways peculiar to his own experience. Thus one man may come to believe that hard work is a threat to health, and another to believe that idleness is a threat to health. Both men may long for good health, but their response to a speaker who advocated the strenuous life would be quite different. Similarly, one man might come to believe that emotional security belongs to those who achieve wealth; that in the words of a cynical aphorism, "It is better to be rich and healthy than poor and sick." Another man might link emotional security to freedom from the pursuit of material things. The two men share a common human need, but they are likely to react quite differently to a speech on "Ten Ways to Become a Millionaire."

Theoretical accounts of the nature and development of human behavior help us to understand why a public speech may succeed greatly with some listeners, and fail greatly with others. Such accounts are also important to the person-to-person persuader, who is able to adapt his discourse to the unique perceptions of a particular listener. But intensive study of the nature and development of human behavior tends to direct the attention of the public speaker to the behavior of individuals rather than the behavior of audiences, and to leave unsolved the speaker's problem of adapting his discourse to a specific audience, most of whose members may be unknown to the speaker.

The Audience as a Group

We suggest that the public speaker seldom knows his audience as an assembly of particular persons, each possessed of somewhat unique perceptions and attitudes. In some cases the speaker may have such intimate knowledge of his listeners. He may address a small audience of people he knows well. But for the most part the speaker is denied the particular knowledge that a salesman may have of a customer, or a conversationalist of an acquaintance. And even if the public speaker could know each person in his audience, the idea of a public speech somehow adapted to the unique needs of each member of an assembly is absurd.

The public speaker addresses a group. He talks to his concept of the purposes, positions, attitudes, and expectancies of that group. In other words, the speaker knows his audience not as the summation of the characteristics of ten, or fifty, or two thousand individuals, but as an assembly which reflects the characteristics of one or several societal groups. Thus the speaker's knowledge of the audience reflects his assumptions about the way in which Democrats or Republicans, college students or businessmen, farmers or workers, teachers or churchmen, etc., will think about the substance of the speaker's discourse.

GROUP STRUCTURE IN SOCIETY AND THE NATURE OF THE AUDIENCE

Aristotle, in his *Rhetoric,* observed that a general theory of finding the means of persuasion in a given case had to rest not on the study of the behavior of individuals, but on the study of the probable behavior of persons belonging to certain groups. "Individual cases," he wrote, "are so infinitely various that no systematic knowledge of them is possible . . . the theory of rhetoric is concerned not with what seems probable to a given individual like Socrates or Hippias, but with what seems probable to men of a given type." [1]

The Athenian philosopher thought that public speakers needed to know about those things that Athenians at a given point in history generally thought to be good or true or desirable; about the kinds of reference likely to arouse pity, indignation, envy and the like; about the differences in the perceptions of young men, elderly men, and men in the prime of life; of men of wealth and men of power as opposed to those less fortunate.

[1] Aristotle, *Rhetorica,* translated by Y. Phys Roberts (Oxford: The Clarendon Press, 1924), I.2, p. 1356b.

The contemporary speaker needs a somewhat more elaborate theory of groups than that proposed by Aristotle. This elaboration is partly the product of the increasing complexity of our social organization. It also reflects the increasing attention social scientists now give to the way in which each person's group affiliations help to determine his positions, values, and attitudes.

A contemporary view of the relationship of individual behavior to group membership can be stated as follows: each person organizes a significant part of his behavior by thinking and acting in ways he believes appropriate to his membership in one or more groups. Thus the person who has or seeks membership in certain political, religious, economic, or social groups will reflect in his own behavior the purposes, positions, values, and attitudes which he thinks appropriate to membership. In this sense, the groups with which each person seeks affiliation become his "reference groups"; the individual "refers" to the positions, values, and attitudes of some group in choosing his own positions, values, and attitudes.

The importance to public speaking of the concept of "reference groups" should be apparent. We observed in Chapter 1 that organized groups, or social institutions, are the product of communication, and that these groups preserve and sometimes transform themselves by further communication. Thus public speeches occur primarily not as the product of the autonomous needs of individuals, but as the product of efforts to organize, sustain, and shape, the life of groups, or social institutions. The public speaker is likely to be known in part to his audience through the groups with which he may be identified. The occasion for his speech is likely to have been defined by the action of some group, whether political, economic, religious, educational, or social. The speaker, in turn, is likely to know his audience by reason of the reference groups he assumes to be represented in his listeners. The extent to which assumptions about group purposes, positions, values, and attitudes determine the knowledge that speakers and listeners have of one another is clearly indicated by many of the clichés of the public-speaking situation: by the introduction which refers to the speaker as a Democrat or scholar or business leader or college student; or by the speaker who addresses his "fellow Republicans," or who finds himself "happy to be talking to the business leaders of this fine community."

The Politician and His Audience

Political candidates provide a good illustration of the practice of viewing an audience in terms of its reference-group affiliations. Candidates for public office are notably self-conscious seekers after effective discourse. If the candidate seeks national office, the audience he concerns himself with is much larger and more complex than those faced by the generality of public speakers. But the politician's need is the same as that of any public speaker—to know as much as possible about his audience.

In his Pulitzer Prize winning book on the 1960 American Presidential election, Theodore H. White asserts that all wisdom about the behavior of American voters in a political campaign can "be boiled down to a single sentence of truth, beyond which we know not: *Every American election summons the individual voter to weigh the past against the future.*"

"The past," White writes, "consists variously of the voter's ethnic stock, the way his father voted, the tales his mother told him, the prejudices he has accumulated on the way of life, the class and the status he has attained or inherited. And the future consists of his fears and dreams; if he is a farmer, his fear of being squeezed out; if he is a Negro, his aspiration for libertarian equality; if he is a businessman, hope and fear for his enterprise; if he is a pensioner, his dependence on the social security system; and for all, the future course of America in war and peace." [2]

The verbal assaults of political candidates upon voters, White suggests, start with analysis of the voters' past. The past, with its massive influences on what the voter can become or will permit himself to become, must somehow be joined to the future that the candidate hopes that voters will choose. It is to the subtle dialectic between what the voter is and what he may become that the candidate addresses his rhetorical skill.

The Speaker's Audience

White's comment on the political candidate's audience, impressionistic as it may be, is instructive. "The politician's map of America," says White, "differs from the geographic map." The politician's map of the voters whom he addresses is formed by calculating approximately the various *reference groups* in which voters find membership. The voter is not thought of as an individual, possessed of a unique set of purposes, needs, attitudes, and values. Rather he is thought of as a member of a variety of groups, each of which has some level of significance to him, and each of which defines in some way the purposes, needs, attitudes, and values with which the voter identifies. The candidate's voter is not Tom, Dick, or Harry. He is Democrat, Republican, or independent; con-

[2] Theodore H. White, *The Making of the President 1960* (New York: The Atheneum House, Inc., Giant Cardinal Edition, 1961), p. 234.

servative, liberal, or moderate; black, red, yellow, or white; Protestant, Catholic, or Jew; old, young, or middle-aged; businessman, white-collar worker, laborer, union member, farmer, doctor, lawyer, teacher, unemployed, or retired. He is rich, poor, or middle-income; city-dweller, small-town resident, or suburbanite. Despite the fading of immigrant ties, he is still German-American, Scandinavian-American, Afro-American, Mexican-American, Polish-American, Italian-American, Puerto Rican-American, or Japanese-American. The map of the audience set up by such groupings provides only the grossest approximation of the groups in which large numbers of voters find membership. Any such set of groups could be elaborated. But the important fact about this description of the way in which the politician sees his audience is not that his map of reference groups may be unsophisticated. It is rather that the audience is in fact perceived as an assemblage of reference groups—a gathering of various political, ethnic, economic, social, religious, educational, and cultural groups.

The groups in which individuals find membership may be formally organized, highly self-conscious associations, as in the case of a church, a political party, a club, a business organization, or a labor union. They may also be much more amorphous sets of associations—a social, educational, or economic class. They may be associations based on similarities of age or sex or recreational preferences. The individual's perception of his membership in certain groups is likely to be accompanied by a contrasting recognition of groups with which he feels little or no identification. And given human propensity to satisfy one's own ego by feeling superior to or despising others, the awareness of membership in some groups may sometimes be accompanied by hostility toward other groups. Thus, one may see himself as young rather than old; as a Democrat rather than as a Republican; as black rather than white; as Catholic rather than Protestant, Jew, or agnostic; as educated rather than ignorant; as cultivated in taste rather than a lowbrow.

THE DATA PROVIDED BY REFERENCE GROUPS

Three generalizations will serve to summarize the way in which a speaker may discover, appraise, and interpret the knowledge about his audience made available by the reference groups represented in that audience. First, reference groups are significant producers of public and private discourse. They sustain themselves by the communications originating with and addressed to their members. Accordingly, the public speaker does have available a source of information about the positions, values, and attitudes of various reference groups. Second, the position a speaker chooses to espouse is likely to be directly relevant to the positions taken by some of the reference groups represented in his audience. Through the use of reference-group data, it is possible for the speaker to know at the time he develops his discourse that the position he takes is likely, for example, to be popular with Republicans and unpopular with Democrats, or popular with college students and unpopular with their parents, and so forth. Third, inferences from reference-group data about the positions, values, and attitudes represented in a given audience are necessarily quite imprecise. Nevertheless such inferences can be drawn, and can be trusted at some level of probability. We shall examine each of these three generalizations in turn.

Reference Groups Produce Data Concerning Their Positions, Values, and Attitudes. As we have previously observed, organized groups are developed, maintained, and modified through public speaking, as well as through other acts of public and private discourse. One finds conservatives talking to conservatives about the positions, values, and attitudes of conservatism. Similar self-definition is commonplace in the talk of Democrats to Democrats, Republicans to Republicans, Catholics to Catholics, students to students, and so on. In like manner, organizations prepare and distribute printed materials. Newspapers and magazines frequently acknowledge their identification with various religious sects, economic groups, social or educational groups, or other groups determined by age, sex, or occupation. Thus the public speaker who reads and converses widely concerning the subject matter of his discourse has ready access to an understanding of the positions, values, and attitudes that various reference groups hold toward his topic. Speakers are normally advised to read widely in order to become well informed about the matters they talk about in public. They should also be advised to read widely in order to become sensitive to the way in which various reference groups are likely to view the speaker's chosen subject matter.[3]

The Speaker's Position Is Likely to Be Relevant to the Positions of

[3] In observing that a speaker's major source of information about his audience is the public discourse of reference groups represented in the audience, we have omitted discussion of the influence on each listener of positions, attitudes, and values common to the small social groups in which he finds membership—his family, and circles of friends. Such primary social groups influence powerfully the response of members to the discourse of others. But public speakers have little direct access to the particular dynamics of the small social groups to which members of an audience may belong. Hence they must draw most of their inferences about audience positions, attitudes, and values from the discourse of the public reference groups represented in the audience. For discussion of the way in which primary social groups influence the effects of public discourse, see Elihu Katz and Paul Lazarsfield, *Personal Influence* (Glencoe, Illinois: The Free Press, 1964), pp. 1–12, 15–47.

Various Reference Groups. The public speaker seeking a position will seldom find that his topic is unrelated to positions developed by various reference groups which may be represented in his audience. For example, the speaker talking on the topic of "Law and Order" during the 1968 Presidential election campaigns would have available a mass of information on the positions of reference groups in America. This information would be readily at hand in the speeches of the three major Presidential candidates—Richard Nixon, Hubert Humphrey, and George Wallace; in the response of various ethnic and economic groups to the three candidates; in commentary on the topic by religious leaders, lawyers, policemen, students, criminologists, journalists, and so forth, as reported in the mass media or in magazine articles. The speaker could know that the achievement of law and order through application of requisite force was a major position of George Wallace's American Independent Party. He could identify the types of community organizations attracted to Wallace. He could learn that the position attracted favorable response from major segments of the membership of labor unions despite attacks on Wallace by national union leaders; from citizens in middle class, white neighborhoods in the central city area of large metropolitan complexes; from members of police departments and veterans' groups; and from segments of rural, white America. The speaker could know that support of the goal of law and order was also a major, if less salient, theme in the candidacy of the Republican leader, Richard Nixon. He could know that Nixon stressed support for police departments, and restraint in judicial protections of accused persons. He could know that the Democratic candidate, Hubert Humphrey, likewise supported the goal of law and order, but gave still less relative attention to this topic and stressed the position that law and order was a consequence of progress toward justice and economic opportunity. The speaker could observe that black activist leaders treated the phrase "law and order" as a covert sanction for racial injustice, and that activist college students saw emphasis on this theme as an intention to use force in suppressing their activities in support of various social causes. Armed with knowledge about the positions of various reference groups, including knowledge of the nuances in stance assumed by people who supported law and order as a goal, the speaker would be able to estimate how a particular position he might choose would be viewed by constituencies represented in his audience.

Inferences from Reference Group Data Are Precarious but Possible at Some Level of Probability. The prudent public speaker will not assume that the official positions, values, and attitudes of a given reference group will be reflected fully and univocally by all persons who affiliate with that group. For a variety of reasons, inferences from reference-group data concerning the preconceptions of group members are somewhat tenuous.

The difficulty starts with the fact that some large reference groups deliberately seek to maintain the affiliation of members whose opinions on public issues vary greatly. This is conspicuously the case with the two major American political parties, both of which try to maintain the widest range of members of different economic, social, racial, religious, and vocational groups. To know that the members of an audience are Democrats or Republicans may tell us little about their attitudes toward specific issues of public policy unless we know other additional facts about their reference group affiliations. To know that the audience includes Mississippi Democrats rather than Minnesota Democrats may tell us more about the meaning of the affiliation in relation to such issues as states' rights and segregation. Similarly the knowledge that an audience consists predominantly of well-to-do businessmen, with Republican party leanings, can provide the basis for predicting certain attitudes of this audience on governmental fiscal policy, tax policy, and governmental regulation of labor union activity. Thus knowledge of party affiliation joined to knowledge of other reference groups represented in an audience may provide the speaker with a basis for predicting positions, attitudes, and values present in his audience.

In short, group affiliation does not predict the positions, values, and attitudes of any single member of the group with any high degree of accuracy. Only a remarkably naive speaker would suppose that all members of a political party, economic class, vocational group, or religious sect will think alike on specific public issues. But membership in a group does predict group tendencies. And the intersection of a particular set of memberships in a single audience may become the basis for increasingly accurate predictions.

There is a second difficulty in formulating prudent estimates of audience expectancies and preconceptions from knowledge of group memberships. Audience members may be affiliated with two or more reference groups holding conflicting attitudes toward some position of importance to the speaker's position. In such instances, knowledge of multiple affiliations, rather than increasing the security of prediction, may increase the ambiguity of the knowledge to be interpreted. For example, a speaker might take a position on American economic aid to Poland, a nation with a communist government, to an audience whose members were generally affiliated with both the Democratic party and the American Legion. In general since World War II, the leaders of both the Democratic and Republican parties have supported such aid. The position of the leadership of the American Legion, however, has opposed such aid.

In the example cited, the speaker might have to accept the ambiguity of his information about the probable attitude of his audience toward his subject matter. On the other hand, the occasion for the speech could indicate whether the particular audience had assembled by reason of Democratic party affiliation, American Legion affiliation, or neither of these. The educational level of the audience could be significant; in general, the assumptions underlying the use of limited economic aid to communist satellite nations have been more strongly supported by well-educated Americans than by those with less education. Knowledge of religious affiliations predominant in the audience could also aid in interpreting the attitudes of a particular audience. Some religious groups have been more uniformly militant in opposing aid to communist-governed nations than have other religious groups. The speaker might also consider how strongly the two reference groups represented in his audience feel about aid to communist nations. Opposition to American aid to communist nations has been an important and strongly proclaimed article of faith for the American Legion since World War II. By contrast, support for such aid has not been a salient position of either American political party. Thus for the issue in question, the Legion affiliation could be more important to audience preconceptions than political party affiliation.

A final difficulty in interpreting the meaning of audience reference-group affiliations lies in the fact that the meaning of any reference group to its members changes through time. Groups change both as a result of the historical circumstances in which they find themselves, and as the product of communication within the group leading to reformulation of group purposes, positions, attitudes, and values. For example, in 1932 most members of the medical profession in America opposed all kinds of insurance against medical costs. In 1964, the great majority of members of this profession supported voluntary insurance plans for the payment of medical costs, while remaining opposed to compulsory insurance plans operated by the government. By 1966 substantial numbers of medical doctors acknowledged or supported the inevitability of some system of governmental support for the costs of medical care. Opinion within the medical profession had become diverse on this issue. One could observe in the 1960's a similar diffusion of opinion within each of the major political parties on the issue of American involvement in the war in Vietnam, and a growing diffusion of opinion within the Catholic church on issues as complex as the forms of religious worship, population control, the appropriateness of clerical participation in civil rights demonstrations, and the merit of celibacy as a pre-condition of clerical service.

Clearly it is not possible to chart the expectancies and preconceptions of any given group at any particular point in time, and then expect that the chart will remain true throughout history. The judgment a speaker makes of his audience must be based on current knowledge of the internal discourse of reference groups.

We have emphasized the difficulty of moving from knowledge about reference groups to knowledge about the positions, values, and attitudes present in an audience affiliated with such groups. The speaker's knowledge of a particular audience when based on such inference is necessarily tenuous. Nevertheless the speaker who seeks genuine knowledge about the current positions, values, and attitudes of major reference groups; who is attentive to the multiple group affiliations present in any audience—and the possible inconsistencies of such affiliations; who understands that few reference groups achieve anything resembling monolithic loyalty to the group from all its members; and who understands that opinions and attitudes in any audience are likely to be distributed— such a speaker will have achieved a better-than-chance understanding of the audience he addresses.

Additional Aids to Judgment

Given the difficulty of knowing the preconceptions and expectancies of a given audience, speakers need to exploit all possible sources of such knowledge. Thus far we have observed that inferences drawn from knowledge about reference groups is a major source of such knowledge. It is also a source available to all public speakers. We have also emphasized that engaging in, listening to, and reading the discourse produced by various reference groups can give knowledge of the positions, values, and attitudes of these groups. This knowledge is most available to the speaker who looks consciously for the regularities of thought and style which seem to provide the "social glue" for any reference group.

But speakers seeking engagement with large audiences, with high stake in the success of their discourse, and with strong financial resources, may turn to a much more systematic effort to gain knowledge about an audience.

The right arm of the political speaker in mid-twentieth-century America has become the opinion poll. The political candidate speaks for high stakes. A shift in the voting behavior of a relatively few members of his audience may spell the difference between victory and defeat in his search for office. His search for office is often well-financed; a senatorial campaign in a large state may involve the expenditure of from two to four million dollars, and a portion of this sum will usually be spent on opinion polls designed to gain information about the nature of the speaker's audience. Political candidates are voracious consumers of the information provided by the independent polling agencies active in contemporary American society. If a particular poll shows a candidate to be unpopular with a majority of the voting public, the candidate is likely to be loud in his denunciation of the inaccuracy of polling. He is not insensitive to the rhetorical importance of a public statement that the majority of Americans view his opponent more favorably than they view him. But his public abuse of the accuracy of polls is seldom accompanied by a failure to use polls intensively in an effort to improve his estimate of the nature of his audience. The candidate wishes to know: "What are the primary concerns of suburbanites, city-dwellers, farmers, businessmen, housewives, white-collar workers, members of various racial and religious groups, and so forth; what are the attitudes of members of these groups toward the proposals I am making in my campaign?" The candidate could base his rhetoric on inferences drawn from the study of reference-group affiliations, previously suggested as useful to any speaker; but he wishes to sharpen his inferences with data provided by direct questioning of a selected sample of the members of various groups.

Public speakers who lack the resources of time, money, and organization for conducting formal research on their audiences may nevertheless engage in a variety of informal versions of the opinion poll. The speaker who converses with members of his audience before addressing them can readily uncover some of the dispositions his listeners bring to the occasion. Moreover, the speaker who addresses a reasonably small audience may wish to pose certain questions and hear a sampling of audience opinion before he develops his own answers to these questions. A reasonable rule of thumb for the public speaker is this: if you don't know much about your listeners, ask them some questions.

THE AMERICAN AUDIENCE

To this point we have been viewing the American public as a composite of reference groups, and a particular audience as composed of persons having a set of reference-group affiliations. This is the reality confronted by every public speaker. But the very concept of "reference group" invites question as to whether or not American society as a whole is in any sense a reference group for Americans generally. That is, are there purposes, positions, attitudes, and values so generally shared by American society that knowledge of these can be useful in judging the nature of any audience? The question is like the question raised in Chapter 6 as to whether or not there is a general American style of public speaking widely preferred in our culture. And the answer to the question posed in this chapter takes the same form as the earlier answer. In general, the most conspicuous feature of any American audience is the plurality of purpose, positions, attitudes, and values represented by its members. But it still may be possible to find some fabric of expectancies and preconceptions binding American culture as a whole. The possibility is sufficiently intriguing that, despite the hazards of the enterprise, a variety of pollsters and scholarly investigators engage in a continuing search for general statements about the nature of American culture, as well as statements about the shared attitudes and values of important segments of that culture.[4]

To illustrate the possibilities and limitations of general descriptions of the American audience, we turn to a somewhat free version of the judgments about the emerging values in American society made in 1958 by anthropologist Clyde Kluckhohn.[5]

Kluckhohn summarizes a variety of studies of values revealed in segments of American society, and then seeks to generalize about some values characteristic of American society as a whole. He believes that the following trends are visible:

(1) Strictly personal values are receding in importance and the more publicly standardized "group values" are emerging. That is, Americans tend to adopt as personal beliefs the values of an organization, a community, a social class, a profession, a minority group, or an interest group with which they identify. "Conservatism" in the sense of a preference for values and beliefs already well established as opposed to a militant desire for rapid change seems to be increasing.

(2) Americans are tending increasingly to take the machine as the model for human behavior. That is, individuals are perceived as behaving in certain ways because of the part they play in some larger organization or system in which they operate.

(3) The importance given to such concerns as "mental health" and the education and training of children has increased markedly. Self-

4 For example, the serious student of public speaking will find intriguing conceptions of the American audience in such studies as:
Phillip E. Jacob, *Changing Values in College* (New York: Harper, 1957), p. 174.
Francis X. Sutton, Seymour E. Harris, Carl Kaysen, and James Tobin, *The American Business Creed* (Cambridge: Harvard University Press, 1956), p. 414.
Don A. Martindale, *American Social Structure* (New York: Appleton-Century-Crofts, 1960), p. 521.
5 Clyde Kluckhohn, "The Evolution of Contemporary American Values," *Daedalus*, LXXXVII (Spring, 1958), 78–109.

cultivation has become an ascendent value, although the self-cultivation preferred seeks less the achievement of uniqueness and more the achievement of similarity.

(4) The once strong value given to "future success" by Americans has receded . . . "in favor of 'respectable and stable security' seen in shorter time range." That is, Americans are less concerned with the distant future, whether earthly or heavenly, and more concerned with immediate status and security.

(5) Aesthetic values have been given greatly increased status, reflected in increased attention to the arts and to the cultivation of fashionable cultural and leisure-time pursuits.

(6) There is a great increase in the value placed on institutionalized religious affiliation, although this seems to reflect the need for group membership and social stability rather than the value given to . . . "intensified personal religious life."

(7) The acceptance of heterogeneity in society is increasing; that is, despite the value given to seeking membership in stable groups, Americans are increasingly less aroused or disturbed by the presence of a varied subculture. One might expect the tolerance of heterogeneity to be unstable in the presence of a threat to social stability or security.

(8) The acceptance of the American woman as an equal, participating in the same range of activities and according to the same assumptions as men is increasing. This shift in values is related to changing attitudes toward the code governing sexual behavior.

(9) Greater overt concern for abstract standards of conduct and policy is emerging; that is, . . . "greater value is placed on (holding) explicit values" as a justification for behavior or choice.

From the perspective of the turbulent 1960's, Kluckhohn's 1958 generalizations seem partly prophetic, and partly archaic. He does anticipate the instability of American tolerance of heterogeneity in the presence of a threat to social stability or security—an instability clearly evident in 1968 in relation to the problems of race relations and the Vietnam war. However, he forecasts a declining desire for rapid social change for a society which ten years later attends to militant and powerful calls for rapid change.

In many ways, Kluckhohn's description of American values in 1958 mirrors the characteristics of the general American style of public speaking discussed in Chapter 6. Thus, speaking which emphasizes easy informality, a search for cordial relationships with the audience, an avoidance of stridency, a pleasant acknowledgment of the merit of differences of opinion—such discourse would seem appropriate to the values described by Kluckhohn. But these values do not mirror the voices of dissent emerging in the 1960's, whose speaking is marked by assertiveness, angry attacks on established institutions and customs, and the substitution of aggressiveness for cordiality. In this sense, the central tendencies in American values at any point in history serve not only as the source for one style of public speaking, but as the stimulus for quite different styles seeking to change or transform those values.

Thus, a considerable body of public discourse in the 1960's advocates that individuals "do their own thing" rather than accepting behaviors which serve the efficiency of large-scale organization. The goal of immediate security is subordinated to the more amorphous goals of immediate freedom and personal fulfillment. Still other speakers call for an emphasis on varieties of "inwardness" in religious behavior, together with a de-emphasis on institutionalized religious practice. And yet others find the machine, or more especially the computer, less an attractive model for human behavior than a threat to distinctively human values. If Kluckhohn's 1958 generalizations were perceptive, then it would seem that some public speakers did more than accommodate their discourse to the values generally supported in their culture. They moved to oppose these values, seeking to organize opinion and behavior in support of alternative positions.

THE SPEAKER'S RELATIONSHIP WITH HIS AUDIENCE

Speakers do not use knowledge of an audience in any single way. The speaker's knowledge of an audience should aid him in the preparation of utterance useful to his purpose. The ratio between that already given in an audience and that which is added by a particular speaker will affect materially the speaker's actual influence. Thus speeches which add nothing to the existing knowledge or values or actions of an audience deserve to be described as inconsequential.

But we have not yet discussed the various choices available to speakers concerning the relationship they seek with a given audience. To get at these options, we shall examine some of the roles speakers play vis-à-vis their audiences and the modalities of relationship implied by these roles.

1. The Speaker as Agent: The Mode of Flattery

The simplest and most straightforward accommodation by the speaker to the expectancies and preconceptions of the audience rises from those situations in which he is content simply to serve the purposes of the audience. Such situations require a relatively homogeneous audience with relatively clear-cut purposes. Given such an audience, the speaker can seek total accommodation—the development of utterance that says of the audience what the audience wishes to hear about itself, that affirms the values and attitudes already present in the audience, and that pretends to novelty, originality, or energy of thought only for the purpose of assuring the audience that its thoughts are novel, original, or dynamic. Speakers may seek this form of accommodation in order to elicit the affection or high regard of the audience. Graceful and total accommodation to the purposes of a united and confident audience is likely to win the speaker much personal approval. Such speaking can be considered a path to personal advancement if the audience is one whose good opinion is useful to the speaker. The general modality of such accommodation is unabashed flattery. The audience feels good because a speaker has succeeded in assuring its members that they are worthy people whose thoughts are indeed sound and profound.

2. The Speaker as Catalyst: The Mode of Management

The speaker may face an audience which is potentially homogeneous, but vague about its purposes or beliefs. Nothing in the situation suggests division within the audience, nor tension between speaker and audience. The audience is amiable and well-disposed, but unable to articulate its desires.

The audience finds through the speaker who serves as catalyst the affirmation of that which it wants to believe, but which it had lacked skill to affirm for itself. For example, President Franklin Roosevelt, in 1933, was inaugurated before a listening national audience whose confidence in the nation's future had been shaken by the impact of a prolonged economic depression. Roosevelt's confident assertion, "we have nothing to fear but fear itself," seemed to capture an attitude toward the future that many in his audience had sought. Roosevelt became spokesman for an attitude which was latent but unrealized in his audience.

The speaker as catalyst is also exemplified in the speech delivered by Martin Luther King, Jr., in August, 1963, to an audience of some 200,000 black and white Americans gathered in Washington, D. C., to support racial equality. King's conclusion is one of his best known public statements:

. . . I still have a dream. It is a dream deeply rooted in the American dream that one day this nation will rise up and live out the true meaning of its creed—we hold these truths to be self evident, that all men are created equal.

I have a dream that one day on the red hills of Georgia, sons of former slaves and sons of former slave-owners will be able to sit down together at the table of brotherhood.

I have a dream that one day, even the state of Mississippi, a state sweltering with the heat of injustice, sweltering with the heat of oppression, will be transformed into an oasis of freedom and justice.

I have a dream my four little children will one day live in a nation where they will not be judged by the color of their skin but by content of their character. I have a dream today!

I have a dream that one day, down in Alabama, with its vicious racists, with its governor having his lips dripping with the words of interposition and nullification, that one day, right there in Alabama, little black boys and black girls will be able to join hands with little white boys and white girls as sisters and brothers. I have a dream today!

I have a dream that one day every valley shall be exalted, every hill and mountain shall be made low, the rough places shall be made plain, and the crooked places shall be made straight and the glory of the Lord will be revealed and all flesh shall see it together.

This is our hope. This is the faith that I go back to the South with.

With this faith we will be able to hew out of the mountains of despair a stone of hope. With this faith we will be able to transform the jangling discords of our nation into a beautiful symphony of brotherhood.

With this faith we will be able to work together, to pray together, to struggle together, to go to jail together, to stand up for freedom together, knowing that we will be free one day. This will be the day when all of God's children will be able to sing with new meaning—"my country 'tis of thee; sweet land of liberty; of thee I sing; land where my fathers died, land of the pilgrims' pride; from every mountain side, let freedom ring"—and if America is to be a great nation, this must become true.

So let freedom ring from the prodigious hilltops of New Hampshire.

Let freedom ring from the mighty mountains of New York.

Let freedom ring from the heightening Alleghenies of Pennsylvania.

Let freedom ring from the snow-capped Rockies of Colorado.

Let freedom ring from the curvaceous slopes of California.

But not only that.

Let freedom ring from Stone Mountain of Georgia.

Let freedom ring from Lookout Mountain of Tennessee.

Let freedom ring from every hill and molehill of Mississippi, from every mountain side, let freedom ring.

And when we allow freedom to ring, when we let it ring from every village and hamlet, from every state and city, we will be able to speed up that day when all God's children—black men and white men, Jews and Gentiles, Catholics and Protestants—will be able to join hands and to sing in the words of the old Negro spiritual, "Free at last, free at last; thank God almighty, we are free at last." [6]

[6] Reprinted by permission of Joan Daves. Copyright © 1963 by Martin Luther King, Jr.

The modality of the accommodation sought by the speaker who serves as catalyst is that of *management*. In formulating his discourse, the speaker draws from the audience but goes beyond that which the audience is able to verbalize for itself.

3. The Speaker as Mediator: The Mode of Management

Abraham Lincoln, in his first inaugural address, spoke to a nation sharply divided into the strongly led factions which were to carry the nation into a civil war. Lincoln sought to unify this audience, not by managing vaguely held purposes, but by mediating between strongly held and conflicting purposes. His address was surely one of the most skillful ever devised by an American President, although it failed to achieve his immediate end. Lincoln sought to transcend factionalism in his audience by avoiding partisan assertion of the positions on slavery taken by some leaders of the party which had elected him President. He appealed to the hopes for avoiding national disintegration which were found in leaders of both sectional factions. He sought affirmation of pride in the nation—a position which encompassed sectional differences by going beyond them. Lincoln was handicapped in his purpose by his public identification with the full range of purposes carried by one of the two major national factions. Comment from southern newspapers on his inaugural address made it clear that many listeners could not really hear what Lincoln said, since they were so firmly convinced in advance of the speech that they knew what he stood for.

By contrast, Charles de Gaulle became Premier of France in 1958 at a time when the French nation was sharply divided over the issue of independence for the French colony of Algeria. France also seemed on the brink of civil war. And De Gaulle, like Lincoln almost a century earlier, called for devotion to values which were found in both of the violently divided factions of France—devotion to love of country, to domestic peace and order, and to the proposition that a strong and united France could assume its historic position as a leading world power. De Gaulle was greatly aided in his role as mediator by the fact that he had maintained sufficient ambiguity concerning his position on Algerian independence so that both factions regarded him as sympathetic to their purposes.

The speaker who confronts a sharply divided audience, who wishes or is expected to speak to the point of the divisions, and who seeks some unification of the audience, is cast in the role of mediator.

The modality of the speaker who serves as mediator is also that of *management*. The speaker must seek a strategy which will take account of the differences present in his audience and seek either to resolve these differences or to move beyond them. Thus the speaker may seek to help the audience reach a compromise position—one which gives divided groups a chance to claim some part in formulating the position around which unity can be built. Or the speaker may seek unified support for some procedure which will move toward a resolution of differences. Or, in the manner of Lincoln and De Gaulle, the speaker may seek to unify his audience by acknowledging the existence of difference, but seeking a purpose common to all which is more important than the positions, attitudes, or values which divide the audience.

4. The Speaker as Defendant: The Mode of Management

In the Athens of Socrates and Plato, any citizen might be called on to defend himself before an assembly of his peers to answer charges brought by a fellow citizen. The charge might be based on anything in the conduct of a given citizen that one of his neighbors thought worthy of censure or punishment. Trials were frequent, and they accounted in part for the enormous interest Athenians had in learning to speak effectively in public.

The formality and complexity of the contemporary American legal system has all but eliminated the possibility that citizens will defend themselves in court, rather than seeking the services of a lawyer. Nevertheless, the situation in which a speaker is in some sense "required" to answer to criticism still occurs. Any person answerable for his conduct to a group of fellow citizens may find himself in a speaking situation in which he must defend his record, or his conduct of office, or his position, against the possiblity of censure. In March of 1917, Senator George Norris of Nebraska was one of twelve Senators who led a successful filibuster against passage of a bill for arming American merchant ships. The twelve Senators, who were called "willful men" by President Wilson, came in for enormous public abuse from a nation which was moving swiftly toward war with Germany. Criticism of Norris from his home state was so violent that he wrote the Governor of the state offering to resign his Senate post should a special recall election show the voters no longer desired him as Senator. Norris then traveled to Lincoln, Nebraska, to speak to an open meeting in justification of his actions as Senator. The situation seemed hostile; no prominent Nebraskans offered to appear with him on the platform or introduce him, and many warned him against any public appearance before an open audience. Norris appeared alone before the audience, and began his talk with a memorably direct statement, "I have come home to tell you the truth." His management of his own defense was a model of direct engagement with his critics. His management had started before the speech, with his expressed willingness to leave office should it be really true that the majority of the voters lacked confidence in him. It continued with his appearance as an isolated man, totally convinced that he had possession of the truth about the pressures that were moving America toward war, and asking only that his side of the story be given a fair hearing. The speech evoked a strongly affirmative response from the immediate audience, and led to requests from all parts of the state for further speeches by the Senator. The Governor of the state laid aside all proposals for a special recall election. One cannot isolate the impact of a single speech or series of speeches on the totality of factors affecting public opinion in Nebraska. But Norris was reelected to the Senate in November of 1918, even though subsequent to the filibuster against the armed ship bill, he also was one of six senators voting against the declaration of war against Germany.

Accommodation to the audience in a situation requiring defense again requires the modality of management. The speaker must seek to know the nature and strength of the charges or doubts that he confronts, the force with which they will be pressed, and the extent to which they are credited by his audience. He seeks to unify personal support in his audience, either by meeting directly the causes for any doubts directed toward him, or, as in the case of Norris, by moving beyond these doubts to seek a base for support which exists despite specific doubts.

5. The Speaker as Critic: The Mode of Confrontation

The situations discussed thus far are alike in one sense. In each of them the speaker seeks to unify his audience and to achieve support for his position and person drawn from positions, attitudes, or values latent in the audience as a whole. In each case the speaker seeks a direct accommodation with his audience.

But speakers often enter into a more complex relationship with an audience. An illustration of this is the situation in which the speaker takes a critical posture, attacking directly positions, attitudes, or values held by the audience or some part of the audience. The speaker seems to be seeking, not unity with his audience, but a sharp division with it. The situation thus seems to find the speaker inviting a personal disaster; however, this is not necessarily the case, as an examination of some varied actions involving the speaker as critic will illustrate.

The speaker may represent a force with which the audience seeks accommodation. The speaker's personal stature, or the power or threat posed by the group he represents, or his capacity to stir reactions of guilt or shame in his audience may make his aggressiveness effective.

In some cases the division of speaker and audience may be more apparent than real. Some of the sermons of Jonathan Edwards to New England audiences in the eighteenth century seem remarkably aggressive—assertions about the absolute sinfulness of his listeners joined to painful descriptions of the punishment they faced. The powerful effect of the sermons suggests, however, that they were well adapted to the listeners, who accepted their sinfulness and both the merit and opportunity provided by criticism. The guilt-ridden or insecure audience may welcome criticism and experience catharsis by accepting it.

In other cases the speaker may force division with his audience as a means of clarifying for the audience the intransigence and depth of his own commitments. By "telling it like it is," the speaker may hope that his audience will achieve greater understanding of the depth and gravity of the divisions they confront—an understanding which may be glossed over if the speaker engages in flattery or management. In the 1960's, militant spokesmen attacking racism in American society and attacking American involvement in the war in South Vietnam turned increasingly toward such an aggressive posture.

The mode of accommodation for the speaker who acts as critic is that of *confrontation*. The speaker chooses to express his position, his outrage, or anger, and his vision of the future without overt accommodation to his audience. The task of accommodation, if it is to be achieved, is made the responsibility of the audience. The speaker presumably enjoys the emotional catharsis of uninhibited verbal aggression; he gambles with the possibility of violent counterattack or of isolation from the processes of decision by which others may move to restore the fabric of order and good manners characteristic of a stable society.[7]

6. The Speaker as Leader: The Mode of Transcendence

Emerson held that the highest purpose of the public speaker was to achieve the transformation of his listeners. The speaker who seeks such transformation accommodates not simply to that already present in the audience, but to that which man may become regardless of the claim his past makes. As leader, the speaker is not content to leave his audience as he found it, seeking only personal gain from the good opinion of his audience. Nor is he content to unify his audience in terms of positions, attitudes, or values already latent in the audience. His object is genuine novelty. He seeks belief and action not predicted by the past of his lis-

[7] For a more detailed description of the modality of confrontation, see Robert Scott and Donald Smith, "The Rhetoric of Confrontation," *Quarterly Journal of Speech,* February, 1969.

teners, nor manifestly latent in that past. The modality of his accommodation is that of transcendence, a search for the concept by which man may exceed himself.

The vision of leading an audience to that which is genuinely new may loom more brightly than a realistic view of the possibilities of public speaking would support. The best empirical evidence we have of the relationship of speakers and listeners underscores the intransigence with which the past in an audience lays claim to the shape of the future. Listeners, we know, have remarkable success in forgetting information which threatens their prior beliefs. They are ingenious in distorting threatening information so that it becomes nonthreatening. They are alert to learning only those new things which serve to confirm the rightness of positions already held. In this sense, the speaker who serves as catalyst or mediator may provide the leadership genuinely possible for any society.

Yet it would be unjust to suggest that all this evidence demonstrates the impossibility of genuine transcendence. Societies and individuals are transformed, and they are transformed through discourse. Individuals report the transformation of personal values and actions as the product of effective speech. Perhaps the seeming paradox is created by the amount of contextual information we bring to bear in interpreting the effects of particular speeches. If we knew everything about the past of an audience, then the seemingly novel or transforming speech could be seen to have its roots in the past. Since we cannot know this full account of the past, some speeches will seem to succeed in transcending that which is already present in the audience.

The leader has been defined as one who is far enough ahead of his audience so that he brings a new form to their actions or beliefs, but not so far ahead that his audience finds no grounds for identification. The speaker who seeks seeming transcendence for his audience risks total failure, but he also chooses to seek more than straightforward adaptation to or management of that which is already given to his audience.

THE MODALITIES OF THE SPEAKER-AUDIENCE RATIO

In discussing the various roles played by the speaker vis-à-vis his audience, we have called attention to four fundamental modalities of relationships: flattery, management, confrontation, and transcendence. The four modalities are not mutually exclusive. Many speeches contain elements of each, and most speeches will reveal more than one modality of relationship.

The four modalities vary in terms of the degree of risk accepted by the speaker and in terms of the amount of freedom from the audience which he asserts. Thus, in the modality of flattery the speaker accepts little risk, but he becomes a creature of his audience rather than an independent force. In seeking to manage an audience, the speaker risks more, but emerges as a force in social action if he succeeds in energizing latent values, or unifying amorphous or divided audiences. The speaker who seeks to confront or transcend his audience risks much. Isolation, total failure with the audience, or martydom are possible consequences of his posture. There is evidence that some speakers find emotional satisfaction in such consequences. They are drawn by the claim of total freedom from the past as represented by their audience, by the heroic possibilities in a successful assertion of their freedom, and by the almost equally satisfying posture of heroic failure.

SUMMARY

The action of a speech is completed in an audience. Accordingly, the accommodation of discourse to its end in the audience has long been accounted essential to effective utterance.

The speaker needs to know his audience. But his manner of knowing it is seldom the product of knowledge about the expectancies and preconceptions of each member of the audience. Rather, he knows an audience through the expectancies and preconceptions of the groups with which they affiliate. Knowledge about the audience inferred from knowledge of the reference groups present in the audience does not result in precise information. At best it permits the speaker to make assumptions about his audience at some level of probability. Knowledge of the expectancies and preconceptions of reference groups is available to the speaker through reading or conversation with group members, and in some cases the knowledge can be made more precise through the use of polling techniques.

The most accurate view of the American audience observes the plurality of that audience: the existence of multiple reference groups with different positions, attitudes, and values. It is possible, however, to propose some general tendencies in the American audience as a whole. These generalized positions, attitudes, and beliefs seem to be the counterpart of a general American style of speaking.

Speakers enter into a number of different relationships with audiences, each of which implies a somewhat different problem in accommodation to the audience. Thus the speaker may relate to his audience as agent, as catalyst, as mediator, as defendant, as critic, or as leader. The major modalities of accommodation in all situations are flattery, management, confrontation, and transcendence. All of these modes of accommodation may be found in a single speech. In the first, the speaker risks little but chooses to assert little of his possible freedom as an individual. In the latter modes, confrontation and transcendence, the speaker risks much but chooses freedom from the claims of his audience.

CHAPTER 8

The Question of Ethics

VIRTUE AND SKILL

Quintilian, the most famous Roman teacher of rhetoric, thought that an orator must above all things study *morality*. Without knowledge of "all that is just and honorable," he wrote, "no one can either be a good man or an able speaker." [1]

Quintilian thus declared his view that the orator's search for skill and virtue were somehow intertwined. But he did little to clarify the nature of this relationship. If all men skilled in speaking were in fact virtuous, then the ethical questions frequently raised by successful public speakers would be of little consequence. If the most successful speakers were always more virtuous than those less successful, then we would know that the society which cultivated speaking skill would also be cultivating ethical men. This happy relationship does not exist. History presents us with too many examples of greatly skillful speakers whose virtue was doubtful.

In this chapter we shall join Quintilian in suggesting that the study of public speaking and the study of ethics are essentially intertwined. We will not say, as the Roman rhetorician seemed to imply, that virtue is prerequisite to speaking skill. Nor shall we say that a skillful speech is necessarily a moral rather than an immoral action. But we shall contend that a public speech is inherently a moral or immoral action, and that speaking skill cannot therefore be conceived as an ethically neutral capability. We shall further contend that speakers and their auditors are necessarily engaged in complex moral choices as they produce or respond to discourse. And we shall also observe that speaking skill is prerequisite to certain ethical purposes. Thus, the inept speaker may conduct an immoral action because of his lack of skill rather than his unworthy purposes. In this sense, the man who would fulfill himself as a moral agent must seek skill in speaking.

The argument supporting these positions is necessarily complex, but

[1] Quintilian, *Institutes of Oratory*, translated by J. S. Watson (London, 1856), XII, ii, 1.

provides a critical perspective on the conduct and interpretation of public speeches. After definition of the key terms, *ethics* and *moral,* we will explore the concept of speaking skill as an ethically neutral human capacity—a concept to be rejected. We will then examine a variety of efforts to establish and apply ethical standards to judging public speeches, seeking understanding of the potentialities and limitations of these efforts. And finally we will consider the sense in which speaking skill supports certain important ethical purposes, thus making the search for such skill an avenue to moral fulfillment.

Definitions

By *ethics* we mean the set of value statements which identify the standards of conduct which an individual may acknowledge as constitutive of his person or personality, or which a group or society may acknowledge as constitutive of its character. We take it that men and societies universally acknowledge such systems of values. To be sure, some men cannot verbalize the system they acknowledge. They have no facility for saying "this is what I believe to be the standard against which I can judge the virtue of my actions." But all men implicitly espouse a system of values in their actions, and all recognize a system in their willingness to judge the actions of others as good or bad.

The term *moral* is used to describe actions which support, or do not deny, the standards of an ethical system. Thus when we say that a speaker's action is moral or immoral, we are implicitly pointing to an ethical standard which justifies such a judgment.

THE PERCEPTION OF SPEAKING SKILL AS ETHICALLY NEUTRAL

Speaking skill is frequently studied as an ethically neutral instrument available for man's use. Thus the skill is likened to any instrumental power, such as skill in shooting a rifle. From this point of view, speaking skill per se is neither good nor bad. The skill can be used by good persons or bad persons. It can be put to the service of good purposes, bad purposes, or purposes which seem so innocuous that they do not need to be viewed as either good or bad. Certain problems and purposes in studying speechmaking make the ethically neutral view of speaking skill attractive.

By distinguishing a speaker's method or technique from his purposes, the speech critic may be aided in achieving a relatively dispassionate understanding of method. He may be able to observe the extent to which the speaking practices of great scoundrels resemble those of obviously virtuous men. The distinction also encourages precision in separating questions about the effect of a speech from questions of ethics. Too often when a critic says, "that was a good speech," it is not clear whether he is commending the speaker for his success in moving the present audience, is making an ethical judgment, or is doing both. Since a speech can be effective and unjust, or ineffective and just, some reasonable care would seem to be in order in distinguishing comment about the value or "goodness" of a speech from comments about its effectiveness.

One primary question which leads us to an understanding of a speaker's method is this: Given the speaker's person, purpose, and situation, should he have chosen to conduct his utterance differently? This question uncovers the fact that a speaker may confront so many constraints in a speaking situation that he can only choose the least obnoxious of several disagreeable options. The speech which seems a rather poor effort may be the most artistic speech possible to the total situation. We are all too ready to deny any virtue to a speaker whose person or purposes irritate us, or to a speaker who faces a situation which presents him only with disagreeable options. But such denial of merit may be unjust and may call for a more objective treatment of the speaker's action. By deliberately neutralizing our tendency to apply ethical judgments to the totality of a speaking situation, we may extend our power to perceive clearly the method or technique used by the speaker and the options faced by the speaker.

Aristotle's Approach to the Ethics of Rhetoric

Aristotle's *Rhetoric* provides an excellent example of a dispassionate analysis of the art of public speaking. For this reason the Greek philosopher is often asserted to have treated public speaking skill as ethically neutral. A better reading of Aristotle is that he succeeded in examining objectively the method by which public speeches achieved effectiveness. But at the same time he revealed the sense in which a public speech is intrinsically an ethical action.

Aristotle's search for an objective analysis of the art of speaking is revealed in his definition of rhetoric as "the faculty of discovering in the particular case what are the available means of persuasion." [2] The strategy of the definition seems clear enough. The means of persuasion are examined by Aristotle with a minimum of effort to pass ethical judgment. The means are observed to be available to both virtuous and evil men. But this fact, Aristotle thought, was no reason for objecting to the study of rhetoric or the search for speaking skill. "If it be urged that an

[2] *The Rhetoric of Aristotle,* Lane Cooper, translator and ed. (New York: Appleton-Century-Crofts, 1932), I.2.

abuse of the rhetorical faculty can work great mischief," he wrote, "the same charge can be brought against all good things (save virtue itself) and especially against the most useful things such as strength, health, wealth, and military skill. Rightly employed, they work the greatest blessings; and wrongly employed, they work the utmost harm." [3]

Although Aristotle viewed speaking skill dispassionately, he did not treat speaking as an instrumental or ethically neutral action. To the contrary, he asserted strongly that the study of rhetoric was essentially entangled with the study of ethics and the assertion of values. Aristotle saw rhetoric as an ". . . offshoot, on the one hand, of Dialectic, and on the other of that study of Ethics which may properly be called 'political.' " [4] He thus placed rhetoric as a study concerned with the conduct of men in groups. Moreover, he saw all public speeches as concerned ultimately with human preferences or value choices. The ends of forensic speaking were justice and injustice; those of political speaking were expediency and inexpediency; and those of *epideictic* or ceremonial speaking were honor and dishonor. Thus for Aristotle public speaking was a human action essentially asserting the values of speakers, and seeking to organize the values or preferences of listeners. And thus also he saw the search for public speaking skill as serving ethical purposes. Such skill served both the moral purposes of the state and the individual for four very tangible reasons: (a) because things that are true and just have a natural tendency to prevail over their opposites—if truth and justice are to prevail, they need to be served by speaking skill as artistic as that which serves error or injustice; (b) because people cannot be instructed or led to knowledge save through speaking skill; (c) because speaking skill helps us argue out both sides of any question of probability, thus clarifying the nature of any dispute and promoting the discovery of truth; and (d) because speaking skill is needed to defend oneself. [5]

Public Speaking Is Inherently a Moral Action

Two facts about a public speech make it clear that a speech cannot be viewed ultimately as an ethically neutral or instrumental act.

First, a speech is essentially an action involving the well-being of other persons. In this sense the act of speaking is different from instrumental acts, and skill in speaking is different from instrumental skills. We have earlier referred to skill in shooting a rifle or pistol as an instrumental skill. Such skill may of course be exercised in acts that involve

---

[3] *The Rhetoric of Aristotle,* I.1.
[4] *The Rhetoric of Aristotle,* I.2.
[5] *The Rhetoric of Aristotle,* I.1, p. 1355a.

the well-being of other persons. Shooting at bank robbers or the use of weapons in time of war certainly makes the act of shooting a moral choice. But moral choice is not essential to the act of shooting: one may shoot at targets, clay pigeons, tin cans, and chicken hawks. In actions employing an instrumental skill, the use of the skill *does* determine whether or not the act is ethically neutral or involves some moral choice.

But in public speaking, moral choice is an inherent condition of the action. When a speaker takes responsibility for asking others to believe or feel or behave in certain ways, then his action is inherently moral or immoral and is susceptible to judgment according to some set of values. To be sure, many public speeches are ethically innocuous. They leave undisturbed the values accepted by the speaker and his listeners. Accordingly, no one is likely to observe that an ethical issue has been raised. But the issue is there; the speaker and his listeners have chosen to act according to certain ethical assumptions.

Second, a speech not only affects the welfare of its audience, but also announces, either explicitly or implicitly, certain values. The expository speaker says in effect, "this is the right time and place for an exposition on cellular biology," and "this is the truth about such matters insofar as it can be known." The persuasive speaker says, "these are the propositions one should affirm, or the actions one should take." The ceremonial speaker says, "these are the values by which we praise or reject some person, institution, or event." Each speaker has chosen to assert certain preferences and to ask others to join in these preferences. Richard Weaver states the same point as follows: "Rhetoric, seen in the whole conspectus of its functions is an art of emphasis embodying an order of desire. Rhetoric is advisory; it has the office of advising men with reference to an independent order of goods with reference to their particular situation as it relates to these. The honest rhetorician therefore has two things in mind: a vision of how matters would go ideally and ethically and a consideration of the special circumstances of his auditors. Toward both of these he has a responsibility." [6]

We can no more conceive public speaking abstracted from moral choice than we can conceive biological life existing apart from metabolism. The speaker chooses to act in a certain way and his choice affirms or denies certain ethical standards; he assumes responsibility for the well-being of others, and his speech therefore, as a condition of its being, is moral or immoral. We have observed that it is useful for certain purposes to examine a public speech as though its action were ethically

[6] Richard Weaver, "Language is Sermonic," from Roger E. Nebergall, ed., *Dimensions of Rhetorical Scholarship* (Norman, Oklahoma: Department of Speech, University of Oklahoma, 1963), p. 54.

neutral. Such a perspective promotes insight into the sources of effectiveness available to all public speakers, whether their preferences be good or evil. But in the final analysis, the speaker's examination of his own choices is incomplete until he perceives such choices to be moral or immoral. The listener's response to a speech is incomplete until he perceives that the speaker is asserting or denying some system of values. Skill in public speaking is not an ethically neutral capability. It is a skill which grows in intrinsic relationship to the moral growth of the speaker. Accordingly, we turn next to an examination of a series of ethical perspectives used by speakers and their listeners in judging the moral quality of acts of public speaking.

APPROACHES TO ETHICAL JUDGMENT

We are all remarkably adept at finding that speeches which displease us are somehow highly unethical. By contrast, our moral sensibility is likely to be dormant in the presence of the shabbiest speech if the speaker happens to be saying things that please us. Thus, we are outraged when a speaker calls a political leader we admire "a slippery scoundrel." "Name-calling," we assert, "is unethical. Only a rascal lacking any moral sensitivity would engage in name-calling." We overlook the irony that we have denounced "name-calling" by calling the act a name and denounced the "name-caller" by calling him a name. The truth is we disliked the name because we thought it unjust; but rather than accepting the invitation to demonstrate the greater accuracy of a different name, we sometimes seek to silence those with whom we disagree by alleging that they are morally reprehensible.

The self-serving use of ethical judgments, which raises more ethical questions than it answers, is commonplace enough to assure confusion in discussion of the ethics of public speaking. Such judgments often take the form of an explicit or implicit labeling of some speaking practice which is held to be universally unethical. The label is used as an ethical norm or standard which is held to be universal in its application. Thus if a speaker engages in a practice which denies the asserted ethical standard, his practice is immoral by definition. The difficulty is that even the most avid labelers seldom want to apply a particular standard to all speeches and all speaking situations. The norm is selectively applied; there are exceptions to the rule; and the so-called universal standard becomes in actuality a contingent one. To illustrate this point we will take two common ethical standards and examine the complications that arise when they are applied to particular speaking situations.

The Value of Truth

The first standard holds that speakers are responsible for telling the truth, the whole truth, and nothing but the truth. The value proposition implicit in such a standard may be formally stated: it is morally wrong for a speaker to speak less than the whole truth as he knows it, or to engage in deliberate deception by false reporting or by withholding information for the purpose of giving a false impression. The value thus expressed is a durable one. It is found in the biblical commandment against bearing false witness; in courtroom oaths administered to witnesses; in the discourse of parents seeking to elicit an accurate report from their children, teachers wanting to know what happened in the classroom in their absence, and investigators wanting to get the facts about some crime or potential public scandal. The American legal system, which assumes that justice can be served by truth, gives a variety of legal recognitions to the value. There are laws against slander or libel— against public false witness bringing harm to another person. There are laws against perjury so that the witness under oath who knowingly testifies contrary to the truth is subject to legal sanctions. There is even the Fifth Amendment to the United States Constitution, which permits a witness under oath to refuse to answer questions if he believes an answer might tend to incriminate him. This civil liberty may be said to encourage witnesses to tell the truth by permitting them recourse to silence in circumstances which would place the witness under heavy pressure to be less than candid. Most political campaigns produce accusations among competing politicians that their opponents are untruthful and therefore unworthy. Indeed, accusations of deliberate falsification are so commonplace in political public speaking and so bipartisan in distribution as to make one curious about the possible gap between ethical theory and moral practice in campaign oratory.

Truth is an important value in public speaking. One can observe that the very enterprise of communication becomes all but impossible unless people who talk with one another can trust the candor of the one who speaks. Because of our need for communication, for organization, for cooperation with others, we must accept with candor much of what is said to us or else abandon the whole possibility of constructive human interaction. The person who assumes that all that he reads in all newspapers is false is left without current information. The person who believes that all public speakers should be mistrusted, or that he has no basis for sorting out truth from falsehood, finds it impossible to join in effective group action. Lack of trust among speakers poisons the well-spring of constructive communication, and the speaker who deliberately violates any listener's trust also poisons the spring. Anatol Rapoport has observed both the difficulty encountered in conversation which starts with mistrust, and the gamesmanship used in such encounters. In his book *Fights, Games, and Debates,* he relates an anecdote to illustrate this point:

> Where are you going?
> To Minsk.
> Shame on you! You say this to make me think you are going to Pinsk. But I happen to know you *are* going to Minsk.[7]

Difficulty in Applying the Standard of Truth

Truthfulness may be the most used ethical standard for judging the morality of public speeches. But great difficulties attend application of the standard to particular acts of speaking. The difficulties become clear when we remember Richard Weaver's injunction that a speaker has responsibility not only for talking about an order of reality external to his person, but also for taking into account the situation of his listeners.

In examining the speaker's responsibility for the situation of his listeners, we are likely to ask that he observe two values, either of which may qualify or even oppose the value of truth.

The first of these qualifying values is tact or courtesy. When we ask a speaker to be tactful, we are probably asking him to be less than candid about his own preferences or attitudes—to tell less than the full truth as he sees it or feels it. Most of us would be reluctant to criticize a speaker who engaged in modest praise of an audience, even when he believed many of its members to be sunk in ignorance, greed, or self-deception. Indeed, if we observe that the speaker seems to lessen the ignorance of some listeners by his skill in obtaining their good will, we might find his tact to be eminently moral. Moreover, we could observe that the tactful or courteous speaker may have acknowledged some truths about himself and others that are of larger importance than his candid judgments of those with whom he talks. For example, he has acknowledged that few people think ill of themselves and that those who do profit little from having their defects pointed out publicly. He has also acknowledged that the speaker who treats his listeners with respect may find them more worthy of respect than he had imagined.

A second value which sometimes comes into conflict with the value of truth is that of prudence in judging how much of the truth a particular

7 Anatol Rapoport, *Fights, Games, and Debates* (Ann Arbor: University of Michigan Press, 1960), p. 105.

audience can usefully confront. It is not altogether certain, for example, that a medical doctor should immediately tell every patient who has acquired a fatal disease that his days are numbered. Prudence, and concern for the well-being of another person, asks that the doctor judge the readiness of his patient to handle the news, or that he prepare the patient for truth before he produces it. In similar vein, Brembeck and Howell in the book *Persuasion* ask if we should expect a speaker to avoid falsification to an audience in circumstances when telling the truth might precipitate violence or mob action.[8]

Again, what shall we say of the wartime national leader who conceals evidence of military disaster from his citizenry on the grounds that the truth would affect morale to the point of hazarding national purpose? One might object to this latter example on the grounds that, given the absolutely immoral context of war, one should expect a series of specific immoralities to follow. Nevertheless speakers constantly face unpleasant historical realities, and they must assume responsibility for the actual condition of their listeners and not their condition as the speaker would like it to be.

The speaker's responsibility for his listeners clearly limits the virtue of simple truthfulness or candor. But even if this were not the case, the problem of applying the standard of truth to particular acts of speaking would remain.

We properly ask a speaker to avoid deliberate misrepresentation of facts, or to avoid alleging the truth of events when he lacks good evidence of such truth. But while the factual accuracy of a speaker's statements is important, such accuracy is the lesser part of his obligation to truth. Public speakers necessarily select and arrange the information they present. Such selection and arrangement is inseparable from the act of speaking and involves the speaker in choosing a particular picture of reality. The speaker cannot tell the whole truth about any subject, and the truth he chooses to tell is always one among several possible patterns of selection and arrangement. We can observe that discourse can be factually accurate but quite misleading in the impression created by the selected facts. For example, accurate quotations taken out of context may give a totally false impression of the meaning intended by the person quoted. Thus public officials frequently allege that they have been victimized by newspaper accounts of their utterance or by quotations "torn from context" and used immorally by their political opponents.

When we confront the decisive role played by selection and arrangement in determining the truth told by a speaker, it becomes clear that a speech containing factual inaccuracies could conceivably be less deceptive in its total impress than a misleadingly ordered speech free from such inaccuracies. It is also clear that when we judge a speech to be deceptive or untrue, we are making a judgment based on some selection of an order of reality different from that used by the speaker. Our judgment may be better and therefore more ethical than that of the speaker. But the judgment is not an easy or automatic one.

We can also observe the problem of judging the truthfulness of a speech by recalling the variety of stylistic variations used by speakers. The speaker who uses hyperbole engages in deliberate exaggeration of some features of reality. But shall we say that he has been untruthful? Or is it the case that he has opened our eyes to some aspects of reality which we might otherwise have overlooked? The speaker who uses irony is indirect; he seems to say less than he means, or to say one thing while meaning another. But should we accuse him of lacking candor, and therefore of being unethical? Or is it the case that he has made vivid for us a dimension of reality we might otherwise have missed? And if an audience misunderstands the irony of a speaker, shall we fault the speaker for failing to understand the condition of his listeners or fault the listeners for failing to understand properly the order of reality pictured by the speaker?

In summary, application of the value of truth to particular acts of public speaking is a difficult enterprise. The difficulty does not mean that the value is unimportant. We have already observed that some residue of trust between speaker and listener is a necessary condition of human communication. And the speaker who violates that trust by deliberately misleading his listeners does some injury to the health of his society. The same injury is done by the speaker who inadvertently violates the confidence of his listeners by talking from less knowledge than might be available to him or with less forethought than prudence might dictate.

The Value of Reason

A second value pervasively applied to the ethical criticism of public discourse is that which praises use of evidence and reasoning, and condemns use of emotive language. The value is so ambiguous as to raise a serious question as to whether its existence is not more productive of confusion than insight.

The appeal of the value seems reasonably clear. The whole history of western civilization has demonstrated the power of man's reason to achieve control over his environment, to accumulate and communicate new knowledge which in turn seems useful to human purposes. There is no doubt that the power of speech confers the power of rational behavior. Moreover, the historically demonstrated power of such behavior has been greatly augmented in recent centuries by the development of the natural sciences. "Science" has itself become a major value term, with overtones suggesting that man's ascendancy over other animals derives from his capacity to reason.

We can readily understand the value status given to discourse which reveals an apt management of evidence and reasoning. But great confusion rises if we propose that discourse which is highly emotive is therefore irrational and ethically suspect. Discourse may be highly emotive if it presents a listener with images, facts, lines of argument, or stylistic characteristics capable of inducing high levels of emotional response in the listeners. In a given situation, with a given audience, some kinds of utterance are more likely to induce heightened emotional response than other kinds. But it is perfectly clear that a speaker's utterance may be highly emotive in a given situation and also highly demonstrative of the effective use of evidence and reasoning. It is simply not the case that speeches which are informative and well reasoned are thereby necessarily lacking in emotive power, or vice versa. Accordingly, giving value to reasoned discourse does not imply censure for highly emotive discourse.

The confusion is compounded by a rather common misapprehension about the nature of language. This misapprehension holds that words are in themselves emotional or nonemotional, and that certain words which automatically generate an emotional response in listeners are therefore emotional appeals. This is of course a naive view about the nature of words and their relationship to the context in which they are used. Words are not in themselves emotional. Men may utter words while in a state of emotional arousal. They may be aroused by hearing certain utterance in certain circumstances. But we should avoid the assumption that any word is inherently either emotive or rational. For example, stripped of all context the word "fire" has a variety of potential meanings. However, Supreme Court Justice Oliver Wendell Holmes held that to cry "fire" in a crowded theater was to exceed the right conferred by the Constitution's guarantee of free speech. The context would make the utterance emotive and give it a dangerous potentiality. A condemned spy facing a firing squad no doubt regards the command, "fire," as highly emotive. The same term seems placid enough if one visualizes a scoutmaster telling his charges, "You can start a fire by rubbing two sticks together, although the use of matches is less tiring."

Since all meaningful utterance is in some sense rational, and since words become emotive only with reference to a given context of utterance, we might wonder at the frequency with which speeches are subjected to ethical criticism because the speaker used "emotion rather than reason." The source of this kind of judgment seems to be a reaction to the spectacle of a powerful speaker moving an audience deeply toward ends or actions thought unworthy by a critic. Adolf Hitler unquestionably moved Nazi audiences to extravagant devotion to a corrupt and bloody political program. This might seem a reason to distrust an emotional speaker or emotive language. Effective demagogues throughout history have had a similar relationship with audiences. This might seem to reinforce our distrust of emotive utterance. But while we often object to the emotionality of demagogues, we seldom object to speakers who give emotive power to a cause we believe just. Americans do not object to the emotive force of the Declaration of Independence. Churchgoers do not object to the sermon which moves them deeply. Men generally do not object to the proposition that they should feel deeply about matters that are important to them, and that they should seek utterance charged with such feeling.

The truth is that reason and emotion are not antithetical properties of human utterance. All discourse is in some sense rational; that is, the speaker pictures some order of reality for his listeners. All discourse is also an expression of preference; that is, the speaker reveals his feeling for events and people. When we object to the emotionality of a demagogue we are in fact objecting to his affection for causes we believe to be unjust or to his unbridled enthusiasm for an order of reality we believe untrue or destructive. When we say that the discourse of the demagogue is irrational, we mean that the order of reality he provides seems to us contrary to the order that men should prefer.

We may properly assert reason as a value in public speaking when we mean only this: that speakers who wish to give a true and just order to reality should have an affection for the best evidence available to them, and should use care in interpreting this evidence. In this sense the value of reason, properly understood, becomes indistinguishable from the value of truth. But to assume that rational discourse is opposed to emotive discourse, or that rational discourse is virtuous while emotive discourse is corrupt, is to perpetuate confusion.

THE INSTITUTIONAL BASIS OF ETHICAL STANDARDS

Public speakers and their listeners undoubtedly profit from prudent contemplation of the relationship of values such as truth and reason to particular speaking situations. But they may also wish for less abstract ethical norms to guide their practice and their judgment. One method of reducing the level of abstraction of the ethical norms we apply to discourse is to approach ethical analysis by observing the relationship between particular public speeches and the social institutions supported and served by these speeches. In earlier chapters we observed that public speeches are usually generated by social organizations, groups, or institutions. Speeches create organizations, and sustain and transform these organizations. Thus it is commonplace for a social group or organization served by a certain kind of public speaking to concern itself with the ethical standards which should guide the speaker who is linked to the particular organization. When an organization or social institution begins to examine the ethics of the speaking done by its members, we generate not an ethical system applicable to all public speeches, but a system applicable to teaching or to preaching or to salesmanship or to courtroom speaking, and so forth. The ethical system set forth by a particular organization or group to guide the speaking practice of its members will be linked directly to the purposes of the particular organization. The system is likely, therefore, to be less abstract than a system which might be applicable to all acts of discourse. We can illustrate the way in which social organizations form ethical systems to guide the discourse of their members by a brief discussion of two group or institutional settings in which a sizable number of public speeches are given.

1. The Ethics of Classroom Lecturing

The first setting is that of the classroom lecture. College teachers are presumably professional persons who practice their profession in part by making speeches. In common with other professional groups, teachers set ethical standards for the actions of members of their profession. A variety of such ethical codes have been developed by groups of American teachers, and we shall examine two values common to many of these codes.

The college teaching profession commonly enjoins its members to be dispassionate or objective in examining the information and concepts included within the subject matter of their academic discipline. That is, the teacher is asked to examine the information and generalizations provided by scholars in his area, and to judge the trustworthiness of the information, and the validity of the generalizations drawn from the evidence. In presenting subject matter to students, the teacher should make clear the evidence on which he bases any generalizations he presents, and should call attention to any limitations in this evidence or to the existence of contradictory evidence. He should also be at all times willing to hear critical analysis of his own discourse, including the presentation of evidence and generalizations contradictory to those he has advanced; and he should show respect for the ideas of those who differ. By giving special value to discourse which is dispassionate and open to criticism, the teaching profession seeks to influence the conduct of classroom lecturing.

A second ethical standard advanced by the teaching profession is found in the 1940 statement on academic freedom adopted by the American Association of University Professors. This standard asserts that the teacher should not introduce "into his teaching controversial matter which is not related to his subject matter." In other words, the teacher in the classroom is not ethically free to advance opinions on any topic which interests him; he is free only to offer his judgments on controversial questions germane to the subject matter he professes. Thus the teacher in the classroom is ethically less free in his utterance than the teacher acting as citizen outside the classroom.

We have described two values asserted by the teaching profession to illustrate the way in which a group or organization may propose ethical standards for the discourse of its members. These standards are not ordinarily proposed as applying to all utterance. They are proposed as having peculiar relevance to the purposes of the group for which they are intended.

2. The Ethics of Courtroom Speaking

The legal profession also advances ethical standards for the discourse of its members. Some of the ethical standards developed by the legal profession contrast with those set forth by the teaching profession. These contrasts are instructive since they reveal the extent to which ethical standards set by particular groups are not intended to be universal systems of ethics, applicable to all discourse. Rather, these ethical standards are adapted to the purposes of a particular group of speakers operating in a particular social context.

One context in which much legal speaking takes place is provided by the courtroom under the familiar adversary system of seeking justice. In a criminal trial, for example, the system asks that the alleged criminal be prosecuted by one speaker or group of speakers and defended by another speaker or group of speakers. In this system the end of justice is supposedly best served if the competing adversaries argue their cases as vigorous partisans. That is, each adversary is expected to make the best possible case for the side he represents. Under this system the legal adversary may ethically minimize every weakness in his own case, and every strength in his opponent's case. He should emphasize strength in his case and weakness in his opponent's case. Moreover, a defense attorney need not believe in the innocence of the client whose acquittal he seeks. Indeed, the system prescribes that justice is served if even a person who seems manifestly guilty receives thorough and devoted defense.

Courtroom speaking is more heavily governed by rules than the speaking of teachers. Whereas teachers admonish one another not to talk about irrelevant matters in a classroom, lawyers confront strict rules of procedure enforced by a judge who limits the kind of evidence they may introduce, the way in which it may be introduced, the point at which interpretations of data may be presented to judge or jury, and so forth. The adversary lawyer speaks as an intense partisan. But he also speaks within an institution organized to make skillful partisanship serve the ethical purpose of justice.

We have now examined two institutional settings for public speeches. The differences in the ethical standards applied to speaking in these two contexts illustrate the way in which a society composed of many groups will develop multiple standards particularly adapted to the utterance which sustains and advances the various groups. This fact emphasizes the need to examine the morality of any act of speaking with careful attention to the whole context of the speech. We do not use the same value structure in judging classroom lecturing that we use in judging courtroom speaking. We should not expect that the same value structure will apply equally to speeches by candidates for public office, men holding office, ministers, salesmen, popular lecturers, or commencement speakers. The morality of any speaker's action is likely to be better understood if we also understand the values served by the institution or organization which provides the context for his utterance.

We have not said that all groups in our society have been equally attentive to the problem of developing ethical standards for the discourse of their members. But groups do have different histories and purposes, and they do develop particular ethical systems affecting the utterance of their members.

The link between ethical standards affecting speechmaking, and the purposes of groups served by speeches also calls attention to a further point about the ethics of public speaking. Speeches are moral or immoral acts, but they are not simply this. They are also value-forming acts. The speaking activity associated with any group announces the values sought or achieved by members of that group. Thus public speeches may remind the group of its ethical responsibilities, and may reinforce the values shared by its members. The ethical health of any group or organization may be reflected by the vitality with which its members discuss their ethical responsibilities.

THE AMERICAN POLITICAL SYSTEM AND THE
ETHICS OF PUBLIC SPEECH

The most general institutional framework for American public speaking is that provided by the American political system as a whole. Not all citizens are lawyers, teachers, or preachers. But all participate in some way in the public address associated with the formation and modification of the nation's political system. The values of this system as a whole should therefore provide ethical standards relevant to the largest body of American public discourse. Professor Karl R. Wallace, in an article entitled "An Ethical Basis of Communication," seeks to show how the value assumptions underlying the form of American society as a whole generate ethical standards for public communication.[9] Professor Wallace's analysis asks first about the fundamental values underlying a free society. Presumably our nation seeks to be a free society and has sought political forms and standards effective in achieving this goal. Presumably also the rationale for a free society holds certain assumptions about the nature of man, and the way in which men should organize and conduct their relations with one another. Wallace stipulates four values which he believes underlie the idea of a free society. From these he derives four values to be used in judging the morality of acts of communication. Acts of communication adhering to these values would presumably help America to achieve a free society; acts of communication departing from these values would handicap or embarrass this achievement.

Professor Wallace's analysis is theoretical. That is, he does not ask what values American citizens generally express in their statements or conduct, nor does he ask what values are generally revealed in American public discourse. He does, however, state the value concepts commonly revealed in public commentary about the goals and forms of American democratic society. We will summarize Wallace's analysis and provide some extensions.

As to the assumptions underlying a free society, Wallace postulates that "A free and democratic society, first of all, is built on the notion that the individual has dignity and worth." This idea that each person has value, that his person and values deserve the respect of others, and that he should not be used simply to serve others, is one of the fundamental cut-lines between the idea of a free society and the idea of a totalitarian state. All societies assume that they are doing good for their

9 Karl R. Wallace, "An Ethical Basis of Communication," *The Speech Teacher,* January, 1955, pp. 1–9.

members, but only a free society assumes that each person should have some voice in deciding what is good for him and some protection from the notion that the state, or society as a whole, should determine what is good for him.

The idea that each individual has worth leads to a second assumption: that each person should enjoy equality of opportunity within society. The statement "all men are created equal," asserted in the Declaration of Independence, rests on this assumption. The statement does not claim that all men are born to equal circumstances nor that they have identical mental and physical capacities, but it does propose that insofar as possible society should be organized to permit each man the opportunity to make the most of his capacities. The idea of free public education as developed in the United States is perhaps the most tangible expression of society's effort to assure equality of opportunity.

The third assumption is that each person should have freedom to act as he chooses as long as his actions do not impinge on the freedoms proper to others. The Bill of Rights of the American Constitution was a fundamental effort to protect the rights of individuals from invasion by the state. And a considerable body of public discourse in America is devoted to a continuous dialogue about the line which divides proper exercise of personal liberty from improper invasion of the rights of others. We speak of this line in terms of the difference between "liberty and license," or between "freedom and responsibility."

Wallace's fourth assumption is that a free society believes that each person is capable of understanding his society at a level sufficient to enable him to participate constructively in the determination of public policy. This assumption is underwritten in American society by election procedures which presumably give each citizen one vote in choosing public officials. It is also underwritten by the system of free public education presumed useful in providing each citizen with the information and understanding necessary to his participation in the affairs of state. Most Americans believe in their own fitness to help determine public policy. However, they often express considerable doubt about the capacity of many persons they know to join usefully in the decision-making process of the nation. A recurrent theme in public discussion in America relates to the question of who should actually participate in the election of public officials. For example, should the voting age be lowered to age 18? Should citizens empowered to vote be required to demonstrate minimal literacy?

From the four ideals of a free society, Wallace derives four standards to guide the ethical conduct of communication or to be used in judging the morality of particular acts of communication.

The Ethical Speaker Must Be Fully Informed. First, since a free society assumes an informed electorate, Wallace believes that a communicator's responsibility for being fully informed about his subject matter is not simply intellectually desirable; it is ethically required. As Wallace observes, a public speaker is, during his utterance, the sole source of argument and information available to his listeners. To the extent that the speaker places misinformation or invalid reasoning into the public domain, he has performed a disservice to his society. His action is not merely a failure of intellect, it is also a moral failure. If being well informed before speaking is an ethical requirement, then many public speakers might find silence more moral than public utterance.

The Ethical Speaker Must Be Accurate and Fair. Second, the communicator must be both accurate and fair in his presentation of information and opinion. This value is similar to the value of *truth* previously discussed in this chapter. In a democratic society it derives from the assumption that since all people have worth, they deserve to have their opinions fairly reported. And since sound decision-making rests best on accurate information, society is ill served by each inaccuracy.

The Ethical Speaker Must Reveal His Purposes and His Sources. Third, Wallace asserts that the communicator in a free society should reveal the sources of his information and opinion, and the purposes which underly his utterance. The speaker who pretends to impartiality when his purposes are partisan is acting immorally; he is denying to his listeners information which would be useful to them in judging the merit of that which they hear. The speaker who uses information from biased sources and conceals this fact also acts immorally.

The Ethical Speaker Must Defend the Free and Open Discussion of Ideas. Finally, since a free society assumes an open marketplace of ideas and information and since every person in such a society has worth, the ethical communicator will do all that he can to promote a fair hearing for all information and opinions. The ideal of free discussion may be considered the master value for a free society. This value, if held to, provides public correction for misinformation, for unfair selection of information and opinion, and for concealment of sources or motivations. It suggests that the speaker acts immorally if he refuses to share his platform with speakers who may criticize or oppose him; that he acts immorally if he uses his utterance to seek to organize opinion or action to suppress the public expression of others; and that he acts immorally if he seeks unfairly to label others with names which automatically bring into question the accuracy or respectability of any public statements made by these persons. It is at this latter point that the name-calling activity of a public speaker needs to come under close ethical scrutiny. For a speaker to call a person with whom he disagrees a rascal or know-nothing, a reactionary or radical, is a *relatively* innocuous business in the somewhat muscular atmosphere of American political campaigning. Yet such names deserve scrutiny when used, and if they are unfair, they deserve to be refuted. The first two names, rascal and know-nothing, have enough overtones of moral and intellectual disreputability so that a teacher who applied them to other teachers would be making a serious and professionally damaging accusation, one not to be taken lightly. In the political arena, however, such names are commonplace, and do not seem to prevent a fair hearing for the speaker so named. On the other hand, the contemporary politician who calls his opponent a Communist or Fascist or knowing conspirator has selected damaging labels. Those accusations suggest that the labeled persons are not merely slippery or ignorant, out of the mainstream of American thought, or grossly mistaken. They suggest that the persons in question are knowing enemies of the society in which they seek to be heard, that they are capable of systematic deception in order to mislead listeners. The names, if credited at all, are sufficient to deny many public platforms to the persons so branded. They work to destroy decisively the public credibility of those named. Such names, therefore, operate not to sustain the value of free discussion, but to limit the range of opinions that may be heard. They seek not simply criticism of another person's thinking, but destruction of his person, his capacity to earn a living, and his capacity to be fairly heard.

THE QUESTION OF ETHICS IS INHERENTLY CONTROVERTED

We have examined several sources for ethical standards which may be used in judging the morality of public speeches. None of the standards or systems of standards can be applied easily or unambiguously to a given speech, although each may be used strategically to reveal certain qualities of the speech, and to raise a specific ethical issue concerning speech. We should not be surprised that the question of ethics as applied to the practice of public speaking uncovers moral problems rather than resolving them. Speeches are not instrumental acts to be judged against the standards existing outside the speech. They are essentially moral acts which propose certain values, either implicitly or explicitly. The public speaker may reflect value standards in his society, but he also may criticize or seek to modify these standards. He is engaged in an act of moral choice which frequently involves an effort to modify or create ethical standards. He necessarily addresses himself to such eternally controverted questions as: What are my proper obligations to those whom I address? What is the order of reality I wish to share with them?

SPEAKING SKILL AND ETHICAL POTENTIALITY

Much of the discussion about the ethics of public speaking assumes that the problem of ethics is posed only because some speakers are both effective and immoral. For example, Plato's censure of the Sophists of ancient Greece did not include censure of Greeks who spoke ineptly, but only of those who used their skills to achieve immoral ends. Ineffective speaking, apparently, has seldom been viewed as ethically suspect or as a threat to the moral order. And the possibility that skill in speaking is itself a value with moral implications has been treated lightly, if at all. Yet the question of a possible relationship between a man's speaking skill and his ethical stature needs to be raised. The question may be stated as an issue: Are there certain moral obligations faced by men which cannot be met save through effective speaking? Or is it rather the case that the decision to speak ineffectively is an option without ethical implications?

The issue thus posed should not be treated lightly. A considerable body of inept public speaking in our society goes without ethical censure, or even enjoys ethical approval as a reciprocal of its ineptness. For example, the man who speaks the truth as he sees it is often praised as one who has discharged his responsibility to himself. If his choice of matter and manner promotes misunderstanding, then the responsibility is assumed to rest with those who listened. If the misunderstanding foments public confusion, then the responsibility is still with those who listened. And if the listeners who misunderstand abuse the speaker, the speaker may even be credited with special moral virtue for having the courage to speak his "truth" even if it meant that he would be abused. By way of contrast, the arts of effectiveness—the speaker's study of his audience and situation, his adaptation of forms of enforcement by reason of this analysis, and his selection of purpose and position in terms of that which is possible for an audience rather than simply in terms of that which the speaker might wish—all these arts are treated as compromises a speaker might have to make for reasons of effectiveness. But these compromises are often viewed as limiting or embarrassing the morality of the speaker.

The perspective which wholly dissociates the search for effective communication from the search for virtue, or which even views the search for effective communication as a necessary deterrent to virtue, is commonplace. It is also grossly distorted, and for three very important reasons.

In the first place, the public speaker's action is symbolic. The signs produced by the speaker are not in and of themselves a "truth" corresponding to nature; rather they are a means of ordering some part of nature, or some perspective on reality, in a form capable of being shared with others. The speaker who says, "I spoke the truth, and care not if others misunderstand" implies a profoundly ignorant point of view about the nature of speech. At best he spoke *his* truth, in language which he understands. But if he was misunderstood by others, his language served to conceal his truth from others.

Second, a public speech purports to be an interpersonal action, undertaken not simply for the exercise it affords the speaker, but because of a responsibility toward those who listen. A recluse may speak ethically if he talks only to himself and avoids deception. The moral burden of such action is not great. On the other hand, a public speaker who claims integrity for his own person must acknowledge absolutely the integrity of others with whom he has undertaken communication. He cannot acknowledge the integrity of others without attention to the choices that will make effective communication possible, or without cultivation of the skills which serve such effectiveness. The inept speaker has the option of silence, but if he cannot or will not accept this option, he is in position to discharge his moral responsibility for those who hear him only if he seeks and achieves reasonable skill in his art.

Finally, there is a category of truth available to men which is not external to speech, but is created in the very act of successful communication. The phenomenon created when two or more people understand one another fully has unique reality for those who share in such moments. We are accustomed to think of public speeches as participating in the broad dialectical process in which propositions are controverted, and through which men seek either agreement or understanding of their differences. But speeches also participate in some measure in the dialogue through which men seek a genuine experience with community. Those moments in which groups find the symbols which evoke their sense that they belong to one another, that they share a common humanity, may be more often discovered in conversation than in the public forum. But this experience with community is sometimes achieved by speakers and their audiences. When achieved, the experience is a truth for those who share it.

Ineptness in speaking skill, no less than ignorance of subject matter, has its moral consequences. The speaker who is inept through personal limitation or through error in judgment deserves our forgiveness as much as the speaker who is ignorant through mischance or defective education. His speeches may have immoral consequences, but the consequences derive from the speaker's limitations rather than from his purpose. The speaker who chooses ineptness, either through lack of attention to developing his skills or through lack of attention to the rhetorical choices which underlie effective practice, merits no such sympathy. If he chooses to be complex for people who have no capacity to interpret complexity, if he is casual for those who expect formality, if he is deliberately outrageous in situations constructed for propriety, he chooses in some measure to symbolize his contempt for others. He chooses also to deny to himself and others the truth to be found only in the experience of community. Skill in speaking does not assure moral action. But ineptness forestalls the possibility of moral achievement in the vast number of situations in which men talk to one another.

SUMMARY

Ethical questions are raised about a public speech when some value is applied to the judgment of that speech. The ethical judgment describes the speech as in some sense either moral or immoral. Speaking skill is often treated as an ethically neutral capacity. In this sense speech is viewed as an instrumental action available for good, bad, or morally neutral ends. This point of view is useful in uncovering the sources of effect in acts of speaking. However, the point of view is incomplete and, ultimately, inaccurate. As an action involving others, a speech is intrinsically moral or immoral and cannot be properly compared with instrumental actions which may or may not involve the welfare of others. All speeches select and arrange some order of reality held to be good; they also make judgments about the condition and needs of listeners. Thus speeches are not simply acts to be judged by some ethical system external to the speech. They are acts participating in the work of defining, modifying, and creating values.

Ethical analysis of public speaking is often confused by the self-serving application of standards of judgment only to speakers who assert positions or attitudes distasteful to the critic. Thus the critic uses an alleged ethical standard to denounce the speech he dislikes, but accepts analogous practices without censure when he finds the speaker's position or attitudes agreeable.

Two of the most common values applied to public speeches are the value of truth, or avoidance of deception; and the value of reason, or avoidance of emotive language. Each of these values is important, but the application of either to particular acts of speaking is difficult. Affirmative valuation of reason is further confused by the assumption that a speech is rational only if it fails to engage the emotions of an audience. Neither the nature of speech, nor the nature of speaking generally held to be ethical, justifies the assumption that a speech which is powerfully emotive is therefore ethically suspect.

We may perceive systems of values for controlling or judging speeches rising out of the purposes of the reference groups which are formed and sustained in part by public speaking. Thus groups set standards for the type of speaking held appropriate to their nature and purpose, and these standards become appropriate for understanding and judging speeches in particular contexts. The most general set of institutional values for judging speeches may be drawn from the values held useful or necessary to a free and democratic American society.

No single system of values for judging public speeches can be proposed which will be readily applicable to all speeches. Rather, public speeches reflect a variety of personal and group ethical standards. And they also engage in the criticism and development of these standards. Public speeches are thus not merely events to be judged; they are actions participating in the dialogue by which values are formed and altered.

Skill in communication is often held to be irrelevant to, or a limitation on, the possibility of moral action. A proper view of the nature of public speaking reveals that such skill is prerequisite to the achievement of certain moral ends. Ineptness in speech, like ignorance of substance, may have immoral consequences.

FOR FURTHER STUDY

SPEAKING, WRITING, OR DISCUSSION EXERCISES

1. Describe the style revealed in the language of an important speech in terms of the dimensions of style discussed in Chapter 6. Cite passages from the text of the speech to support your description.
2. Describe the public manner of a speaker you have heard on one or several occasions in terms of the dimensions of style discussed in Chapter 6. Support your description with references both to the speaker's language and to his delivery. Call attention to whether or not the speaker's language and manner support a unified image of his style.
3. Contrast and compare the public images of two important public figures in the political, business, educational, or religious worlds. For example,

compare Presidents John Kennedy and Lyndon Johnson; President Charles de Gaulle and President Dwight Eisenhower; Pope John XXIII and Pope Paul VI; Vice Presidents Hubert Humphrey and Richard Nixon. Identify particular aspects of the public manner of the persons described which seem to have been most important in developing their public image. Discuss the reference groups with whom each person may be effective or ineffective.

4. Describe changes over a period of time in the positions reflected in the public statements of spokesmen for various reference groups. For example, describe position changes in leaders of a civil rights group, a religious group, college student groups, a political party. Do you see the changes in the positions taken by group leaders as reflecting opinion change in their constituencies or as seeking to influence opinion change in their constituencies?

5. Analyze a significant public speech from the point of view of the extent to which the speaker fulfilled what you believe to be his ethical obligations. Consider whether or not you believe the speaker has provided the best available "order of reality" for his listeners, and has taken proper accounting of the condition of his listeners. Consider both the speaker's purpose and his methods as involving moral choices. Your analysis will be more interesting to others if you start with a speaker who has aroused strong moral approval or disapproval, or both, because of his speaking practices.

READINGS

1. For a thorough summary of the topics and terminology used by classical rhetoricians in the study of style, see:
   Edward J. R. Corbett, *Classical Rhetoric for the Modern Student* (New York: Oxford University Press, 1965), pp. 384–534.

2. In 1852, the English scientist and philosopher Herbert Spencer published an essay on style in which he sought to derive all particular generalizations on the attributes of good style from the single principle of economy. Spencer's method and advice contrast interestingly with twentieth-century efforts to analyze stylistic attributes associated with effective speaking and writing. Read:
   a. Herbert Spencer, "The Philosophy of Style," in Dudley Bailey, ed., *Essays on Rhetoric* (New York: Oxford University Press, 1965), pp. 147–172.
   b. Rudolph Flesch, *The Art of Readable Writing* (New York: Harper and Brothers, 1949).
   c. Walker Gibson, *Tough, Sweet and Stuffy* (Bloomington: Indiana University Press, 1966).

3. For some contemporary discussions of the analysis of style, see:
   a. Walker Gibson, "A Note on Style and the Limits of Language," in

Walker Gibson, ed., *The Limits of Language* (New York: Hill and Wang, 1962), pp. 104–113.

b. Louis T. Milic, "Metaphysical Criticism of Style," and Monroe C. Beardsley, "Style and Good Style," in Martin Steinmann, Jr., ed., *New Rhetorics* (New York: Charles Scribner's Sons, 1967), pp. 161–175; 191–213.

4. The power of metaphoric expression to illuminate thought has led modern critics to give detailed attention to the structure and properties of metaphors. See:

a. I. A. Richards, *The Philosophy of Rhetoric* (New York: Oxford University Press, 1936; Galaxy Books paperback edition, 1965), pp. 89–138.

b. C. S. Lewis, "Bluspels and Flalansferes," in Max Black, ed., *The Importance of Language* (New Jersey: Prentice Hall, Inc., 1962), pp. 36–50.

5. For varied approaches of speaker-audience relationships, see:

a. Raymond A. Bauer, "The Communicator and the Audience," in Lewis A. Dexter and David M. White, eds., *People, Society and Mass Communication* (New York: The Free Press of Glencoe, 1964), pp. 125–140.

b. Kenneth Burke, "Rhetoric—Old and New," in Martin Steinmann, Jr., ed., *New Rhetorics,* pp. 59–76.

6. The sense in which speaking is more than exercise of an ethically neutral technique is developed in:

a. Richard M. Weaver, "Language is Sermonic," in Roger Nebergall, ed., *Dimensions of Rhetorical Scholarship* (Norman, Oklahoma: Department of Speech, University of Oklahoma, 1963), pp. 49–63.

b. Karl R. Wallace, "The Primacy of Substance and Ideas in the Teaching of Practical Discourse," *The English Journal,* LIII (January, 1964), 1–9.

c. Franklyn S. Haiman, "Democratic Ethics and The Hidden Persuaders," in Haig A. Bosnajian, ed., *Readings in Speech* (New York: Harper and Row, 1965), pp. 195–207.

7. The public man, charged with mediating the motives and positions of others, may face inherent conflicts in the values he holds as a person, and those he assumes publicly. For interesting reflections on such conflict see: Dag Hammarskjold, *Markings,* translated by Leif Sjoberg and W. H. Auden (New York: Alfred Knopf, 1964), p. 222.

PART II

Preparation and Action

*When imaginings and illusions are over, the possible and
inevitable meeting of man with himself is able to take place
only as the meeting of the individual with his fellow man.*
—MARTIN BUBER

INTRODUCTION

Part I examined public speaking from the perspective of one who
stands outside acts of public discourse seeking to understand their nature. But because we experience public speeches as participants in an
action, the inquiry in Part I moved necessarily into consideration of the
problems of judgment and choice confronting both those who speak, and
those who listen.

Part II examines public speaking from the perspective of the person
preparing and presenting a public speech. The action we have been
examining now becomes the action to be undertaken.

If there is much that can be said *about* public speeches, there is less
that can be usefully said in a public way to people engaged in the immediate process of creating and presenting a particular discourse for a
particular audience. For one thing, we know too little about the actual
processes by which human beings move from their varieties of purposes
and perceptions into the moment of public utterance. Moreover, if there
are regularities in the habits of preparation and presentation acquired by
skillful speakers, these regularities are not readily apparent in the reports such speakers give of their own experience. About the most that
can be said with much certainty is that most successful speakers seem to
have taken their responsibilities seriously, to have devoted great energy
both to preparation and action, and to have sought out opportunities for
engaging audiences. If every man must be his own teacher on matters of
speech preparation and presentation, it follows that no one teaches himself unless he gives both purpose and energy to repeated use of the public platform.

Part II treats the advice and associated commentary which may be useful for people seeking self-consciously to improve their skills of speech preparation and presentation. In order to give focus to such advice and commentary, the materials in Part II are related to the preparation and presentation of speeches in a particular context—in this case, the college classroom. The strategies of preparation and presentation appropriate to the classroom are treated as a special instance of the strategies of preparation and presentation which might be adapted to any specified context. Thus as we observe the way in which the expectancies, possibilities, and limitations characteristic of the classroom affect a speaker's choices, we can perceive by inference how a different set of expectancies, limitations, and possibilities might be treated.

The materials in Part II are compressed since the commentary and advice touch on many matters commonly studied in secondary school courses in English or speech. Thus Part II may be, for many college students, a review of matters studied before. The materials are presented in three chapters: "Classroom Speaking: The General Scene," "Preparing the Speech," and "Delivery and Criticism."

CHAPTER 9

Classroom Speaking: The General Scene

THE TRADITION OF CLASSROOM SPEAKING

Students of public speaking traditionally prepare and present public speeches to their fellow students. This tradition is a venerable one. Isocrates, contemporary of Plato and Aristotle, was reputedly more successful than other teachers of his day in teaching public speaking because he insisted that his students engage in speaking as well as attend lectures on rhetorical theory. Roman education, for almost half a millennium, was grounded in an elaborate system of exercises in speaking and writing. These exercises supported the belief that the end of education was the development of the orator-statesman—a man whose highest natural aptitude, that of speech, was to be both cultivated and disciplined. It is worth noting that the entire conception of "discipline" in the classical world was somewhat at variance with the usual definition given to the term in modern education. We are apt to think of a discipline as an orderly body of knowledge. The Greeks and Romans, however, had no such static view. Discipline for them was the mark of the educated man, defined by the way he conducted himself, and by the substance and manner of his action. One did not simply learn a discipline as a body of information; one acquired discipline through the exercise and development of his natural powers.

The education of the speaker as a central and universal mission of higher education persisted in the medieval and renaissance university. As recently as the latter half of the nineteenth century, it was common for all students in an American college or university to prepare and present speeches for the examination of some patient faculty member, or to justify their claim to a baccalaureate degree by the final public presentation and defense of a thesis. At Columbia College, until growing enrollments in the latter half of the nineteenth century made the task too burdensome, the president of the college judged the ability of all his students to speak in public. And until late in the nineteenth century, candidates for graduation at several American colleges and universities were expected to demonstrate through a public lecture their fitness for a degree.

There is considerable merit in the 2,500-year-old educational tradition which asserts that an educated man or woman assumes a responsibility for public leadership and should, therefore, be reasonably disciplined in the art of public communication. But a number of theoretically meritorious educational traditions, ranging from the reading of Greek and Latin to universal familiarity with Shakespeare and Plutarch's *Lives,* have fallen prey to the immense elaboration and specialization of contemporary education. Students surveying the range of public speaking skills presented by their college instructors, their clergy, their doctors and attorneys, and their statesmen will have no difficulty in deducing that the possession of a college degree—even an advanced one—no longer implies discipline in public speaking.

If college students are no longer universally required to seek discipline in public speaking, the opportunity to engage in such a search is nevertheless almost universally available in American colleges and universities. The theoretical merit of the tradition which viewed skill in communication as an essential mark of an educated man is seldom disputed. And the assumption that the search for such skill requires participation in speaking exercises continues equally without serious dispute.

The reason that speaking exercises should be part of the study of public speaking seems too evident to require lengthy discussion. As we observed in Chapter 1, skill in public speaking is so useful in a variety of contexts in public life that few persons care to study the art without giving attention to the condition of their own skill. While one may study poetry without ever intending or desiring to write poems, few persons study public speaking without expecting that they are likely to be called on to make speeches. And it is unquestionably true that the range of speaking abilities most of us wish to acquire can no more be attained through contemplation of the art of speaking than the ability to paint great pictures can be attained by a reflective tour through art galleries.

Many students, however, are less ready to believe that there is any very fundamental relationship between practicing an art and coming to have knowledge of the art. "After all," they observe, "there are very skillful public speakers who have never studied the art of public speaking in any formal sense. Similarly, there are painters whose wisdom is in their eye and hand, but who don't have two coherent ideas about the nature of art. There are men who play a musical instrument beautifully, but who couldn't define the difference between a semitone and a diminished seventh. Knowledge and skill are two different things." Since there unquestionably are such speakers, such painters, and such musicians, the argument seems plausible enough; and it gives force to an illusory separation of the search for skill in an art and the search for knowledge or understanding of that art.

Let us dismiss the untutored but skillful man as the Greeks did. Who knows, they said, how high such a man might have risen had he become a student of his art? But is it not also true that the practicing of an art is an important avenue to understanding an art? To speak in public, if the experience is reflected upon, is to see the action of a speech from the inside. Assuredly such experience enables a student to *know more* of the problems and possibilities of public speaking than could possibly be known to one who only observed, listened to, or read speeches. To take an example from another field, painters have been known to comment angrily on the shortsightedness of the critic who has never submitted himself to the discipline of the art he judges. Actors and directors may also carry on a persistently acrimonious dialogue with critics whom they believe have never known, from the inside, the nature of theater. To *know* fully the nature of any art, one must have in some sense experienced its discipline, and thus have learned the limitations and possibilities of its action. In this sense the most complete knowledge about public speaking is available only to the student who joins his study of theory to reflection about his own speaking experiences.

One of the important objectives of participation in classroom speaking exercises, therefore, is the search for understanding of the nature of public speaking. This objective is not antithetical to the search for personal skill, but it is clearly more important. The student who hopes that from a few classroom speaking exercises he can complete his discipline as a public speaker hopes for the impossible. What he can realistically hope for is that he will find the form and direction he would like his own development to take; that he will move in some measure along the selected direction and toward the selected form; and that he will acquire such knowledge of the art he seeks to practice as to enlighten all his subsequent experience as speaker, audience member, or interpreter of the communication practices of his society.

THE CLASSROOM SPEECH AS A "REAL" PUBLIC SPEECH

To see classroom speaking as unrelated to knowledge is a serious misconception. One other misconception often limits the usefulness of classroom experience. Classroom speeches are often called "exercises."

The label is proper if it implies that such speeches are instrumental in an educational process which has ends beyond life in the classroom. But if one holds that classroom speeches are not "real" speeches—that they differ in basic ways from the speeches which are given in the "real" world—then a serious misinterpretation has occurred.

The classroom speech is as real as any other speech. It brings together a speaker and an audience. The speech incorporates purpose, position, movement, structure, forms of enforcement, and style. It has consequences.

To be sure the occasion of the classroom speech sets certain limits on the choices available to the speaker. But all speakers must deal with circumstances limiting their freedom of choice. In this sense preparing and presenting a classroom speech is to engage in a type of thinking and acting characteristic of all public speaking. The speaker encounters contingencies and seeks to take account of them. He makes choices. To a greater or lesser extent he is successful in encompassing the diverse elements of the situation into an action in which purposes and meanings are shared. To the extent that he understands the successes and failures of his effort, he understands a mode of thought and action which will serve him in all speaking situations.

Before considering speech preparation and presentation, it will be useful to see how the classroom creates particular opportunities and limitations for the speaker. Our analysis will illustrate, in brief form, the way in which a speaker might start a study of the contingencies affecting any speech.

SPECIAL OPPORTUNITIES AVAILABLE IN CLASSROOM SPEECHES

Perhaps the greatest single opportunity available to the classroom speaker is that of "trying out" ways of action which are for him new or experimental. Such experimentation is extraordinarily important to the speaker who seeks to understand his public role. But outside the classroom situation the pressures against such experimentation are very heavy. As we observed in Chapter 1, each of us finds a self through interaction with others; we find our public self through trying public behaviors and internalizing those which seem to establish our relationship with others in a satisfactory way. But the repertory of behaviors we establish early in life are likely to become a fixed limit to our public conduct unless we seek out and make use of opportunities to "try on" different roles or different behaviors in public situations.

When we experiment with different roles or behaviors in public, we are of course taking a chance. The effort to do something different, or be in some sense a different person, may not work too well the first time we try it. We may feel awkward, and even seem awkward. Outside the classroom we are naturally reluctant to experiment with our public behavior. We can scarcely expect a church gathering to understand if the pastor says, "Ordinarily I am a quiet and sentimental person. I build my talks around a few simple ideas supported by my personal experiences. Tonight for the first time I am giving a speech based on extensive research in which I shall try to make my central thesis as forceful as possible through the use of the best evidence and reasoning I can bring to bear. Be patient with me, because I have never before really tried to speak in this way." Perhaps the audience would accept a speaker who did this, but the approach would be unusual.

By contrast, the classroom is in part an experimental laboratory. No speaker need explain that he is trying to be different from or better than his "good old underdeveloped public self." Every speaker is in some way supposed to be seeking change from that which is simply customary or habitual to him. The search for improvement is presumably a purpose shared by the group, and the speaker who shows evidence of genuine search faces no real threat if some of his efforts are failures. The political speaker who has an established speaking routine which has been successful for him in winning elections scarcely dares change this routine. Failure is too punishing. The classroom speaker may depart from his established routines with confidence. Failure is a source of learning as well as success. Experimentation is the order of the occasion. The risk in trying to do something new is minimal. The potential gain is maximal.

A second opportunity characteristic of classroom speaking is that of receiving reasonably candid reactions from one's audience. Outside the classroom it would be an unusual listener who would rise at the end of the speech to say, "I found it almost impossible to follow your speech because of the abstract and technical language you used. It was the longest five-minute speech I have ever heard." Such a comment would wound the speaker. It would probably make other members of the audience uncomfortable. What a boor this listener was! True, the speech *was* all but unintelligible, but the social conventions surrounding public-speaking situations outside the classroom respect the term "tact." One praises the speaker or remains silent.

By contrast, the classroom speaker and audience, bound by the common pursuit of excellence and understanding, can value candor in a way impossible outside the classroom. The listener who speaks honestly to us in the classroom is our "best friend." He best understands the purpose all members of the class have accepted as legitimate to the occasion.

Under circumstances permitting listeners to be candid in their responses, speakers have the best opportunity for discovering the reality of their effect on others.

The classroom offers another special opportunity. We usually try out new ways of speaking as an imagined action. That is, we rehearse internally how we shall appear in public before the time of appearance. The major stimulus to our imagination is observation of the actions of others. In the classroom, the listener-speaker can observe a remarkable variety of speeches in a decently short interval of time. To see the same range of actions outside the classroom might require one to devote the better part of some years joining various public audiences.

The classroom audience sees the noisy speaker and the quiet speaker, the colloquial speaker and the literary speaker, the reflective and the impetuous, the clown and the preacher, the warm speaker and the cold speaker, the fearful and the aggressive, the well-read and the poorly read, the tactless and the tactful. The listener observes disorder and obvious order, the supported assertion and the asserted assertion. In short, he sees much of the range of human possibilities in public speaking illustrated in some measure, and he has the opportunity to observe the special merits and limitations of each possibility. He may, if he watches and listens carefully, see himself in another person, or see what he seeks in another person.

CONSTRAINTS OF THE CLASSROOM-SPEAKING SITUATION

If the classroom-speaking situation presents unique opportunities, it also presents other unique contingencies which constrain the speaker's choices. A proper taking into account of these contingencies becomes an important measure of the speaker's success.

A notable constraint is the accidental nature of the audience and occasion. Each classroom speaker confronts listeners who did not gather just to hear him speak; nor did they gather because the word went out that a speech on the Vietnam conflict was being given at 9:30 a.m., February 7, in Room 214 of Old Main. The situation faced by the speaker is extraordinarily unstructured. He has no right to assume prior interest or experience with his subject by all members of the audience. He has no reservoir of goodwill to trade on by reason of having been invited to speak. He is not being paid to talk, and the audience has no financial stake in pretending that his speech is outstanding. Such structure as has been given to the situation may have been provided by an assignment and may be quite unrelated to the speaker's background or special talents. The varsity football player may be asked to present a propositional speech on some social or political problem. The major in biological sciences may be caught up in the philosophic enterprise of praising or blaming some notable historic personage. The audience, aware of the assignment, may entertain expectations about the speaker's action. And the speaker must take these expectations into account even though he senses that they ask him to do things he has never attempted.

This situation places heavy responsibility on the speaker for turning his loosely assembled classmates into a genuine audience. He cannot assume that the audience came to hear him talk; he must seek to have them believe that he has earned the right to their time. The speaker cannot assume that the audience understands how the speaker's ideas are important to their interests; he must establish the relevance of his ideas to the interests of his listeners.

A second constraint in the classroom speech is that it takes place in an academic environment. This fact seems sometimes to be ignored by student speakers, although it may take on great importance to their instructor and certain members of the class. It is clear that colleges and universities were not established for the conduct of conversation about trivial matters. The trivial speech is as unsuited to such an environment as a discourse on the preparation of hybrid corn seed would be out of place at a convention of aeronautical engineers—and for the same reason. The environment of a speech, the kind of institution or organization which gives rise to the speech, limits the speaker's range of appropriate choice. There is nothing intrinsically wrong with a speech on the art of canoe paddling, or the wrapping of Christmas packages; but such speeches, unless they serve only as context for an artistic exercise of wit or some philosophic observations about the nature of man, are grossly inappropriate to a college setting.

If an academic setting condemns trivia, it has its own positive demands. The college or university campus holds rationality in high esteem. The speeches and written works of academicians are often charged with being overly cautious and incredibly dull. But caution and dullness may stem in part from the historic insistence of institutions of higher learning that assertions ought to be grounded in evidence and reasoning, and that there ought to be a decent relationship between the claims one makes publicly, and the amount of reputable information one can bring to bear in support of these claims.

If the academic environment is cautious about ill-founded assertions, it is extraordinarily receptive to new or unorthodox ideas. The academic ideal holds that a man should state those conclusions to which his best study and thinking have led him, and that it is no criticism of an idea to say that it is new or unusual.

The student must work within the contingencies of the academic environment if he is to take proper account of the occasion. He will recognize soon enough that not all members of his audience understand equally or share equally the predispositions of academic institutions. Nevertheless, to the extent that the virtues of curiosity, openness to new ideas, and respect for reflective thinking operate at all in American culture, they are more likely to operate in the context of the institution of higher learning. This is the setting for which the classroom speech should be appropriate.

A final constraint for classroom speeches is that they are characteristically short speeches, presented under sharp and strictly enforced time limitation. A three-minute speech may be called a short speech in the classroom; a five-minute speech may be considered standard; and a ten or fifteen minute speech, considered rather long. In some classes the instructor may conclude that the size of the class does not permit a "long" ten- or fifteen-minute speech. While five-minute and ten-minute speeches have their counterparts in situations other than the classroom, they are not typical in American public life.

Brevity requires certain kinds of planning from the speaker. The short speech needs a carefully limited purpose so that the magnitude of the end sought is not disproportionate to the means that can be used. If it is to seem a finished and yet artistically formed speech, its introduction and conclusion must do their work quickly lest the speech becomes all introduction or all conclusion. The classroom speech needs a structure that will move toward its purpose with a minimum of wasted language. All speakers are to some extent redundant, and this is not a grave fault in a leisurely speech; but it can turn the short speech into a thin and unsubstantial morsel. The speaker has little or no time for digression. Digressions are commonplace in longer speeches, and often are used to good purpose—to rest the audience, or to relieve the tension of an extended period of seriousness, or to take account of special circumstances attending a speaking occasion. But digression is a doubtful choice for short speeches.

One could view enforced brevity as a contingency which justifies an insignificant or trivial speech. But this is a poor accounting to take of brevity. Properly conceived, the short speech calls for the utmost discipline on the part of the speaker in clarifying his thinking to achieve the kind of economy of statement which will permit both form and substance to be accomplished quickly.

THE NATURE AND USE OF ADVICE ON SPEECHMAKING

Public speaking seems to have stirred more men to set down more advice than any other branch of human conduct. The advisers range from philosophers such as Aristotle, Francis Bacon, or Ralph Waldo Emerson; to successful orators such as Cicero, William Gladstone, or Norman Thomas; to teachers such as Isocrates, Quintilian, or John Quincy Adams. The volume of advice given through history by reputable men seems not to have discouraged the constant appearance of new advice-givers. Nor has the accumulation of advice through history resulted in any constant accumulation of wisdom. There may be good reason for the fact that each generation produces its own group of advice-givers, none of whom seem greatly wiser than the advisers of earlier generations.

The reason is to be found in the fact that advice on speechmaking is always given within the context of some particular culture. This culture produces its own set of speaking customs, speaking situations, and audience expectations. And thus the adviser, if he wishes to be practical or specific, will inevitably include some recommendations on the conduct of speeches which cultural change will quickly render obsolete. An interesting example of this is the fact that Cicero felt it necessary to caution Roman speakers against use of the left hand for gesturing while speaking. The advice seems to have been based on the commonsense fact that young Romans practiced the art of oratory before they wore the Roman toga, and that since the toga was supported from the left shoulder, violent gesturing with the left arm might at best produce disarray in the speaker's attire, and at worst cause serious embarrassment. Interestingly enough this culture-bound advice persisted in works of rhetoric for some centuries after the toga became obsolete. Some medieval writers cautioned against use of the left arm apparently for no better reason than the fact that Cicero had so written, and what was good enough for Cicero was good enough for them. Others made a curious cultural adaptation of this advice, calling attention to the sinister and negative symbolism of the left arm, and recommending its use only for dramatizing allusions to corrupt ideas.

Cicero's advice on gesture seems only an historical curiosity today. While his advice on courtroom speaking also seems in part culture-bound, in part it is relevant to legal pleading in our own age. One cannot learn much from the great Roman advocate about the rules of evidence which constrain the speaking of lawyers and witnesses in contemporary American courts; one *can* learn much from him about the way in which a lawyer in our own age might discover the lines of argument most likely to produce a decision favorable to his client, and about the most effective way of ordering and presenting such lines of argument. Thus Ciceronian advice, so admirably suited to the contingencies of his own age, becomes a mixture of observations about effective speaking made obsolete by time, and observations durable enough to be useful even today. And thus one senses how inevitable it is that each society or culture must produce its own advice-givers on the art of speaking, none of whom may add much of enduring importance to the wisdom of earlier advisers, but any of whom may, in proportion to his own wisdom, produce advice peculiarly suited to speakers of his own age.

A contingency other than cultural change limits sharply the status of the "wisdom" that can be accumulated in the form of advice to others as to how they ought to conduct themselves as speakers. In one sense advice is not wisdom at all except to the person for whom it seems to work. And it is an invariant condition of even the best advice that it works for some people, and doesn't work at all for others.

Our understanding of the contingent and all too perishable nature of advice on speechmaking has been greatly sharpened in twentieth-century America by two interacting forces. As a society, we place a high value on individuality—committed as we are to a political and social system which argues that each person is in some sense unique, that his uniqueness is valuable, and that it should be respected. In a culture with such presuppositions we should neither expect nor wish that all men should resemble one another when they perform as public speakers. Moreover, the studies of human personality and conduct carried out by our social scientists seem to reinforce our belief that individuality is not merely a thing to be desired in mankind; it is rather the very shape of reality. People should differ from one another, and they do differ. Such individual differences as we observe in the quality of voices and the fluency with which speakers articulate words are not merely the product of different environments. To some extent such differences are forecast in the muscular and neurological raw material with which speakers come into this world. Individuals differ in physical energy, in intellectual aptitude, in the capacity for aesthetic response, and in myriad other ways which will be reflected in their speaking. Is it possible at all to advise people generally how they ought to speak?

Perhaps in the final analysis it is impossible to tell another person how he should go about preparing and presenting a speech. As we observed in Chapter 1, a person's speech is better viewed as intrinsic to his nature, rather than as an outer garment to be changed at will. For this reason the advice-giver can tell another person "how I prepare my speeches." (Suggestion: this works for me and it might work for you.) Or he can tell another person "how Emerson thought speeches should be prepared and presented." (Suggestion: try Emerson's advice. He was a wise man, and his advice might work for you.) But finally each speaker must discover for himself the methods of preparation and presentation which seem best suited to his own possibilities and limitations, his own person and purposes. Advice, properly conceived, is not wisdom to be learned and followed, but the wisdom of another person, to be tested against experience, to be used as it proves useful, to be modified by one's own person and purposes. To say this is not to say that advice is useless. We learn to act in part by observing the actions of others, and by seeing imaginatively certain aspects of the actions of others that we can appropriate to our own way of life. But finally we must search for our own rhetoric—our own theory of speechmaking— just as we must search for understanding of ourselves. No one can tell us who we are in the sense of relieving us of the burden or pleasure of self-discovery. No one can tell us how to speak in the sense of freeing us from the search for a discipline uniquely suited to ourselves.

Our cautionary notes about advice are intended as a properly philosophic frame of reference for interpreting the remaining materials in this and the following chapter. In the pages that follow we shall consider the question of how a speaker should go about preparing and presenting a classroom speech. The advice will be presented in compressed form, without extensive illustration. Presumably much of it will be familiar to students reading this book, since it represents the sort of "received wisdom" about speechmaking which has some common currency in American education. The advice is intended as a review of the study of speechmaking from the point of view of the speaker, and as a preliminary to the task of preparing and presenting classroom speeches. Although most closely related to classroom speaking, the suggestions also describe procedures in preparing and presenting speeches outside the classroom. The student should approach such advice thoughtfully, prepared to screen its usefulness against his experiences in the work of preparing and presenting speeches.

THE CENTRAL ACTION OF A CLASSROOM SPEECH

At a certain time in the public-speaking class, the instructor calls on Mr. Jones to speak. The moment is seldom one of high drama. Mr. Jones has not traveled far for this occasion. Neither band music nor prayers have preceded his address, and his only status as he approaches his audience is represented by his claim to equal status with his listeners

—a claim which he can either substantiate or refute with his speech. Nevertheless, the calling of his name creates certain expectancies. Jones is expected to appear—and he usually does. He is expected to talk for a brief period of time. According to the ground rules laid down in the assignment, he may be expected to answer questions during or after his speech, or remain before the group for oral criticism.

It is expected that his period of talk will not be one of free association. Rather Mr. Jones should have (a) identified the purpose or purposes of his action; (b) selected his topic with due consideration for his capabilities, the nature of the audience, the nature of the assignment, and the limitations of time and physical setting; (c) planned his talk in terms of some central position, and in order to give it form and structure; (d) discovered a suitable range of supporting materials for his ideas; and (e) prepared himself carefully for the most effective delivery of which he is capable. These expectancies define the types of activity that Jones will have gone through if his speech has been carefully prepared, and we shall consider each in turn. But before undertaking such consideration, is there any more general description we can give to the nature of the action to be represented in Jones's speech?

Ideally, Jones's speech can convert the somewhat amorphous and loosely structured society of the classroom into an audience. To do this, Jones must do more, however, than simply agitate the air and light waves of the classroom. He must somehow bind himself and the audience in a state of mutual attention and regard for one another, and in the common act of considering some area of human affairs defined by his subject. "Here is a subject," he says in effect, "with which I am concerned, and for which I want your concern. I shall make known the nature of, and perhaps the private reasons for, my interest in this subject as it relates to your lives. I shall have considered the ways in which I can make my ideas available to you, and interesting to you, because I see this occasion as belonging to you just as much as it belongs to me."

Ideally, Jones seeks an action which will encompass the classroom situation, and bring speaker and audience into a state of common activity.

If the speech is to realize its potential, the relationship of speaker, audience, and subject must be fully established. The speaker cannot use his subject as an excuse for removing himself from concern for or attention to his audience. His concern for his subject is for the subject as made publicly available to others. The audience, properly, is as interested in the speaker as in his subject. Listeners seek not only knowledge or a point of view about some subject, but also to know another person more completely. Within this view of the action, common movements by the speaker become significant. He may seek to show his regard for the audience in his manner of looking at them. He may open his speech with the story, experience, or fact which seems to him the most memorable and exciting facet of his subject. This story or fact announces the nature and quality of his own involvement in the subject, and he may hope that it will link his audience to the subject. If some kind of private or personal experience led the speaker into his subject, he may wish to make this clear to the audience, so that they may better know the speaker and the path that brought him to this subject. Either explicitly or implicitly the speaker seeks to answer the inevitable questions which must be answered if the relationships present in the speaking situation are to be fully established: (a) Why am I speaking? (speaker and subject); (b) How do I view our relationship? (speaker and audience); and (c) Why should you listen? (audience and subject matter).

These relationships may sometimes be established implicitly. The speaker whose enthusiasm for his subject permeates his manner of address, and whose regard for his audience is evident in the warmth of his manner, may completely bind together the elements of the situation. But classroom speakers often err in depending too much on the relationships implicit in the occasion and too little on making these relationships explicit. The speaker who "lectures" on the critical nature of Soviet-American relationships in Berlin, and who fails to mention his own experience in Berlin is simply withholding from his audience access to information that would help them to understand him better. The speaker who believes that his information or his ideas have specific values for members of the audience should make known to the audience the benefit they may expect from careful listening.

We have now reviewed the rationale for classroom speeches, their particular contingencies, the perspective from which advice about speechmaking must be viewed, and the general conception of the classroom occasion. In the next chapter we shall consider "received advice" on public speaking and its application to the preparation of classroom speeches.

SUMMARY

Preparing and presenting classroom speeches is an ancient and much honored practice in higher education. Such practice should be considered not merely as an avenue to personal speaking skill, but also as a means of understanding the nature of speechmaking.

The classroom speech is no more artificial than any other speech. It operates within a set of contingencies, and the speaker who understands and adapts to these contingencies uses a method of thinking appropriate to any speaking situation. If classroom speeches are in some ways unique, the same truth holds for any speech anywhere.

The classroom occasion is useful for the development of personal skill in speechmaking because it offers opportunity for experimentation, opportunity for receiving candid reactions to one's speaking, and opportunity for observing a variety of speech practices in a brief period of time. The classroom speech must meet the contingencies of the accidental nature of the audience, the expectancies created by assignments, the expectancies created by the purposes of academic institutions, and the pressure created by the need for brevity.

History has produced voluminous advice on the preparation and presentation of public speeches. The advice has been culture-bound, and has not produced any progressive accumulation of imperishable wisdom. Such "received advice" nevertheless is necessary to every culture and can be useful if the speaker screens the advice against the uniqueness of his own capabilities and purposes.

The classroom speaker must act to encompass the particular situation he enters. He is expected to (a) observe limitations set by the assignment; (b) define his purpose(s); (c) define his central position; (d) seek subject matter, structure and movement, forms of enforcement, and style relevant to his position; and (e) prepare himself for the most effective delivery of which he is capable.

CHAPTER 10

Preparing the Speech

. . . there are three kinds of authors. First those who write without thinking. They write from a full memory, from reminiscences; it may be, even straight out of other people's books. This class is the most numerous. Then come those who do their thinking whilst they are writing . . . there is no lack of them. Last of all come those authors who think before they write. They are rare.

—ARTHUR SCHOPENHAUER

THE RECOLLECTION AND DISCOVERY OF SUBJECT MATTER

A series of complaints often voiced about public speeches may have a common origin. "The speaker does not seem really concerned about his subject," says one critic. "He recites words, but I have no sense that the words are part of him." Another critic observes: "The speaker's subject seemed trite and unexceptional. I have heard those same ideas about the best way to reduce traffic accidents a hundred times. In fact, I think he got his speech from the same article in the Sunday supplement that I read last week." One critic seems to be reacting to the speaker's manner or delivery; the other to the speaker's subject matter. Yet the speaker's difficulty may begin in both cases with the way in which he has chosen and prepared his subject matter.

The primary source of the subject matter for effective public speeches rests in the reflective experience of the speaker. A speech growing from the speaker's reflective experience belongs to him; he is a part of it and can become a person talking to people rather than a physical presence trying to seem real. Speakers commonly seem most alive and most real when relating incidents from their own lives. But this fact does not reveal the full significance of the concept of reflective experience.

The source of reflective experience may rest in the events of one's own life. These events when recalled become experience. They become reflective experience when they have been thought about and interpreted

269

—when their meaning has been understood, or when one has come intellectually to know how the experience affected his life and can judge its importance or insignificance. We tell the story of the death of our dog and this is an experience recalled. But the experience is essentially trivial, a mere piece of conversation, unless we have discovered its significance. Reflection—the search for the meaning of the experience—may assure us only that the experience was indeed trivial, or it may inform us that this was our earliest experience with the nature of death, its paradoxical opposition to life, its effects on the living, its possible meaning. Then we know that the experience, far from being trivial, touched on one of the most profound themes of existence.

But the overt or dramatic events of our past are not the only basis for reflective experience. Obviously the products of our reading, viewing, and listening may take on the quality of reflective experience. We attend a play or read a novel, and participate imaginatively in the experience of so-called fictional persons. Through reflection we may discover that literature has offered us understanding of the complex motivations involved in human existence, or understanding of the problems of choice faced by all men, or understanding of the way life seems to persons whose background differs from our own. The knowledge that literature offers us becomes part of our own life, however, only as we reflect on the meaning of the literature for our own life, or our own way of viewing the lives of others.

Similarly, through reflection we may convert intrinsically inert facts about the world about us into part of our own experience with the world. For example, one may know certain facts about population growth in various areas of the world without any serious effort to comprehend the possible import of these facts. But one can also take possession of the facts through reflection in a way that makes this information part of a personal point of view toward such diverse intellectual topics as population control, public health measures, land use, urban planning, economic growth, or the relationship of population density to patterns of living. The facts possessed or appropriated in this way become part of one's personal experience with his world. In this sense, one hundred men may present a public speech supporting federal aid to education; all may use some of the same bits of information and some of the same lines of argument. Yet each speech can be a personal possession of the speaker provided he has come to see his own life as involved in his utterance. The tragedy of the speaker who seems uninvolved in his subject, or whose speech seems trite or lacking in originality, is not simply that he is parroting the public expression of others. To be sure, using the words and ideas of others without acknowledging their source is a form of plagiarism. Plagiarism can be a cause for legal action if the ideas or language taken from others have some demonstrable uniqueness and value; it is always a grave offense against the spirit and purpose of an academic institution. But the person who speaks without involvement offends most seriously his own person; he has chosen to act without reality—to give part of his life to some empty pretense.

If we understand that every good speech is the product of reflective experience, the potential sources of materials become enormous. The speaker needs to drive his thinking back upon himself as he seeks subject matter. What do I believe? he may ask himself. Why do I believe these things? What kinds of experiences have I had which have changed me? Have I had personal experiences which have a meaning worthy of public discussion? Have I read a magazine article lately which caught my attention? Why did it catch my attention and interest? If I can find the importance of the article for me, can I not also find how to make it important for others? What kinds of information and problems have I encountered in my college study? Have I learned things of importance in this study? If I can discover its importance, can I not also bring knowledge to my classmates, and have them understand its interest and importance?

There are many ways in which the speaker can stimulate either his recollection of reflective experience, or his entry into the task of reflection. The contemplation of one's own life may be an excellent starting point. A trip to the library to read articles in journals of opinion and information such as *Harper's, The Atlantic Monthly, The National Review,* or the *Saturday Review* may set off reflection or stimulate the recall and development of half-formed experiences. Conversation with interesting people may uncover the subject the speaker wishes. The search proceeds with the certain awareness that every person, to the extent that he has attitudes and positions toward his world, is capable of finding the subjects for public speeches. Every person is in some sense an "expert"—possessed of corners of knowledge and ways of seeing the world which belong more to him than to anyone else. The student who says, "I haven't anything to talk about," has made a more dismal statement about himself than he perhaps intends. If his statement were true he would be saying: "I have learned nothing in my years of schooling; I understand nothing of importance about my world; I find neither truth nor falsehood in the world of opinion, nor wisdom, nor foolishness; I live not as a man but as a conditioned organism which functions without thought or understanding; I am the original model and the ultimate form of The Hollow Man."

The knowledge that all speeches worth giving start as reflective experience calls attention to a certain paradoxical quality in the subject matter of public speeches. On the one hand the good speech must be in some sense original—the reflection of the mind of the speaker and of the form that mind has placed upon age-old questions of human conduct, personal values, and public policy. But the originality necessary to effective speech should not be confused with the originality achieved by the speaker who deals only with exotic or little-known subjects. One can achieve a reputation for originality by talking only of such subjects as "the arts of necromancy in the middle ages," or "the art of parboiling the Mediterranean squid." And if this form of exotica is not often chosen by student speakers, another form frequently appears. The speaker may announce his originality by choosing positions notable for their capacity to "shock" certain listeners. The speaker who on one occasion calls for the legalization of the sale of alcoholic beverages to twelve-year-olds, on another for the legalization of obscenity, and on a third for the legalization of narcotic drugs is less likely to be revealing the originality of his own reflective experience than his desire to be thought unusual.

The paradoxical nature of genuine originality is that its subject matter may involve hundreds or thousands of speeches which have treated the same topics. The questions which are of genuine concern to people in any given era of history may be few in number. The fact that they are much discussed in books, magazines, and newspapers is a sign, not of their inherent triteness, but of the fact that they involve the experience of many people. The more that is being said and being said in public about a subject, the more likely it is that any person may find himself able to take genuine possession of some part of this subject and make an original contribution to public thought.

Exploratory research thus becomes a stage in the possession of appropriate subject matter. This kind of study, supplementing the recollection of past events and of past reading and conversation, serves both to locate more precisely the exact subject and to uncover the various kinds of information and arguments useful in developing this subject. A speaker may begin with an inclination to talk on censorship in the motion-picture industry. He may be certain that the subject interests him, and that he has an inclination either to possess the available information on censorship, or to take a public position toward censorship. But he may also be aware of the poverty of his present knowledge and of the relative triviality of his thinking on the subject. A trip to the library, exploratory reading, conversation with friends, and further reflection are all indicated as he seeks the exact subject matter for his speech.

In brief, there are three primary questions a speaker should ask himself in choosing subject matter:

(1) _Have I chosen a subject which in some sense belongs to me?_ Unless the subject is the product of reflective experience, the speech will lack genuineness. Its action will not be that of a person talking to people, but of a person posturing or parroting the materials produced by another.

(2) _Is my subject under discussion in current public literature, and if so have I explored reflectively this literature?_ The best test of the genuine worth of subject matter is this: Has the subject been widely discussed? One often finds his own truth as he explores the positions and information of many people who have been concerned with the same subject matter.

(3) _Is my subject appropriate to the occasion?_ In Chapter 3 we consider the contingencies of the classroom-speaking situation: the expectations created by the assignment, the audience's receptivity to experimentation, and its expectation that subject matter would avoid triviality. Avoiding triviality may well be the speaker's most difficult task.

If the speaker has lived without much reflection, he will find it difficult to generate reflective thought on short notice. Yet he would do well to remember that his audience welcomes experimentation, and will be receptive to any genuine effort to grapple publicly with important matters. The speaker should also be aware of probable audience reaction to subject matter chosen merely because it promised an easy solution to the problem of filling five minutes with talk. Suppose, for example, the speaker announces that he will urge his listeners to take their next vacation in Glacier National Park. What can he expect from his listeners? Some will doubtless react with the amiable and vague attention they reserve for dull lectures. Others may concentrate on the color clash in the speaker's necktie and shirt. Some may hope that the speaker's announced intention is only a mask for his real purpose; that the speaker has done some thinking and proposes to philosophize on the union of man and nature. After all _Walden Pond_ seems an unlikely topic for important thought, but Thoreau had some success with the subject. But —unhappy prospect—the speaker may mean only to tell his listeners that he had a wonderful time in Glacier National Park last summer, and therefore recommends the trip to everyone. Now the discomfort of his audience is assured. "I would be glad to go to Glacier Park next summer," thinks one listener, "but I've promised to visit my rich uncle in upper New York." "Is he a paid agent for the state of Washington?" asks a local patriot. "I don't have enough money to visit the suburbs let alone a national park; I'd rather hear a talk on the poverty bill," thinks a third dispirited listener. Others wonder if the next speech will be a "how to do it" demonstration on canoe paddling or on the art of putting, and the instructor is likely to review somberly the events that led him into teaching. The speaker may fill time with animated sound and gesture. But he has chosen to ignore the meaning of the setting for his utterance, and he should not need spoken criticism to announce the magnitude of his failure.

PLANNING THE SPEECH

The actual planning of the classroom speech begins as the speaker formulates the purpose he hopes to achieve. It culminates when the speaker has prepared an outline or text representing the position, movement and structure he chooses for his speech, and the major forms of enforcement he intends to use.

The Purpose

A carefully formulated purpose represents the speaker's end or goal with his audience. Since the action of a speech is completed in its audience, a statement of purpose helps the speaker define the substance of the speaker, subject, and audience relationship he hopes to achieve.

The speaker's purpose is most usefully formulated as an "I want my listeners to . . ." statement. A purpose statement can be both illuminating and concise. For example:

"I want my listeners to know about the kinds of evidence supporting the idea of extrasensory perception."

or

"I want my listeners to support the policy of federal aid to parochial-school education."

or

"I want my audience to understand the philosophic objections conservative thinkers raise to the constant expansion of the role of the national government in American life."

or

"I want my listeners to view favorably the thesis that the United States is investing insufficient money in public facilities: schools, roads, parks, waterways, and welfare services."

A cursory examination of these four purpose statements would permit their grouping into two broad categories of purpose. The two statements proposing that the audience come to "know about" and to "understand" seem to indicate that the two speakers intend *to inform* the audience. We might anticipate that if the speakers use a method suitable to their stated purpose, their speeches will be *expository* in nature: they will provide clear and possibly interesting exposition of information. The two statements proposing that the audience come "to support" or to "view favorably" seem to indicate that the speakers hope to persuade their listeners. The method of the speech will result in persuasive utterance, seeking a change in audience attitude or action. The persuasive speakers will provide statements, evidence, or lines of reasoning thought likely to influence the attitudes or actions of the present audience.

A specific purpose statement provides the ground for looking realistically at audience predispositions, time limitations, and other factors of the occasion. For example, a speaker who intended to support federal aid to parochial-school education might well ask about the practicality of his goal. He could guess that for an audience including persons of different political and religious backgrounds, his proposal is likely to arouse strong opposition from some listeners. His reading should have revealed the strong emotions aroused by any discussion of public aid for religious schools. Does he really believe that he can change anyone's mind about federal aid to parochial-school education in five minutes? Is not so large and optimistic a purpose likely to lead our speaker into emotive blasts at those who oppose him? Will such an action really achieve the purpose stated? Such considerations might cause the speaker to formulate a more modest aim, such as: "I want my audience to view more favorably the position of those who support federal aid to parochial-school education." Or perhaps if the speaker really purposes a five-minute harangue, stating his own fervent support of aid to parochial education in the strongest possible language, then he might want to ask objectively about his real purpose. Could it be that his real purpose is to cheer those who support him, and to confront others with the strength of his feeling, and his low esteem for their views?

Carefully formulated purpose statements often forecast one of the most general sources of failure in public speaking—that of attempting too much in too short a period of time. The speaker who seeks to win the world to his way of thinking in five minutes or five hours is either seeking the martyrdom of certain failure, or nursing the illusion that his powers of persuasion exceed those of all speakers in history. A speaker who states, "I want my audience to believe that God exists because of the irrefutable nature of the rational proofs of his existence," might be asked: "Do you propose to secure belief in five minutes? The controversy into which you enter is an old one, and religious or nonreligious beliefs are notably durable in the presence of conflicting arguments." Perhaps this speaker would do better by limiting his purpose to: "I want my audience to understand one of the major rational proofs for the existence of God, and to appreciate the force of this proof."

The purpose statement just quoted seems to be a double statement. It seems to propose both an expository purpose ("to understand") and a faintly persuasive purpose ("to appreciate"). The idea that a speech can well contain more than one purpose needs some explanation. Speech theory traditionally holds that a good speech can seek only one central purpose. The wisdom of this advice rests in the often observed fact that nothing vitiates the force of a speech as much as diffuseness of purpose. The speaker who runs after multiple goals may achieve no goal, and the notion that a strong sense of purpose is a prerequisite to efficient conduct seems synonymous with the notion that a strong purpose is a unified or single purpose. However, the transparent virtues of unity are too easily translated into an assumption that the explicit purpose of a well-designed speech can always be most accurately perceived as a single point—a one-dimensional and uncomplicated line of development. Many speeches reveal multiple purposes, and as long as those purposes are mutually supportive they need not detract from the unity of the speech. Thus a speaker may propose to make the major portion of his speech informational in nature but to conclude the speech with a movement shaped by a persuasive purpose. Perhaps, if required to do so, he would identify one or the other purpose as "central," or dominant, and its companion purpose as preliminary or supplementary. But such a choice could be an artificial one in some cases. In the summer of 1961, President John Kennedy went on television to address the American people concerning the gathering crisis between Russia and the United States over the future of West Berlin. The speech had unity, but it had multiple purposes. These were generally stated by commentators as: "to arouse the American people to a sense of the seriousness of the crisis; to assure Russia that we would meet our commitments in Berlin with force if necessary; to reassure our Allies in Europe that we intended no hasty action, and would seek all possible avenues of negotiation." The President had multiple audiences and multiple purposes which somehow had to be bound together.

The Speaker's Position and Statement

The speaker may or may not state his purpose as part of his utterance. He needs to formulate his purpose carefully, however, as a step necessary to developing the position that he hopes to assume, and the planned set of movements through which he will carry his discourse. In building a plan or outline, the speaker will find it useful to formulate a statement which provides the most central declaration of his position, and which will be enforced or developed by the materials of his discourse. We use the term *statement* as a general name for the assertion (or declaration, thesis sentence, central idea, proposition) which is most central to the speaker's entire utterance. In this sense, the speaker's statement becomes the controlling concept of his discourse. It is central to the position he is assuming and serves to control the selection of the materials to be included in the utterance.

In persuasive speeches, and in some expository speeches, the statement may be an assertion—a simple declarative sentence which the speech is designed to enforce, support, prove, or make plausible. Typical persuasive statements would take such form as: "The American home is excessively dominated by women," or "Status symbols play too big a part in our lives," or "The United States should expand the operations of its information and propaganda agencies," or "Excessive violence in television programming threatens basic American values."

Many speeches use an assertion as the organizing concept of the speech, but others are built around a statement which simply forecasts the general type of informational materials to be presented, and the number of divisions within which these materials will be ordered. For example: "The United States now has three major delivery systems for nuclear warheads" is a statement which announces the speaker's topic and anticipates three divisions for the body of the speech.

Finding the Organizational Pattern

With his statement firmly in hand, the speaker next seeks a pattern of movement for his utterance which will provide a form or structure for the entire speech. This form can be viewed in retrospect as encompassing some principle of organization.

The discovery of a speech pattern involves the speaker in a kind of internal conversation involving the relationship of his position and statement, the available subject matter, and his knowledge of various possible patterns of organization. In some cases the speaker's statement will suggest the major structural components of his speech. Suppose the speaker states: "I am going to explain the three types of hypodermic injections now used by doctors." He has already forecast that the body of his speech will be divided into three parts, to explain the subcutaneous injection, the intravenous injection, and the intramuscular injection. He will need to consider an introductory movement for his speech, a transition into his statement, and a concluding movement. He will also need to organize a pattern of development for each of the three major divisions. But the overall pattern of his speech seems almost inevitably to emerge from his statement.

Not all statements forecast explicitly the structure of a speech. Suppose a speaker wishes to support the statement that "Degrees from Ivy University should be granted on the basis of comprehensive examinations rather than credit hours and course grades." The speaker's statement forecasts and limits the subject matter appropriate to his discourse, but the speech could be developed in a number of different patterns. For example, the speaker could treat the course-credit and grading system of Ivy University as an educational problem calling for an imaginative solution. Alternatively he could provide an exposition comparing the typical systems for granting degrees used by British and American universities, and proceed to weigh the merits of these contrasting systems. In such cases, the speaker's selection of pattern might be influenced by the position he wishes to assume. If he wants to act as a persuader who is strongly critical of Ivy University's practices, calling for vigorous reform, he may wish to use a problem-solution pattern for his discourse. If he wishes to assume a more contemplative position, and engage primarily in an exposition on comparative educational practices, leading to an evaluation, he may choose a pattern of comparison. The speaker's consideration of his audience and of his own level of information may also affect his choice. Thus, if his familiarity with the faults of Ivy University outruns his knowledge about the practices of English universities, he may prefer a problem-solution pattern, using his reference to English practices only as an illustration of a solution he proposes. Familiarity with various organizational patterns will also help the speaker in choosing a pattern. The speaker who uses only one general pattern is handicapped in generating a pattern appropriate to his position, audience, and subject matter.

In Chapter 4 we gave extensive consideration to some of the fundamental patterns found in public speeches, and to the variety of adaptations possible in the use of these patterns. It will be useful here to confirm part of the discussion in Chapter 4; to point to some of the relatively simple patterns of organization commonly used by public speakers; and thus to observe once more that the speaker who is familiar with a variety of speech patterns is aided in choosing the pattern most appropriate for a particular discourse.

The "Good Reasons" Pattern

A very simple plan for a persuasive speech is one in which the statement (an assertion in this case) is supported by a series of reasons for accepting or believing the assertion. With an introduction and conclusion attached, the pattern of the speech can be represented by the following schema:

   I. Introduction
  II. Statement
     A. First reason for accepting this statement
     B. Second reason for accepting this statement
     C. Third reason for accepting this statement
 III. Conclusion

This plan can be readily adapted to an expository speech in which the statement is presented as an assertion accepted by the speaker, or by some other source, and the "good reasons" are treated as an exposition of the reasons which seem compelling to the speaker or the source of the assertion.

The Problem-Solution Pattern

This is a popular form for the discussion of social issues. The speaker whose subject concerns some aspect of juvenile delinquency may wish to devote the first part of his speech to the nature of the problem faced by our society, and the second part to one line of action designed to help alleviate this problem. Thus:

   I. Introduction
  II. An important problem we all confront
 III. A way of alleviating this problem
 IV. Conclusion

The Pro-Con Analysis

This is a simple form for presenting an exposition of the conflicting evidence and lines of reasoning brought to bear in the public discussion of some controversial issue. For example, the speaker who wishes to discuss the concept of the "negative income tax," which provides direct federal aid to low-income families, may wish to summarize the major arguments developed by both the proponents and opponents of such a tax. If the speaker's purpose is purely expository, he may wish to conclude either with a summary, or with a forecast of the policy he thinks most likely to emerge from the public debate. If his purpose is also persuasive, he may wish to evaluate the arguments he has compared, and indicate his own position. Thus:

I. Introduction
II. Statement of the public issue
III. The most important arguments and evidence favoring an affirmative answer to the issue
IV. The most important arguments and evidence opposing an affirmative answer
V. Conclusion

System or Process Analysis

This pattern can be used for exposition of the functioning of some physical or social process. For example, the speaker wishing to talk on "Interpersonal Communication" may ask his audience to understand an act of communication as a structure of several interacting events, each influencing the occurrence, form, and consequences of the total act. The pattern of his speech could be described as follows:

I. Introduction
II. A gross description of an act of communication, naming the parts of the whole
III. Analysis of the process or system in being, showing the interaction of the several parts
IV. Conclusion

Since process or system analysis is likely to involve a relatively complicated discourse, the pattern is often aided if the speaker grounds his descriptions in one or more concrete examples, or if he provides a chart showing the set of terms he will use in his description and the lines of interaction he will describe.

These four illustrations of simple speech patterns will serve to recall the sense in which speakers may visualize alternative plans as possibilities for arranging the materials of a particular speech. As their sense of speech patterns develop, experienced public speakers find it possible to give simple schematic descriptions and titles to a great variety of such patterns.

A Technical Plan for Classroom Speeches

In developing a sense of structure or pattern, the speaker may find it useful to develop a number of speaking exercises through application of a specific technical plan which will require him to carry out certain steps in the development of his speech. The technical plan which follows is adaptable to either persuasive or expository speeches; it permits the use of various organizational patterns in the body of the speech; and if intelligently applied, it will result in a speech with clear and obvious organization. Speeches developed with such a plan usually reflect good workmanship. If they sometimes seem lacking in artistry or inspiration, this is surely a lesser fault than the chaos achieved by the speaker who talks without any sense of progression or design.

TITLE OR SUBJECT:

PURPOSE STATEMENT:

SPEECH MATERIALS:

I. INTRODUCTION (Here the speaker seeks to interest the audience; to direct attention to his subject; and to provide a transition to . . .)

II. STATEMENT (Here the speaker asserts the idea his speech will develop or support.)

III. OVERVIEW (Here the speaker makes known the plan he will follow in developing his statement. An explicit overview should enable the audience to follow the main divisions of the speech easily. The fact that the speaker can present such an overview is assurance that he has a clear organizing pattern for his presentation.)

IV. BODY (Here the speaker follows through on the major divisions of his speech as indicated in his overview. This may mean the presentation of a series of reasons for believing his assertion, or a description of a problem, followed by a proposed solution; or a series of divisions within which a unified body of information may be presented.)

V. CONCLUSION (Here the speaker may summarize the most important points of his speech; or restate his assertion, asking for agreement or support of action; or provide some other statement which will provide a sense of finish or completion to his speech.)

A Sample Outline Using the Technical Plan

Classroom speeches which are carefully constructed according to some technical plan help the student acquire a sense of structure. The student can achieve a close relationship between the categories of a technical plan and the actual movements in his speech by using a split-page technique in outlining the speech. In this technique, the technical plan is arranged along the left one-third of the page, and the speech outline appears on the right two-thirds of the page. The following sample outline will illustrate the form for such preparation.

SAMPLE TECHNICAL PLAN AND OUTLINE

TITLE OR SUBJECT: Academic Freedom

PURPOSE STATEMENT: I want the audience to accept the tradition of academic freedom as an important guarantee both of their own "liberty to know" and of intellectual progress.

SPEECH MATERIALS: The Greek philosopher Socrates was
  I. INTRODUCTION   sentenced to death by the freest society of the ancient world because, among other things, it was charged that he corrupted youth by his teaching.

Familiar historical   A. Plato's account of the trial and
example: death of Socrates reveals that Socrates asked his students to raise questions, to doubt ideas that were not constantly examined, and to seek virtue; and that Socrates preferred death to a life in which he could not speak the truth as he saw it.

Summary of example: B. The death of Socrates remains one of the most profound experiences of western civilization with the brutality and futility of suppression of free inquiry.

Transition: C. Yet the lesson this experience should teach has not been fully learned; our American colleges and universities still face repeated pressure for the suppression of "dangerous" thoughts. Against this pressure college and university teachers offer the concept of academic freedom.

II. STATEMENT

The concept of academic freedom is an essential guarantee of a teacher's right to do his proper work, of a student's right to learn, and of society's need for knowledge.

III. OVERVIEW
Partition of the
two major movements:

To further our understanding of the importance of this guarantee, let me first define the rights and responsibilities implied by the concept of academic freedom, and second show why the concept merits our support.

IV. BODY

The concept of academic freedom defines both rights and responsibilities of teachers.

Authority for definition:

A. This is clear from the definition offered by the American Association of University Professors, which makes six essential points:

1. The teacher should be free to discuss his subject matter without limitation from other persons.

Comparison:

   a. This is a right supported by his professional competence, analogous to the doctor's right to treat illness without outside direction.

2. The teacher should avoid classroom discussion of controversial materials not related to his subject matter.

Hypothetical example:

   a. Avoid politics in a physics class and vice versa.

3. The teacher should be free to carry out and publish the product of his research.

Historical example:

   a. Example of restriction on publication of research comparing margarine and butter.

4. The teacher should observe at all times the respect for reason, for care in making judgments,

and for other persons appropriate to his profession.

   a. Intellectual standards define responsible scholarship.

5. The teacher should enjoy the freedom of speech and association in his life outside the classroom guaranteed to all citizens.

Hypothetical example:

   a. There should be no restriction on physicists discussing politics outside the classroom.

6. The teacher should make clear that when he speaks as a citizen he does not speak as a teacher or officer of his college.

Supporting authority:

B. These same concepts appear in the statement on academic freedom and responsibility issued in 1961 by the American Association of Universities.

C. The definition, like most definitions of freedom and responsibility, has some ambiguity.

1. How do we judge when research impinges on the rights of other persons?

Historical example:

   a. Example of research into the effects of drugs at Harvard University.

2. How do we judge when the teacher outside the classroom fails to observe the respect for reason appropriate to his profession?

   a. Example of professor questioning loyalty of American President.

3. Because application of the definition will always involve controversy, teachers, like members of other professions, ask that judgments on the teacher's pro-

fessional conduct be made by
other members of the profession.

Comparison:
         a. Comparison to law and med-
icine.

Transition:
D. If we now have general understanding of the concept of academic freedom, we should continue by examining the merit or importance of the
concept.

    1. The teacher's right to teach is
linked to the student's right to
know.

Historical example:
         a. Cite harm to students of ge-
netics in the Soviet Union
from suppression, by the Soviet government, of theories
other than those of Lysenko.

Historical example:
         b. Cite harm to students of sup-
pression of such books as
Orwell's *1984* and Hersey's
A Bell for Adano after public
attack on their use in instruction in literature.

    2. The teacher's right of inquiry is
linked to the process by which a
democratic society seeks truth.

Authority, plus deductive
argument on the danger of
suppressing alleged error:
         a. John Stuart Mill's statement
on the need for free inquiry
from his essay *On Liberty*.

Analogy:
         b. The free marketplace of ideas
promotes intellectual growth
like the free market of goods
promotes economic growth.

Historical examples:
         c. Examples of yesterday's here-
sies that have become today's
orthodoxies: Galileo, Pas-
teur, Darwin.

Authority as summary
and transition:
    3. The point that J. Frank Dobie,
the well-known American historian, has made about censorship
applies with equal force to all
efforts to restrict freedom of in-

quiry: "Censorship is never to let people know but always to keep them in ignorance; never to bring light but always to darken. It is, and for thousands of years has been, a main force used by dictators and all manner of tyrannical governments from Nero to Khrushchev."

V. CONCLUSION

The power to learn is man's most important capability, and the right to learn his most precious freedom.

Historic example linked to introduction:

A. Socrates preferred to drink hemlock rather than flee from Athens because he believed his life less important than his right to seek after truth through free inquiry.

B. The concept of academic freedom is addressed to the same right Socrates so valued. We are unlikely to be asked to suffer loss of life in defense of this concept, but we should not value it less than did this wisest of teachers.

The Speaker's Outline

The sample technical plan here presented includes the major statements which will give order and movement to the intended speech, but it does not include all the language the speaker will use. For example, the plan offers opportunity for the speaker to contrast the formidable punishment exacted of Socrates with the somewhat more mild punishment that might accompany suppression of a teacher in our own age; it also offers opportunity for supplanting or supplementing some of the historical or hypothetical examples with examples drawn from a campus familiar to the speaker and audience. Thus the plan is neither a manuscript nor a rigorous outline of all the possible materials that might be woven into the speech as delivered. However, the plan does give evidence that the hypothetical speaker preparing it has prethought his purpose, his statement, his method of beginning and ending his discourse, the order and materials of the movements central to the speech, and his method of getting from one part of the speech to the next. With sufficient rehearsal based on the plan, the speaker should be able to convince most listeners that his utterance is thoughtful, orderly, and nontrivial.

As brief as the plan is, it is yet more extensive than the well-prepared speaker will need at the time of his speech. After several rehearsals with the speech, the speaker should have little need to take more to the plat-from than a few 3″ x 5″ cards or a single sheet of paper with the main divisions of his speech indicated. Thus, the speaker's outline might consist of the following:

I. Introduction.
   A. Socrates' trial.
II. Statement: The concept of academic freedom is an essential guar-antee of a teacher's right to do his proper work, of a student's right to learn, and of society's need for knowledge.
III. Overview: Definition of rights and responsibilities of academic freedom; why this concept merits support.
IV. Body
   A. Six point definition, A.A.U.P.
     1. Teacher's freedom to teach his subject.
     2. Responsibility to stay within his subject in class.
     3. Freedom to do and publish research.
     4. Responsibility to speak, write, and act in accordance with standards of profession.
     5. Right to ordinary freedom outside class.
     6. Responsibility to keep clear role as teacher and role as citizen.
   B. Support from A.A.U.
   C. Ambiguity in definition; procedure for interpretation.
   D. Why important?
     1. Linked to student's right to know.
       —Lysenko; Orwell; Hersey.
     2. Linked to democratic process for seeking truth.
       —Mill argument; Galileo; Pasteur; Darwin.
     3. Quote J. Frank Dobie.
V. Conclusion
   A. Return to Socrates.
   B. Ask audience support.

To this basic speaker's outline, the speaker may wish to add certain note cards for special uses. For the speech on academic freedom, a card with an exact quotation from John Stuart Mill, and a second with the quotation from historian J. Frank Dobie would be obvious choices.

There is little reason for a speaker to strain his memory recalling word-for-word quotations, or, if the speech requires, detailed statistical information. But in general the well-prepared speaker will need few if any notes at the time of presentation. If his speech has been put into a simple and coherent structure, if it includes only a few major movements, and if it has been rehearsed until the structure seems natural and inevitable to the speaker, then extensive notes will simply stand between the speaker and his audience.

PROBLEMS OF ENFORCEMENT

The speaker who is able to tell all he knows about his subject in the course of a five-, or even a thirty-minute speech, is likely to have acted in a way that will be little noted and unremembered. Many speeches seem to reflect more than anything else the limited resources of information and imagination which the speaker brought to the occasion. They seem thin—the ideas are few and commonplace. The information included seems borrowed from the most available pool of common information—
—from newspaper headlines, the lead story in last night's newspaper, or a single article from some popular journal. Both content and treatment seem unimaginative. One senses not an active mind at work in the clarification and amplification of thought, but a passive mind parroting the ill-formed banalities of impromptu conversation.

Clearly the speaker who has formulated his purpose has gained control of his statement, and has found the structure within which he wishes to conduct his utterance faces yet another problem. How can he make his listeners feel that he has selected the best available methods of enforcing his ideas? How can he assure the audience that his information is the most relevant and significant for the enforcement of his statement? How can he indicate that his regard for the audience and occasion caused him to seek the most vivid and memorable manner of utterance rather than the easiest and most commonplace?

Both research and reflection can assist the speaker to escape thin and unimaginative utterance. We have already considered the need for *exploratory* research as a part of the process by which the speaker seeks his statement and position. A second type of research, which we shall call *intentional research* may be needed before the speech is ready for rehearsal. From his plan the speaker can usually visualize types of supporting materials which would be useful in fulfilling the intent of the plan. "I would like an apt quotation about the blessings of solitude as a fitting close for my talk," he may say. Or, "I need the latest statistics on the extent of alcoholism in America to buttress my discussion of this social problem. I have some statistics, but they are five years old, and better and more recent statistics must exist." Or, "I need a specific and vivid illustration of the extent to which automated factories can operate without a working force."

Intentional research can be used to find the exact type of supporting material the speaker visualizes as most useful to his effort. *Bartlett's Familiar Quotations* may contain the apt quotation on solitude. A search of *The Reader's Guide to Periodical Literature* should uncover recent magazine articles on alcoholism, and thus provide access to an article by a reputable authority summarizing the latest statistics. The example of automation may also be found in a recent article concerning this subject. We do not seek to review here the range of research possibilities for uncovering specific kinds of supporting materials for the speech. Students have had some experience in using libraries, and they can ask librarians to assist them. Rather, we emphasize the importance of intentional research in final preparation. Doubtless there are speakers who begin preparation with such a surplus of resources that no further study will be needed for final preparation. But most speakers realize that their speeches would be strengthened by specific additions of data, examples, or supporting authority. They must then choose between presenting a speech that is thin and unimaginative, or engaging in the research and reflection needed to uncover the additional materials.

Just as a speaker's knowledge of various speech patterns will assist him in developing the pattern appropriate for a particular speech, so will his familiarity with a variety of forms of enforcement direct him toward the intentional research needed to extend the clarity, plausibility, and imaginativeness of his discourse. We have already considered in Chapter 5 the major "lines of argument" which serve as primary forms of enforcement in public discourse. At this point we can recall this earlier discussion, and extend it somewhat by a brief discussion of some of the specific forms of enforcement commonly used by public speakers and the problems of managing these forms.

1. The Extended Example

The example may be the most used and most useful form of enforcement available to the speaker. Personal experiences, the experiences of others, experiences taken from literature, or created experiences (hypothetical examples) all serve to make ideas clearer and more interesting by rooting the ideas in some concrete situation. But the well-told experience may do more than make an idea clear and interesting; it may also add to the plausibility or seeming truth of the idea thus amplified. If the speaker's example is one with which listeners can identify—an experience which they feel to be genuine—then the example suggests strongly the truth of whatever generalization it serves to illustrate.

The potential of the extended example to interest, to enforce a generalization, and to evoke agreement is well illustrated in the opening passage of J. S. Bronowski's essays on *Science and Human Values,* first presented as public lectures:

On a fine November day in 1945, late in the afternoon, I was landed on an airstrip in southern Japan. From there a jeep was to take me over the mountains to join a ship which lay in Nagasaki Harbor. I knew nothing of the country or the distance before us. We drove off; dusk fell; the road rose and fell away, the pine woods came down to the road, straggled on, and opened again. I did not know that we had left the open country until unexpectedly I heard the ship's loud speakers broadcasting dance music. Then suddenly I was aware that we were already at the center of damage in Nagasaki. The shadows behind me were the skeletons of the Mitsubishi factory buildings, pushed backwards and sideways as if by a giant hand. What I had thought to be broken rocks was a concrete power house with its roof punched in. I could now make out the outline of two crumpled gasometers; there was a cold furnace festooned with service pipes; otherwise nothing but cockeyed telephone poles and loops of wire in a bare waste of ashes. I had blundered into this desolate landscape as instantly as one might wake among the craters of the moon. The moment of recognition when I realized that I was already in Nagasaki is present to me as I write, as vividly as when I lived it. I see the warm night and the meaningless shapes; I can even remember the tune that was coming from the ship. It was a dance tune which had been popular in 1945, and it was called "Is You Is Or Is You Ain't Ma Baby?"

These essays, which I have called *Science and Human Values,* were born in that moment. For the moment I have recalled was a universal moment; what I met was, almost as abruptly, the experience of mankind. On an evening like that evening, some time in 1945, each of us in his own way learned that his imagination had been dwarfed. We looked up and saw the power of which we had been proud loom over us like the ruins of Nagasaki.[1]

Examples are not limited to narrative experiences. Descriptive examples may be used to exemplify the nature and worth of a speaker's proposal. In discussing government health insurance the speaker may say, "Let me describe the workings of the British national health plan. This will illustrate my meaning." His example could be developed in such a way as simply to clarify the way in which government health insurance operates, or in a way designed to emphasize the merits, demerits, or

[1] J. Bronowski, *Science and Human Values* (New York: Harper and Row Publisher, Harper Torchbook, 1965), pp. 3–4.

both of the British system. If descriptive examples are used to support or attack some idea, the speaker is presumably contending that his example typifies the way this idea works out in practice.

We refer to this form of enforcement as an "extended example" to emphasize the fact that speakers using such examples usually seek enough colorful detail in their examples to give the listener the sense of participating in a full experience, or of visualizing the whole of some situation or operation. In this sense the example differs from the allusion or "specific instance," which may be given only brief reference.

The speaker who relates an extended example clearly and colorfully is likely to be successful in gaining the attention and interest of his listeners. This kind of success with an audience is so rewarding that it may serve to obscure some of the problems implicit in the use of long narrative passages, personal experiences, and the like. For example, the speaker who bases the problem he wishes to discuss with an audience solely on his own experience runs the risk of seeming to ask a public audience to take action in order to relieve the personal worries of the speaker. Thus, the speaker who wants to reform the grading system of his college because, as he tells the story, he has been the victim of countless unjust grades, may entertain his audience. But unless his experiences confirm those of his listeners, this speaker may set off less speculation about grading reform than about his fitness as a student. Similarly, the speaker calling for reform of the police department because of his constant troubles with the law provides his audience with some interesting questions about whether it is the police department or the speaker who needs reformation. For such reasons the speaker who chooses to give over large segments of his speaking time to narrative materials should be certain that his narration will serve his purpose, and not merely serve to gain attention.

2. Statistics

An example enforces an idea if the listener accepts the example as embodying some truth, or as typical. But often an idea cannot be enforced simply by an example, or even a series of examples. The speaker who wishes to produce generalizations about the behavior of whole categories of events may wish to clarify the meaning of his generalization with an example, but he may also need to demonstrate the credibility of his generalization by producing the statistical information which justifies it. Thus, the speaker who says that "ten percent of all Americans live in a condition of abject poverty," may wish to impress upon his listeners the human meaning of "living in abject poverty" by a specific example. But he has made a generalization based presumably on some body of statistical information, and his listeners may well want to know the figures on which he bases his claim, the source of the figures, and the criterion used for classifying those said to be living in poverty. The astute listener may also want to know whether or not the specific example used by the speaker typified living conditions for all those whom he categorizes as living in abject poverty, or was rather an extreme and an atypical member of the class.

Since data gathering is both omnipresent and necessary in our complex society, contemporary public speeches abound in statistical information: trends in family income, in the gross national product, in the national debt; in marriage rates, divorce rates, birthrates, and death rates; in voting tendencies; in public opinion; in construction costs; in tax rates; in college attendance, church attendance, motion picture attendance; in television viewing habits; and in the incidence of various diseases, crimes, and other pathologies affecting both man and animals. The speaker who says, "60 percent of Americans don't know the meaning of the first amendment to the federal Constitution," may have some evidence to back his claim, possibly provided by some test items administered to a certain sample of the American population. If the claim was important or disturbing to an audience, the speaker would strengthen its credibility by explaining how the statistic was derived.

Speakers and listeners who give most thought to statistical information are likely to become highly sensitive to the difficulty of moving from a set of numbers to a proper interpretation of those numbers. The speaker who says, "the average farmer in Greenvalley County earns only $4,000 per year," has done little to clarify the economic position of Greenvalley County farmers. His statement contains a statistic which seems clear enough but is nevertheless wholly ambiguous. Is the speaker talking about net income or gross income? Is he talking about cash income or cash income plus product consumption? And what is an "average" farmer? Does the speaker intend to say that the arithmetic mean of the income of all farmers in Greenvalley County was $4,000? Or is he saying that $4,000 is the median income, with as many farmers earning more than that amount as the number earning less? Or is $4,000 the approximate modal income of Greenvalley farmers—that is, the figure closest to the income of the greatest number of farmers in the sample? How many farmers were in the sample, and what is the range of their incomes? If there were only five farmers in Greenvalley County, one of whom earned $20,000, and four of whom earned nothing, the comment on the "average farmer" becomes a foolish statistical illusion. One is reminded of possible illusion in talk about "averages" by such statements as "the average American family includes 3.19 children."

The problems of interpreting a statistic are increased when the speaker generalizes from the behavior of a certain sample of a population to the probable behavior of an entire population. Thus, when a newspaper story says that "fifty million Americans heard the President of the United States speak on Thursday evening," the number is likely to be an extrapolation from data collected from a small sample of American television viewers—perhaps as few as 1,000—extended to the total population of potential viewers. Polls of public opinion similarly extend the responses of a selected sample of citizens to the probable distribution of response for all citizens. The reliability of such data rests very heavily on the competence and impartiality of the persons providing the data. Thus the Abner Zilch Poll may assert that "four out of five voters prefer candidate O'Henry as the next Governor of Minnesota," but if one learns that the Zilch poll was taken from a sample of citizens attending a rally for candidate O'Henry, the interpretation of the data becomes somewhat questionable. Once more we should observe that if the speaker uses figures which will be important or disturbing to his listeners, he should give close attention to the reputation of the source of his data, and to the care with which he interprets that data. He should also share with his audience the grounds which cause him to believe his data and interpretations to be reliable.

The management of statistics. The credibility of a statistic and its interpretation is the major problem facing the public speaker in his selection of data and his presentation to an audience. But the problems of clarity and impressiveness also loom large, and speakers who use statistics in their utterance should observe certain commonsense possibilities in such use. First, spoken discourse should not be crowded with numbers. An audience cannot be expected to contemplate a large array of numbers, and observe the interrelationships and interpretations of such numbers in the course of a spoken presentation. If the speaker's mission requires the use of elaborate data, he should provide such data through visual projections or charts, or in written materials handed to the audience. If such elaboration is unnecessary to the speaker's mission, he should reduce his use of numbers to the few figures necessary to support his generalizations.

Second, speakers should generally use easily remembered approximations of large or complex numbers, rather than using numbers accurate to the third figure after the decimal point. Thus, if the arithmetic mean of teachers' salaries in the United States is $6,971.43, the speaker planning to use such a figure can speak of this as "approximately $7,000," and increase the likelihood that his listeners will understand and recall the figure.

Finally, if the speaker wishes a particular number to be made impressive to his listeners, he may well use a variety of devices for increasing the memorability of the number. One such device is that of simple repetition of the statistic in a variety of relationships, as in such statements as: "More than 50,000 Americans died on the nation's highways last year. Our neighbors die at the rate of approximately 4,400 every month, or 140 every day, or 6 in every hour. The population of our city is about 100,000. If you visualize half of the men, women, and children of this city as dying in an automobile accident last year, you will get some idea of the slaughter we perpetrate." Another device, similar to the final sentence in the preceding illustration, is the application of a large number to some simple, visual consequence of that number. Thus, "If the present rate of population increase in the world is maintained, within six centuries there will be less than one square meter of land for each living person on this earth."

3. Testimony

In Chapter 5, "argument from authority" was discussed as one of the lines of argument common to public speeches. And in the foregoing treatment of statistics, we have emphasized the extent to which the credibility of data is involved in the credibility of its source. The public speaker's utterance as a whole provides his own testimony for an audience, but he is well advised to seek the enforcement of others to establish the reliability of his evidence, or the fact that his opinions or interpretations of evidence are shared by reputable persons. Some part of the speaker's intentional research may, therefore, be devoted to a search for useful witnesses.

In using testimony, the speaker should give attention to the extent to which the audience knows and respects the person or organization he cites. The speaker who quotes an opinion by Professor Snodgrass on the conflict in Vietnam has done little to enhance the stature of that opinion if his audience has never heard of Professor Snodgrass, or if it holds the professor in low esteem. If Snodgrass is unknown, the fact that he has authored three books on the social structure of Southeast Asia, or that he has recently returned from a year-long study of social and economic change in Vietnam, may help to make his opinion more significant. If Snodgrass is held in low esteem by the audience, then the speaker might better seek testimony from a different witness.

The speaker using testimony should also consider whether he cites a source primarily because the reputation of the source will enhance the speaker's utterance, or because of the unusual felicity of a statement attributed to the source. If there is special merit in the language used by a witness to develop an idea, the speaker may wish to quote this language directly. On the other hand he may find that the language of his witness is excessively complex or abstract, and prefer to paraphrase the testimony.

Speakers should be aware of the possible merit of both negative testimony, and testimony from witnesses who might seem unfriendly to the speaker's cause. Listeners who are asked to believe some data or adopt some opinion are properly concerned with the nature of the persons and groups who also believe the data or hold the opinion. Listeners may be equally concerned to know the names of the witnesses they are being asked to oppose if they agree with a speaker. Thus, the speaker who points out that his ideas are opposed by persons held in low regard by his listeners has enforced his ideas through negative testimony. Listeners may also find particular force in the testimony of a person who might be expected to testify differently. Thus, the words of a politician praising some member of the opposite political party are likely to be more frequently used as testimony than praise coming from an expected source. Similarly, if a football coach praises the educational value of football, his testimony is weakened by the fact that his opinions seem a matter of self-interest even though he is presumably expert in the area he discusses. By contrast, a professor of philosophy praising the educational value of football gives testimony which seems strengthened by the fact that his opinions would not seem automatically congruent with the witness's self-interest.

4. Figurative Language

Chapter 6, on style, illustrated a number of figures of language through which speakers seek greater clarity or memorability for their utterance. In preparing his discourse for rehearsal, or during rehearsal, the speaker should seek apt phraseology to convert mundane or pallid statements into more vivid or colorful forms. This is a part of the speaker's intentional research in which he draws on the resources of his own imagination to add force to his discourse.

A speaker may propose to say that a potent idea which he finds distasteful has "a kind of malignant energy." He can add metaphoric color to his description by saying "the same kind of energy as crabgrass or cancer." A speaker wishing to discuss the effect of the Beatles on American popular music could say, "the Beatles have had a profound effect on the tradition of American popular music. Peter Schrag chose to put the matter more vividly by writing in the *Saturday Review* that 'Ever since the Beatles first hit the United States three years ago, the Moon-June-Spoon tradition in pop music has sounded about as vital as Mary

Poppins next to Anna Karenina or Tom Swift alongside Humbert Humbert.' " [2]

The danger in intentional search for vivid or colorful language is that the speaker will be drawn to embellish his language by collecting worn-out figures of speech which have lost their impact. Too many speakers have referred to their nation as the "ship of state" to make the expression any more than a tired cliché. The speaker who hits upon this weary figure, and goes on to talk of the President as helmsman, and to invite the audience to join the crew, only extends the original tedium.

5. Visual Aids

The intentional search for apt methods of enforcement should often lead to the use of visual aids. Few experienced speakers wishing maximum clarity for complex statistical information, geographic relationships, complex systems of interaction, or interpretations of artistic artifacts would choose to talk without supporting visual materials. The speaker wishing to describe American military action in Vietnam without support from a map of the region, or a blackboard representation of a map, is obviously failing to use available resources for communication. The speaker wishing to show trend lines in college populations between 1946 and 1976 without use of a graph plotting numbers of students against a time line is similarly handicapped. Few teachers of chemistry would choose to talk about molecular structure without the resources of both charts and models; few astronomers would attempt description of a complex pattern of motion such as that represented in the solar system without charts, and preferably a model.

The occasions when a speaker could scarcely succeed at all without use of visual aids are obvious; the occasions when success would be greatly accentuated by appropriate aids may be less obvious. The sight and sound of a strange word reinforces its recall beyond sound alone; the visual representation of the key ideas in a speech similarly reinforces recall and the perception of relationships among ideas. Intentional exploration of the possibilities of enforcement in any speech should not stop short of the search for visual supporting materials. And in an age when most speakers have ready access to slide projectors; overhead projectors; flip charts permitting the quick creation of graphs or charts; and opaque projectors permitting the enlargement of maps, pictures, or pages from books, the failure to use visual aids often represents a failure in thorough planning.

[2] Peter Schrag, "Voices in the Classroom," *Saturday Review*, August 19, 1967, p. 61.

SUMMARY

Genuine subject matter for public speeches is the product of reflective experience. Through reflection the speaker can take possession both of his own experience, and also of public information and opinion. He is able to formulate purposes to be supported by his public utterance which are in some sense his own.

The preparation of a public speech starts with the recollection and discovery of subject matter, and proceeds through the process of planning the speech. Planning includes such steps as stating the purpose or purposes of the utterance, finding a statement which controls the selection of subject matter, finding an appropriate pattern of organization, and using both reflection and intentional research to discover the strongest possible forms of enforcement or amplification for the speaker's ideas. Knowledge of certain hypothetical patterns of speech organization may aid the speaker in discovering a pattern best suited to a particular body of subject matter, and knowledge of the common forms used for supporting or amplifying ideas may aid in the intentional search for effective subject matter. The initial steps of speech preparation may result in a speech plan which is subject to review and reconstruction during rehearsal of the speech for delivery. We therefore turn in the next chapter to the problem of rehearsal, and to certain additional considerations affecting the actual presentation of the classroom speech.

CHAPTER 11

Delivery and Criticism

The unrehearsed public speech may not be worth delivering. Rehearsal tests the adequacy of the entire process of preparation and uncovers changes needed in outline or language prior to actual presentation. In this sense rehearsal is integral to the process of speech preparation, and essential if the speaker is to fulfill his audience's expectancy that he will act with forethought.

THE PROCESS OF REHEARSAL

Ideally, the rehearsal is conducted with the speaker standing as he plans to appear before his audience, and talking aloud as he would wish to talk with his audience. Circumstances and well-established habits may cause speakers to use a different procedure. The speaker rehearsing at full voice might prove an annoyance or object of curiosity to family or friends, or even create a disturbance in his neighborhood. In such cases the speaker may wish to rehearse *sotto voce*—uttering all the language he intends, but using little or no voice. Some speakers prefer to walk during the first few rehearsals. The physical activity sometimes prompts a better flow of language. Other speakers prefer to sit and talk to themselves for the first few trials, seeking full control over the movement and structure of the speech before a final rehearsal in which they will stand and talk aloud. While no single pattern of rehearsal can be considered best, rehearsal itself is essential if a speech is to realize its full potential. Each speaker needs to discover the pattern of rehearsal which is effective for him.

THE EFFECTS OF REHEARSAL

Rehearsal tests the structure of the speech. The movement of ideas which seemed right as the speech was being outlined or written may prove awkward as the speech is rehearsed. The speaker may need to recast his organization during rehearsal to bring the plan into line with the progression of ideas and materials which seems to flow most readily.

Sufficient rehearsal will give the speaker the sense that the plan for his speech is the "only" way in which the materials of this speech should be ordered.

Rehearsal perfects the language of the speech. With sufficient rehearsal for extemporaneous speaking, the speaker may find the single phrase which clarifies a particular idea and which can replace the series of phrases first used. In the case of manuscript speaking he finds the passages which seem awkward when read aloud, or which seem to use language suitable to the printed page, but ill-suited to conversation. The speaker should rehearse not with the notion that he will not alter some words or phrases at the moment of actual presentation, but rather with the search for certainty that he has full possession of all the language he will need to carry through the action he has visualized, and that he is thus free to seek an immediate and direct relationship with his audience. In an extemporaneous speech, this means that the speaker will have achieved freedom from his notes, and indeed, that in a short speech he may dispense with notes altogether. In a manuscript speech, such freedom means that the manuscript is less an artifact to be read aloud than an evidence that the speaker has prepared himself carefully, while remaining ready to respond extemporaneously to signs of audience doubt, or pleasure, or incomprehension.

Rehearsal engages the speaker in the search for the public manner, or manner of delivery which he believes most suitable to his person, his utterance, and the occasion he anticipates. In seeking the development of delivery skills, the speaker who rehearses with the full manner he anticipates using with his audience enjoys obvious advantages in gaining control over the details of his delivery. But he makes use of these advantages only if his rehearsal is animated by a vision of himself as a man speaking, assuming a particular public role, and carrying out that role through appropriate physical and vocal behavior. Repetitious rehearsal of a speech does not guarantee improvement in the speaker's delivery if the rehearsal lacks clear purpose. The rehearsal may serve simply to confirm inadequate delivery habits. But repeated rehearsal guided by a speaker's desire to find the public form for the tone and attitude he wishes for his material and audience can lead to improvement.

DEVELOPING EFFECTIVE DELIVERY

In the discussion of style in Chapter 6, we observed that a speaker's manner is reflected both in his choice and ordering of words, and in his delivery. Delivery, or the speaker's use of voice and physical action, is only part of his total manner. Accordingly, it becomes difficult to talk in the abstract about the qualities of effective speech delivery, and the way in which these qualities may be developed. If we say that a speech was poorly delivered because the speaker seemed physically and vocally listless, we might discover on more thorough inspection that the speech was flawed from its very inception: that the speaker lacked a clear sense of purpose, that he had not developed a clear position, and that the language used for verbalizing vague thoughts was itself listless and feeble. Powerful delivery might make such a speech ludicrous rather than effective.

Nevertheless, it is possible to observe speeches in which the speaker's substance seems ill served by his physical and vocal manner. The potentially good speech can be destroyed in its delivery. And for this reason some isolated inquiry into the problem of delivery is warranted.

The Qualities of Effective Delivery

The general qualities of effective speech delivery combine behaviors required by a speaker's need to be heard, and behaviors expected by audiences in terms of the general role assumed by public speakers in American society. The qualities of *animation, directness, cordiality,* and *control* will serve to summarize these requirements.

The speaker seems *animated* when he uses a wider range of variation in pitch and force than usual to conversation, and when he makes full use of the language of gesture, reflecting variation in attitude in his facial expression, and gesturing both to emphasize and illustrate ideas. Effective public speakers will normally give an abundance of physical and emotional energy to the moments of delivery, thus achieving the force which may be necessary to reach all members of an audience. Thus the speaker who wishes to talk in a conversational way to an audience needs to remember that his physical separation from many members of that audience requires heightened energy. He needs also to remember that his audience has conferred on him a position of leadership and that he is expected to take charge of the situation, demonstrating through the force and variety of his delivery that he is prepared to act as a leader.

The speaker seems *direct* when he seeks eye contact with his listeners, and when he seems willing to reveal his attitudes and emotions to his listeners through appropriate variety of facial expression and gesture. Presumably the quality of directness symbolizes the speaker's desire to communicate with his listeners, and his concern for their response. Effective public speakers are ordinarily direct not only because directness fulfills an audience expectation, but because it fills a need of the speaker. The speaker must be alert to signs that his statements have puzzled or bewildered some of his listeners, or that he has provoked others, or induced sleep in still others. The speaker who notes response in his audience, and responds appropriately in turn, establishes the community of meaning which unifies speaker and audience.

Cordiality of manner is a common expectation audiences hold for public speakers. This quality of delivery is a concomitant of directness, with the added feature that the speaker reveals in his facial expression and vocal intonation that he likes and respects his listeners, and enjoys the rare opportunity of talking to them for some minutes without interruption. Few listeners have the capacity to like and respect a speaker who manifestly is either unconcerned with their welfare, or who is hostile. Faced with such a speaker, listeners generally will withhold effort to understand the speaker or give a fair hearing to his ideas.

Finally, the speaker needs to seek *control*—over vocal intonation, rate, quality, and force, and over gesture and facial expression. Vocal and physical energy and variety give the impression of animation in the speaker, but such animation must be controlled if it is to enforce the speaker's utterance rather than serve as a distraction.

When listeners are asked to name the qualities in speech delivery which they believe most important to the speaker's effectiveness, they are likely to give first position to the quality of *sincerity*. In many ways listeners seem to use the word "sincerity" to describe the effect achieved by the speaker. Animation, directness, cordiality and control all seem to rise from a genuine concern for both his subject matter and his listeners. Thus we are reminded that even the most technically proficient delivery achieves little if it seems superimposed upon the whole action of the speech. We are reminded also that audiences forgive many technical insufficiencies in the speaker who seems to believe deeply in his utterance, and in the welfare of those who listen.

Seeking Effective Delivery

The search for effective delivery starts from a realization that vocal and physical manner are the outward form for one's beliefs, attitudes, and emotions. Thus, effective delivery begins with the selection and preparation of subject matter in which the speaker has confidence, and with the cultivation of attitudes of affection and respect for other people.

The search continues with the speaker's self-conscious effort to give vocal and physical form to the beliefs, attitudes, and emotions he holds. Many of us have observed public speakers who seem stiff, impassive, and withdrawn while presenting a prepared talk, but who become animated and direct in conversation with friends, or in a question-and-answer period following their prepared comments. Such speakers know how to deliver a speech. But they have not brought to bear in their public utterance the attitudes of trust and cordiality they give to friends, or the deep concern for ideas that they may express in response to a challenging question. For the most part, public speakers do not need to learn the range of vocal intonation, facial expression, and gesture needed to support effective delivery. These resources are already part of their repertory of behaviors. What they do need to learn is to develop a conception of their role as public speaker which permits heightened use of the vocal and physical symbolism which they would employ quite unselfconsciously in conversation.

Finally, the search for effective delivery should include attention to the elimination of distracting vocal and physical habits which the speaker may have acquired. Many persons experience great tension in public speaking, and they may acquire distracting mannerisms as a reflex of such tension. Thus, we observe the speaker who paces as he talks, and who may give listeners in small auditoriums the sensation of watching a ping-pong match. Or, we observe the speaker who plays nervously with tie, handkerchief, or pencil, or who grips every available lectern as if it were a prized personal possession. Speakers who wish to eliminate such habits should welcome the comments of listeners who call attention to such details and should work self-consciously in rehearsal to avoid the distracting behavior.

The Extemporaneous Mode of Delivery

We have referred thus far to the two most common modes of delivery in public speaking: extemporaneous speaking and speaking from manuscript. Of the two, the extemporaneous mode is most commonly practiced, and may be considered fundamental to the development of skill in speaking from manuscript. The general assumption underlying the extemporaneous mode is that the speaker has prepared his speech carefully, including rehearsal for delivery, but that he has not written a manuscript or memorized the language of the speech. Many ill-prepared speeches are delivered extemporaneously, and this fact occasionally traps speakers into the mistaken assumption that the directness, liveliness, and personal quality of extemporaneous speaking is the product of poor preparation. Careful preparation, however, supports the most direct and spontaneous manner of delivery. The speaker who exploits most fully the resources of the extemporaneous mode will find that he achieves his greatest ability to talk directly and personally with his audience when he has prepared himself most carefully. The speaker who has complete possession of the language he intends is free to adjust his utterance to unanticipated audience reactions.

Speaking from Manuscript

Speaking from manuscript is extensively practiced in American society, and the student who has command of the extemporaneous mode of delivery should also seek competence in manuscript preparation and in delivery using a manuscript. The popularity of manuscript presentation is readily understandable. Men who hope their ideas will have a larger audience and longer history than that possible to an extemporaneous speech may turn to a manuscript. If a speech text is to be published, advance preparation of a manuscript is likely to be an economical use of the speaker's time. Few speakers wish to have typescript prepared from an extemporaneous speech published without extensive editing; extemporaneous prose may be clear enough, but it is likely to violate frequently the syntactical conventions of writing. Moreover, persons who must choose carefully the words they utter in public will prefer the discipline of a manuscript to the possible error in emphasis that might occur in an extemporaneous presentation, however carefully prepared. Thus a person holding high public office, or one facing an audience filled with reporters likely to give critical scrutiny to the speaker's alleged wisdom, may well seek the security that a manuscript provides. The manuscript assures the speaker that his careful choices on position, structure, forms of enforcement, and style will not be lost under the pressures of audience stimulus.

Yet effective manuscript delivery is unquestionably more difficult than effective extemporaneous delivery. If the speaker is not skilled in using his manuscript he may lose the sense of direct, person-to-person communication which is essential to effective delivery. He may seem unresponsive to audience reactions, and at worst may seem less interested in talking with his audience than in giving voice to some language which is not really his own, or not really intended for his listeners.

Such defects in manuscript delivery are commonplace and account for the negative response many listeners give to the mere appearance of a manuscript. Yet they are defects which are the product of lack of skill in preparation and delivery rather than the product of some condition inherent in speaking from manuscript.

Effective manuscript delivery starts with a manuscript prepared in the speaking style of the person who speaks. He must write the speech as he would talk with an audience, asking of each sentence, "Is this the way I would say it?" Given typescript which reflects the speaker's manner of talking, he will find the manuscript not so much a document to be read, as a prompting for the talking he wishes to do. The qualities of directness and spontaneity, the sense of something happening here and now, can and should be maintained. If these qualities are present in the language of the manuscript, then style of delivery should differ little from the style of effective extemporaneous speaking. If the speaker can achieve this style, he loses little of the power of directness possible to extemporaneous speaking. In fact, he gains much from the economy and precision of language the manuscript may provide, and from the sign the manuscript creates that he has taken the occasion and audience most seriously.

Effective delivery from manuscript requires that the speaker be ready to react to unanticipated response in the audience. Experienced speakers, using manuscripts, frequently make slight departures from the text—partly to acknowledge moments of doubt or delight they sense in their listeners, partly to add to the air of immediacy in their presentation. They may also attach extemporized introductions to their presentation, in response to remarks of another speaker, or topical aspects of the occasion.

The fully prepared manuscript speech and the fully prepared extemporaneous speech move toward the same goals. The process of preparation differs. The extemporaneous speaker seeks possession of vivid and precise language as the product of repeated rehearsal. The manuscript speaker seeks earlier to secure the language he wishes, and then through rehearsal to adjust the language to the form most consonant with direct and spontaneous delivery. He rehearses to take such possession of his language that his delivery is free from any sense of being bound to the printed page.

Just as the extemporaneous mode of public speaking suffers from the occasional assumption that its virtues are linked to poor preparation, so manuscript speaking suffers from the assumption that this mode of speaking can save hours of time for the busy executive. Thus persons who find little time for speech preparation, but frequent occasion to speak, may turn to the services of a speech writer for preparation of their utterance. The ghost-written manuscript speech presented by a man who has not participated in developing the position and structure of the speech, who has taken neither the time nor trouble to make sure that its idiom is the language with which he feels comfortable, and who has not taken possession of the manuscript through rehearsal, is likely to produce a drab speech. Indeed, the prevalence of such speeches in contemporary American society contributes much to the sense of desolation many audiences experience at the very sight of a speaker, manuscript in hand, marching to the rostrum. The sense of desolation is not always confirmed. Manuscript speaking does not necessarily entail a manuscript-bound reading of the half-possessed words of another man, accompanied

by such flourishes as the rereading of certain sentences to get the proper accent. Such skillful public speakers in our century as President Franklin Roosevelt and Sir Winston Churchill demonstrated repeatedly the fact that a manuscripted speech could live as fully in the moment of delivery as any extemporaneous speech. And President Roosevelt, who made extensive use of the help of speech writers, demonstrated that the man who used such assistance could take possession of all the language of his utterance: by participating in the initial planning of the text, by repeatedly editing the language to make it his own, and by careful rehearsal for delivery.[1]

Impromptu Speaking and Speaking from Memory

We may dismiss quickly the possibilities of impromptu public speaking and speaking from memory. The former mode is a probable fiction and the latter little practiced in contemporary society.

As to impromptu speaking, there are occasions when the speaker seemingly must speak on the spur of the moment, to take part in a debate, or to answer a question at a public meeting. In such situations we properly say that the speech is impromptu—given with little or no prior calculation or rehearsal. When a speaker performs brilliantly in such circumstances—with vivid language, clear organization, and apt use of enforcement, his performance is likely to be much admired. We would emphasize the fact that the seeming impromptu speech which is artistic in design and presentation is not likely to have been impromptu at all. Able parliamentary debaters may perform brilliantly in the allegedly impromptu give and take of debate, but it is well to remember that these debaters may have spent hundreds of hours in developing this skill, during which time the lines of argument, the illustrative materials, the apt quotations all have become readily available parts of the speaker's repertory of utterance. The debater's grace and wit is no more impromptu than the comments used by a veteran night club comedian in dealing with hecklers from the audience. He has learned by arduous rehearsal, some of it anticipatory, some of it painfully carried out in public when he was less expert, the commonplaces he can use effectively. Skill in so-called impromptu speaking is likely to be the product of hours of rehearsal, some of it provided in conversation about public issues, some the product of a wealth of experience with prepared speeches.

A final possible mode of delivery is that of speaking from memory. This mode is little used in contemporary America other than in some

[1] For an interesting discussion of President Roosevelt's use of speech writers, see Waldo Braden and Mary L. Gehring, *Speech Practices: A Resource Book for the Student of Public Speaking* (New York: Harper and Row, 1958).

speech contests, although the orators of ancient Greece and Rome, who practiced their craft as a high art, were apparently skillful in memorized delivery and spoke to audiences who expected such skill. To be sure, speakers who give approximately the same talk on repeated occasions may move toward memorization. Whether speaking extemporaneously or using a text, they achieve a control over their utterance which is the product of such frequent rehearsal that they could be said to be talking from memory. In such cases, however, the audience is unlikely to perceive the speech as memorized. And it is paradoxically the case that if a speech is effectively delivered from memory, the audience must be unaware of the memorization. Nothing is more ruinous to effective delivery than the spectacle of a speaker struggling to recall words when he should be talking with people.

THE MANAGEMENT OF SOCIAL FEARS

We are accustomed to notice speakers who seem remarkably self-confident or who, conversely, reveal timidity. We say of the confident speaker that he has poise. He seems to enjoy the opportunity for speech. If his manner is spontaneous and friendly, if his confidence does not turn toward arrogance or indifference, we properly conclude that he possesses personal resources which will serve him well. An excess of social timidity on the other hand may seem to all but disable the person for the role of public speaker. We observe the speaker who trembles, though he has no history of malaria; whose eyes seek the comfort of the ceiling, the floor, or the window; whose voice loses force and color; or whose face becomes masklike; and we say, "this person suffers from stage fright."

The obvious confidence of some speakers and the obvious timidity of others may mislead us as to the nature of the emotional relationship of speakers to the speaking situation, and as to the nature of our own response in a speaking situation. To the extent that we are misled in interpreting the nature of social confidence or social fear, our capacity to manage our own emotional responses while speaking may be lessened.

The Speaking Situation and Tension

Speakers who seem confident tend to create an illusion in the minds of the less confident who observe them. The illusion is that such speakers have never lost a moment of sleep worrying about a speech, have never been unable to eat heartily before speaking, have never felt their pulse rate increase, or their stomach tighten as the moment of speaking approached. In other words, we may think that this confident speaker has somehow escaped the disease called "social fear" or "stage fright," which many other people have caught.

Doubtless there are some speakers who experience no great tension before speaking in public, but they are unlikely to be among those whose confidence seems notable. The person who experiences no tension at the prospect of a public speech is more likely to be noted for his mediocrity or ineptness. Such persons have a confidence resembling the courage of the monkey who pulls the pin on a hand grenade—not so much because he is too brave to worry about having his paw blown off as because he is too unaware of the situation to act prudently.

The speaking situation is inherently tension-producing. The speaker must *act* in a public situation. To some extent his reputation with those in the immediate audience is at issue. He is asking much of his audience —their time and attention. He works with the most powerful and fragile of human behaviors. At best, he will not be perfectly understood by any members of his audience, and he is assuredly going to be misunderstood rather dramatically by some. The speaker faces a problem in achieving any part of the response he wishes from his audience, and if he seriously seeks to meet that problem he will experience tension. With some audiences on some occasions the speaker's sense of the importance of the occasion may magnify his perception of the problem he confronts. His tensions will be magnified accordingly.

Tension as Physiological Readiness

Stripped of such evaluative terms as "confidence" or "fear," the experience of tension in the presence of a problem may be accurately viewed as a "readiness" reaction in the organism. The nature of this reaction is well known and universally experienced. The body's readiness for action is achieved through increased secretion of adrenalin, accompanied by an increased pulse rate, some increase in respiration, and adjustments which slow the activity of the stomach and viscera to make blood and oxygen more available to the brain and the large muscles. This is the primitive "run or fight" reaction of the body. Our ancestors doubtless experienced it when confronting a saber-toothed tiger; we experience it in scores of social situations. One could interpret the effects of this *readiness* reaction in the speaking situation by saying that the confident speaker has chosen to "fight." He has used the energy potential of his tensions in the process of preparing himself thoroughly to speak, and in the action of the speech itself. The very high level of tension reported in many successful public speakers is instructive. Edward R. Murrow, at the time he was the most successful news commentator in American radio and television, was noted for the amount of tension he experienced in preparing and presenting a newscast.

Tensions Not Inherently Unpleasant

It is an illusion to assume that speakers who seem confident don't experience tension. It is equally an illusion to assume that tension-provoking situations are inherently unpleasant and to be avoided. Either introspection concerning our own life or the observation of others assures us that many of our most memorable and pleasurable moments are those accompanied by a high level of tension. The person who enjoys acting does so partly because of his ability to take proper action in response to the tension; and the football player who experiences great tension just before a game is likely to judge that he is ready for effective play.

Evaluation of Tension a Key Reaction

The tensions we all experience at the prospect of speechmaking are subject to vastly different evaluations by different persons. Tension interpreted or evaluated as a state of *readiness* for speaking may direct the speaker to the useful effort of planning and rehearsal, and toward the pleasure many speakers experience from their utterance. Tension evaluated as *fear* becomes an immediate threat to the speaker's capacity to prepare and act. The person who says "I'm afraid" has proposed an evaluation of the speaking situation which will assuredly cast a subtle poison into his pattern of response to the situation. The workings of the poison may be observed in some of the characteristic avoidance activities of speakers who evaluate themselves as fearful. The speaker may spend energy worrying about the prospect of speaking rather than in preparation and rehearsal. Many speakers who say they are fearful and who exhibit strong evidence of withdrawal in the speaking situation also seem to engage in the projection of fear-provoking qualities into the speaking situation. "The audience is waiting for me to make a mistake," they allege. Nothing could be further from the truth concerning most audiences, whose members fervently wish the speaker all success, and who are as eager for the trust and good opinion of the speaker as the speaker is for their trust and good opinion. "I will be ridiculed," says the speaker. The circumstance is unlikely in a classroom situation. Occasionally one of the speaker's *ideas* or *statements* will be the object of satire, but this is far from ridicule of the speaker's person or his worth as a person.

It would seem useful for speakers who believe themselves handicapped by fear to practice some conscious effort at making useful or productive evaluations of the situation, rather than disruptive evaluations. In short, such speakers should seek to perceive their tensions as a readiness reaction and to convert the energy from such tension into a condition of actual readiness.

The Causes of Misevaluations May Not Be Knowable

Why some speakers have come to evaluate social tensions as fear has been a subject for considerable speculation among students of speech and psychology. That speakers do make such evaluations, we know. That the evaluations are disruptive and damaging, we also know. The exact genesis of such evaluations, however, is not always knowable. Fearful speakers often report various experiences in which they have failed. Such experiences range from childhood speaking efforts that were ridiculed by adult members of the family, to school or public occasions in which the speaker met criticism which he was unable to understand or use. Fearful speakers display an interesting and almost unpredictable pattern in their evaluations and in their manifest responses to these evaluations. Some persons will welcome the prospect of taking part in a play and take pleasure in this activity; yet they report fear at the prospect of a public speech. Other persons reverse these evaluations. Some persons are fearful in the presence of a microphone and confident in the presence of an audience; others have reverse reactions. The red eye of the television camera is likely to produce unusual turmoil in the nervous system of even the most experienced speaker—at least at the first experience. The manifest evidence of the speaker's fear also varies widely. Some speakers' voices tremble and their hands do not; others experience a tremor in the muscles of the arms and legs but their voices are steady and full. In the face of such disparate patterns of evaluation and reactions, the problem of knowing how the pattern came to be is all but insurmountable.

In most cases, "the unknowable" need not be known for the speaker to take action appropriate to effective public speaking. Whatever the cause of the harmful evaluations, and whatever the responses they set off, the speaker can know that certain types of deliberate, conscious activity on his part will be likely to aid him in making useful evaluations of his tensions and useful patterns of response in tension-provoking situations.

(1) The tension normal to any social situation in which one is expected to act may be converted into anxiety (social fear) if one is unprepared to take action. It follows that the most positive action any speaker can take to avoid anxiety is that of thorough preparation. The well-planned and carefully rehearsed speech provides the speaker with a

firm course of action to follow in response to the tension aroused by the speaking occasion.

(2) Anxiety feeds upon itself. To say to oneself "I'm afraid," is to project danger into a situation. Since the danger in the speaking situation is at best problematic and may be no more than the counterpart of an exaggerated hope for great success, such projection gives full room for the imagination to create vast and shadowy perils which are altogether illusory. Anxiety allowed to flourish may cause the speaker to spend time in worry that ought to be spent in preparation. In this sense the anxiety takes on the quality of a self-fulfilling prophecy: the prophecy that we will fail encourages the kind of preparation which assures failure.

Tensions evaluated as "fear" set in motion the processes of disabling anxiety. Tensions evaluated as "readiness" set in motion processes of preparation for action—the processes that lead to genuine readiness. The speaker should practice healthy and objective evaluations of the speaking situation, the expectations of audiences, and the processes by which a speaker is able to fulfill those expectations.

(3) Anxiety may be experienced suddenly in a speaking situation as the product of past experiences in which an effort to communicate met with painful consequences. Or it may appear suddenly as the product of an unfamiliar or unexpected aspect of the speaking occasion—the presence of a microphone, the abence of a speaker's stand. To understand the propensity of certain forgotten experiences or certain new dimensions in the environment to create anxiety is to take the first step toward controlling anxiety. To understand that unexpected experiences accompanied by anxiety really should be expected, and that they seem to be experiences shared by all people is to place unpredictable experiences in proper perspective. Such experiences reinforce the desirability of careful preparation in which the speaker gives attention to as many possible contingencies as he can anticipate. They suggest also the desirability of building up as much speaking experience as possible in as many contexts as possible.

(4) Finally, all of us have known occasions when speaking proved a source of real pleasure. Many of these occasions may have been conversations with close friends. We therefore know that the act of achieving genuine communication with other people can be a source of rich satisfaction. We should avoid considering any particular kind of communicative activity as sharply different from the pleasant and satisfying experience of friendly conversation. We should perceive the possibility of achieving in public speaking the same direct and open relationship with

other persons that we have found possible in some of our private speaking.

Public Speaking Training as Therapy for Social Fear

This book emphasizes the study of public speaking as a form of practical art. Such an art should not be viewed as primarily a therapeutic practice through which persons lacking in social confidence acquire confidence. While confidence may be a condition necessary to the person who would achieve his maximum potential in public speaking, it is not a condition sufficient for either good or effective speaking. Indeed, the merely confident speaker, whose confidence is unsupported by thorough understanding of the art which he practices, is a greater social liability than the person who avoids public speaking at whatever cost. Accordingly the student of public speaking who sees his study as primarily or exclusively the search for poise or confidence both demeans the importance of his art and sets his aspirations too low. He confuses a prerequisite to effective performance with the fulfillment of effective performance.

Nevertheless, it is true that the study and practice of public speaking tends to increase the general level of confidence which one may bring to a variety of public occasions. The study of public speaking is not primarily therapeutic, but it may have important therapeutic by-products for many students.

THE SPEAKER, HIS AUDIENCE, AND THE CONDUCT OF CRITICISM

We have been examining the act of classroom speaking from the point of view of the person preparing and carrying through such an action. A unique dimension of the classroom speech, however, is the criticism of speeches. The classroom speaker recognizes two purposes. He seeks not only growth in his own ability as a speaker but also in his own understanding of the nature of public speaking. He needs, therefore, as much explicit reaction from his audience to his speech as the exigencies of time and inclination will permit. It is desirable, therefore, that both speaker and audience hold a common understanding of the object and nature of post-speech classroom discussions.

Written and Spoken Criticism

The speaker is likely to receive both written and spoken responses to his utterance. The general concepts about the conduct of criticism which will follow apply equally to both forms of rejoinder. But before these concepts are considered some of the practical limitations and possibilities present in written and spoken criticism may be observed.

Written response to a speech provides the speaker with a full cross section of audience reaction. If all listeners address themselves to a common question, such as identification of the speaker's statement, or the structure of his speech, or the quality of his delivery, then the speaker may be able to judge the relative extent of his success or failure in controlling certain specified audience responses. Impromptu written comments, however, suffer from the disability of most impromptu writing. Critics make vague and general statements, difficult to interpret at best and at worst impossible to read. In general written comments are best if the critic limits his commentary to a few selected aspects of the speech heard and if he tries to make his statements as specific as possible.

Spoken reactions permit the speaker to sense the tone or attitude of the critic and to seek immediate clarification of vague or ambiguous comments. In discussion, speaker and critic may come better to understand why they have understood or misunderstood one another. On the other hand, the speaker usually can hear only a few critics in spoken discussion, and their response may not be typical of the entire audience.

Structured and Unstructured Comments

Critical discussion of a speech, whether in speech or writing, may follow some preestablished structure or may roam freely over any aspect of the action. For example, the instructor may structure criticism by announcing that after a certain speech, he will call on some critic to discuss one or more specific topics, as: the clarity and appropriateness of the speaker's statement, the nature and clarity of the speech structure; the forms of enforcement used by the speaker—their sufficiency and appropriateness; and so forth. In such instances criticism is structured in the sense that the aspects of the speech to be considered by the critic are specified and limited.

On other occasions, critics may be permitted to respond to the speaker in any way that seems important or useful. The critic may aver his pleasure in a particular analogy used by the speaker, praise the spontaneity of the delivery, express his irritation with an argument, or add some evidence from his own reading which affirms or contradicts evidence provided by the speaker. The criticism is unstructured in that it may be a reaction to any feature of the speech. Unstructured criticism, unless guided by questions from the speaker himself, may not touch on features on which the speaker desired response. But it has the merit of informing the speaker as to those aspects of his action which stimulated the greatest amount of overt audience response.

Basic and Expert Criticism

Professors Thonssen and Gilkinson, in their text *Basic Training in Speech*,[2] distinguish two points of view a critic may take toward his role as critic. In giving *basic* criticism, the critic reports his own reactions to aspects of the speech and insofar as possible he tries to explain his reaction. "I liked your introduction," he says. "I thought your experience with the giant cat fish was colorful and interesting, and it led me easily into a consideration of your statement."

In giving *expert* criticism, the critic tries to advise the speaker on ways in which his speech would affect an audience—perhaps some specific audience. "I wasn't too disturbed by your slighting reference to President Eisenhower," says the critic, "but I think many Republicans might have been, and many Americans who admire the General might have been. After all he is a very popular man." The critic is thus predicting how other listeners would have reacted to some aspect of the speech; he is taking the role of an expert.

While both kinds of criticism are likely to appear in the discussion of any speech, it is probably sound advice that listeners try to perform their role as *basic* critics conscientiously before seeking the more tenuous role of the *expert*. The speaker should seek first of all knowledge about the genuine reactions of his present audience. This is the kind of information that his critics are best able to provide, since any listener can report "as a fact," his own reaction to a particular aspect of the speech. His suggestions about how others might react are at best inferences.

Reactions to Substance vs. Reactions to Form

We can abstract from any speech certain reactions which seem to be responses to the form of the speech, and others which are reactions to its substance. Reactions to formal matters would include consideration of the speaker's delivery or manner, the structure of his speech, the organization of the speech, and the forms of enforcement used in the speech. Reactions to substance would include responses to his subject matter, including the strength or weakness of the speaker's position, the adequacy of his proof, or the merit of his purpose. Clearly it is impossible to draw an unambiguous line between reactions to form and substance, since in the action of the speech, form and substance exist together. Nei-

---

[2] Lester Thonssen and Howard Gilkinson, *Basic Training in Speech* (Boston: D. C. Heath and Company, 1953), pp. 6–9.

ther is found in nature without the other. We perceive substance only within some form; we perceive form only as it shapes some substance. Efforts to limit the discussion or criticism of classroom speeches to matters of "form" are probably misdirected. If the speaker's arguments for supporting capital punishment are unpersuasive or even irritating to his listeners, he needs to know this. The counterarguments of his listeners inform him concerning the difficulty of the purpose he set for himself with this speech, and concerning the nature of responses to his substance which he needs to know and consider in the design of further speeches. Nevertheless it is possible to become so involved in a dialogue about the subject raised by the speaker that the form of the speaker's action is forgotten.

Rhetorical Judgments vs. Philosophic Judgments

In order to avoid drifting too far from the purpose of the public-speaking classroom, listeners need to remind themselves that each speaker carries both the right and responsibility for choosing the kinds of purposes he wishes to achieve in his speaking—and thus the kind of public role he wishes to assume. Speakers who are Democrats do not take public-speaking courses in order to have Republican listeners persuade them that their political choices are unsound and that they ought to seek a different political allegiance. They do seek information from their audience which will enable them to speak more artistically in support of their purposes. They need to know when and in what sense and to what degree their statements affect Republicans, but they need not engage in an extension of a political argument which begins with the speech but soon goes far beyond it.

It is useful for members of a classroom audience to seek to *lend* themselves to the speaker's purpose, and to ask about his method as it relates to their reactions. "Here is a Democrat talking to me, a Republican," says the listener to himself. "If I accept the speaker's right to be a Democrat, and to support a point of view which he finds congenial, what can I say of his method? I doubt that he could change my mind on the Democratic administration's program for federal aid to education, but has he chosen a method most likely to catch my attention, and to command my respect for his intelligence, his goodwill, and his responsibility? If I report to him that a certain aspect of his speech seemed ineffective to me, can I suggest an alternative choice which I think he could have made which would have had a better prospect of reaching his goal?"

The listener who lends himself to the speaker's purpose in this way is engaging in rhetorical criticism in the ancient, Aristotelian definition of rhetoric. Aristotle called rhetoric "the faculty of discovering in the particular case what are the available means of persuasion." The rhetorical critic accepts the nature of the "given case," and asks whether or not the speaker has found and used the best means of persuasion (or exposition) available to him, and thus has found the best way of fulfilling his purposes. Within such a context listeners may wish to voice their opposition to certain arguments of the speaker, but to do so because they believe the speaker could have found better evidence or a better line of argument for achieving the same purpose. Within the same context the speaker should not feel constrained to advance or add to the argument produced in his speech. Rather he should consider whether or not there were better choices available to him than those he made for his speech. A rhetorical orientation to classroom speaking will make discussion of a speech primarily a consideration of the speaker's choices screened against possible alternatives.

There will be occasions when the listener will want to go beyond the limits of rhetorical criticism and engage in philosophic discussion of the fundamental terms on which the speaker bases his public identity. Such discussion is not directed to the speaker's method, nor to the appropriateness or prudence of the specific purpose of a speech presented in particular circumstances. Rather the discussion asks the speaker to consider whether or not he is right in choosing to be a Democrat, or Republican, or Christian, or agnostic, or idealist, or realist, and so forth. The speaker can use the responses of listeners who challenge not simply his rhetorical method, but challenge the worth of his fundamental assumptions. At the very least, such challenges give the speaker insight into the way in which his public identity may be rejected by some of his listeners; the speaker thus confronts the truth that men do differ fundamentally in their conceptions of what a man's life should stand for and that communication among persons whose fundamental assumptions differ is at best incomplete. But both speakers and their listeners should recognize that a challenge to the fundamental public identity of the speaker is an invitation to philosophic dialogue concerning the nature of reality and of man's obligations. In the public-speaking class, such philosophic dialogue should not be prolonged in the discussion of a particular speech. It can be profitably continued by a speaker and his critics in their subsequent public speeches. The basic rhetorical question a listener should raise for discussion after a given public speech is this: *If I were this speaker, holding his purposes in life and possessed of his capabilities, would I have chosen a different position and method for my discourse?*

Seeking Maximum Candor

The classroom-speaking situation provides an exceptional opportunity for both speaker and audience to extend their understanding of the nature of the speech act. This opportunity is realized only to the extent that the group both seeks and values candor. Ideally, critics ought to report their own reactions and interpret those reactions as honestly as they can. Speakers ought to welcome such reactions, seek to understand them, and value them. Such an ideal is difficult to achieve since it runs counter to established social conventions governing speaker-audience relations. The social convention demands that the speaker be reassured; that he be praised politely. Speakers sometimes are greeted by a member of the audience who says, "you made an excellent speech, and I want you to know that I really mean it." The last phrase—I really mean it—unfortunately suggests that the critic often says "you've made an excellent speech" when he doesn't mean it at all. The ideal also asks of the speaker that he suspend an inclination to seek personal reassurance in the higher interest of seeking accurate information. It is difficult for a speaker to view the man who honestly though caustically dissects his speech as a "real friend." Yet the speaker genuinely interested in extending his own understanding would have to recognize that tactful praise stemming not from candor but from sympathy cannot lead to knowledge. The speaker's attitude toward the discussion of his speech will have much to do with encouraging or discouraging candor in his audience.

A final barrier to achieving complete candor is the audience's perception that fearful speakers seem to need encouragement, and to have less need for the candor which might seem to nourish their anxieties. Clearly it is impossible to demand of an audience that it practice the same level and form of candor with all speakers. The best that can be done is to ask all speakers and audience members to respect the ideal of candor, and to work toward it as rapidly as their sense of joint participation in the search for genuine understanding permits.

The Student of Speech as Critic

The ability of the student of speech to act as critic is the measure of his understanding of the nature of public speaking. To be able to see the speech of another person as it is; to see the choices of the speaker and to compare those choices with other possible choices; to see how this or that choice carries certain merits and also carries certain liabilities— these skills represent insight into the nature of a speech. The student who acquires capacity as a discerning critic is ready to direct his own

growth in speaking ability. From the limited environment of the classroom he can gain an understanding of speech which will enable him to
profit from subsequent speaking experiences in all of the possible situations he may confront. None of us fails to realize our potential as a
speaker through lack of opportunity to speak. Many of us fail either
through withdrawal from experience or through inability to evaluate the
meaning of our experience.

The Critic as Participant

In the final analysis the speech student who becomes a capable critic
also enlarges his capacity to participate fully in the public affairs of his
society. Throughout this book we have treated public speaking as a
human action encompassing the speaker, his utterance, and his audience. The man who listens to a speech is not simply the object of language; he is participant in an action. His expectations shape the behavior of speakers and his judgment shapes the consequences of the
speaker's utterance.

In his provocative lecture entitled "What is Man?" [3] Martin Buber
asks the modern world to go beyond the categories of the individual, and
the assembly or the collective, and to give attention to the category he
calls *between*. The truths men need to find, he suggests, lie not in one
man alone, nor in men subsumed in a crowd. Rather, they lie *between*
men, to be sought in acts of communication in which the listener, no less
than the speaker, becomes a full participant. If all speakers seek to
understand their listeners, all listeners must seek equally to understand
those who address them.

SUMMARY

Rehearsal for delivery tests the planned structure and language, and
may lead to extensive reconstruction of the speech. Rehearsal also engages the speaker in a search for a public manner consistent with general
audience expectations about the role of a public speaker, and consistent
with the speaker's image of himself as a public person.

Rehearsal for the two most common modes of delivery, extemporaneous speaking and speaking from manuscript, seeks the same goals of
full control over the structure and language of the speech, and freedom
to talk directly with the audience. The extemporaneous mode seeks control over the speech's structure and language as the product of repeated
rehearsal; the speaker using a manuscript seeks control over structure

[3] Martin Buber, *Between Man and Man* (New York: The Macmillan Company,
1965), pp. 118–205.

and language first, and then through rehearsal achieves such adjustment and control of the language as to make possible direct and spontaneous delivery. The best-prepared extemporaneous speeches, and the best-prepared manuscript speeches will not differ greatly in structure, language, or manner of utterance.

The management of social fears is also an important consideration for many speakers, and such management begins with the understanding that the public-speaking situation inherently produces tensions. Such tensions may be viewed as a *readiness* reaction, providing energy useful to the speaker, or as a *fear* reaction. The latter evaluation handicaps both the speaker's habits of preparation and delivery. Practice in public speaking can and does assist students to develop social confidence. But while confidence is necessary to effective speaking, it is not sufficient. A good speech is too important an event to be viewed as an activity undertaken as a form of personality therapy.

The usefulness of classroom speaking to the development of speaking skill depends on the form and spirit of classroom criticism. Ideally, speakers and listeners in the classroom should practice the maximum candor permitted by particular situations, and should seek mutual appreciation of such candor. The emphasis in classroom criticism should be on basic reactions of listeners as well as on their reactions as experts; it should be addressed to the rhetorical question of method more frequently than to philosophic questioning of the speaker's purpose.

The test of one's understanding of public speaking is skill as a critic. Such understanding is the surest foundation for making effective use of speaking experience. But to be a capable critic of speech in the fullest sense is to become a person able to participate fully in any speaking event, to shape its form, and to share in its consequences.

FOR FURTHER STUDY

THREE SPEAKING EXERCISES

Following are assignments for three classroom public-speaking exercises. Each of these assignments is a "technical exercise" in the sense that it asks students to undertake preparation and presentation of a speech dealing with a specified type of subject matter managed in a specific way. Such exercises give experience with certain linguistic problems and with the structure of discourses seeking to deal with these problems. Conduct of the exercises should extend the analytical resources available to the speaker or the speech critic.

While all of the exercises have been used successfully with college classes, certain cautions should be observed in their use. For example, each exercise *permits* the student to prepare a stimulating public speech. But some students working within the constraints imposed by these assignments will not produce the most agreeable or successful speech of which they are capable. A speaker asked to manage an intellectual problem which he has never before sought to manage is being asked to talk in ways which may seem strange or unnatural to him. The more resolutely he tries to fulfill the terms of the assignment, the more this awkwardness may affect his utterance. Hence, while such technical exercises promote development of the linguistic resources of many speakers, they also limit the immediate effectiveness of some.

The exercises are not proposed as a full set of assignments which might accompany a college public-speaking class. They are best used when intermingled with other assignments giving students opportunity to engage in acts of persuasion, exposition, or ceremony wholly of their own invention.

The exercises have been designed for speeches meeting a ten-or-fifteen-minute time limit. They can be adapted to shorter or longer speeches as a class schedule permits, and they can be adapted either to extemporaneous or manuscript speeches.

Exercise Number 1: A Speech Analyzing a Question of Fact

General Purpose

To identify a specific and significant question of fact; to perform a thorough critical investigation of the evidence available to answer the question and of the method of inquiry which produced the evidence; and to report the product of the investigation in a public speech.

The Assignment

1. Identify a specific *question of fact* which has been the subject of public discussion because of its significance to some larger question of value or policy confronted by persons or groups in American society.
2. Determine the types of evidence which have been used to support varying answers given to this question of fact, and the methods of inquiry used to provide such evidence.
3. Evaluate both the methods of inquiry which have been brought to bear on investigation of the fact in question and also the evidence produced by such methods.
4. Prepare a speech in which you
   a. Establish the nature and significance of the question of fact you have investigated. The importance of the specific question to larger issues of value or policy may serve as the basis for audience involvement in your speech.
   b. Discuss the major methods of investigation which have been used

to provide answers to the question, and the evidence produced by such investigation.

c. If, as is probable, existing investigations to which you have access have not provided a conclusive answer to the question, discuss the nature of a possible investigation which might produce a more reliable answer than you can determine, and/or the nature of the problems that may inhibit the search for a reliable answer.

d. Present the most responsible answer you believe possible to the question you have raised. You may wish to propose an answer which you believe is affirmed by the preponderance of available evidence. If you do this you should indicate the level of confidence which your answer warrants. Or, you may wish to indicate that you believe it impossible, given the state of available evidence, to provide any answer to the question.

e. You may wish to conclude by discussing the implications of your answer to the larger questions of value or policy to which the question of fact relates.

Rationale

Questions of fact are those which presumably permit a conclusive answer based on publicly verifiable evidence. The answer to a question of fact would be an assertion or statement of fact. Both questions of fact and their answer can be distinguished from questions and assertions of *value* or *policy*. Questions of fact are concerned with what *is* the case; questions of value with what should be thought good; and questions of policy with what actions should be undertaken by persons or social groups.

Although questions of fact presumably permit a conclusive answer, many such questions are posed for which no conclusive answer can be given on the basis of existing evidence, or to which different persons give different answers. A question for which a conclusive and generally accepted answer exists would not be a proper question for detailed investigation or detailed exposition in a public speech. For example, the question, "In what year did Columbus land in the West Indies?" is one for which an obvious and generally acceptable answer exists. Similarly, the question, "What was the population of the United States in 1960?" can be answered in a way which permits little controversy, although the method used to provide the statistical basis for an answer is subject to analysis. In general, questions such as the foregoing would not result in other than a sleep-provoking speech.

On the other hand the question, "Does fluoridated water have any harmful physiological effects on persons who drink it over a period of years?" is a question which has stimulated a variety of answers. Despite the range and intensity of the investigations made of this question, persons familiar with the evidence and presumably skilled in its interpretation continue to give different answers to the question. Since the "fact" in this case looms large in any public discussion about the advisability of the policy of fluoridating the water supply of any given community, the discussion of this question of fact has been prolonged and often heated.

The type of question of fact to which this assignment is addressed, therefore, is the type which cannot readily be answered conclusively on the basis of existing evidence, or one concerning which considerable disagreement exists as to the nature of a responsible answer. The assignment is also addressed to questions which are involved in larger issues of value or policy under public discussion in American society. Because of this latter criterion, many of the questions of fact available will be formulated in ways that involve use of some qualitative or evaluative terminology, and therefore invade to some extent a question of value. For example, the question posed on the effects of fluoridation uses the term "harmful," which is a "value" concept definable according to some qualitative judgment. We should expect that many of the questions selected for investigation will include some problems of qualitative definition. A series of further examples will serve to clarify useful types of questions.

1. Was President John F. Kennedy's religion linked causally to the popular vote he received for President in 1960?

   Evidence on voting behavior in 1960 has been cited both to affirm and deny the thesis that religion was an important determinant of this behavior. The question of fact has been related to the larger issue of whether or not the religious preference of candidates should be a factor in determining their fitness for office, and if it should not, how such an issue can be kept out of political campaigns.

2. Is the military strength of the United States relative to that of the Soviet Union increasing?

   Assertions of fact on this question abounded in the 1960 and 1964 Presidential campaigns. The term "strength" has a qualitative dimension, and the question poses some serious problems as to the availability of reliable and relevant evidence.

3. Is cigarette smoking an established cause of lung cancer?

   This question has become somewhat hackneyed, and some consensus as to the proper answer seems to be emerging in the scientific and medical community. Some controversy persists as to the form a responsible answer to the question should take; and this difference of opinion represents the importance scientists attach to the methods of investigation used to supply evidence relevant to the question, and to the importance of keeping assertions of fact within the limits permitted by existing evidence. The question and its answer are involved in public controversy over such policy issues as restrictions on advertising, the labeling of packages with health warnings, and the conduct of educational ventures.

4. In proportion to population, is juvenile crime increasing in the United States?

The assertions given in answer to this question tend to provide an affirmative answer which is purportedly conclusive. An investigation of the evidence and the method by which it is gathered, however, may reveal some questions about the type of assertions of fact permitted by the evidence.

5. Were urban riots in the United States during the 1960's wholly spontaneous, or were they in whole or in part deliberately planned?

This question has elicited a large number of opinions, but little "hard" evidence has appeared to support a definitive answer. Analysis of the kind of evidence that might be gathered, and of the possibility of its being gathered, would be productive.

6. Was American military intervention in South Vietnam an intervention in a civil war, or a response to armed invasion of South Vietnam by North Vietnam?

This question invites analysis of the data on which conflicting interpretations are made of the character of United States' military action in South Vietnam. Analysis might reveal the difficulty of obtaining the evidence needed for a definitive interpretation.

7. Is the threat of capital punishment a deterrent to certain categories of crime?

This is a well-worn question which is periodically revived when discussion about the use of capital punishment is aroused for any reason. Despite the age of the question, and the freedom with which assertions are made in answer to it, the available evidence has not generated any generally acceptable answer.

8. Does the American high school graduate write (spell, read, speak, carry out mathematical computation, etc.) less well than the average graduate of 1920?

> This question includes a qualitative dimension in the definition given to the term "less well." Assertions of fact about the decline or improvement of secondary school instruction abound in public discussion of educational policy. The assertions conflict, and the nature of the evidence on which they are based invites exploration.

These eight questions will illustrate the type of question of fact which might prove suitable for this assignment. But such questions abound in every area of value or policy under discussion in American life, and the student searching for a particular question would be well-advised to start his search in an area of discussion in which he is broadly interested.

Two final and somewhat philosophic points may help understanding of the nature of the discourse sought through this assignment. First, the assignment directs attention to "how we know" certain things to be true or untrue, in distinction to the question of "why we believe" certain things to be true or untrue. All men need to believe many things about themselves, their neighbors, their universe, the nature of the good and the bad, and about public policy. Our need to believe generally exceeds our capacity to "know" in any scientific or publicly demonstrable way. Hence much of the public discourse in our society takes the form of speakers or writers revealing what it is that they believe, and the reasons for their beliefs. These reasons may or may not relate to any careful analysis of the question of how men generally may know something to be true or untrue. It has been a characteristic impulse of science to concentrate on the question of "how" things can be known; hence the emphasis of science on the posing of questions in forms which will permit the discovery of evidence relevant to an answer. Science concentrates on the methodology of investigation to assure reliability for the evidence adduced; and science characteristically raises doubts about the reliability of many assertions of fact which find popular acceptance and affirms the need to keep assertions of fact available for reconstruction in the light of new evidence. This speaking exercise invites participation in an act of investigation and discourse which partakes of the scientist's emphasis on how facts are to be known, of the scientist's attention to the method by which evidence is adduced, and of the scientist's concern for the extent to which certain types of evidence warrant confidence in certain assertions of fact.

The final point is one of caution about the relationship between assertions of fact, and assertions of value or policy linked to such alleged facts. In general, statements about what *is* the case do not lead logically to any particular statement about what *should* be the case. Such linkages are made in public discourse when a speaker assumes that the fact of a large number of automobile accidents demonstrates the need for new public policies to curb the incidence of such accidents; or when a speaker assumes that the fact that many men gamble proves that gambling should be legal. All such linkages make certain assumptions about the relationship of the facts in question to the policies in question. If the assumptions are accepted by an audience, the speaker's linkage will seem logical enough to his auditors; but if it is not accepted, then the real problem of relating the *is* to the *ought* will be uncovered.

We have emphasized in this assignment that the speaker should seek questions of fact which are embedded in public discussion of questions of value or policy, and that he may wish to explore some of the value or policy implications of the answer he gets to his question of fact. Such exploration should be mindful of the need to make explicit any assumptions needed to tie a particular assertion of fact to any given assertion of value or policy.

Exercise Number 2: A Speech Analyzing a Conflict in Values

General Purpose

To identify in a specific public dispute or issue, a conflict in two opposing values which have been brought to bear on answers to the issue; to show how each of the conflicting values is used in public discussion of the issue in question; to propose and support a personal position on the value which should be given most importance in judging the issue in question.

The Assignment

1. Identify a case or incident, either contemporary or historical, which has provoked controversy over the relative importance of one or the other of two generalized and conflicting values. Two kinds of cases or incidents, and two sets of conflicting values, provide the most suitable subject matter for analysis:

   a. Cases or incidents involving dispute over the limits, if any, society may properly set to the speaking, writing, or other actions of individuals, especially when such actions reflect the personal beliefs of the individual. Such cases often bring into conflict the value we assign to personal liberty versus the value we assign to public order, or to the safety and peace of the community.

   b. Cases or incidents involving dispute over the relative value assignable to tradition, and to innovation in judging a wide range of human actions, social customs, and works of art. Dispute over the merit of any new art form usually involves conflict in the values of tradition and innovation. Disputes over innovations in public or economic policy often involve this same value conflict, as in the case of the destruction of historic buildings or traditional communities in acts of urban renewal, or in the destruction of some natural habitat in some act of economic expansion.

2. Analyze public comment on the case selected to discover how the two conflicting values have been brought to bear in judgment of the case in question. For example, in analyzing comment on a case allegedly involving freedom of speech, one should seek to identify the lines of argument used by persons who give precedence to the freedom of the individual, and the lines of argument used by those who give precedence to the protection of society.
3. Evaluate the relative merit of the conclusions reached by giving precedence to one or the other of the conflicting values.
4. Prepare a speech in which you
   a. Summarize the facts about the case or incident with which you are concerned, seeking to establish the importance of the issue involved in the particular case.
   b. Define the two opposing values which different critics have brought to bear in their judgments about the case in question.
   c. Summarize the way in which these values are used in opposing lines of argument leading to opposing judgments about the case.
   d. Present your own judgment about the case in question, supporting the merit of giving preference to one of the conflicting values in this particular case, and in similar cases.

Rationale

Fundamental conflicts in value underlie many of the persistent controversies in any society. These conflicts are often confusing because both parties to a value dispute may acknowledge the merit of the opposing values brought to bear on the dispute. For example, most Americans believe that an individual should act according to the dictates of his own conscience. The worth or dignity of the individual is an important American value. They also believe that citizens should defend the security and stability of their society. Responsibility for social order and the rights of society as a whole is also an important value. One might believe in both of these values, and then confront a situation in which a citizen refuses to support his government in time of war because he believes, as a matter of conscience, that war is unjust. In judging such a case or incident, if one gave priority to the value of individual conscience, one might ask that the conscientious objector be allowed to go his way, free from both legal constraint and public criticism. If one gave priority to the security of the state, however, he might support either legal constraint or public censure of the conscientious objector.

As most of us have learned, it is relatively easy to talk about our values in the abstract. One can support both the integrity of the individual and the security of the state in the abstract, but the presence of a particular case in which one man refuses duty to the state as a matter of conscience forces us to judge in a concrete historical situation which value we consider more important to the moment. Similarly, one may support both the values of free *and* responsible speech in the abstract. But confronted with a speaker whose comments seem so distasteful and irresponsible to some listeners as to make the speaker a public danger, one must again choose in a concrete historical situation whether he believes in free speech without qualification, or free speech up to a point, and, if "up to a point," how this point is to be determined.

This exercise is designed to focus attention on the conflicts in value which underlie most public disputation, and to promote understanding of the way in which particular cases of human choice or action force men to choose between values, both of which they may consider worthy. In this exercise, the speaker is asked to make a choice and defend that choice, but to do so only after showing that he understands fully the merit of the opposing values that might be brought to bear on the case in question. In this sense the speaker's primary obligation is to provide a clear analysis of the value conflict present in the different judgments brought to bear on a particular human action, and only secondarily to argue the merit of his own choice.

In carrying out this exercise, the student should be aware that he is seeking understanding of the process by which every society seeks to establish the values which its members will share, and the way in which these values will be brought to bear in judgment. The process involves a continuing dialectic or dialogue in every society. That is, such eternal antinomies as the rights of the individual versus the rights of society, the claims of personal conscience versus the claims of the state, or the claims of tradition and order versus those of innovation and social renewal are constantly being reinterpreted by every society. The dialectic is as ageless as it is essential.

Exercise Number 3: A Speech About a Speech

General Purpose

To identify a significant public speech, either historical or contemporary; to study the utterance, the speaker, the audience, and the occasion in order to be able to understand and appraise the act selected for study;

to choose a particular perspective on the speech useful in enlarging an audience's understanding of the speech; to prepare a public speech developing this perspective.

The Assignment

1. Select a public speech which you believe of some interest and importance to you and the members of your classroom audience. Speeches frequently anthologized in historical collections are suitable actions to study,[1] as are contemporary speeches bearing on important public issues.

2. Through study of the speaker, his utterance, his purpose, his audience, the immediate occasion for the speech, and the historical-cultural setting in which it was given, seek to develop a thorough understanding of the nature of the action chosen for study.

3. Select the particular perspective for commentary on the speech which you believe most revealing of the speaker's art, or lack of art, or which you believe most interesting as the basis for a general comment on the art of public speaking. For example, you might choose to comment on a difficult problem faced by the speaker because of the relationship he held to his audience, or the relationship of his purpose to purposes present in the audience, or the nature of the opposition he faced. From such a perspective, an analysis of the way in which the speaker sought to manage his problem, and an appraisal of the merit of the speaker's choices would be in order. Other possible perspectives would be

    a. An analysis of the speaker's style, or manner, including appraisal of its merit.

    b. An analysis of the speaker's purpose including its clarity, its appropriateness to his age, and its merit as judged by the worth of such purpose to society.

    c. An analysis of the speaker's method of supporting or amplifying his major assertions, together with an appraisal of the merit of such methods for the particular audience, or in the light of more reflective analysis.

4. Prepare a speech in which you

    a. Reconstruct briefly for the audience the speech chosen for analysis,

---

[1] See, for example, speeches in such collections as:

Carroll C. Arnold, Douglas Ehninger, John C. Gerber, *The Speaker's Resource Book* (Chicago: Scott, Foresman and Company, 1961).

A. Craig Baird, *American Public Addresses, 1740–1952* (New York: McGraw-Hill Company, 1956).

Carl G. Brandt and Edward M. Shafter, *Selected American Speeches on Basic Issues* (Boston: Houghton Mifflin Company, 1960).

Wil A. Linkugel, R. R. Allen, and Richard L. Johannesen, *Contemporary American Speeches* (Belmont, California: Wadsworth Publishing Co., 1965).

Ernest J. Wrage and Barnet Baskerville, *American Forum: Speeches on Historic Issues* (New York: Harper and Row, 1960).

seeking to enlist audience interest in the speech, and audience understanding of the proximate nature of the action selected.
  b. Announce the particular perspective from which analysis is to be conducted.
  c. Carry out the analysis of the speech in terms of the selected perspective.
  d. Conclude with any generalization about the art of public speaking which seems warranted by your analysis.

Rationale

We have emphasized the point of view that a public speech is a social action; that understanding of this action involves perception of the relations among speaker, purpose, utterance, audience, and occasion; and that judgment of a speech proceeds from perception of the options or choices available to the speaker, and from comparison of the speaker's choices with other possible choices. One of the best procedures for making these abstract ideas concrete is the careful study of a particular speech with full attention to interrelationship of the variables of person, purpose, audience, and occasion within which the speaker made his choice of utterance. Such study is particularly illuminating when the speech under study is a significant one in the sense that the speaker was under heavy pressure to choose wisely, either because of his reputation, the importance of the occasion, or the historical importance of his purposes.

While a "speech about a speech" cannot hope to encompass all that might be said with profit about the object of study, it can select a particular perspective which illuminates one aspect of the problem of choice confronting every public speaker. Thus this exercise is an opportunity both to test one's skill in applying public speaking theory to a particular case of practice, and to engage in further instruction on the nature of the public speaker's art.

Index